The *ACRC Exam Certification Guide* uses real-world scenarios with exercises, challenging questions, detailed explanation of exam objectives, and a test simulation on the accompanying CD-ROM to help you master all 73 ACRC exam objectives. All exam objectives are covered and are pointed out like the following example:

Objective 66: Configure source-route translational bridging (SR/TLB).

You'll be tested with challenging questions before and after the chapters:

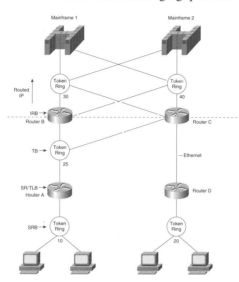

Q&A: In an SR/TLB bridging configuration, how does the source route bridging network appear to the transparently bridged network?

Scenario-based exercises at the end of each chapter test your knowledge and ability:

Scenario: Given the network setup in the accompanying diagram, configure Router A for SR/TLB. Ensure that you include:

• Transparent and source-route bridging configuration

• The use of the multiport utility

• SR/TLB configuration

CD-ROM Exam Questions: The CD-ROM provides a simulation of the ACRC exam with multiple-choice questions to help ensure your mastery of the exam objectives. For example:

Q. What command will enable an Ethernet segment to bridge to Token Ring when using SR/TLB?

a. ring-group

b. bridge-group

c. source-bridge srb

d. source-bridge transparent ring-group pseudo ring bridge-number tb-group

e. source-bridge transparent ring-group pseudo ring tb-group bridge-number

This book's chapters are organized by topic area: Managing Scalable Network Growth; IP Addressing; IP Routing Protocols; OSPF Configuration; EIGRP, BGP, and Redistribution; WAN Options: ISDN, DDR, and Configuration; Bridging; and AppleTalk and ISDN Options. By working through the information, exercises, and questions, you should feel confident as you prepare to take the exam and move on to achieve your CCNP or CCDP certification.

ACRC Exam Certification Guide

Clare Gough, CCIE #2893

with Kevin Downes, CCIE #1987

Cisco Press
201 West 103rd Street
Indianapolis, IN 46290 USA

ACRC Exam Certification Guide

Clare Gough

Copyright© 1999 Cisco Press

Cisco Press logo is a trademark of Cisco Systems, Inc.

Published by:
Cisco Press
201 West 103rd Street
Indianapolis, IN 46290 USA

Printed in the United States of America 1 2 3 4 5 6 7 8 9 0

Library of Congress Cataloging-in-Publication Number: 99-90202

ISBN: 0-7357-0075-3

Warning and Disclaimer

This book is designed to provide information about the ACRC exam. Every effort has been made to make this book as complete and as accurate as possible, but no warranty or fitness is implied.

The information is provided on an "as is" basis. The authors, Cisco Press, and Cisco Systems, Inc., shall have neither liability nor responsibility to any person or entity with respect to any loss or damages arising from the information contained in this book or from the use of the discs or programs that may accompany it.

The opinions expressed in this book belong to the author and are not necessarily those of Cisco Systems, Inc.

Trademark Acknowledgments

All terms mentioned in this book that are known to be trademarks or service marks have been appropriately capitalized. Cisco Press or Cisco Systems, Inc., cannot attest to the accuracy of this information. Use of a term in this book should not be regarded as affecting the validity of any trademark or service mark.

Feedback Information

At Cisco Press, our goal is to create in-depth technical books of the highest quality and value. Each book is crafted with care and precision, undergoing rigorous development that involves the unique expertise of members from the professional technical community.

Readers' feedback is a natural continuation of this process. If you have any comments regarding how we could improve the quality of this book, or otherwise alter it to better suit your needs, you can contact us through email at ciscopress@mcp.com. Please be sure to include the book title and ISBN in your message.

We greatly appreciate your assistance.

Publisher	John Wait
Executive Editor	John Kane
Cisco Systems Program Manager	Jim LeValley
Managing Editor	Patrick Kanouse
Development Editor	Andrew Cupp
Project Editor	Dayna Isley
Copy Editor	Keith Cline
Technical Editors	Mike Bevan, CCIE
	William V. Chernock, III, CCIE
	Tom Deevy
	Vincent Lamb
	Brian Morgan
	Gary Rubin
	Deborah A. Smith
Team Coordinator	Amy Lewis
Book Designer	Scott Cook
Cover Designer	Karen Ruggles
Production Team	Argosy
Proofreader	Megan Wade
Indexer	Kevin Fulcher

About the Author

Clare Gough is a Cisco Certified Internetworking Expert (CCIE #2893) and a Cisco Certified Systems Instructor. She worked with the developers of the ACRC course and taught the first commercial offering of the course. She holds a master's degree in Education and one in Information Systems. Over the past 14 years, she has developed and taught a variety of networking and internetworking courses throughout the world. She moved from England in 1991 and now lives in San Francisco with her family.

About the Technical Reviewers

Mike Bevan is a Systems Engineer for Cisco Systems, Inc. Prior to joining Cisco, he was a Cisco Certified Systems Instructor, teaching ICRC, ACRC, and Internetworking Troubleshooting with GeoTrain Corporation. Mike earned his CCIE in September 1995 while working as a network specialist for UB Networks (formerly Ungermann-Bass, Inc.). Mike joined Ungermann-Bass in 1982 as a networking jack-of-all-trades with no prior knowledge of computer networks and no college education. Only in America can an uneducated bum make it so far.

William V. Chernock, III, CCIE, is a senior consultant specializing in network architecture and design. During the past eight years, he has constructed large-scale strategic networks for top 10 companies within the financial and health care industries. William can be reached at wchernock@aol.com.

Tom Deevy is director of Jiratek Pty. Ltd., a consulting company specializing in internetworking with Cisco routers. Tom has previously been a communications network manager for the second largest electricity supplier in Australia. He has project managed network mergers, installation of EDI (Electronic Data Interchange), video conferencing systems, and business resumption sites, to name a few. Tom is a Certified Cisco Instructor teaching ICRC, ACRC, SNAM, CIT, and CLSC. He is also a Certified Cisco Network Associate on his way to CCIE certification. When Tom is not delivering training or consulting services, he's busy delivering babies. Tom is the proud father of five children from age 13 down to 2 years of age.

Kevin Downes is a senior network systems consultant with International Network Services (INS). His network certifications include Cisco CCIE (#1987), Cisco CCDA, Bay Networks CRS, Certified Network Expert (CNX) Ethernet, and Novell CNE. He has published several articles on the subjects of network infrastructure design, network operating systems, and Internet Protocol (IP).

Vincent Lamb is a freelance instructor and consultant specializing in networking. His network certifications include Master Certified NetWare Engineer as well as Microsoft Certified Systems Engineer. He has written computer-based training courses on OSPF, BGP, dial-on-demand, Frame Relay, and LAN troubleshooting and protocol analysis for Learning Tree International. He currently lives and works in Edinburgh, Scotland.

Brian Morgan is a Certified Cisco Systems Instructor and a CCNA. He is Senior Instructor for GeoTrain Corporation, Cisco's largest training partner. He has been with the company for two years. He teaches ICRC, ACRC, CATM, and Cisco Voice over Frame Relay, ATM, and IP. He is a representative member of the ATM Forum. Prior to his teaching career, he spent a few years with an IBM subsidiary known as TSS in large LAN/WAN troubleshooting arenas. During that time, he also became a Novell MCNE and Microsoft MCSE.

Gary Rubin is president of Information Innovation, Inc. (III), a Cisco-oriented training company. He is also a Certified Cisco Systems Instructor who has taught for Cisco Systems, US West, and many other domestic and international training companies. He has taught the ACRC class for five years and has helped Cisco develop each successive version of the course. He has received degrees from Berkeley and Stanford, worked for IBM, programmed the AutoPilot of the NASA Space Shuttle, traveled to more than 40 countries, and helped excavate a seventeenth-century shipwreck.

Deborah A. Smith is a Certified Cisco Systems Instructor at GeoTrain Corporation, where she teaches Advanced Cisco Router Configuration and other Cisco-related courses. She has degrees in physics and philosophy and has taught physics at Idaho State University. She has worked at the Stanford Linear Accelerator Center, American Microsystems, Inc., and Intel Corporation. When she's not consulting on network engineering and systems management, Debi "makes steam" (runs the boilers) for the reciprocating steam engine on the *S.S. Jeremiah O'Brien* (a restored WWII cargo ship in San Francisco) and works on the restoration of her and her partner's 50-foot wooden sailboat.

Dedications

This book is dedicated to Jack Sebastian and David, my inspiration and support.

Acknowledgments

I have been given a great deal of encouragement and help from many people, but would particularly like to mention the staff at Cisco Press who made this book come together. My thanks go to the many members of the team who helped produce this book, especially John Kane, the Executive Editor, and Drew Cupp, the Development Editor, without whose patience, kindness, and expertise this book would never have been written.

I would also like to thank the following people:

Wendell Odom, not only for giving me the opportunity to write this book, but also for so generously sharing his wealth of technical expertise.

The technical editors, whose advice, careful attention to detail, and depth of knowledge greatly improved this book. They include Mike Bevan, Bill Chernock, Jeff Doyle, Tom Deevy, Vince Lamb, Brian Morgan, Gary Rubin, and Debi Smith.

Kevin Downes, for coming to the rescue at the eleventh hour to review the book.

Dayna Isley and Keith Cline, for the project and copy editing.

Imran Qureshi of Cisco Systems, for lending me equipment so that I could test configurations and version-specific details.

Finally, I wish to thank my husband David and our son Jack for their love and support throughout everything.

Contents at a Glance

Table of Contents

Overview of Certification and How to Succeed with This Book

Professional certifications have been an important part of the computing industry for many years and will continue to become more and more important. Although many reasons exist for these certifications, the most popularly cited reason is *credibility*. All other considerations held equal, the certified employee/consultant/job candidate is considered more valuable than the one not certified.

Cisco Certifications: Training Paths and Exams

The *Cisco Certified Internetwork Expert (CCIE)* certification program has been available since the early 1990s. This long-standing certification has maintained a high degree of credibility and is recognized as a certification that lives up to the name "expert." The CCIE certification process requires passing a computer-based test and then passing a two-day hands-on lab. Recertification is required every two years to ensure that the individual has kept his or her skills up to date.

Many problems were created by having one highly credible, but difficult-to-pass, certification. One problem was that there was no way to distinguish between someone who is almost ready to pass CCIE and a novice. The CCIE lab test is meant to prove that the individual not only has mastery of many topics, but that the individual also has the ability to learn and unravel situations quickly and under pressure. Many highly respected engineers have failed the CCIE lab on their first try. Employers wanting to reward employees based on certification, employers looking at prospective new employees, and network managers trying to choose between competing consulting companies have had too few Cisco-related certifications on which they could base their decisions.

Certification Exams

In an effort to solve these problems, Cisco Systems has created several new Cisco Career Certifications. Included in these new certifications is a series of certifications related to routing and switching. The *Cisco Certified Network Professional (CCNP)* and *Cisco Certified Design Professional (CCDP)* certifications, accomplished by passing computer-based exams, are two of these certifications oriented toward routing and switching. *In addition to other exams, you must pass the ACRC exam (or the very similar ACRC portion of the FRS exam) to achieve CCNP or CCDP certification.* The ACRC exam is used to prove mastery of the features used in more advanced and complicated large networks.

Figure I-1 lists the various Cisco certifications that relate to routing and switching, along with the exams that must be passed for such certification (including the exams in addition to ACRC that you must pass to become a CCNP or CCDP). Note that no matter which combination of exams you choose to become a CCNP or CCDP, you will need to master all the ACRC objectives.

Figure I-1   *Cisco Certifications and Exams on the Routing and Switching Career Track*

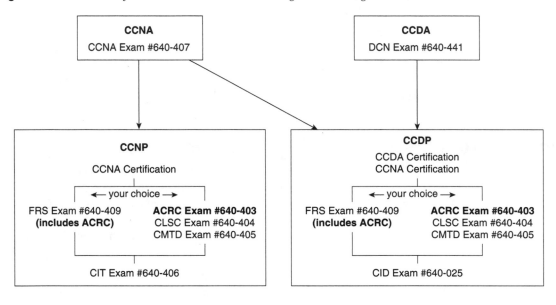

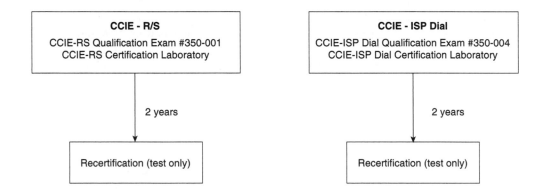

In addition to those certifications and exams listed in Figure I-1, a CCNP can choose to go on to one of five career specializations. These specializations are Security, LAN ATM, Voice Access, SNA Solutions, and Network Management. These specializations require CCNP certification and that the candidate pass a specific exam. See Cisco's Web site for exam details.

Some reasons for passing the ACRC exam and achieving CCNP or CCDP certification are as follows:

- To prove your mastery of advanced networking concepts

- To create a more impressive entry in your résumé

- To prove that beyond just taking a Cisco-certified course you have actually understood the topics in the class

- To demonstrate that you have equivalent experience and expertise to those who have taken the Cisco-certified courses

- To obtain a Cisco certification while you gain the experience needed to pass the CCIE Routing and Switching or CCIE ISP Dial certification (unless you want to shoot for the stars and take a CCIE test now)

- To encourage self-discipline in your study as you try to become CCIE certified

- For consultants, to provide a marketing edge over your competitors by asserting that a Cisco-certified individual will be working with a particular prospective client

Certification Training Paths

Cisco suggests training paths that include courses and exams for each certification.

The *Cisco Certified Network Associate (CCNA)* certification is used to prove mastery over network implementation issues for basic networks. Cisco suggests the following courses as the training path for CCNA certification:

- Internetworking Technology Multimedia (ITM) course (CD-based)

- Either the Cisco Routing and LAN Switching (CRLS) course (instructor-led) or both of the following courses:

  Introduction to Cisco Router Configuration (ICRC) (instructor-led) and

  High-Performance Solutions for Desktop Connectivity (HPSDC) (CD-based)

Because the CCNA certification is the entry-level Cisco certification, candidates may find that they have ample training through on-the-job experience to become a CCNA. Finally, Cisco's Networking Academies are designed for high school and university students. These academies seek to provide their students with valuable Cisco skills—skills ready to use in the marketplace at CCNA level.

The *Cisco Certified Networking Professional (CCNP)* certification is used to prove mastery of more complex networks. In this case, *complex* means topics covered in the prerequisite courses. Like the CCNA, the CCNP certification is oriented toward proving the skills needed to implement internetworks. *CCNA certification is a prerequisite to becoming a CCNP. You must pass the ACRC exam to become a CCNP.*

Cisco suggests the following courses as preparation for the CCNP certification exam:

- A training path leading to CCNA certification
- The Advanced Cisco Router Configuration (ACRC) course
- The Cisco LAN Switching Course (CLSC) course
- The Configuring, Monitoring, and Troubleshooting Dialup Services (CMTD) course
- The Cisco Internetwork Troubleshooting (CIT) course

The *Cisco Certified Design Associate (CCDA)* exam is used to prove mastery over network design issues for basic networks. It is similar to CCNA, but is focused on design issues. This certification is particularly important for those with presales-oriented jobs.

Cisco suggests the following courses as preparation for the CCDA exam:

- The Internetworking Technology Multimedia (ITM) CD-based course
- The Designing Cisco Networks (DCN) course

The *Cisco Certified Design Professional (CCDP)* exam is used to prove mastery over design issues for more advanced networks. This certification proves mastery of design issues in complex networks. In this case, complex means topics covered in the prerequisite courses. This certification is particularly important for those with presales-oriented jobs. *CCDA and CCNA certification are prerequisites to becoming a CCDP. You must pass the ACRC exam to become a CCNP.*

Cisco suggests the following courses as preparation for the CCDP certification:

1 A training path leading to CCDA and CCNA certification
2 The Advanced Cisco Router Configuration (ACRC) course
3 The Cisco LAN Switching Course (CLSC) course
4 The Configuring, Monitoring, and Troubleshooting Dialup Services (CMTD) course
5 The Cisco Internetwork Design (CID) course

A Few Words on the Various Cisco Certifications

You should note the following when considering CCNA, CCNP, CCDA, and CCDP Cisco routing and switching certifications:

Most people will not pursue all four of these certifications: CCNA, CCNP, CCDA, and CCDP—Most people will follow a track of getting CCNA and then focusing on either the design certifications or the implementation certifications.

None of these certifications require you to take any Cisco classes—However, the new certification exams happen to cover the content taught in Cisco Systems Certified Courses; so there is a definite benefit to taking the courses suggested by Cisco before attempting the exam.

The old CCIE is now CCIE-Routing and Switching (R/S)—Cisco added the designation R/S for routing and switching, which includes both LAN and ATM switching. This is the CCIE of old. A separate CCIE-ISP Dial certification covers dial issues in more depth, as well as exterior routing protocols. CCIE-WAN, which entails a separate career path of recommended courses and exams altogether, covers WAN switching and voice.

Only the CCIE certifications require a hands-on lab exam—CCIE-R/S, CCIE-ISP Dial, and CCIE-WAN all require passing a hands-on lab exam, after passing a written (computer-based) exam. Recertification for CCIE of any kind currently does not require a hands-on lab, but rather a more detailed written test on an area of specialization.

Recertification is not (yet) required for CCNA, CCNP, CCDA, and CCDP—Because these certifications were announced in early 1998, there is not yet a need for recertification rules. In my opinion, Cisco will eventually require recertification for these, probably with a written (computer-based) test.

In the future, CCNA might be required before taking CCIE—Today, you can take the CCIE written exam at any time. The reason these new certifications are not required before taking the CCIE exam today is that there would be complaints from people who have prepared for CCIE, but would have then to back up and take other tests. It is possible that one day Cisco will require CCDP or CCNP certification before taking the CCIE written and lab exams. Of course, the CCNP certification requires CCNA certification first, and the CCDP requires the CCDA and CCNA certification first.

There is also a WAN Switching Career Certifications path—There is a whole other set of certifications with the acronym WAN in the title, which refers to the WAN switching topics and the functions of what was once the Stratacom product line (which was bought by Cisco). CCNA-WAN, CCNP-WAN, CCDP-WAN, and CCIE-WAN are the certifications; only a CCDA-WAN is missing as compared to the routing/switching certifications outlined previously. These certifications are similar in concept to the others outlined previously; because the technology concerned is WAN switching, however, there are different exams and courses for the Career Certification levels. See Cisco's Web site (http://www.cisco.com) for more details.

Objective of This Book

The objective of this book is to help you fully understand, remember, and recall all the details of the topics covered on the ACRC exam. If that objective is reached, passing the ACRC exam should follow easily. The ACRC exam will be a stepping stone for most people as they progress through the other Cisco certifications; passing the exam because of a thorough understanding and recall of the topics will be incredibly valuable at the next steps.

This book prepares you to *pass the ACRC exam* by doing the following:

- Helping you discover which test topics you have not mastered

- Providing explanations and information to fill in your knowledge gaps

- Supplying exercises and scenarios that enhance your ability to recall and deduce the answers to test questions

- Providing practice exercises on the topics and the testing process via online test questions (delivered on the CD-ROM)

Who Should Read This Book?

This book is not designed to be a general networking topics book, although it can be used for that purpose. This book is intended to tremendously increase your chances of passing the ACRC exam. This book is intended for an audience who has taken the ACRC course or has an equivalent level of on-the-job experience. Although others may benefit from using this book, the book is written assuming that you want to pass the exam.

So, why should you want to pass ACRC? To get a raise. To show your manager you are working hard to increase your skills. To fulfill a manager's requirement (before he will spend money on another course). To enhance your résumé. Because you work in a presales job at a reseller, and want to become CCDA and CCDP certified. To prove you know the topic, if you learned via on-the-job experience rather than from taking the prerequisite classes. Or one of many other reasons.

Have You Mastered All the Exam Objectives?

The exam tests you on a wide variety of topics; most people will not remember all the topics on the exam. Because some study is required, this book focuses on helping you obtain the maximum benefit from the time you spend preparing for the exam. You can access many other sources for the information covered on the exam; for example, you could read the Cisco Documentation CD. This book is, however, the most effective way to prepare for the exam.

You should begin your exam preparation by reading Chapter 1, "What Is ACRC?" and spending ample time reviewing the exam objectives listed there. Check out Cisco's Web site for any future changes to the list of objectives.

How This Book Is Organized

The book begins with a chapter that generally defines the topics that will be covered by the ACRC exam, including all of the objectives. Before studying for any exam, knowing the topics that could be covered is vitally important. With the ACRC exam, knowing what is on the exam is seemingly straightforward; Cisco publishes a list of ACRC objectives. However, the objectives are certainly open to interpretation.

Chapters 2–9 directly follow Cisco's ACRC exam objectives and provide detailed information on each. Each chapter begins with a quiz so that you can quickly determine your current level of readiness.

The appendix provides the answers to the various chapter quizzes. Also, example test questions and the testing engine on the CD-ROM allow simulated exams for final practice.

Approach

Retention and recall are the two features of human memory most closely related to performance on tests. This exam preparation guide focuses on increasing both retention and recall of the topics on the exam. The other human characteristic involved in successfully passing an exam is intelligence; this book does not address that issue!

Adult retention is typically less than that of children. It is common for four-year-olds to pick up basic language skills in a new country faster than their parents can pick up these skills. Children retain facts as an end unto itself; adults typically need either a stronger reason to remember a fact or must have a reason to think about that fact several times to retain that fact in memory. For these reasons, a student who attends a typical Cisco course and retains 50% of the material is actually quite an amazing student!

Memory recall is based on connectors to the information that needs to be recalled. If the exam asks what ARP stands for, for example, we automatically add information to the question. Because of the nature of the test, we know the topic is networking. We may recall the term *ARP broadcast*, which implies it is the name of something that flows in a network. Maybe we do not recall all three words in the acronym ARP, but we recall that it has something to do with addressing. Of course, because the test is comprised of multiple-choice questions, if only one answer begins with the word *address*, we have a pretty good guess. Having read the answer "Address Resolution Protocol," we may even have the infamous "A-ha" experience, in which we are then sure that our answer is correct (and possibly a brightly lit light bulb is hovering over our heads). All these added facts and assumptions are the connectors that eventually lead our brains to the fact that needs to be recalled.

Of course, recall and retention work together. If you do not retain the knowledge, it will be difficult to recall it!

This book is designed with features to help you increase retention and recall. It does that in the following ways:

- Providing succinct and complete methods of helping you decide what you already know and what you do not know.

- Giving references to the exact passages in this book that review those concepts you did not recall. These references enable you to quickly remind yourself of a fact or concept.

- Including exercise questions that supply fewer connectors than multiple-choice questions provide. This format helps you exercise recall and avoids giving you a false sense of confidence (as a multiple-choice–only exercise might do). Fill-in-the-blank questions require you to have better recall than multiple-choice questions, for example.

- Finally, including a CD-ROM that has online, exam-like multiple-choice questions. Therefore, you can practice taking the exam and accustom yourself to the relevant time restrictions.

Features and Conventions of This Book

This book features the following:

Cross Reference to ACRC Objectives—Cisco lists the objectives of the CCNA exam on its Web site. That list is included in Chapter 1 of this book. A section of each core chapter will include a reference to the ACRC objectives discussed in that chapter. Each major section also begins with a list of the objectives covered in that section.

Do I Know This Already? Quiz—This beginning section of each chapter is designed to thoroughly quiz you on all topics in that chapter. Use your score on these questions to determine your relative need to study this topic further.

Foundation Topics—This section in each chapter explains and reviews topics that will be covered in the exam. If you feel the need for some review of the topics listed in that chapter, read through the explanations in this section. If you do not feel as much need to review these topics, review the "Foundation Summary" section in each chapter and then proceed directly to the exercises at the end of the chapter.

Foundation Summaries—Most of the major facts covered in each chapter are summarized in tables and charts within each chapter. This format enables you to review a chapter quickly, focusing on these summaries, without having to read the text. If you want to learn more, pause and refer back to the "Foundation Topics" section that covers the material in question. This shortcut is just one of the methods used in this book to enable you to make maximum use of your preparation time.

Q&A—Thinking about the same fact in many different ways increases recall; during a timed test, recall is a very important factor. During study time, increasing retention is most important (so there is something in memory you can recall in the future). These variously styled end-of-the-chapter questions focus on recall, covering topics in the "Foundation Topics" section.

Scenarios—Each chapter ends with scenarios that include a battery of questions. These scenarios are intended for use after you have reviewed the chapters and are ready to validate your mastery of the ACRC topics. If you get a high percentage of these questions correct, you should feel very confident about the ACRC exam.

Test Questions—Using the "Test Preparation" test engine on the CD, you can take simulated exams. You can also choose to be presented with several questions on a topic that you need to work on more. This testing tool will provide you with practice that will make you more comfortable when you actually take the ACRC exam.

Guidance Using Each Chapter—Chapters 2–9 can be used to discover gaps in your knowledge, fill those gaps, and practice recalling the new information. Figure I-2 outlines a general approach that can be used with each of these chapters.

By following this process, you can gain confidence, fill the holes in your knowledge, and know when you are ready to take the exam.

Knowing Cisco is not enough. Knowing Cisco and being able to prove that you know it—both at your job and with credentials—is vitally important in the job markets of the 21st century. The days of working an entire career at one firm are most likely gone; your skills, both professional and technical, will be invaluable as your career evolves. Being certified is a key to getting the right opportunities inside your company, with your clients, and with your next job!

Figure I-2 *How to Use Each Chapter*

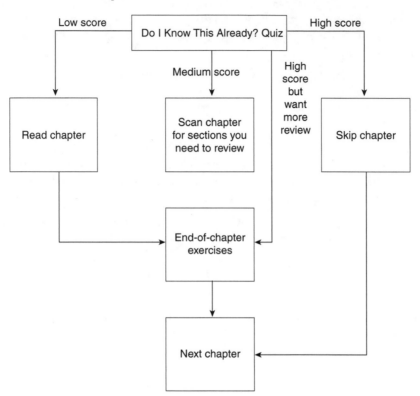

CHAPTER 1

What Is ACRC?

The ACRC exam evaluates the internetworking knowledge of network administrators, network specialists, and technicians who configure and support multiprotocol internetworks. Candidates attempting the ACRC exam must posses the skills to perform the following tasks:

- List and describe issues inherent in large and growing multiprotocol internetworks.

- Configure the Cisco IOS software to control multiprotocol routed traffic, routed protocols, and WAN traffic in a scalable network.

- Use VLSMs to extend the use of an IP address within a large internetwork.

- Configure OSPF and EIGRP in a growing enterprise network environment.

- Connect remote office routers to corporate backbone routers by configuring dial-up WAN connectivity and demonstrating end-to-end connectivity.

- Given a network problem, determine which bridging service to use and describe the required configuration.

The ACRC Exam and CCNP and CCDP Certification

The Cisco Certified Network Professional (CCNP) and Cisco Certified Design Professional (CCDP) certifications, accomplished by passing computer-based exams, are two of the certifications oriented toward routing and switching. *In addition to other exams, you must pass the ACRC exam (or the very similar ACRC portion of the FRS exam) to achieve CCNP or CCDP certification*. The ACRC exam is used to prove mastery of the features used in more advanced and complicated large networks.

Skills required for CCNP certification include the ability to install, configure, operate, and troubleshoot complex routed LANs, routed WANs, switched LANs, and dial access services.

Complex networks are defined as those utilizing IP, IGRP, IPX, asynchronous routing, AppleTalk, extended access lists, IP RIP, route redistribution, IPX RIP, route summarization, OSPF, VLSM, BGP, Serial, IGRP, Frame Relay, ISDN, ISL, X.25, DDR, PSTN, PPP, VLANs, Ethernet, access lists, 802.10, FDDI, and transparent and translational bridging.

The target audience for CCNP certification includes the following:

- Gold- or Silver-certified partners
- CCNAs who want to progress for reasons such as increased earning power, professional recognition, job promotion, and so on
- Level 1 network support, central operations staff in a large enterprise who want to further develop technical expertise

A CCNP's training and real-world experience will enable him or her to accomplish the following:

- Install and configure a network to increase bandwidth, quicken network response times, improve reliability, and improve quality of service
- Maximize performance through campus LANs, routed WANs, and remote access
- Improve network security
- Create a global intranet
- Provide access security to campus switches and routers
- Provide increased switching and routing bandwidth as well as end-to-end resiliency services
- Provide custom queuing and routed priority services

Skills required for CCDP certification include the ability to design complex routed LANs, routed WANs, and switched LANs. This certification exam assumes the prerequisite knowledge and skills to install, configure, and operate these networks.

The target audience for CCDP certification includes the following:

- Gold and Silver partners
- Level 2 network consultants or analysts in a large enterprise
- Technicians who need to learn and apply design methodology
- CCDAs and CCNAs who want to progress for reasons such as increased earning power, professional recognition, job promotion, and so on

As well as the base level of technical knowledge, CCDPs must also demonstrate proficiency in the following areas:

- Network-layer addressing in a hierarchical environment
- Traffic management with access lists and hierarchical network design
- VLAN use and propagation

- Performance considerations (including required hardware and software, switching engine, and memory)
- Cost minimization

The ACRC exam tests all the skills listed in this section. (Other exams required for CCNP or CCDP certification also test these skills.) See the section "The ACRC Exam Objectives" later in this chapter for a list of the specific skills tested on the ACRC exam. This book discusses all these skills in detail.

Suggested Prior Preparation—Cisco Training Paths

This book assumes that you have a familiar level of understanding of the ACRC objectives, either through the ACRC course or an equivalent level of on-the-job training, and that you are now ready to master the ACRC exam objectives and become a CCNP or CCDP. Table 1-1 outlines the three training paths you can take to become a CCNP, including the various courses available.

Table 1-1   *The Training Paths for Becoming a CCNP*

Training Path	What Is Involved
1. CCNP Path #1	As defined by Cisco Systems, this involves taking the following courses:
	Advanced Cisco Router Configuration (ACRC) Cisco LAN Switch Configuration (CLSC) Configuring Monitoring and Troubleshooting Dial-Up Services (CMTD) Cisco Internetworking Troubleshooting (CIT)
	The candidate must then take a test for each course attended. (Note that the ACRC, CLSC, and CMTD exams can be taken all together; the exam is called the Foundation Routing and Switching [FRS] exam.)
2. On-the-Job Training	On-the-job training, without the courses described in the preceding path. The courses are not required to take the exams, but the exams require a large amount of specific knowledge. Candidates who have not taken the courses should use this book to make sure that they are familiar with all the objectives.
	The candidate must then take the same exams listed in the preceding path.

The CCDP training path is the same as the CCNP path, but it substitutes a Cisco Internetwork Design (CID) course and exam for the Cisco Internetworking Troubleshooting (CIT) course and exam. Both CCNP and CCDP require mastery of the ACRC exam objectives.

ACRC Exam Philosophy

The exam objectives are a great tool for preparation. Making sure that you can address all objectives is an obvious thing to do if you are going to prepare only slightly. Be aware, however, that *what each objective means and the breadth of questions that might be based on an individual objective are open to interpretation*. This book generally follows the ACRC course to determine the depth of coverage for various objectives. This is the safest bet.

Cisco will probably never identify exactly which topics are on the exam. Cisco does want candidates to succeed at passing the ACRC exam, but not at the expense of making the Cisco career certification an easily attained paper diploma. Cisco's goal is that passing the ACRC exam should reflect the fact that you have internalized and mastered the concepts, not that you can read a book and memorize well. To protect you against the ACRC slowly losing credibility due to people just reading a book and passing the test, Cisco will probably always avoid an exact definition of the topics on the exam. By giving a general definition only, Cisco rewards those who understand networks. Those who prefer to memorize will be less likely to pass the test.

The objectives will change as time goes on. As this happens, a higher percentage of the test questions will not be in the list of objectives found in this book. Of course, Cisco will change or add to the objective list at their discretion; therefore, pulling the latest ACRC objectives list from Cisco's Web site is worth the effort.

The ACRC exam topics will closely match what is covered in the recommended prerequisite training course. Cisco Worldwide Training (WWT) is the Cisco organization responsible for the certifications. Many of the certification exams evolved from exams covering a particular course. It is reasonable, therefore, to expect that ACRC and the other certifications will cover the topics covered in the prerequisite classes. Knowing that, I have made choices about which topics to focus on and which to ignore.

The following list encapsulates the basic philosophy behind preparing for the ACRC exam based on what Cisco is willing to disclose:

- Although open to interpretation, the ACRC objectives define the main topics covered on the exam. At a minimum, you should know about each subject covered in these objectives.

- The depth of knowledge on each topic is comparable to what is covered in the prerequisite courses. This book attempts to cover the topics to a slightly deeper level, to make sure that you know more than enough.

- Getting the latest copy of Cisco's ACRC objectives from their Web site is very useful. By comparing that list to the one used for this book, you can know which topics you need to spend additional time studying.

- Do not expect to pass the exam if your only preparation has been to read this book. One of the suggested training paths should be used. For the best chance at success, you should also work with routers and switches.

ACRC Exam Preparation

This book contains many solid tools to help you prepare for the ACRC exam. The next few sections outline some of the key features that help you prepare.

Chapters Follow the Objectives

Each chapter clearly follows the ACRC exam objectives so that you can stay on track with the material that will be covered on the exam. You will know clearly which objective each section is covering.

Determining Your Strengths and Weaknesses

You may feel confident about one topic, and less confident about another. That may be a confidence problem, however, not a knowledge problem. One key to using your time well is to determine whether you truly need more study, and if so, how much?

The chapters guide you through the process of determining what you need to study. Suggestions are made as to how to study a topic, based on your personal strength on the topics of that chapter. Each chapter begins with a quiz that helps you decide how well you recall the topics in that chapter. From there, you can choose to read the entire chapter, ignore that chapter because you know it already, or settle for something in between. Much of the factual information is summarized into lists and charts in the "Foundation Summary" section of each chapter; therefore, a review of the chapter is easy. Also, exercises at the end of each chapter provide an excellent tool for practice and for quick review.

Questions and Exercises That Are Harder Than the Actual Exam

The exercises in this book are intended to make you stretch beyond what the exam requires. Do not be discouraged as you take the quizzes and exercises in the book; they are intended to be harder than the exam. If by the end of your study time you are getting 70–80 percent of these harder non-multiple-choice questions correct, the ACRC exam should be easier to handle. You will probably want to validate your readiness by using the testing engine included on the CD-ROM that accompanies this book.

This book's exams are harder than the ACRC exam not because they ask for facts or concepts that you will never see on the ACRC exam, but because they ask for information in ways that do not imply the correct answer. You will get some questions correct on the ACRC exam just because the multiple answers will trigger your memory. The exams in this book ask non–multiple-choice questions and also ask for the same information in different ways, and thus exercise your memory. This style of review will make the multiple-choice exam easy!

Scenarios for Final Preparation

If all you do is focus on your weaknesses, your strengths may suffer. Scenarios at the end of each chapter include exercises that cover all the topics in the chapter. These give you an opportunity to exercise all your knowledge and skills, both strong and weak. These scenarios will also help to remind you one last time of some facts that you may have forgotten.

Simulated Testing on the CD-ROM

Of course, if you never practice using actual exams, you will not be fully prepared. The Test Prep test engine on the accompanying CD-ROM can be used in two ways to help you prepare for the actual test. First, it will give you a timed test of the same length as the actual ACRC exam and score the exam for you. Second, you can tell the tool to feed you questions on a particular subject so that you can do some intensive review.

The ACRC Exam Objectives

Cisco System's published ACRC exam objectives are currently listed on Cisco's Web sight at www.cisco.com.

The objectives intend to test the ability to install, configure, operate, and troubleshoot complex routed LANs, routed WANs, switched LANs, and dial access services.

The ACRC exam includes 73 objectives, testing the candidate on the following areas:

1 Issues inherent in large and growing multiprotocol internetworks

2 Configuring the Cisco IOS to control routed traffic, routed protocols, and WAN traffic in a scalable internetwork

3 The use of VLSMs to extend the use of an IP address within a large internetwork

4 Configuring OSPF and EIGRP in a growing enterprise network environment

5 Connecting remote office routers to corporate backbone routers by configuring dial-up WAN services

6 Issues surrounding the choice of a bridging technology

List of the ACRC Exam Objectives

Table 1-2 lists all the ACRC exam objectives. These are the objectives this book will help you master to pass the ACRC exam. Each chapter also begins with a list of which objectives are covered in that chapter. Each major section of the chapters also begins with a list of the objectives covered in that section. Note that the ACRC Foundation Routing and Switching objective numbers are also listed for the benefit of those choosing the FRS testing route. This book helps you prepare for either, although the FRS exam covers additional objectives for which you will also need to be prepared. Also provided in this list (in italics) are the categories into which Cisco places these objectives. These categories are for organizational purposes and are not individual objectives. Finally, the table includes the number of the chapter that covers each objective.

Table 1-2   *List of ACRC Exam Objectives, Including the Corresponding FRS Objective Numbers*

ACRC Objective	FRS Objective	Objective	Chapter
	81	Upon completion of this course, you will be able to configure Cisco routers for scalable operation in large or growing multiprotocol internetworks. [This objective is listed in the FRS list of objectives and not the ACRC list. This book covers this very general objective throughout the book by covering the more specific objectives that follow.]	2
Overview of Scalable Networks			
1	82	Describe the key requirements of a scalable internetwork.	2
2	83	Select a Cisco IOS feature as a solution for a given internetwork requirement.	2
Introduction to Managing Traffic and Access			
3	84	Describe causes of network congestion.	2
4	85	List solutions for controlling network congestion.	2
5	86	Introduction to managing traffic and access.	2
6	87	Configure IP standard access lists.	2
7	88	Limit virtual terminal access.	2
8	89	Configure IP extended access lists.	2
9	90	Verify access list operation.	2
10	91	Configure an alternative to using access lists.	2
11	92	Configure an IP helper address to manage broadcasts.	2
Managing Novell IPX/SPX Traffic			
12	93	Describe IPX/SPX traffic management issues.	2
13	94	Filter IPX traffic using IPX access lists.	2
14	95	Manage IPX/SPX traffic over WAN.	2
15	96	Verify IPX/SPX filter operation.	2

Continues

Table 1-2   *List of ACRC Exam Objectives, Including the Corresponding FRS Objective Numbers (Continued)*

ACRC Objective	FRS Objective	Objective	Chapter
Configuring Queuing to Manage Traffic			
16	97	Describe the need for queuing in a large network.	2
17	98	Describe weighted fair queuing operation.	2, 7
18	99	Configure priority.	7
19	100	Configure custom queuing.	7
20	101	Verify queuing operation.	7
Routing Protocol Overview			
21	102	List the key information routers needed to route data.	4
22	103	Compare distance vector and link-state protocol operation.	4
Extending IP Addresses Using VLSMs			
23	104	Given an IP address, use VLSMs to extend the use of the IP address.	3
24	105	Given a network plan that includes IP addressing, explain if a route summarization is or is not possible.	3
25	106	Define private addressing and determine when it can be used.	3
26	107	Define network address translation and determine when it can be used.	3
Configuring OSPF in a Single Area			
27	108	Explain why OSPF is better than RIP in a large internetwork.	4
28	109	Explain how OSPF discovers, chooses, and maintains routes.	4
29	110	Configure OSPF for proper operation.	5
30	111	Verify OSPF operation.	5
Interconnecting Multiple OSPF Areas			
31	112	Describe the issues with interconnecting multiple areas and how OSPF addresses.	4
32	113	Explain the differences between the possible types of areas, routers, and LSAs.	4
33	114	Configure a multiarea OSPF network.	5
34	115	Verify OSPF operation.	5

Table 1-2   *List of ACRC Exam Objectives, Including the Corresponding FRS Objective Numbers (Continued)*

ACRC Objective	FRS Objective	Objective	Chapter
Configuring EIGRP			
35	116	Describe Enhanced IGRP features and operation.	6
36	117	Configure Enhanced IGRP.	6
37	118	Verify Enhanced IGRP operation.	6
Optimizing Routing Update Operation			
38	119	Select and configure the different ways to control route update traffic.	6
39	120	Configure route redistribution in a network that does not have redundant paths between dissimilar routing process.	6
40	121	Configure route redistribution in a network that has redundant paths between dissimilar routing processes.	6
41	122	Resolve path selection problems that result in a redistributed network.	6
42	123	Verify route redistribution.	6
Connecting Enterprises to an Internet Service Provider			
43	124	Describe when to use BGP to connect to an ISP.	6
44	125	Describe methods to connect to an ISP using static and default routes, and BGP.	6
WAN Connectivity Overview			
45	126	Compare the differences between WAN connection types: dedicated, asynchronous dial-in, dial-on-demand, and packet switched services.	7
46	127	Determine when to use PPP, HDLC, LAPB, and IETF encapsulation types.	7
47	128	List at least four common issues to be considered when evaluating WAN services.	7
Configuring Dial-on-Demand Routing			
48	129	Describe the components that make up ISDN connectivity.	7
49	130	Configure ISDN BRI.	7
50	131	Configure Legacy dial-on-demand routing (DDR).	7
51	132	Configure dialer profiles.	7
52	133	Verify DDR operation.	7

Continues

Table 1-2   *List of ACRC Exam Objectives, Including the Corresponding FRS Objective Numbers (Continued)*

ACRC Objective	FRS Objective	Objective	Chapter
Customizing DDR Operation			
53	134	Configure dial backup.	7
54	135	Verify dial backup operation.	7
55	136	Configure MultiLink PPP operation.	7
56	137	Verify MultiLink PPP operation.	7
57	138	Configure snapshot routing.	7
58	139	Configure IPX spoofing.	7
Bridging Overview			
59	140	Define routable and nonroutable protocols and give an example of each.	8
60	141	Define various bridging types and describe when to use each type.	8
Configuring Transparent Bridging and Integrated Routing and Bridging			
61	142	Configure transparent bridging.	8
62	143	Configure integrated routing and bridging (IRB).	8
Configuring Source-Route Bridging			
63	144	Describe the basic functions of source-route bridging (SRB).	8
64	145	Configure SRB.	8
65	146	Configure source-route transparent bridging (SRT).	8
66	147	Configure source-route translational bridging (SR/TLB).	8
67	148	Verify SRB operation.	8
Managing AppleTalk Traffic			
68	149	Identify potential sources of congestion in an AppleTalk network.	9
69	150	Configure zone filters.	9
70	151	Configure RTMP filters.	9
71	152	Configure NBP filters.	9
Configuring T1/E1 and ISDN PRI Options			
72	153	Identify channelized T1 and E1 configuration.	9
73	154	Identify ISDN PRI configuration commands.	9

Cross Reference to Objectives Covered in Each Chapter

Table 1-3 lists the chapters in this book and the corresponding ACRC objectives that each chapter covers.

Table 1-3   *Chapter Roadmap of ACRC Objectives as Covered in Individual Chapters*

Chapter	ACRC Objective
2	1 to 17
3	23 to 26
4	21, 22, 27, 28, 31, 32
5	29, 30, 33, 34
6	35 to 44
7	17 to 20, 45 to 58
8	59 to 67
9	68 to 73

Where Do I Go from Here?

After passing the ACRC exam, you should try to pass all the exams required for you to be a CCNP or CCDP (refer to the exams listed in Table 1-1). Then, with the proper amount of experience and training, the CCIE exam should be your next step.

The objectives for the ACRC exam for CCNP or CCDP certification are taken from the Cisco Web site at http://www.cisco.com/training, under the heading "Cisco Career Certifications and Training." The following table shows the ACRC exam objectives covered in this chapter and also provides the corresponding Foundation Routing and Switching exam objective number. The objective(s) that are explained within a chapter section are also listed at the beginning of that section.

ACRC Exam Objective Number	Corresponding FRS Exam Objective Number	Description
	81	Configure Cisco routers for scalable operation in large or growing multiprotocol internetworks.
1	82	Describe the key requirements of a scalable internetwork.
2	83	Select a Cisco IOS feature as a solution for a given internetwork requirement.
3	84	Describe causes of network congestion.
4	85	List solutions for controlling network congestion.
5	86	Introduction to managing traffic and access.
6	87	Configure IP standard access lists.
7	88	Limit virtual terminal access.
8	89	Configure IP extended access lists.
9	90	Verify access list operation.
10	91	Configure an alternative to using access lists.
11	92	Configure an IP helper address to manage broadcasts.
12	93	Describe IPX/SPX traffic management issues.
13	94	Filter IPX traffic using IPX access lists.
14	95	Manage IPX/SPX traffic over WAN.
15	96	Verify IPX/SPX filter operation.
16	97	Describe the need for queuing in a large network.
17	98	Describe weighted fair queuing operation.

CHAPTER 2

Managing Scalable Network Growth

How to Best Use This Chapter

By taking the following steps, you can make better use of your study time:

- Keep your notes and answers for all your work with this book in one place for easy reference.

- Take the quiz, writing down your answers. Studies show that retention significantly increases by writing facts and concepts down, even if you never look at the information again!

- Use the diagram in Figure 2-1 to guide you to the next step.

"Do I Know This Already?" Quiz

These questions are designed to test not just your knowledge, but your understanding of the subject matter. It is therefore important to realize that getting the answer the same as stated in Appendix A, "Answers to Quizzes and Q&As," is less important than your answer having embodied the spirit of the question. In this manner, the questions and answers are not as open and shut as will be found on the exam. Their intention is to prepare you with the appropriate knowledge and understanding to give you mastery of the subject as opposed to limited rote knowledge.

1 List four symptoms of network congestion.

_____

_____

_____

2 Which of the queuing techniques offered by the Cisco IOS are manually configured?

_____

_____

_____

Figure 2-1 *How to Use This Chapter*

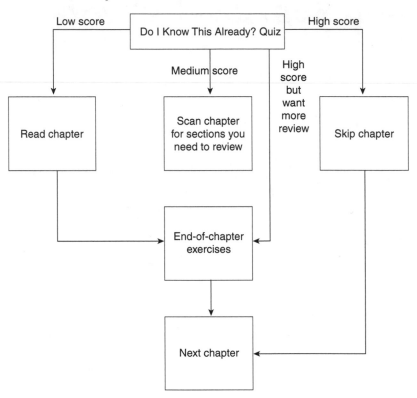

3 In an IP standard access list, what is the default wildcard mask?

_____

_____

_____

4 At which layer of the OSI model do Standard Access Lists work?

_____

_____

_____

5 State three uses of access lists.

_____

_____

_____

6 In the hierarchical design suggested by Cisco, at which layer are access lists not recommended?

_____

_____

_____

7 What does the established keyword do in an extended access list?

_____

_____

_____

8 What is the access list number range for SAP filter access lists?

_____

_____

_____

9 Explain **ip helper address**. What is its function?

_____

_____

_____

10 If a packet does not match any of the criteria in an access list, what action will be taken?

_____

_____

_____

11 On a LAN, where does the IPX node/host address come from?

_____

_____

_____

12 How would you restrict Telnet connectivity to the router that you were configuring?

_____

_____

_____

The answers to this quiz are found in Appendix A, "Answers to Quizzes and Q&As," (see page 453). Review the answers, grade your quiz, and choose an appropriate next step in this chapter based on the suggestions diagrammed in Figure 2-1. Your choices for the next step are as follows:

- Read this chapter.

- Scan this chapter for sections you need to review.

- Skip to the exercises at the end of this chapter.

- Skip this chapter.

Foundation Topics

Introduction to Corporate Networks—Growth, Scalability, and Congestion

Company networks are growing at a dramatic rate. When designing a network, the challenge is to create a system that will grow with the company and be able to deal with increased demand. Obviously, the size, nature, and maturity of the business will affect the demand for increased network resources.

Networking is still young. It has only very recently extended to the home and small business. Therefore, it is a safe assumption that networks and the demand for network traffic will continue to grow for some time.

In addition to the increase in the number of users, applications have become more complex, evolving into highly graphic and often interactive packages.

If the design and implementation of the original network has been well managed, network growth increases dramatically within the first year. Networks must therefore be adaptive to change in order to allow growth. (Instead of constantly having to buy new clothes for the sprouting child, we can just let down hems and lengthen sleeves.) Companies cannot afford either the capital investment nor the hours involved in accommodating a network that must be redesigned frequently.

The consequence of having a network incapable of scaling is that as it grows it becomes constricted, just like the child squeezed into a coat that is too small. The result within your company would be *network congestion*.

Identifying the Problem of Network Congestion

The ACRC objectives mastered in this section are as follows:

ACRC Exam Objective Number	Corresponding FRS Exam Objective Number	Description
1	82	Describe the key requirements of a scalable internetwork.
3	84	Describe causes of network congestion.
4	85	List solutions for controlling network congestion.

Network congestion results, literally, when too many packets are competing for limited bandwidth. The result is similar to that of heavy road traffic: collisions, delays, and user frustration.

Problems Created by Network Congestion

The problems caused by network congestion are easily identified. By using network-monitoring tools such as Cisco's Traffic Director or a standard protocol analyzer, it is possible to ascertain the traffic volume on either an entire network or on individual segments. It is important to understand the context of the traffic flow within your network so that you can appropriately accommodate the requirements of the users and their applications, designing and building a network that will scale.

The traffic on the network typically follows the organization's business flow, responding not only to peaks and valleys in business cycles, but in the direction of the traffic flow, as well. Necessarily, the communication between the accounting department and the marketing department within the organization must be reflected in network traffic. The appropriate placement of network resources such as servers is another important consideration. The original design of the network and the placement of the servers dictate the traffic flow throughout the company. Poor design inevitably leads to congestion.

The next sections cover the following problems created by network congestion:

- Excessive traffic.
- Dropping of packets.
- Retransmission of packets.
- Routing tables may be incomplete.
- Server lists may be incomplete.
- The Spanning-Tree Protocol may break.
- Runaway congestion.

Excessive Traffic

If the traffic volume outgrows the network capacity, the result is congestion. When this occurs on a single segment, not only is the capacity of the medium overrun—resulting in the dropping of packets—but also the medium can react adversely to excessive traffic. Ethernet has strict rules about accessing the medium. A physical problem—extraneous noise or just too many trying to access too little—results in excessive traffic, causing collisions. A collision requires all transmitting devices to stop sending data and to wait a random amount of time before attempting to send the original packet. Only the nodes involved in the collision are required to wait during the backoff period. Other nodes must wait until the end of the jam signal and the interframe gap (9.6 microseconds). If after 16 attempts the device fails to transmit, it gives up and reports the error to the calling process. If for this or any other reason the device fails to transmit and drops the packet from its buffer, the application typically retransmits the original packet. This may result in increased congestion that grows exponentially, which is often referred to as *runaway congestion*.

Dropping of Packets

One of the effects of congestion is that not all the packets can get through the network. Essentially, the queues and buffers in the intermediate forwarding devices (for example, routers) overflow and have to drop packets, causing a higher layer of the OSI model on either end device (for example, workstation) to timeout. Typically, the transport and/or the application layer has the responsibility to ensure the arrival of every piece of data.

Maintaining the integrity of the transmission requires the communication to be *connection oriented*, giving the end devices the mechanisms to perform error detection and correction (for example, the TCP layer of TCP/IP) through sequencing and acknowledgements.

Retransmission of Packets

If packets are dropped, the layer responsible for the integrity of the transmission will retransmit the lost packets. The session or application layer may not receive the packets that were re-sent in time, however, causing either incomplete information or timeouts.

Routing Tables May Be Incomplete

The application may be unaware that it did not receive all the data; this missing data may just appear as an error or may have more subtle and insidious effects. If the routing table of an intermediate forwarding device such as a router is incomplete, it may make inaccurate forwarding decisions, resulting in loss of connectivity or even the dreaded *routing loop* (see Figure 2-2).

If the WAN connection becomes congested, packets may be dropped, possibly resulting in partial routing updates being received. In Figure 2-2, for example, if Router X hears a full update, the routing table will know subnetworks 10, 20, and 30. Imagine that Router Y does not receive a full update from Router X. It only knows about subnetworks 20 and 30. When Workstation A tries to connect to Server B, Router X can direct the traffic to Router Y. In turn, Router Y can forward to Server B. When Server B responds, Router Y has no way to forward back to Router X, because it has no entry for the remote subnetwork 10. In a more complex environment, routing loops often occur.

Server Lists May Be Incomplete

Congestion results in the random loss of packets. Under extreme circumstances, packet loss may result in routing tables and server lists becoming incomplete. Entries may ghost in and out of these tables. Users may find that their favorite service is sometimes unavailable. The intermittent nature of this type of network problem makes it difficult to troubleshoot.

Figure 2-2   *Incomplete Routing Tables Cause Loss of Connectivity*

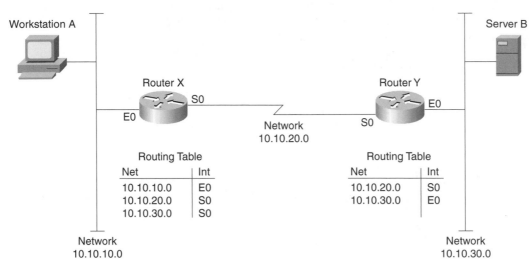

The Spanning-Tree Protocol May Break

The Spanning-Tree Protocol is maintained in each Layer 2 device, allowing the device to ensure that it has only one path back to the root bridge. Any redundant paths will be blocked, as long as the Layer 2 device continues to see the primary path. The health of this primary path is ensured by receiving spanning-tree updates (called Bridge Protocol Data Units, or BPDUs). As soon as the Layer 2 device fails to see the updates, panic sets in and it removes the block on the redundant path, falsely believing it to be the only path available. In a short time, spanning-tree loops and broadcast storms will cause your network to seize up and die.

This is one of the reasons that the industry moved toward a routed network solution. However, organizations are beginning to reintroduce spanning tree into their switched environments without any problems. This is due to the vast improvements in the hardware, the increased bandwidth, the use of VLANs to reduce the size of the broadcast domain, and in a Cisco implementation, due to the spanning-tree domain. Refer to the Cisco design guides for more information on these topics.

Runaway Congestion

When packets are dropped, requiring retransmission, the congestion will inevitably increase. In some instances, this may increase the traffic exponentially; this is often called *runaway congestion*. In relatively unsophisticated protocols, such as the Spanning-Tree Protocol, it is almost unavoidable, although others may have methods of tracking the delays in the network and throttling back on transmission. Both TCP and AppleTalk's DDP use flow control to prevent runaway congestion. It is important, therefore, to understand the nature of the traffic on your network when designing scalable networks.

Symptoms of Congestion

The ACRC objectives mastered in this section are as follows:

ACRC Exam Objective Number	Corresponding FRS Exam Objective Number	Description
1	82	Describe the key requirements of a scalable internetwork.
3	84	Describe causes of network congestion.

The symptoms of congestion are intermittent. If the link is running near bandwidth capacity, and the connected devices are overwhelmed, any additional traffic will cause problems. Because the packets are randomly dropped, it is difficult to track where the problems have occurred. Therefore, the network will have equally random failures. The symptoms of network congestion are consequently difficult to troubleshoot. Because some protocols are more sensitive than others and will timeout after very short delays are experienced, however, the network administrator who knows his network well will soon identify these recurring problems. The following are three symptoms of network congestion:

- Applications timeout.
- Clients cannot connect to network resources.
- Network death.

Applications Timeout

The session layer of the OSI model is responsible for maintaining the communication flow between the two end devices. This includes assigning resources to incoming requests to connect to an application. To allocate resources adequately, idle timers disconnect sessions after a set time, releasing those resources for other requests. Note that although the OSI model assigns these duties to the session layer, many protocol stacks include the upper layers of the stack in the application. TCP/IP is an example of this practice.

Clients Cannot Connect to Network Resources

In a client/server environment, the available resources are communicated throughout the network. The dynamic nature of the resource tables (offering services, servers, or networks) gives an up-to-date and accurate picture of the network. NetWare, AppleTalk, Vines, and Windows NT all work on this principle. If these tables are inaccurate due to the casualty of packets in your network, however, errors will be introduced as a result of decisions made with incorrect information. Some network systems are moving more toward a peer-to-peer system in which the end user requests a service identified not by the network but by the administrator.

Network Death

The most common problem arising from network congestion is intermittent connectivity and excessive delays—users having to wait a long time for screens to refresh; users being disconnected from applications; print jobs failing; errors resulting when trying to write files to remote servers. If the response of the applications is to retransmit, the congestion could reach a point of no recovery. Likewise, if routing or spanning-tree loops are introduced due to packet loss, the excessive looping traffic could bring your network down.

Key Requirements of a Network

The ACRC objective mastered in this section is as follows:

ACRC Exam Objective Number	Corresponding FRS Exam Objective Number	Description
1	82	Describe the key requirements of a scalable internetwork.

When designing a network, it is imperative that the requirements of the network be met. Understanding the business structure and current data flow within the existing environment inform the requirements of the network. The relative importance of each of the following broad categories is determined by the needs of the organization in question. A small, growing catering company may place more importance of efficiency, adaptability, and accessibility than a large financial institution that demands reliability, responsiveness, and security. The sections that follow describe the key requirements of a network, including the following:

- Reliability
- Responsiveness
- Efficiency
- Adaptability
- Accessibility/security

Reliability

For a hospital or bank, the network must be available 24 hours a day, seven days a week. In the first instance, lives are at stake. If network access cannot be granted to the blood bank, it may not be possible to give a life-saving transfusion. For a finical bank exchanging money throughout the international markets and across every time zone, network downtime can cost up to millions of dollars per fraction of an hour. The capability to isolate and limit any problems that occur is as important as solving the problem quickly.

Responsiveness

Excessive latency within a network appears to the end user as a lack of responsiveness. Frustration sets in and often leads the user to reboot or to repeat keystrokes. This is the same response that might cause you to raise your voice to someone who does not answer your question; you assume that he or she hasn't heard your question, so you repeat it more loudly. In the network environment, however, repeating keystrokes generates more network traffic, which increases congestion and delays. Avoiding this is essential for network health. To do so, build in mechanisms to alleviate congestion and to prioritize certain protocols that are more sensitive to delay.

Efficiency

Designing the network and restricting the traffic to allow only the necessary information to be carried across it proves extremely helpful in preventing congestion. The inefficiency in allowing network and service updates to travel to areas of your network that have no need for the information can seriously limit the available bandwidth left for data. Allowing users in Brussels, Belgium to see printers in Palo Alto, California is not very helpful and may saturate the 56k serial link.

Adaptability

It is difficult to anticipate every change your company may make in terms of mergers and organizational structure. Therefore, building an adaptable network protects capital investment. It also increases the reliability of the network. Because network administrators are not issued crystal balls, it is essential that attention be given to the interoperability of both products and applications when designing the network.

Accessibility/Security

Security is a popular topic and a major consideration, particularly as more and more companies connect to the Internet and thereby increase the chance of idle hackers wandering in to the network. The needs of the users to access the network, particularly when remote access is required, against the need to secure the company secrets is a difficult balance that requires careful consideration at the executive level.

Cisco's Hierarchical Design

The ACRC objective mastered in this section is as follows:

ACRC Exam Objective Number	Corresponding FRS Exam Objective Number	Description
4	85	List solutions for controlling network congestion.

Cisco suggests a network design structure that allows for growth. The key to the design is that it is hierarchical. There is a division of functionality between the layers of the hierarchy, allowing only certain traffic—based on clear criteria—to be forwarded through to the upper levels. It is a filtering operation that restricts unnecessary traffic from traversing the network. Thus the network is more adaptable, scalable, and more reliable. Clear guidelines and rules govern how to design networks according to these principles. These guidelines and rules are covered in the Cisco design class as well as design guides provided by Cisco on its Web page. The following section explains how the hierarchical network design proposed by Cisco reduces congestion.

Why Scaling Reduces Congestion

If the network is designed hierarchically, with each layer acting as a filter to the layer beneath it, the network can grow effectively. In this way, local traffic is kept local, and only information about global resources needs to travel outside the immediate domain.

Understanding that the layers are filtering layers begs the question as to how many layers are required in your network. The answer is: It depends.

How Hierarchical Is Hierarchical?

Cisco's design methodology is based on simplicity and filtering. Cisco suggests that the largest networks currently require no more than three layers of filtering.

Because a hierarchical layer in the network topology is a control point for traffic flow, a hierarchical layer is the same as a routing layer. This means the placement of a router or, more recently, a Layer 3 switching device.

The number of hierarchical layers that you need to implement in your network reflects the amount of traffic control required. To determine how many layers are required, you must identify the function that each layer will have within your network.

The Functions of Each Layer

Each hierarchical layer in the network design is responsible for preventing unnecessary traffic from being forwarded to the higher layers (and then being discarded at a higher point in the network or by the receiving stations). The goal is to allow only relevant traffic to traverse the network and thereby reduce the load on the network. If this goal is met, the network can scale more effectively. The three layers of a hierarchy are as follows:

- The access layer
- The distribution layer
- The core layer

The Access Layer

In accordance with its name, the access layer is where the end devices connect to the network—where they gain access to the company network. The Layer 3 devices (such as routers) that guard the entry and exit to this layer are responsible for ensuring that all local server traffic does not leak out to the wider network. Service Advertisement Protocol (SAP) filters for NetWare and AppleTalk's GetZoneLists are implemented here, in reference to the design consideration of client/server connectivity.

The Distribution Layer

The distribution layer is responsible for determining access across the campus backbone, by filtering out unnecessary resource updates as well as by selectively granting specific access to users and departments. Access lists are used not just as traffic filters, but as the first level of rudimentary security.

Access to the Internet is implemented here, requiring a more sophisticated security or firewall system.

The Core Layer

The responsibility of the core layer is to connect the entire enterprise. At the pinnacle of the network reliability, it is of the utmost importance. A break in the network at this level would result in large sections of the organization no longer being able to communicate across the network. To ensure continuous connectivity, the core layer should be designed to be highly redundant and, as much as possible, all latency should be removed. At the core layer, functions relating to connectivity, such as filters, should not be implemented. They should already have been implemented at the access or distribution layers, leaving the core layer with the simple duty of relaying the data as fast as possible to the remote site.

General Design Rules for Each Layer

A clear understanding of the traffic patterns within the organization—who is connecting to whom and when—helps to ensure the appropriate implementation of filtering at each layer. Unless you have a profound knowledge of the current network and the placement of the servers, it is impossible to design networks with hierarchy. Without hierarchy, networks have less capacity to scale because the traffic must traverse every path to find its destination.

It is important for each layer to communicate only with the layer above or below it. Any connectivity or meshing within a layer impedes the hierarchical design.

Organizations often design their networks with duplicate paths. This is to build network resilience so that the routing algorithm can immediately use the alternative path if the primary line fails. If this is the design strategy of your company, care should be taken to ensure that the hierarchical topology is still honored.

Figure 2-3 shows an illustration of the appropriate design and traffic flow.

Figure 2-3 *Redundant Connections between Layers*

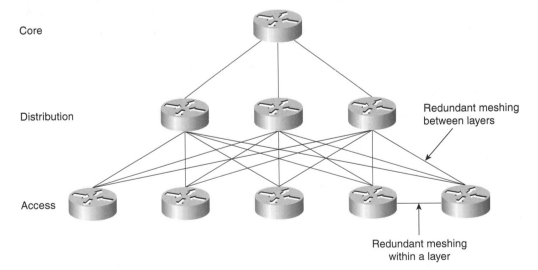

Alleviating Congestion with Cisco Routers

The ACRC objectives mastered in this section are as follows:

ACRC Exam Objective Number	Corresponding FRS Exam Objective Number	Description
	81	Configure Cisco routers for scalable operation in large or growing multiprotocol internetworks.
2	83	Select a Cisco IOS feature as a solution for a given internetwork requirement.
4	85	List solutions for controlling network congestion.
5	86	Introduction to managing traffic and access.
6	87	Configure IP standard access lists.
8	89	Configure IP extended access lists.
9	90	Verify access list operation.

Cisco router features enable you to control traffic, primarily through access lists. Access lists give you "what if" control of the network.

Given that the router operates at Layer 3, the control that is offered is extensive. The router can also act at higher layers of the OSI model. This proves useful when identifying particular traffic and protocol types for prioritization across slower WAN links.

With the assumption of connections between Cisco routers, Cisco has optimized many network operations. The various standards mean that organizations have to tolerate a wide range of variation in the interpretation of a specification. While defying many of the standards that streamline network traffic to a minimum, Cisco has been conscientious by providing the standard solution and a sophisticated method of translation between the standard and the proprietary Cisco solution. The clearest example of this is the use of redistribution between Cisco's routing protocol, Enhanced Interior Routing Protocol (EIGRP), and any other routing protocol such as Open Shortest Path First (OSPF).

Managing Network Congestion for IP

IP is generally considered a well-behaved protocol because its communication is typically peer to peer, removing the necessity for excessive broadcasts throughout the network. The only broadcasts are routing updates and Address Resolution Protocol (ARP) requests. These characteristics can no longer be assumed, however, because client/server technologies are starting to offer IP as a communication protocol. It should be understood that the application demands determine the nature of the traffic on the network. Therefore, if the application relies on broadcasts to locate its server, the protocol used to communicate that broadcast is of little concern. NetBIOS, AppleTalk, and IPX are the obvious examples of client/server applications utilizing TCP/IP as the transport method.

It would be misleading to suggest that there have not been improvements in network utilization by these protocols, which were originally designed for small LAN environments as opposed to the enterprise solutions for which they are now being sold. Nevertheless, it is important to emphasize the need to do careful analysis of the network traffic flow and to understand the communication requirements between the client and the server.

The Implementation of IP Access Lists

Access lists are used to restrict traffic from a specified source to a specified destination. They are also used to implement "what if" logic on a Cisco router. This gives you the only real mechanism of programming the Cisco router. The access lists used for IP in this way enable you to apply great subtlety in the router's configuration.

IP Access Lists Reviewed

Access lists are "linked lists" with a top-down logic, ending in an implicit **deny any** command (which will deny everything). Top-down logic means that the process will read from the top of the access list and stop as soon as it meets the first entry in the list that matches the packet's characteristics. Therefore, it is crucial that careful attention be given to their creation. Writing down the purpose of the proposed access list before attempting to program the system also proves helpful.

Access lists block traffic traversing the router. Remember, however, that an access list will not block traffic destined to the router.

Standard IP Access Lists

The following is syntax for a standard **access-list** command:

```
Router(config)#
access-list access-list-number {permit|deny}
{source [source-wildcard|any]}
Router(config-if)#
ip access-group access-list-number {in|out}
```

Note that the *access-list-number* is within the range of 1–99.

Standard access lists are implemented at Layer 3 and, in general, identify source and destination addresses as criteria in the logic of the list. IP access lists work slightly differently, however; they use the source address only.

The placement of the access list is crucial because it may determine the effectiveness of the control imposed. Because the decision to forward can be made on the source address only, the access list is placed as close to the destination as possible (to allow connectivity to intermediary devices).

You can place an access list on either an incoming or outgoing interface. The default is for the access list to be placed on the outgoing interface.

To ensure that all paths to the remote location have been covered, access lists should be implemented with careful reference to the topology map of the network.

Extended IP Access Lists

Although the same rules apply for all access lists, extended access lists allow for a far greater level of control because decisions are made at higher levels of the OSI model.

The following is syntax of an extended **access-list** command:

```
Router(config)#
access list access-list-number {permit|deny}
{protocol|protocol-keyword}
{source source-wildcard|any}
{destination destination-wildcard|any}
[protocol-specific options] [log]
Router(config-if)#
ip access-group access-list-number
{in|out}
```

The *access-list-number* range is between 100–199.

When using extended access lists, it is important to consider the sequence of conditions within the list. Because top-down logic is employed, the ordering of the list may alter the entire purpose of the list. For more information about access lists, refer to the *CCNA Exam Certification Guide* from Cisco Press.

Guidelines for Writing Access Lists

You should adhere to the following guidelines when writing an access list:

- Write out the purpose to be achieved by the access list in clear, simple language.

- Determine the placement of the access list in reference to a topology map of the network.

- Write out the access list, ensuring that the following is considered:

  1 The most frequent instance of traffic is placed first in the list, if possible, to reduce CPU processing.

2   Specific access is stated before group access is defined.

3   Group access is stated before world access is defined.

4   There is an implicit **deny any** at the end of the list.

5   If there is a **deny** statement in the access list, there must be a **permit** statement in it as well; otherwise, the interface will be shut down for all IP traffic in the direction that the access list was applied. That is, every access list must have at least one **permit** statement; otherwise, it will deny everything.

6   If no wildcard mask has been defined in a standard access list, the mask of 0.0.0.0 is assumed. This mask would match every bit in the address. If the address was that of a subnet rather than an end station, no match would be found and the router would move on to the next criteria line. If that line is the ending **deny any**, problems may occur.

7   The access list will not take effect until it has been applied to the interface. The access list will default to an outgoing access list if a direction is not specified.

- Test the access list with a utility such as ping.

- Use the **show** commands to verify the placement of the access list.

- If the access list needs to be modified, the list will have to be removed from the interface, deleted, and re-created as additional criteria is appended to the bottom of the list.

  It is useful to save the access list to a TFTP server and just edit it offline.

- Note that in some older versions of the IOS, deleting the access list at the global level without removing it from the interface may cause the interface to restrict all traffic through the interface in the direction it was applied. This is because the access list, although still applied to the interface, has no content; therefore, the implicit **deny any** takes effect. Standard system management calls for making changes to the specific before moving back to the general—that is, removing the access group from a specific interface before deleting the global access list.

Figure 2-4 illustrates the process logic used for access lists.

Access lists are extremely powerful when you are configuring the router to tune the data flow through the device. Because access lists take both CPU and memory, however, you must consider alternatives. The following section discusses these alternatives.

Figure 2-4   *Processing of an IP Access List, Incoming and Outgoing*

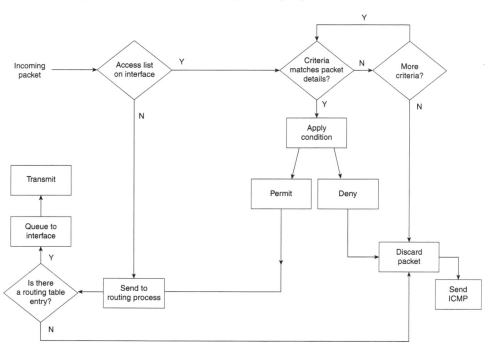

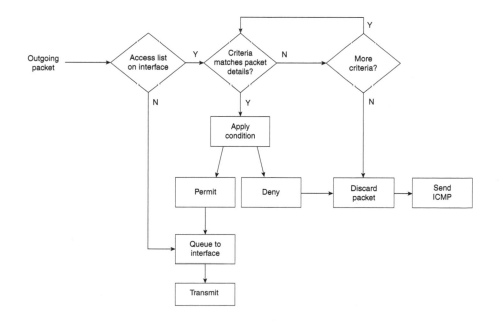

Alternatives to Access Lists

The ACRC objective mastered in this section is as follows:

ACRC Exam Objective Number	Corresponding FRS Exam Objective Number	Description
10	91	Configure an alternative to using access lists.

Because of the resources required to process them, access lists are not always the most suitable solution. The null interface is a good example of when a technology can be used imaginatively to produce a low-resource solution.

Null Interface

The null interface is a virtual interface. It exists only in the imagination of the router. Traffic may be sent to it, but it disappears because the interface has no physical layer. It is a virtual interface that does not physically exist. Administrators have been extremely creative and have used the interface as an alternative to access lists. Access lists require CPU processing to determine which packets to forward. The null interface just routes the traffic to nowhere.

The null interface command syntax is as follows:

```
Router(config)#
ip route address mask null0
```

For example:

```
ip route 10.0.0.0 255.0.0.0 null0
```

Figure 2-5 clearly shows how you might implement a null interface in an organization. The example shows how it can be used to filter the private network from the Internet.

If the router receives traffic to be forwarded to network 10.0.0.0, it will be dropped through null0 into a black hole. Because this is a private address to be used solely within an organization, never to stray on to the Internet, this is a command that may well be configured on routers within the Internet.

Figure 2-5   *The Use of the Null Interface in the Internet*

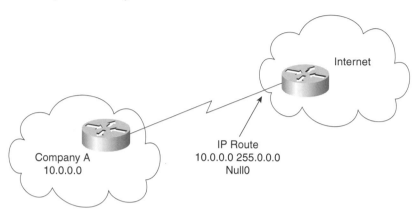

Within the organization, there is often a use for the **null** interface command. Figure 2-6 and the following text explain their use.

Configuring the static route to null0 on an internal company router prevents connectivity to the defined network because all traffic to that destination is forwarded to a "black hole." In Figure 2-6, Workstation A is not able to connect to Server C, the development server used by the Research and Development department. The result is that the Research and Development department can see the rest of the organization. Indeed, the rest of the world can see the Research and Development department in a routing table. Any attempt to direct traffic to the network will be unsuccessful, however. The first router that sees the traffic will statically route it to the null interface, which metaphorically is a black hole. There will be no error messages sent to the transmitting node because the traffic was successfully routed, although unfortunately to a black hole. This is considered beneficial for several reasons, one of which is additional security.

Because the static route is entered into the routing table, it is important to remember that all the rules of static routing apply. If the router hears of the destination route via another source, it is ignored in favor of the static route that has a lower administrative distance (which gives it a higher priority).

Figure 2-6   *The Use of the Null Interface within an Organization*

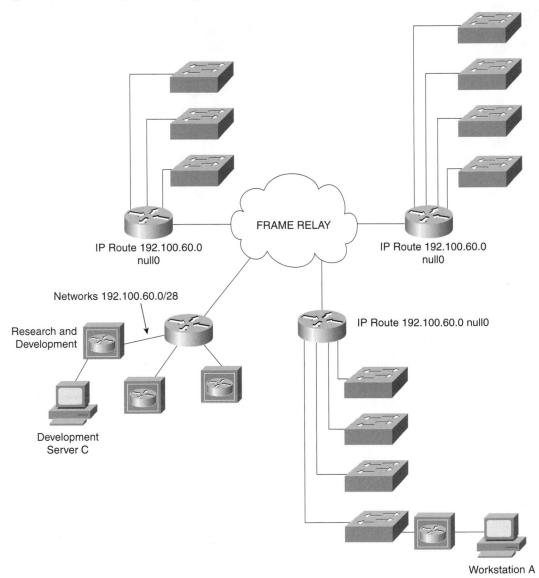

Prioritization

The ACRC objective mastered in this section is as follows:

ACRC Exam Objective Number	Corresponding FRS Exam Objective Number	Description
16	97	Describe the need for queuing in a large network.

Access lists are not used just to determine which packets will be forwarded to a destination. On a slow network connection where the bandwidth is at a premium, access lists are used to determine the order in which traffic is scheduled to leave the interface. Unfortunately, some of the packets may timeout; therefore, it is important to carefully plan the prioritization based on your understanding of the network, ensuring that the most sensitive traffic (that most likely to timeout), such as IBM's System Network Architecture (SNA), is handled first.

Many types of prioritization are available. They are implemented at the interface level and are applied to the interface queue. They are referred to as *queuing techniques*. Some of these techniques are turned on by default and may not be tuned by the router administrator. These include the following:

- **Weighted Fair Queuing**—Turned on automatically by the Cisco IOS, the queuing process analyzes the traffic patterns on the link and transmits traffic on the basis of its conclusions.

- **Cisco Express Forwarding**—This is a very high-end solution and is available on 7500 routers with Versatile Interface Processors (VIPs) and the 8510. It is extremely fast and used for high volumes of traffic. On some of the Cisco platforms, the Cisco processor automatically turns on this feature if the appropriate hardware and software are available.

Those queuing techniques that are manually configured with access lists are as follows:

- **Priority Queuing**—This is a method of dividing the outgoing interface into four virtual queues. Importance or priority ranks these queues. Traffic is queued based on its importance and will be sent out of the interface accordingly. This method ensures that sensitive traffic on a slow or congested link is processed first.

- **Custom Queuing**—The interface is divided into many subqueues. Each queue has a threshold stating the number of bytes that may be sent before the next queue must be processed. In this way, it is possible to determine the percentage of bandwidth that each protocol is given.

These are dealt with in Chapter 7, "WAN Options: ISDN, DDR, and Configuration."

Access lists are mainly used to manage traffic patterns (although it has already been shown that they may have a part to play in security). They are essentially a simple logic based on whether to forward traffic. Certain issues arise when using access lists for security purposes.

Security Using Access Lists

The ACRC objectives mastered in this section are as follows:

ACRC Exam Objective Number	Corresponding FRS Exam Objective Number	Description
2	83	Select a Cisco IOS feature as a solution for a given internetwork requirement.
7	88	Limit virtual terminal access.
16	97	Describe the need for queuing in a large network.
17	98	Describe weighted fair queuing operation.

Cisco recommends that alternative methods to access lists be used for security. Although complex to conceive and write, they are fairly easy to spoof and break through. The 11.3 IOS has implemented full security features and these sophisticated features should be utilized in preference to access lists. The best way to use access lists as security is as a first pass, to alleviate processing on a separate firewall security device. Whether the processing on the firewall device is better designed for dealing with the whole security burden or whether this task should be balanced between devices is a capacity-planning project.

Some simple security tasks are well suited to access lists. Remember, however, that although access lists do not constitute complex security, they will deter the idle user exploring the company network.

Controlling Terminal Access

Because access lists do not prevent traffic generated by the router or traffic destined for the router, another method is required. If the router is being used as an end device for Telnet, an access list can be placed on the virtual terminal line (vty).

Five terminal sessions are available: vty 0–4. Because anticipating which session will be assigned to which terminal is difficult, control is generally placed uniformly on all virtual terminals.

The syntax for vty commands is as follows:

```
Router(config)#
Line {vty-number|vty-range}
```

```
Router(config-line)#
access-class access-list-number {in|out}
```

Standard access lists are used for inbound access because the destination is known. The **access-class** command is the same as the **access-group** command, but is used for terminal access. It could be applied either as an inbound or an outbound list. The access list used has the same structure as the standard access lists; even the range used in the command is the same, 1–99.

When applied as an inbound **access-class** command to the vty, an access list restricts users from connecting to the router from the specified source addresses.

When applied as an outbound **access-class** command to the vty, an access list restricts users who have connected to the router and then attempt to connect to another system from that router. This is because the access list is still using the source address.

Other methods of restricting access are slightly more brutal. It is possible to issue the following command:

```
Router(config)#
no line vty 0 4
```

This command removes all terminal access.

It is also possible to issue the following commands:

```
Router(config)#
Line vty 0 4
Login
No password
```

This requires a password. Because a password has not been sent, however, it is impossible to correctly input a password. The result is no access. In the previous examples, the console is used to configure and manage the router.

Final Connectivity and CPU Considerations

The ACRC objective mastered in this section is as follows:

ACRC Exam Objective Number	Corresponding FRS Exam Objective Number	Description
11	92	Configure an IP helper address to manage broadcasts.

Access lists require CPU processing from the router. The more complex or long the access list, the greater the amount of CPU processing required. In earlier versions of the Cisco IOS, pre-10.3, complex access lists prevented the caching of routing decisions, for example, fast, autonomous, and silicon switching. These functions are now supported, particularly if *Netflow* features are turned on. In this context, switching refers to a Cisco solution that was implemented in the earliest of Cisco's products and that has been consistently enhanced.

To improve the capability of the router to forward traffic—after the routing process has made a routing decision and sent the packet to the appropriate outbound interface—the router holds a copy of the outbound frame in memory along with a pointer to the appropriate outbound interface. This means that incoming traffic can be examined as it comes into the router. The router looks in the cache or memory to see whether a routing decision has already been made for that set of source and destination addresses. If an entry exists, the frame can be switched directly to the outbound interface, and the routing process is bypassed. This not only increases the apparent throughput of the router but also reduces the memory and CPU resources required. The different names for the available switching methods refer to where the cache is stored. For more information on this subject, refer to the Cisco documentation set.

If the router is not caching any of the routing decisions, but is instead processing every packet with process switching, there may be implications on the router's CPU and memory utilization.

Placement of Client/Server

The location of the servers in relation to the clients dramatically affects the traffic patterns within the network.

The current philosophy is to create server farms so that the servers can be centrally administered. If the client finds the server via broadcasts, however, a serious problem will arise if there is a router between the broadcasts: Because routers are a natural broadcast firewall, they treat broadcasts as an unknown address and discard them. In such a scenario, the client sending a broadcast to locate a server will fail in the endeavor.

Even carefully designed centralized server farms on different networks will not work because the intervening router discards broadcasts sent between the clients and the server. The clients will have no connectivity with their servers. The solution is to configure a helper address on the router.

IP Helper Address

The IP helper address removes the broadcast destination address of a UDP packet received on an identified interface and replaces it with a specific destination address. The router has been programmed to say, "If a broadcast comes in on this interface, forward it to this destination address," where the destination address is that of the server.

A helper address is configured on the incoming interface. The destination address may be either an individual server or a subnet address. Multiple helper addresses can be identified, and all broadcasts received on the interface will be forwarded to each destination. This is a good way to create backup servers on different segments. The syntax for the **ip helper-address** command is as follows:

```
Router(config-if)#
ip helper-address address
```

The IP helper address forwards broadcasts for the following UDP ports:

- TFTP (69)
- DNS (53)
- Time (37)
- NetBIOS name server (137)
- NetBIOS datagram service (138)
- BOOTP server (67)
- BOOTP client (68)
- TACAS (49)

In addition to the helper address is the IP forward protocol, which instructs the router to forward broadcasts. By stating the port number, particular types of broadcast may be identified. This is very useful when used in conjunction with the helper address because it identifies those broadcasts to be readdressed to specified destinations. It is possible to either add to the list of broadcasts that will be forwarded with the helper address or remove certain traffic types. You can tailor the **ip helper-address** command so that only necessary traffic is forwarded, which not only optimizes bandwidth but also prevents the servers from being overloaded. (Server overload can result in servers overflowing their buffers; this causes them to slow down or hang.) The syntax for the **ip forward-protocol** command is as follows:

```
Router (config)#
ip forward-protocol {UDP [port]|nd|sdns}
```

Uses of IP Access Lists

Because access lists can be used so subtly in system programming, they are used in many ways to solve many problems. IP access lists are used mainly to manage traffic.

Traffic Control through Routing Updates

Traffic on the network must be managed. Traffic management is most easily accomplished at Layer 3 of the OSI model. You must be careful, however, because limiting traffic also limits connectivity. Therefore, careful design and documentation is required.

Routing updates convey information about the available networks. The updates are sent out periodically to ensure that every router's perception of the network is accurate and current.

Access lists applied to routing protocols restrict the information sent out in the update. Certain networks are omitted based on the criteria in the access list. Remote routers unaware of these networks will not be able to deliver traffic to them. Networks hidden in this way are typically research and development sites, test labs, or secure areas.

These access lists are also used to prevent routing loops in networks that have redistribution between routing protocols.

When connecting two separate domains, the connection point of the domains or the entry point to the Internet are areas through which only limited information needs to be sent. Otherwise, routing tables become unmanageably large and consume large amounts of bandwidth.

It is popular to tune the update timers between routers, trading currency of the information for optimization of the bandwidth. All routers running the same routing protocol expect to hear these updates with the same frequency that they send out their own. If any of the parameters defining how the routing protocol works are changed, these alterations should be applied consistently throughout the network; otherwise, routers will timeout and the routing tables will become unsynchronized.

Across WAN networks it may be advantageous to turn off routing updates completely and to manually or statically define the best path to be taken by the router. Note also that sophisticated routing protocols such as EIGRP or OSPF send out only incremental updates; be aware, however, that these are correspondingly more complex to design and implement.

To optimize the traffic flow throughout a network, you must carefully design and configure the IP network. In a client/server environment, the control of the network overhead is even more important. The following section discusses some concerns and strategies.

Managing Network Access for IPX

The ACRC objectives mastered in this section are as follows:

ACRC Exam Objective Number	Corresponding FRS Exam Objective Number	Description
12	93	Describe IPX/SPX traffic management issues.
13	94	Filter IPX traffic using IPX access lists.
14	95	Manage IPX/SPX traffic over WAN.
15	96	Verify IPX/SPX filter operation.

NetWare, a client/server product, relies heavily on broadcasts to locate servers, to acquire client addresses, and to transmit network information.

In a large network, service updates must be filtered. As a general rule, the router should have no more than 600 SAP service advertisements in the SAP table. This recommendation is concerned with the amount of network overhead that results from communicating all these services between the routers and servers as well as the resources required in the network devices. This number is not rigid; it really depends on the size of the network, the capacity of the network devices, and bandwidth available.

The Implementation of IPX Access Lists

Access lists are used predominantly in the IPX environment to control broadcast traffic. Security concerns are typically dealt with using the NetWare product features.

Access lists are also used for "what if" programming on the Cisco router, primarily in the WAN for dial-up access.

IPX Access Lists Reviewed

All access lists follow the same rules of logic. The previously discussed rules that apply to IP also apply to IPX traffic.

IPX Addressing Reviewed

IPX is a Layer 3 protocol. As such, the address can be broken into two parts: the network portion and the node portion. When implementing IPX, remember that the node address is acquired. The server or router gives the network address on the segment where the network administrator has configured it. The node portion of the address is provided by Layer 2, which lends the MAC address for the interface to complete the Layer 3 address.

Serial interfaces, which have no MAC address, borrow the MAC address from the nearest LAN interface. Although it is often assumed that this is the first Ethernet address, it is not always the case. Therefore, it is wise to check the IPX address on the serial interface before any configuration requiring such things as mapping statements. A Cisco router that has only serial interfaces will have to have a MAC address configured for the router by the administrator.

It is important to understand the addressing structure and corresponding use of wildcards when configuring access lists.

Standard IPX Access Lists

As standard access lists make decisions at Layer 3, the addressing structure and the wildcard determine the scope of restriction defined in the access list. Standard IPX access lists allow control to be applied to both the source and destination addresses. This is unlike standard IP access lists, which only allow the source address to be applied.

Because the standard IPX access list states both the source and the destination, it does not have to be applied as near to the destination as possible. Care should be taken in the use of the wildcard and the placement of the access list in reference to the design topology and addressing of the network. The syntax for a standard IPX **access-list** command is as follows:

```
Router(config)#
access-list access-list-number {permit|deny}
source-network[.source-node[source-node-wildcard mask]]
destination-network[.destination-node[destination-node-wildcard mask]]


Router(config-if)#
ipx access-group access-list-number [in|out]
```

The IPX standard access list number range is 800–899.

Extended IPX Access Lists

Because the extended access list allows for socket numbers to be specified, filtering at Layer 4 and higher is possible (limiting access on an application basis).

Again, it must be stressed that this level of security is typically applied at the server level. Although routers are connectivity devices and offer sophisticated security in some versions (11.3), these features tend not to be implemented in the LAN environment.

The syntax for an extended **access-list** command is as follows:

```
Router(config)#
access-list access-list-number {permit|deny} protocol
[source-network][[[.source-node]source-wildcard-mask]]
[source-socket] [destination-network]
[[[.destination-node]destination-wildcard-mask]] [destination-socket]
[log]
```

Extended IPX filters use an access list range between 900–999.

Uses of IPX Access Lists

IPX access lists are used primarily to control traffic flow. When used in a hierarchical design, these are easily implemented and allow the network to scale very effectively.

Traffic Control

IPX traffic using RIP/SAP updates over IPX has problems scaling. Each SAP packet holds seven service advertisements. The packet is up to 480 bytes in length, without the header. Each server and router will exchange its SAP table every 60 seconds by default.

Imagine an enterprise network with 700 services available worldwide—a moderately sized network. Note that the number 700 identifies the number of services advertised; it does not reflect 700 servers. The servers may number less than 200. However, 700 services is a convenient number because it renders 100 packets—or 48,000 bytes (B), or 48 kilobytes (KB)—of traffic generated by every server or router every 60 seconds.

Within a LAN environment, this amount of traffic would be a consideration. The bandwidth available today diminishes this concern, however. Across a WAN 56 kbps leased line, on the other hand, the amount of traffic would be a major bottleneck—particularly because the 48 KB does not include headers, and the 56 kbps line is bits per second.

For example, consider 100 packets at 480 bytes each, which would be 100×480=48,000 bytes per minute.

Because the speed of the serial line is stated in bits per second and not bytes per second, a conversion is clearly needed:

48,000×8=384,000 bits per minute

How long this would take to send this across a 56 kbps line can be simply converted as:

384,000/56,000=6.86

Therefore, the serial line is busy transmitting SAP network overhead for almost seven seconds out of every minute.

You can also determine the percentage of serial line devoted to the SAP traffic by using the Erlang measurement:

384,000/60=6400 kbps

6400/56,000=0.11

0.11*100=11% of the serial line's capacity is devoted to SAP traffic.

For this network to survive the SAP traffic updates, filtering is essential.

Service Advertisement Protocol (SAP) Filters

A SAP filter is the most common form of filtering used within an IPX environment with NetWare 3.x and 4.x servers that are not using NetWare Directory Services (NDS). Careful design makes it possible to create a network that allows client/server connectivity and yet still has enough bandwidth for data to traverse the network. The syntax for a SAP filter command is as follows:

```
Router(config)#
access-list access-list-number (deny|permit)network[.node]
[network-wildcard mask.node-wildcard mask] [service-type[server-name]]


Router(config-if)#
ipx input-sap-filter access-list-number


Router(config-if)#
ipx output-sap-filter access-list-number


Router(config-if)#
ipx router-sap-filter access-list-number
```

IPX SAP filters use an access list range of 1000–1099.

As seen in the use of access lists in general, the placement of the list is crucial to the effect that it has on the network traffic. With IPX SAP filters, both the placement of the filter and the function of the filter must be considered.

You can assign the filter to the interface as either an input, output, or router SAP filter. The input filter determines what is accepted into the interface and placed into the SAP table. The output filter determines what is allowed out of the interface in SAP updates from the router. The router filter determines which router the SAP updates will be accepted from. Figure 2-7 illustrates the use of SAP filters within an Enterprise network.

Figure 2-7   *The Use of SAP Filters within an Enterprise Network*

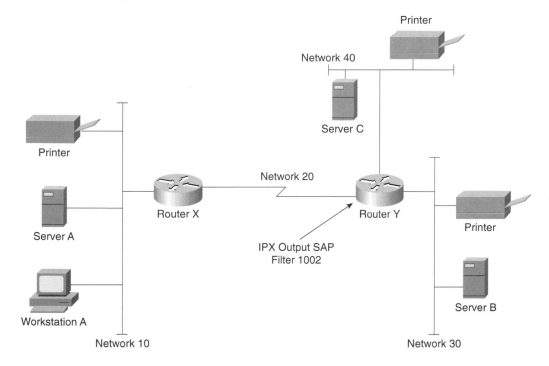

The SAP table on Router Y would have all the services listed on it. If the SAP filter permitted only the File Server Services to be propagated, then although Workstation A could connect to Servers B and C across the WAN, they would not be able to see or connect to the printers on the other side of the serial link. The use of the output filter allows a lot of subtlety in the filtering because each interface can be defined to allow different services in the updates. The input filter is broader in application because it determines how the SAP table is populated.

Get Nearest Server (GNS) Filters

SAP filters are often used in conjunction with the GNS filter. When a client boots up, it sends out a GNS request. The servers and routers will respond. In the case of the servers, the reply will be to advertise themselves as a resource. The router will advertise the server from which it last heard an update, on the basis that it is the most likely to still be available. Note that the manner in which the router responds depends on the version of the IOS. The earlier versions have some problems because the client attaches to the first server that it hears is available. In this race contention, the router, with superior CPU, will provide the server for the client. Unfortunately, the last server the router heard from may be in a distant land across a very slow WAN link. The client could connect to a server 4,000 miles away across an X25 56 kbps link, as opposed to its local server.

In the latest versions of IOS, the router listens for SAP traffic on the LAN and, if it hears none, responds to a client's GNS. If SAP traffic is heard on the LAN, the router will not respond because it "believes" a server is present.

Another solution is to create a GNS filter. This is a LAN filter and as such does not control traffic (because the SAP updates will have been sent across the network). These filters determine what the client will see onscreen, and thus function as a first-level security filter.

The GNS filter is configured as a SAP filter and implemented on the interface as a GNS filter. The access list number will therefore be in the range of 1000–1099. Figure 2-8 shows the use of GNS filters.

Routing Information Protocol (RIP) Filters

Filtering RIP updates using distribute lists makes it possible to determine the networks sent between the routers and servers. It is important to note that although the SAP and RIP protocols are described as independent, they are very dependent on each other. Care must be taken when implementing either SAP or RIP filters to ensure that the required connectivity is available.

NetWare clients learn about services from advertising servers. The first server to respond to the GNS request from the client returns a GNS reply with a list of the services it has learned from the other advertising servers along with the network addresses of the advertising servers. The client then requests the route to the server it is configured to use. If you block the RIP update to a server, it will remove the route from its routing table and no longer advertise services from that location. Consequently, the client will never learn of services where either RIP or SAP updates have been filtered.

Therefore, if the information in the RIP/SAP tables is not synchronized, entries from the tables will drop out and create intermittent and difficult-to-troubleshoot errors. The use and application of RIP filters is very similar to that of the SAP filters. The RIP filters use the standard or extended access list configuration, however, with the list numbers of 800–899, 900–999.

Figure 2-8 *The Application of GNS Filters*

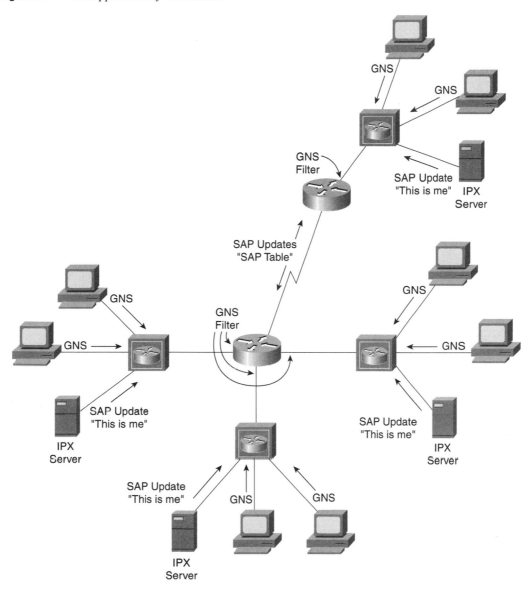

The format of the **ipx input-network-filter** is as follows:

```
Router(config)#
access-list access-list-number {deny|permit}network[.node]
[network-wildcard mask.node-wildcard mask] [service-type[server-name]]


Router(config-if)#
ipx input-network-filter access-list-number


Router(config-if)#
ipx output-network-filter access-list-number


Router(config-if)#
ipx router-filter access-list-number
```

Security

Security within the LAN client/server environment is typically implemented at the server. Within the WAN and in connectivity to the outside world, such as to the Internet, an independent device in the form of a firewall is used.

Other Issues

Advanced and complex configurations may be designed using these filtering techniques. These become particularly relevant in the design of the WAN, where limiting network traffic is a major concern. Careful consideration must be given to the design of the network in relation to the traffic flow and data patterns.

NetWare also supports NetBIOS application traffic. If your network is running these applications, you must consider the following:

- **NetBIOS Filtering**—NetBIOS is a protocol that was developed by IBM. It is an application interface that allows applications to use various transport protocols, such as SPX/IPX.

- **Propagation of Type 20 packets**—Type 20 packets are IPX packets that are NetBIOS broadcasts. If your network is using NetBIOS applications, it will be necessary to allow the Type 20 packets to flood the network so that registration to name servers can happen.

Verifying Filter Configuration

Whenever a network is configured, that configuration must be tested and the changes documented. This enables you to maintain a clear knowledge of the network functionality and is called maintaining *baseline*.

The commands to verify the filter configuration for either IP or IPX filters is most easily accomplished through the **show** commands:

```
Router#
show access list


Router#
show ip interface


Router#
show IPX interface
```

Design of Client/Server

To design an effective network, it is essential to understand the data flow within a network. Where to place the server relative to the clients should be decided only after considering the following factors:

- The frequency of connection to the server
- The duration of the connection to the server
- The volume of traffic sent across the link to and from the server at a specific moment of the day
- The daily quantified average

Analyzing the traffic patterns over time to create a baseline of the network documents how the network functions today and allows the correct determination of server/client placement. Using standard systems analysis methodology, the status of the network must then be set against the future needs of the organization (to ensure the appropriate design of the network). Understand that the design of the network directly influences the traffic patterns experienced within the network.

Enhanced Interior Gateway Routing Protocol (EIGRP)

EIGRP was designed to make efficient use of the available network bandwidth. The routing protocol carries both RIP and SAP information in the updates. The advantage of EIGRP is that it is incremental, sending updates only when a change in the network is experienced.

EIGRP automatically redistributes routing updates into RIP and SAP updates if the IPX RIP/SAP protocol is also configured on the router. EIGRP is proprietary to Cisco and is only understood by other Cisco devices. A powerful use of this technology would be to have EIGRP as the routing protocol between the routers across the WAN and RIP/SAP traffic on the local segments.

It is advisable to use the latest versions of the Cisco IOS when implementing this technology and to ensure that all the devices are running the same version of the protocol. This subject is dealt with in more detail in Chapter 6, "EIGRP, BGP, and Redistribution."

Static SAPs

Another method of restricting unnecessary traffic is to build the SAP table locally and to prevent any SAP update communication between the devices. Although this view is very attractive, it requires manual configuration and removes any concept of dynamic reconfiguration of the network. Used throughout a network, it would severely limit the capability of the network to grow. It is used very effectively across WANs, where connectivity to remote locations is carefully managed, particularly in the dial-up environment where periodic updates interfere with the desired functionality of the connection. The syntax for the static SAP command is as follows:

```
Router(config)#
ipx sap service-type name network.address hop
```

A less-rigid solution is to send the updates less often. Although this reduces the traffic on the network, it also makes the network less responsive to change. The design considerations are therefore centered on the importance of the resource and the utilization of the bandwidth.

If the update timers for SAP and RIP traffic are changed, the effects of this change on the entire network must be considered. In later releases of the Cisco IOS (11.2(4)F and up), the commands for changing the RIP and SAP update timers were integrated into one command. Other commands were added to reduce communication across the WAN to the minimum required for connectivity.

Other commands to research include the following:

- **ipx update interval** {**rip|sap**} {**value|changes-only**}—This command changes the interval at which the updates will be sent. The timer is typically set higher than the default, which is 60 seconds.

- **no ipx linkup-request** {**rip|sap**}—This command suppresses the "General RIP and SAP Query" when the interface comes up. This is useful in a dial-up link because it reduces the communication to one update.

- **ipx update sap-after-rip**—This command automatically sends the SAP update following the RIP update and ensures the synchronization of the two databases. Although this does not reduce the network traffic, it does fix a problem of the past: Because the timers were set differently, networks and servers would appear and disappear from the tables.

Tunneling IPX into IP

Tunneling one protocol into another is the process by which a protocol at a specific layer of the OSI model is wrapped into another protocol of the same layer or one higher in the stack. An example of this would be IPX, which is a Layer 3 protocol being wrapped inside IP, another Layer 3 protocol. Other examples include AppleTalk inside IP and SNA inside IP, which is an example of a Layer 2 protocol being wrapped inside a Layer 3 protocol.

Figure 2-9 illustrates the following steps of the IPX protocol being encapsulated and transported through an IP tunnel:

1   Data from the application layer is passed down the OSI model to the network layer.

2   Once at the network layer, the data is encapsulated in an IPX packet.

3   While at the network layer, the IPX packet is encapsulated into an IP packet.

4   The IP packet is then inserted into the frame format at the data link layer for the media in which the frame will be sent out.

Figure 2-9   *Tunneling IPX within IP*

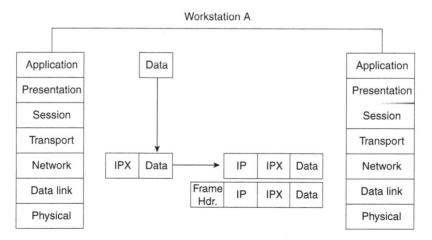

Why would anyone wish to configure anything quite so torturous? Such a configuration certainly will not reduce or control the traffic propagated on to the network. Conversely, it will increase the traffic load because the original data will now have the additional header.

On the end routers, which are responsible for adding this extra header, there are obviously increased CPU requirements.

The reasons for this configuration are not justified on the basis of network optimization, but rather on the ease of management of the entire network.

If the client/server traffic is kept local to the user LAN networks, with traffic to remote networks connected via TCP/IP, the administrator of the core no longer has to understand or worry about the vagaries of the disparate protocols. Instead, the administrator can focus on the one protocol: TCP/IP.

Although the use of IP enables the administrator to utilize all the available optimization tools for IP, it should be understood that the nature of the traffic would still be inherently that of the originating protocol. A NetBIOS application generating a broadcast will be transformed into an IPX broadcast and tunneled in the IP protocol. It would be delivered to the tunnel destination, stripped of the IP header, and the IPX broadcast would be dealt with as normal. Some of the reasons for tunneling IPX through IP include the following:

- The traffic can utilize the advantages of IP and sophisticated routing algorithms.

- The two ends of the tunnel, although in reality separated by many routers, appear as a single point-to-point link.

- The network administrator for the backbone network to which the two LANs connect need only understand TCP/IP.

- The addressing scheme is simplified.

- Simple routing protocols may have a limited hop count, which is extended by the tunnel, which advertises the path across the tunnel as one hop.

Some things to consider when creating an IP tunnel for IPX include the following:

- The delay, or latency, created in tunneling the IPX traffic into IP may cause some applications to timeout.

- Because the tunnel is viewed as a point-to-point link, separate tunnels are required for multiple links. Many tunnels on a physical interface can cause some memory problems on the interface.

- Care must be taken in redistributing routing protocols because the tunnel is often seen as a preferred path. This is because the route is advertised as a single hop. It may involve a much-less-favorable path, however. The tunnel may advertise the path as two hops, one hop through the tunnel and one hop to the destination. However, the one hop actually represents 10 hops across mixed media; the other path, which is rejected because it advertised three hops, is really only three hops away.

Syntax for the tunnel interface command is as follows:

```
Router(config)#
interface tunnel interface-number

Router(config-if)#
tunnel source interface-number|network.node address of Router interface

tunnel destination network.node address of remote network interface
```

Conclusion

Before it is possible to manage traffic flow within your network, it is necessary to understand the network structure and the needs the users and applications have of the network.

A structural topology map of the physical and logical layout of the network is necessary to allow the design and appropriate implementation of the features described in this chapter.

ry

ize the main points of the chapter as well as providing additional points that are not directly related to the exam objectives; these may be useful, however. The intention is that the tables be used to remind you of the key points of the most important subjects that were dealt with in the chapter. If any of the points need clarification, refer to the body of the chapter for greater detail. The additional information is of use to the advanced student, who will see the chapter subjects in a wider context.

In these tables, identify the reasons for congestion within a network and the solution that Cisco proposes. The subsequent tables deal with access lists, including their configuration and application.

Table 2-1   *Network Congestion: Causes and Cisco Solutions*

Causes of Network Congestion	Cisco Solutions
Excessive application traffic	Compression across slow serial links
	Use traffic shaping for Frame Relay with BECN
	Use priority queuing across slow serial links
	Use Serial Backup commands for dual point-to-point links
	Adjust application and other timers so that they do not timeout and retransmit
	Increase the bandwidth using EtherChannel
	Use load balancing, policy routing for IP
	Ensure appropriate server location in network design
Broadcast traffic due to large network	Filter unnecessary networks from routing updates
	Use snapshot routing across dial-up lines
	Manually configure static routes
	Use a sophisticated routing protocol with incremental updates (for example EIGRP, OSPF)
	Use address summarization
Broadcast traffic due to large client/server network	Filter unnecessary servers/services/zones from service updates
	Use a sophisticated routing protocol (for example, EIGRP)

Table 2-2   *Access List Features*

Access List Feature	Purpose
Decision to forward based on: Layer 3 source and destination address (standard access list) Layer 3 and above (extended access list)	Determine packet movement through network or "what if?" programming
Ability to filter on port number, packet size, as well as Layer 3 addresses	Give high level of granularity
Named access lists	Ease of management
Keywords for ports and wildcards	Ease of management
Ability to apply access list as inbound or outbound	Flexibility in design considerations
Ability to prevent ICMP messages from being generated when a packet is denied access	Increased security by making spoofing more difficult
Use of the established parameter to allow outgoing TCP applications, but to restrict incoming attempts	To allow users to Telnet into the Internet while preventing access to anyone trying to initiate a connection from the outside
Ability to filter in TCP/IP by precedence	To speed up the propagation of traffic
Lock and key	Allow users normally blocked to gain temporary access, after the user is authenticated
Reflexive access list	Dynamic filtering at the IP session layer

Table 2-3   *Applications for Access Lists*

Type of Access List	Purpose
Standard	Packet movement through the network or "what if?" programming
Virtual terminal access	Restrict access to and from the VTY line interfaces on the router
Distribute lists	Filtering of networks from the routing updates
Service filtering (for example, IPX SAP, GNS or AppleTalk ZIP, or GetZoneList filters)	Filtering of services from the server updates or from the replies to client requests
Queuing (for example, priority or custom queuing)	To prioritize traffic leaving an interface
Dial-on-demand routing (DDR)	To determine traffic that is defined as important enough to dial the remote site

Table 2-4   *Points to Remember When Configuring Access Lists*

Point to Remember	Consideration
The access list is processed as a top-down link list. The list will be tested for a match. When the first match is found, **deny** or **permit** will be applied and the process terminated.	Place the most specific criteria first. If more than one criteria is specific, place the most frequent match first.
There is an implicit **deny any** at the end of every list.	There must be at least one **permit** statement.
The wildcard uses zeros to indicate bits of the address to match, and ones for those to ignore.	This is the reverse of the use of the subnet mask and is easily confused.
Additional criteria statements are added to the bottom of the access list.	Because there is no editing and placement of the criteria is important, it is advisable to save the access list configuration to a TFTP server where it can be edited with ease.
The access list is not active until applied to the interface.	The access list will not work.

Q&A

The following are questions to test your understanding of the topics covered in this chapter. After you have answered the questions, you will find the answers in Appendix A, "Answers to Quizzes and Q&As." If you get an answer wrong, review the answer and ensure that you understand the reason for your mistake. If you are confused by the answer, refer back to the text in the chapter to review the concepts.

1 State two reasons to use an IP tunnel.

_____

_____

_____

2 Will EIGRP carry SAP updates?

_____

_____

_____

3 Why is it important to ensure the RIP/SAP update timers are synchronized?

_____

_____

_____

4 In configuring an IP tunnel, how many IP tunnels may be created with the same source and destination address?

_____

_____

_____

5 Associate the appropriate IOS feature to solve the network congestion problem experienced on the network in the following table.

Network Congestion Problem	IOS Solution
Large SAP tables on the routers	Routing access list
Clients cannot connect to the centralized servers	Prioritization on the interface

Continues

Network Congestion Problem	**IOS Solution**
Cisco environment in a large network with a large number of WAN connection	Reduce the size of the broadcast domain by adding a router
Large routing tables using RIP for IP	IP helper address
Spanning tree is failing	EIGRP
SNA sessions are failing	SAP filters

6 Which command would prevent the router from forwarding data to a remote network without generating an ICMP message?

_____

_____

_____

7 Identify two commands that might be used to verify the configuration of an IP access list configuration.

_____

_____

_____

8 What UDP ports will the IP helper address forward automatically?

_____

_____

_____

9 If the number of workstations increases on a physical segment, the user may experience delays. Give two reasons why this might occur.

_____

_____

_____

10 State three things to consider when deciding where to place extended IP access lists.

_____

_____

_____

11 What is the function of the access layer?

_____

_____

_____

12 What is the access list number range for IP extended access lists?

_____

_____

_____

13 What is priority queuing?

_____

_____

_____

Scenarios

The following case studies and questions are designed to draw together the content of the chapter and exercise your understanding of the concepts. There is not necessarily a right answer. The thought process and practice in manipulating the concepts is the goal of this section.

The answers to the scenario questions are found at the end of this chapter.

Scenario 2-1

The users are complaining that the network is very slow. They are using an IPX NetWare version 3.12 system. The servers are locally administrated. Each user connects to the local file server and print server and has access to a centralized server for email. The email system is using TCP/IP. There is a gateway server that deals with the translation from IPX to TCP/IP. Figure 2-10 illustrates the network. This diagram has been simplified for the purposes of the exercise. In reality, this network, as drawn, would not generate enough traffic to create congestion problems.

1 Give recommendations for the administrator to implement when trying to solve the problem of network delay.

2 Users on the IPX network no longer have connectivity to the IPX e-mail server. Upon investigation, you notice that the static SAP entry has been changed. List the commands to remedy the situation. The IPX gateway has an address of FAB.082b.0000.1223, the server is four hops away, and the application uses socket 8104 for service type 107.

3 Noticing that someone has been changing the configuration of the routers, you decide to implement some first-line security. State some of the solutions that you might consider.

Figure 2-10   *Network Diagram for Scenario 2-1*

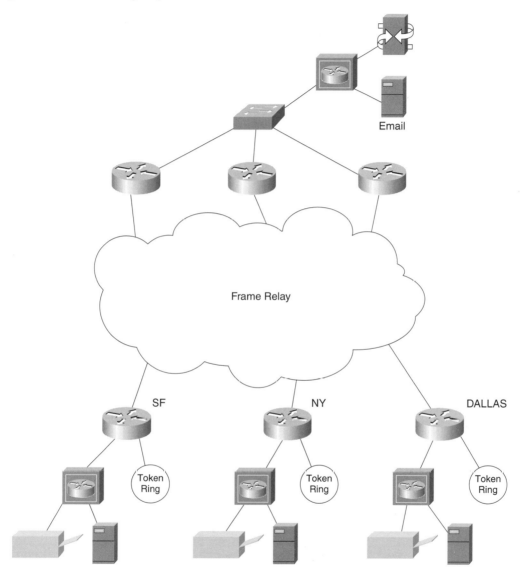

Scenario 2-2

Your company has recently created a lab for you to test TCP/IP configurations and explore new solutions. Although the lab needs to be connected to the entire network, it is important that access to this environment be limited. Although you need to be able to connect from anywhere in the lab to the network, no one else should have this access.

1   Write the access list(s) to achieve this and apply it to the appropriate interface(s) of the appropriate routers(s).

2   Draw a diagram to support your configuration.

Scenario 2-3

In one of the buildings of the network campus, the local administrators have decided that they want to centrally administer the building servers. Each floor of the building is a separate IPX and IP network. The network in the basement is where the server farm is located. The server farm consists of a DHCP server, DNS server, and an IPX file server. None of the clients have been configured with the addresses of the servers.

The IPX network address for the basement network is FAB. The IP network address for the basement is 10.10.10.0.

1   Draw a diagram of the network.

2   What command would allow connectivity of the users to the servers held in the server farm?

3   Write the configuration commands to achieve the requirements stated previously. Make sure this is reflected on your diagram.

4   Which commands would you use to verify the configuration?

Scenario Answers

The answers provided in this section are not necessarily the only possible answers to the questions. The questions are designed to test your knowledge and to give practical exercise in certain key areas. This section is intended to test and exercise skills and concepts detailed in the body of this chapter.

If your answer is different, ask yourself whether it follows the tenets explained in the answers provided. Your answer is correct not if it matches the solution provided in the book, but rather if it has included the principles of design laid out in the chapter.

In this way, the testing provided in these scenarios is deeper: It examines not only your knowledge, but also your understanding and ability to apply that knowledge to problems.

If you do not get the correct answer, refer back to the text and review the subject tested. Be certain to also review your notes on the question to ensure that you understand the principles of the subject.

Scenario 2-1 Answers

1 The administrator could implement the following recommendations to ascertain that delays were being experienced on the network. Also listed here are some possible solutions to the problems.

 • Use a protocol analyzer to verify that there is network congestion.

 • Write an IPX extended access list to prevent users from connecting to any server other than their local server, the e-mail server, or the gateway server.

 • Write an output SAP filter, one that limits service updates, to be placed on the outbound interface of the router.

 • Write a static SAP entry stating the IPX/IP gateway on every local router and prevent all SAP updates.

2 The command to configure a static SAP entry on the router is as follows:

```
Router(config)#ipx  sap 107 MAILSERV FAB.082b.0000.1223 8104 4
```

3 The following are some suggestions of first-line security that could be implemented:

 • Ensure the routers are held in a physically secure environment.

 • Write a standard access list to be applied on the vty line interfaces.

 • Change the passwords on the routers.

 • Turn on logging and accounting at the router.

Scenario 2-2 Answers

1 To permit access from anywhere in the lab for only the administrator, you must apply extended access lists to the fddi 0 interface of Router Y. The access lists would be applied in both the inbound and outbound direction. A diagram has also been included to show the configuration in a simpler environment, where the administrator may well be working from home and dialing in to the network. In this case, the configuration would be the same, but S0 is the interface that has the access lists applied. If the link were a dial-up, there would be additional configuration determining which traffic would raise the line. This is dealt with in the section on DDR later in this book.

2 Example 2-1 shows the commands required to achieve this:

Example 2-1 *Scenario 2-2 Configuration*

```
Router Y
Router(config)#
access-list 102 permit ip 10.0.0.0  0.255.255.255  0.0.0.0 255.255.255.255
Router(config)#
access-list 103 permit tcp 0.0.0.0  255.255.255.255  10.0.0.0 0.255.255.255
➥ established
Router(config)#inter FDDI 0
Router(config-if)# ip access-group 102 in
Router(config-if)# ip access-group 103 out
```

3 Figure 2-11 shows where the access lists described in question 2 would be applied.

Figure 2-11   *Answer to Scenario 2-2, Applying Access Lists*

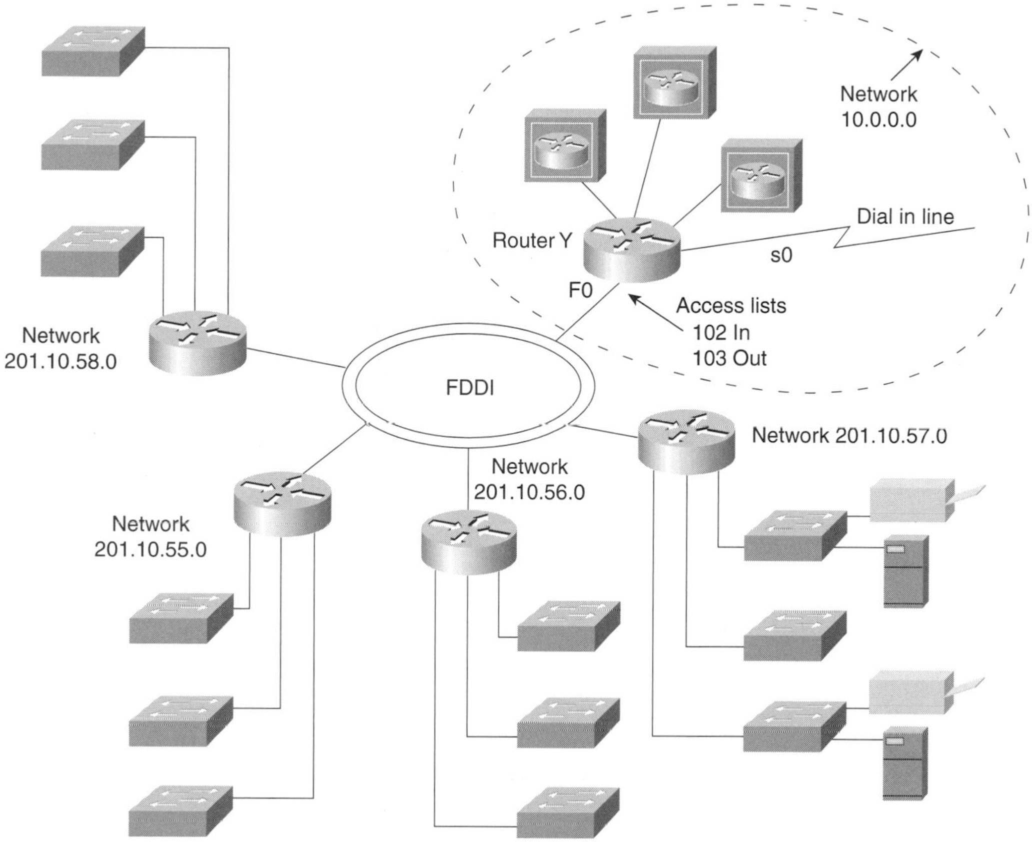

Scenario 2-3 Answers

1   Figure 2-12 shows a diagram of the network.

2   To ensure that the clients could connect to the servers that had been moved to a separate network, the **Helper address** command must be used.

3   The following commands allow the IP clients to connect to the remote servers:

```
Router(config-if)# ip helper-address 10.10.10.255
```

The IPX clients will need no additional configuration because they will find their servers using the normal method of GNS requests and SAP updates.

Refer to Figure 2-11.

Figure 2-12 *Answer to Scenario 2-3*

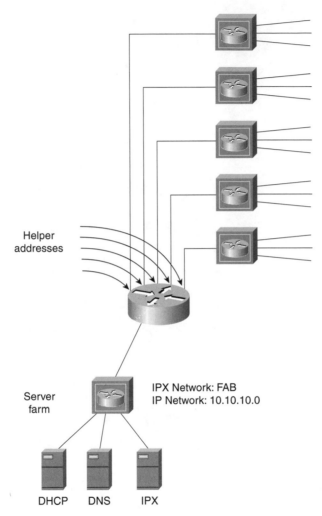

4 The commands that you can use to verify the configuration of the helper addresses are as follows:

```
Router# show startup-config
Router# show running-config
Router# show ip interface
Router# show ipx interface
```

The objectives for the ACRC exam for CCNP or CCDP certification are taken from the Cisco Web site at http://www.cisco.com/training under the heading "Cisco Career Certifications and Training." The following table shows the ACRC exam objectives covered in this chapter and also provides the corresponding Foundation Routing and Switching exam objective number. The objective(s) explained within a chapter section is also listed at the beginning of that section.

ACRC Exam Objective Number	Corresponding FRS Exam Objective Number	Description
23	104	Given an IP address, use VLSMs to extend the use of the IP address.
24	105	Given a network plan that includes IP addressing, explain if a route summarization is or is not possible.
25	106	Define private addressing and determine when it can be used.
26	107	Define network address translation and determine when it can be used.

CHAPTER 3

IP Addressing

How to Best Use This Chapter

By taking the following steps, you can make better use of your study time:

- Keep your notes and answers for all your work with this book in one place for easy reference.

- Take the quiz, writing down your answers. Studies show that retention significantly increases by writing facts and concepts down, even if you never look at the information again!

- Use the diagram in Figure 3-1 to guide you to the next step.

"Do I Know This Already?" Quiz

These questions are designed to test not just your knowledge, but also your understanding of the subject matter. It is therefore important to realize that getting the answer the same as stated in Appendix A, "Answers to Quizzes and Q&As," is less important than your answer having embodied the spirit of the question. In this manner, the questions and answers are not as open and shut as will be found on the exam: Their intention is to prepare you with the appropriate knowledge and understanding to give you mastery of the subject as opposed to limited rote knowledge.

1 If given a Class C address with the requirement to accommodate 14 subnets and 10 hosts on each subnet, what subnet mask would you use?

_____

_____

_____

2 What sort of design scheme does route summarization require?

_____

_____

_____

Figure 3-1   *How to Use This Chapter*

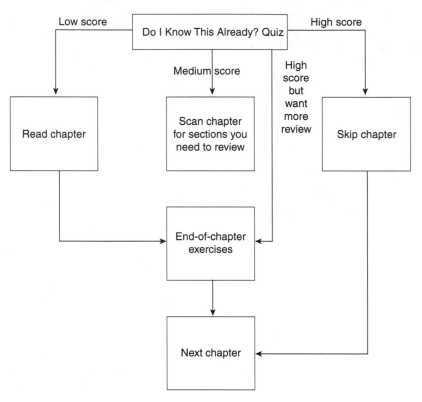

3 Identify two private addresses defined in RFC 1918.

_____

_____

_____

4 Briefly define route summarization.

_____

_____

_____

5 In route summarization, to where is the subnet mask moved?

_____

_____

_____

6 What does VLSM stand for?

_____

_____

_____

7 Where can the software program NAT run?

_____

_____

_____

8 When is NAT useful?

_____

_____

_____

9 When is NAT required?

_____

_____

_____

10 How does summarization allow for smaller routing tables?

_____

_____

_____

11 List the range of hosts available on the 136.122.10.192/28 subnet.

_____

_____

_____

12 Convert the subnet address 56.98.5.0/24 to binary notation and state the class to which it belongs.

_____

_____

_____

The answers to this quiz are found in Appendix A, "Answers to Quizzes and Q&As" (see page 458). Review the answers, grade your quiz, and choose an appropriate next step in this chapter based on the suggestions diagrammed in Figure 3-1. Your choices for the next step are as follows:

- Read this chapter.

- Scan this chapter for sections you need to review.

- Skip to the exercises at the end of this chapter.

- Skip this chapter.

Foundation Topics

Introduction: What Is a Layer 3 Address and How Does It Affect My Life?

A Layer 3 address allows network traffic to be directed to a specific destination. For data to be sent to its destination, the underlying physical structure, or wiring, should support the logical structure, or the Layer 3 addressing. Consider this analogy, for example: The drive from Boston to Chicago is so much easier because roads have already been built and those roads offer a (relatively) direct route. Just imagine driving around the perimeter of the United States and trying to make decisions at every fork in the road as to the best route to Chicago. Network traffic faces such decisions. Therefore, it is important to ensure that the addressing of the network reflects the physical structure of the network so that traffic can be sent directly to the destination.

Both the physical and the logical structure of the network should support the organizational data flow. Without this structure, application data can wander throughout your network inefficiently, clogging up the available bandwidth.

This chapter reviews some of the fundamental concepts of IP addressing. After mastering its subtleties, you will then be able to consider the network management power that results from careful design of the IP addressing scheme.

What Is a Network Address?

The ACRC objective mastered in this section is as follows:

ACRC Exam Objective Number	Corresponding FRS Exam Objective Number	Description
23	104	Given an IP address, use VLSMs to extend the use of the IP address.

Layer 3 provides the capability to address the network. Current approaches to network addressing and design are now challenged by the potential offered by Layer 3 addressing: for example, the ability to override the traditional physical limitations of address allocation with the use of switched environments and VLANs, as well as the use of dynamic addressing with DHCP.

To fully appreciate the power and purpose of the Layer 3 address, it is important to understand the meaning of the term *network* (as defined by Layer 3).

A network address has two parts: the network and the host portions. The host portion of the address identifies the individual device within a group. The network portion identifies a group of individual devices.

Unfortunately, the term *network* is used loosely; and although it is often defined, the term is seldom understood. In addition, the term *network* appears in several different contexts, compounding the confusion.

It is increasingly important to have an accurate definition of a network because new technology—such as VLANs and Layer 3 Switching—have blurred the distinctions between the different layers of the OSI model.

The following list outlines the various uses of the term *network*:

- The piece of wire or physical medium to which a group of devices are connected. This is more accurately defined as a segment.

- A Layer 3 network.

- The LAN.

- The corporate or organizational network.

For our purposes, the term *network* refers to the Layer 3 network.

A Definition of a Layer 3 Network

The network portion of a Layer 3 address is an arbitrary border drawn by an administrator to group end devices. This group is given an identifier or label.

Similar administrative lines are drawn between one city and another, one state and another, and indeed even between countries; these lines, or borders, serve the same purpose as the network portion of a Layer 3 address; that is, they allow rules to be placed on a group of end systems (in the geographic analogy, humans).

Traffic can now be specifically directed. Routing tables serve as maps and road signs. Access lists are the equivalent of immigration officers; access lists are placed strategically in the hierarchical design, where one is challenged at the country level only and not at the local city level. And although "flooding" (excessive broadcasts) might occur at a local level (to continue the geographic analogy, think local-election brochures), these broadcasts can now be contained to ensure that buffers (mailboxes) do not overflow with unnecessary information from further afield.

It is very important to remember to carefully plan the placement of these boundaries to ensure the geographic proximity of the end devices or hosts. Once defined, boundaries seldom change. This is not to say that they cannot change. To remain with the analogy a moment longer, remember that historically, boundaries between cities, states, and counties have been redefined. With the emergence of VLANs in recent years, this is increasingly true of networks.

A Layer 3 network address has the following characteristics:

- It defines a group of end devices or hosts.

- The group of identified devices is given a label to identify the group. This is the network number.

- The group address combined with its unique membership number for that group identifies the end device. This is the host address.

- Although the identifier for the end device may not be unique to the organization, it will be unique to the group or network.

- The address is hierarchical, which allows decisions to be made on groups of devices.

- If the addressing is carefully planned and the addressing scheme allows, groups may be grouped together (cities into states, states into countries, countries into continents, for example). IP subnets are collected into a single address, or addresses are collected into an autonomous system number.

TCP/IP is unique in that the network portion of the address has not been allocated a fixed address space. The number of bits that the network portion may use depends on the number of networks that need to be identified. It is necessary, therefore, to identify how many of the address bits have been allocated to the network portion of the address. A subnet mask is the means of determining the network portion of the address. The question is, from where does the original address originate? Is it from the fertile imaginings of the network administrator or from a higher authority?

The answer to this question solves another puzzle: Why is the Internet so powerful? Without getting into either a deep philosophical, sociological, economical, or indeed political discussion, it safely can be concluded that the power of the Internet emanates from the fact that every end device can have a *unique address* within the global network. (Therefore, my PC in San Francisco, with its address, can find my brother's PC in Tokyo and allow me to continue to pester him as only a little sister can.)

The next question is, where do the unique addresses come from? These addresses, known by various names, are assigned by a governing body that the Internet community has placed in charge of such address allocation. These organizations can then take this address and subdivide it to efficiently identify each network and host within their specific environment.

Unfortunately, the terminology is vague, and the address provided by the Internet community may be referred to by any of the following terms:

- NIC address

- Class address

- Supernet address

- Internet address

- Network address
- Major address
- And others yet unheard

NOTE   For the purposes of this book, the term *Internet address* is used to refer to the unique address of an end device or host so as to avoid confusion with new developments in the addressing structure that the Internet community might apply.

Network and Host Addressing

A TCP/IP address has great flexibility in the ratio of networks to hosts that can be addressed. This flexibility is possible because the address space is 32 bits long and the boundary between the network and the host can be placed anywhere within these 32 bits.

If 10 bits are allocated to the network portion of the address, for example, 22 bits are left to the host portion of the address. In binary, 10 bits can be used to represent 1,024 distinct entities (each being assigned a unique bit pattern or address). The 22 bits left to identify hosts can be used to represent four million hosts (actually, 4,194,304) *on each network*.

The total number of devices that can be addressed is calculated by multiplying the number of hosts' addresses available on each network by the number of networks that can be addressed, as illustrated in Equation 3-1.

Equation 3-1 $4,194,304 \times 1,024 = 4,294,967,296$

The administrator does not have the whole 32 bits to utilize, however. The Internet community, which manages the addresses to ensure their uniqueness, allocates a unique bit pattern to each organization that requests a connection to the Internet. This bit pattern is then used to uniquely identify the organization within the Internet.

The Internet Mask

The Internet community originally identified three classes of organization. Companies or organizations were deemed to fall into one of three sizes, or classes: the small organization, the medium organization, and the large organization:

Table 3-1 shows how the three classes are broken up.

Table 3-1   *The Three Classes of Addresses*

Class of Address	Number of Hosts Address Could Represent on One Network
Class A address	Could represent 16.77 million hosts on one network
Class B address	Could represent 65,000 hosts on one network
Class C address	Could represent 254 hosts on one network

It is the responsibility of an organization's administrator to determine where *their* boundary between the network and host will fall. The Internet community defines an organization with a unique pattern or *Internet address*.

The group within the Internet community responsible for allocating unique Internet addresses is the Network Information Center (NIC), known as the *Internet Assigned Numbers Authority* (IANA). This used to be a government-funded body and most recently was administered by Networks Solutions of Herndon, Virginia. Recently, the growth of the Internet has led to regional organizations. The most recent list follows.

Regional Registries:

- APNIC (Asia-Pacific Network Information Center), http://www.apnic.net

- ARIN (American Registry for Internet Numbers), http://www.arin.net

- RIPE (Reseau IP Europeens), http://www.ripe.net

Domain Registration:

- InterNIC, http://www.internic.net

Once in possession of the Internet address, an organization is responsible for determining the placement of the boundary and addressing the network. This is a complex task, which is an exercise in network design.

After the placement of the boundary between network and host is decided, this boundary will be conveyed to Layer 3 devices in the network via the subnet mask.

The Subnet Mask

The number of networks required relative to the number of hosts per network determines the placement of the network boundary. This determination defines the respective number of bits allocated to both the network and the host portion of the address. This information must be conveyed to the Layer 3 devices (routers), which make decisions based on their tables that state where the network boundary lies. The *subnet mask* is the method of conveying the network boundary to end systems and network devices.

When an address is assigned to an interface, it is configured with the subnet mask. Although represented in a dotted decimal form, the router converts the address and mask into binary and performs a logical AND operation to find the network portion of the address.

A *logical AND* is where the IP address is written out in binary with the subnet or Internet mask written beneath it. Each binary digit of the address is then ANDed with the corresponding binary digit of the mask. The rules of the AND operation are as follows:

- Positive and positive is positive.

- Negative and anything is negative.

This means that

- 1 AND 1 is 1.

- 1 AND 0 is 0.

- 0 AND 1 is 0.

- 0 AND 0 is 0.

The following example illustrates this:

IP address	144.100.16.8
IP subnet mask	255.255.255.0
IP address in binary	10010000.01100100.00010000.00001000
IP subnet mask in binary	11111111.11111111.11111111.00000000
Result of logical AND	10010000.01100100.00010000.00000000

The result is the removal of the host portion of the address, and the subnet address is left intact. Therefore, the host 144.100.16.8 is a member of the subnet 144.100.16.0, which is the result of the logical AND converted to decimal.

With this information, the router can now perform a search on the routing table to see whether it can route to the remote network. Therefore, the correct mask is essential to ensure that traffic can be directed through the overall network.

NOTE   Again, the terms used to describe the mask are numerous and often vague. This book uses the term *subnet mask* when referring to the mask used within an organization and *Internet* or *prefix mask* when referring to the address allocated by the IANA.

Remember these following important points regarding IP addressing:

- The IP address is 32 bits long.

- The network/host boundary can be anywhere in the 32 bits.

- The Internet allocates a unique bit pattern. These bits are the first bits on the far left. These bits are not available for the administrator to use for networks because these identify your organization to the Internet. Those bits that are left untouched (zeroed) are for the organization so that the network can be addressed by allocating the network and host bits.

- The network mask is the identification of the bits allocated to the network, defined on all participating routers.

When determining the subnet mask, certain rules must be followed. RFC 950 outlines these rules.

Familiar Rules

Because originally the routing protocols could not send the mask with the routing update, the original set of rules about applying IP addresses were different than they are now. For the most part, however, these rules still hold true. With the advent of new technology, however, it is now possible to surmount some of the previous limitations set out in RFC 950.

The earlier (and perhaps familiar) rules included the following:

- The network bits do not need to be contiguous, although it is advised to be contiguous.

- The network bits must not be all zeros or ones.

- The decision on the number of bits allocated to the network is made once per NIC number.

The reason for these rules was straightforward: The original routing protocols did not send the subnet mask with the routing update. Each router that received a subnet entry in the routing update had to assume that the mask in use was the same as the one configured on its system. If they were not directly connected to the NIC address (it was not configured on one of the router's interfaces), they would use the mask for the Class A, B, or C network. The class of network was determined by the *first octet rule*.

New technology means that routing protocols can now send the subnet mask with the routing update. Therefore, the earlier rules regarding network classes do not necessarily apply.

The Newer Rules

Because the newer routing protocols can send the mask with the routing update, it is possible to have greater flexibility in the IP addressing design of your network. In particular, it is no longer necessary to adhere to the rule that the subnet mask may only be created once per NIC number. This is because the mask is held with the subnet in the routing table, which allows the distinction between the broadcast address and the subnet address that has been defined. This requires variable-length subnet masks (VLSM).

It is not necessary for either the NIC or the individual organization to conform to the rules of *classful routing*. As long as the address is allocated with a prefix mask to identify the network portion of the address, it is now possible for the NIC to hand out an address without regard for the bit boundary at Class A, B, or C.

The address must be allocated with a prefix mask to identify the network portion of the address. RFC 1812 restricts the flexibility of the addressing slightly, however, by requiring that contiguous bits be used in the mask.

Prefix Routing

Prefix routing is the means by which the Internet identifies the portion of the 32-bit TCP/IP address that uniquely identifies the organization. In effect, this means that the Internet can allocate a group of class networks, which are represented by a single address. This allows for prefix routing and summarization within the routing tables of the Internet. Prefix masks represent a group of TCP/IP network addresses, using the method of address or subnet masks.

This aggregation of Internet addresses is defying the old structure of Class A, B, C addressing, or classful addressing. The aggregation of Internet addresses is, therefore, classless and deals with connectivity between organizations through the Internet, referred to as *interdomain routing*. This technology is called *classless interdomain routing* (CIDR). Table 3-2 shows the RFCs that outline the use of CIDR in an IP network.

Table 3-2   *RFCs on CIDR*

RFC Number	Description
1517	Applicability statement for the implementation of CIDR
1518	An architecture for IP address allocation with CIDR
1519	CIDR: an address assignment and aggregation strategy
1520	Exchanging routing information across provider boundaries in a CIDR environment

CIDR solves the following IP addressing and routing issues:

- Address exhaustion. The Internet was just running out of addresses.

- The network resources required to manage huge routing tables were becoming untenable.

The Internet community found that small companies that wanted to connect to the Internet with 50 hosts needed a Class C address, even though a Class C designation wasted 204 addresses.

Conversely, if an organization has more than 255 hosts but less than 65,000 hosts, the Internet must either waste a large number of addresses by allocating a Class B address or provide multiple Class C addresses. RFC 1466 discusses the low percentage of allocated addresses in use.

The Class A, B, C address structure just does not have enough granularity for today's Internet. Because the Internet has grown in popularity, this has become a pressing problem. In addition, the number of entries in the routing tables of the Internet has reached capacity, although only a small percentage of the addresses allocated have been utilized. The Internet started to reclaim unused addresses, but this was obviously a short-term solution. The implementation of CIDR with prefix routing has solved both problems.

The organization requiring multiple Class C addresses is allocated consecutive Class C addresses, but issues only one address for the Internet routing entry (representing the multiple addresses). This is achieved by pulling the network mask to the left.

The shorter the prefix, the more general the network defined; the longer the prefix, the more specific the identification. Table 3-3 visually demonstrates the use of the prefix. The Internet IP addressing group ARIN (American Registry for Internet Numbers, www.arin.net) typically gives blocks of consecutive addresses to an Internet service provider (ISP) to allocate addresses to organizations that want to connect to the Internet. This reduces the routing tables even further by placing some of the address management responsibilities on the ISP.

WARNING   Connecting to an ISP requires some consideration because the addresses used in your organization have been provided by the ISP. If you change your ISP, that address space will have to be relinquished back to the ISP. This will require readdressing of the network or some software application to translate the addresses.

Table 3-3   *Table to Illustrate the Use of Prefix Masks*

Prefix	Mask	New Address Space
/27	255.255.255.224	12% of Class C
		30 hosts
/26	255.255.255.192	24% of Class C
		62 hosts
/25	255.255.255.128	50% of Class C
		126 hosts
/23	255.255.254.0	2 Class Cs
		510 hosts

Continues

Table 3-3   *Table to Illustrate the Use of Prefix Masks (Continued)*

Prefix	Mask	New Address Space
/22	255.255.252.0	4 Class Cs
		1022 hosts
/21	255.255.248.0	8 Class Cs
		2046 hosts
/20	255.255.240.0	16 Class Cs
		4094 hosts

The following example illustrates one address with a shorter or longer mask. The mask used determines how you get the address space you need.

ARIN provides this address, for example:

200.100.48.0/21

/21 is the equivalent of a mask of

255.255.248.0

When the address and the mask are written in the fashion that the router processes them, which is in binary, it is easy to see that the Internet community has allocated a group of Class C addresses, although they are presented as a single network. Table 3-4 shows an example of an IP address in both a decimal and binary format.

Table 3-4   *An IP Address and Mask Shown in Binary*

Description	Octet 1	Octet 2	Octet 3	Octet 4
NIC Address in Decimal	200	100	48	0
NIC Address in Binary	11001000	01100100	00110000	00000000
Prefix as a Subnet Mask in Decimal	255	255	248	0
Prefix as a Subnet Mask in Binary	11111111	11111111	11111000	00000000

If it were a standard Class C address, the mask would be 255.255.255.0. By making the mask 255.255.248.0, the last three bits of the third octet are essentially giving the organization eight Class C networks.

The bit pattern provided by the Internet cannot be altered. The bits to the right of the unique address given by the Internet are at the disposal of the organization. Figure 3-2 shows the possible combinations of the third octet.

Figure 3-2   *Prefix Routing and the Use of CIDR*

```
          Class C address- - - - -→
                             / 21  | / 24
        110010000.01100100.00110 | 000  | .00000000
                                 | 001  | =  200.100.49.0
                                 | 010  | =  200.100.50.0
                                 | 011  | =  200.100.51.0
                                 | 100  | =  200.100.52.0
                                 | 101  | =  200.100.53.0
                                 | 110  | =  200.100.54.0
                                 | 111  | =  200.100.55.0
```

Although eight Class C addresses are provided to the organization, they are identified to the Internet as one address: 200.100.48.0.

The organization does not have to use the addresses as Class C addresses. In accordance with the original rules, the organization may use the rightmost zeroed bits however they deem appropriate. They must have a routing protocol and TCP/IP stack that can support the latest conventions of classless routing, however.

Prefix routing is used to reduce the size of Internet routing tables. As explained in the preceding example, the Internet gave away the equivalent of eight Class C networks, but just one network entry appeared in the Internet's routing table. In an environment that has more than 54,000 entries in the routing table—at the time of this writing, the size of the routing table in many ISPs has peaked at 54,000 entries—this is a significant reduction in the size of the routing table (which is expressed in terms of CPU utilization, memory, and bandwidth congestion).

In addition to the advantages of the original rules of TCP/IP addressing and subnet design, there is the flexibility granted to the Internet with prefix routing. The Internet no longer needs to abide by the rules of Classes A, B, and C. As shown, with some thought, many NIC networks may be presented as one network, thus reducing the network overhead. It could be said that the Internet has summarized many networks into one network. Figure 3-3 shows the effect of using prefix routing.

An organization can use summarization for the same reasons the Internet uses it with prefix routing: to reduce network overhead. The length of the prefix in this case depends on the number of bits needed rather than the Class A, B, and C structure.

To utilize the power of summarization within an organization, a sophisticated routing protocol that sends the mask with the routing updates is required. The capability to move the network/host boundary is called VLSM.

Figure 3-3   *Summarization of NIC Networks Using Prefix Routing*

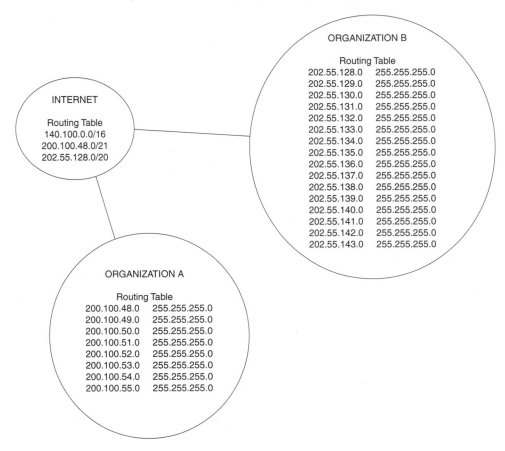

Variable-Length Subnet Masks (VLSMs)

Variable-length subnet masks enable you to allocate required host bits on a granular basis. Because organizations are rarely uniform in the distribution of hosts, it is much more efficient to provide only those host bits to address the number of hosts on a particular network. Consider an example of a company that has been given a Class B address: The company has some satellite offices that connect via point-to-point serial lines. The remote offices have 8 work-stations, 3 printers, and a router connecting them to the outside world. The main site has a building with 10 floors, and each floor has approximately 25 workstations and 4 printers. A server farm in the basement has 3 servers and 2 routers. In this scenario, it is impossible to create a mask that serves all these environments. If you use an older routing protocol, you will waste a considerable amount of the available address space.

TIP	The Cisco feature **ip unnumbered** is useful on the point-to-point serial lines because it saves the use of a subnet.

TIP	Cisco's use of secondary addressing is useful because it provides two subnets to a physical interface and, therefore, more available host bits. Unfortunately, there are some compatibility issues with other TCP/IP stacks.

The other solution is to use VLSM. VLSM requires a routing protocol that supports the sending of the subnet mask.

The following routing protocols support VLSM:

- RIP II
- OSPF
- IS-IS
- EIGRP
- BGP4

The following routing protocols do *not* support VLSM:

- RIP I
- IGRP
- EGP

Rules for VLSM

The rules for variably subnetting an IP address are remarkably straightforward. The key is to remember that a hierarchical design in the addressing scheme is the goal. The physical network design also has to reflect this logical hierarchy (as discussed in Chapter 2, "Managing Scalable Network Growth"). After the physical design is mapped, the logical structure can be placed on top of it.

The following two main rules apply when subnetting:

- A subnet can be used to address hosts *or* it can be used for further subnetting.
- Within the allocation of subsequent subnets, the rule of not using all zeros or ones does not apply.

The two main reasons for using VLSM are as follows:

- To make efficient use of the available addressing.

- To enforce a good hierarchical design, allowing summarization and documentation.

Figure 3-4 illustrates the use of VLSM for summarization and documentation.

Figure 3-4   *VLSM Used to Support the Hierarchical Design*

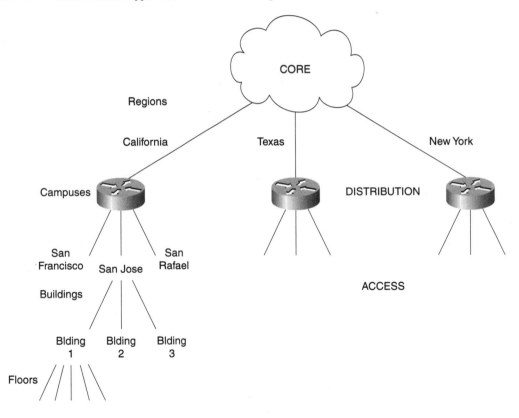

Addressing the Network

To make life more difficult, we will use a Class B address and create an addressing scheme.

If the Internet assigns the address 140.100.0.0, how might you address the network shown in the diagram?

The first task is to determine the number of regions, campuses, buildings, floors, and hosts on each floor. You also need to consider any anticipated growth or change in the network.

For this example, the network is comprised of the following:

- Four regions, but the company has plans to expand into other areas. Any expansion will probably not exceed eight states (adequate to cover the country).

- Within each region/state, there are no more than three campuses.

- Within each campus, there are no more than four buildings. This number might increase, however.

- No building has more than three floors.

- No floor has more than 30 hosts.

With this topology and growth detailed, it is possible to start allocating bits of the network address.

Taking the address 140.100.0.0 and writing the last 16 bits out, you can easily assign them to the different addressing tasks at hand. Figure 3-5 covers assigning IP addressing bits for VLSM.

Figure 3-5   *Assigning IP Addressing Bits for VLSM*

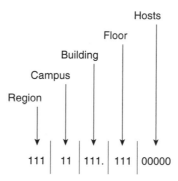

Consideration must be given to the subnetting rules (RFC 950, "Internet Standard Subnetting Procedure," and RFC 1878, "Variable-Length Subnet Table For IPv4") that state there must not be all zeros or all ones in the following:

- The NIC portion of the address

- The subnet portion of the address

- The host portion of the address

The algorithm for calculating the number of networks or hosts available is 2^n-2 (where n is the number of bits).

Only the subnet portion does not have to conform to this rule, however, because of the following two reasons:

- The NIC portion of the address is out of your control, having been defined by the Internet.

- The host portion of the address must conform to the subnet rule as defined; otherwise, it is not possible for the router to distinguish between hosts and broadcast addresses. The host cannot use an IP address of all zeros in the subnet address or all ones in the subnet broadcast address.

WARNING   Although Cisco provides the utility of **subnet zero**, this command should only be used with full understanding of the network devices and the knowledge that there is no device that uses the zero broadcast.

In truth, the subnet does have to conform to the rule as described. With VLSM, however, it is often forgotten that the entire subnet area is considered one subnet. Therefore, the rule needs to be obeyed once, not on each instance of variable subnetting.

In the preceding example, you would choose to obey the rule either in the bits allocated to the region, campus, or building, but not in each hierarchical layer. It would make the most sense to adhere to the rule using the least-significant bits. In this case, three bits have been allocated to the access layer, enabling you to identify eight floors. You have no more than three floors to address in any building, however. To obey the rule on this layer makes sense because you reduce the floors that may be addressed to six, which is still twice as many as required.

Allocating VLSM Addresses

Applying the addressing scheme designed in the preceding example is very simple after the design has been worked out.

Taking the region of California as the example to address, you will now address the entire region.

The following shows the bit allocation that was decided on:

    111|11|111.|111|11111

       | | |

NOTE   Remember that you are going to conform to the rule of reserving the broadcast addresses in the access layer of the network.

Region:

California: 001

Campus:

San Francisco: 01

San Jose: 10

San Rafael: 11

Buildings:

Building 1: 001

Building 2: 010

Building 3: 011

Building 4: 100

Floor:

Floor 1: 001

Floor 2: 010

Floor 3: 011

Floor 4: 100

Floor 5: 101

Hosts:

1–30

NOTE   The buildings have the same bit pattern for each campus. Remember, however, that this bit pattern is unique within the whole address space because the pattern for the campus is unique and the address must be seen in its entirety.

The third host, on the fourth floor of the second building in San Jose, California, will be given the address shown in Figure 3-6.

The address in Figure 3-6 is represented as 140.100.50.131 in dotted decimal.

Figure 3-6 *Example of How to Apply VLSM*

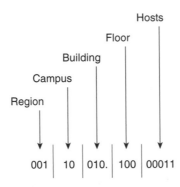

Worked this way, from the physical topology up, it is very straightforward. Many people are given the address 140.100.50.131 and work backward, which is very confusing. To avoid confusion, it is extremely helpful to document the addressing scheme within the organization's network (to make management of the network easier and to help maintain the administrator's sanity).

This use of VLSM shows clearly that when allocating addresses in IP it is necessary to reduce the address to binary and to disregard the octet boundary. Reducing the address to binary and disregarding the octet boundary creates just a continuous set of bits to be applied as appropriate to address the network.

Summarization

Having assigned IP addressing based on a hierarchical design, you can now consider the full weight of the advantages. The primary advantage is the reduction in network traffic and the size of the routing table. The reasons that the Internet implemented CIDR are equally pertinent in the individual organization. VLSM and CIDR use the same principles, VLSM just being an extension of CIDR at the organizational level.

At the top of the hierarchical design, the subnets in the routing table are more generalized. The subnet masks are shorter because they have aggregated the subnets lower in the network hierarchy. These summarized networks are often referred to as *supernets*, particularly when seen in the Internet as an aggregation of class addresses. They are also known as *aggregated routes*.

Figure 3-7a shows the physical network design for the case study discussed earlier. Figure 3-7b shows the allocation of addresses using VLSM to support summarization for this network design.

Figure 3-7a *The Application of Summarized Routes on a Hierarchically Designed Network*

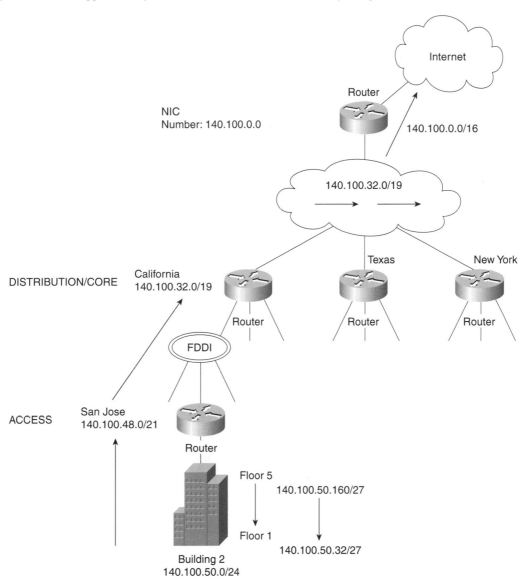

Figure 3-7b *The Binary Calculation of the Hierarchical Addressing for the Organization*

```
NIC Number
140.100.0.0

Region: 000    140.100.0.0/19
        001    140.100.32.0/19
        010    140.100.64.0/19
        011    140.100.96.0/19
        100    140.100.128/19
        101    140.100.160.0/19
        110    140.100.192.0/19
        111    140.100.224.0/19 ─┐
                                 │
                                 ▼
            Campus
            001/00    140.100.32.0/21
               01     140.100.40.0/21
               10     140.100.48.0/21
               11     140.100.56.0/21 ─┐
                                       │
                                       ▼
                Building
                001/10/000    140.100.48.0/24
                      001     140.100.49.0/24
                      010     140.100.50.0/24
                      011     140.100.51.0/24
                      100     140.100.52.0/24
                      101     140.100.53.0/24
                      110     140.100.54.0/24
                      111     140.100.55.0/24 ─┐
                                               │
                                               ▼
                    Floor
                    001/10/010./000    140.100.50.32/24
                            001        140.100.50.64/24
                            010        140.100.50.96/24
                            011        140.100.50.128/24
                            100        140.100.50.160/24
                            101        140.100.50.192/24 ─┐
                            110                           │
                                                          ▼
                        Hosts
                        001/10/010./100/00000    140.100.50.128
                                    00001        140.100.50.129
                                    00010        140.100.50.130
                                    00011        140.100.50.131
                                    00100        140.100.50.132
                                    00101        140.100.50.133
                                    00110        140.100.50.134
                                    00111        140.100.50.135
                                    01000        140.100.50.136
                                    01001        140.100.50.137
                                    01010        140.100.50.138
                                    01011        140.100.50.139
                                    01100        140.100.50.140
                                    01101        140.100.50.141
                                    01110        140.100.50.142
                                    01111        140.100.50.143
                                    10000        140.100.50.144
                                    10001        140.100.50.145
                                    10010        140.100.50.146
                                    10011        140.100.50.147
                                    10100        140.100.50.148
                                    10101        140.100.50.149
                                    10110        140.100.50.150
                                    10111        140.100.50.151
                                    11000        140.100.50.152
                                    11001        140.100.50.153
                                    11010        140.100.50.154
                                    11011        140.100.50.155
                                    11100        140.100.50.156
                                    11101        140.100.50.157
```

The Advantages of Summarization

The ability to summarize multiple subnets within a few subnets has obvious advantages. In reducing the size of the routing table, the updates are smaller, demanding less bandwidth from the network. A smaller routing table also requires less memory in the router or CPU in the routing process itself because the lookup is quicker and more efficient.

The recalculation of the network is also simplified by maintaining small routing tables.

If the routing table contains a summary of the networks beneath it, any changes in the network at these levels are not seen. This is both a good and a bad thing. If the network in the earlier example—140.100.50.128/27, the subnet on the fourth floor of the second building in San Jose, California,—were to go down, the router at the core would be oblivious of the LAN problem. This is beneficial because there are no additional updates or recalculation.

The disadvantage is that any traffic destined for that subnet is sent on the assumption that it exists. To be more accurate, the core router sees the inbound IP packet destined for 140.100.50.131 and instead of applying the /27 mask, it uses the mask it has configured. It employs the /19 mask that sees the subnet 140.100.32.0/19, although in reality the destination subnet is 140.100.50.128/27. If the subnet 140.100.50.128 is no longer available, all traffic is still forwarded to the subnet, until it reaches a router that holds the same mask as the IP packet and, therefore, is aware that it is no longer available. An ICMP message that the network is unreachable is generated to the transmitting host. The host may stop transmitting upon hearing that the network is down.

Although unnecessary traffic will traverse the network for a while, it is a minor inconvenience compared to the routing update demands on the network and the CPU utilization on the routers in large networks. Summarization allows networks to grow because the network overhead can scale.

Configuring Summarization

In the newer routing protocols, summarization must be manually configured; this manual configuration lends greatly to its subtlety and strength. Each routing protocol deals with summarization in a slightly different way, and how summarization works or is configured depends on the routing protocol used. This is discussed in detail in the Chapter 4, "IP Routing Protocols."

All routing protocols employ some level of summarization. The older protocols, RIP and IGRP, automatically summarize at the NIC or natural class boundary. They have no choice because the subnet mask is not sent in the routing updates. When a routing update is received, the router looks to see whether it has an interface in the same class network. If it has one, it applies the mask configured on the interface to the incoming routing update. With no interface configured in the same NIC network, there is insufficient information and the routing protocol uses the natural mask for the routing update. The first few bits in the address are used to determine to which class of address it belongs and then the appropriate mask is applied. This is known as the *first octet rule*.

Both EIGRP and OSPF are more sophisticated: They send the subnet mask along with the routing update. This feature allows the use of VLSM and summarization. When the routing update is received, it assigns the mask to the particular subnet. When the routing process performs a lookup, it searches the entire database and acts on the longest match, which is important because it allows the following:

- The granularity of the hierarchical design

- Summarization

- Discontiguous networks

Discontiguous Networks

A *discontiguous network* refers to when another NIC number separates two instances of the same NIC number. This can happen either through intentional design or a break in the network topology. The problem that can occur with a discontiguous network is that the router does not know where to send the traffic. If it resolves the address down to the NIC number, it appears as if there is a duplicate address. The same NIC number appears twice, but in different locations. In most cases, the router will load balance between the two paths if they are of equal cost. The symptoms that the network will see are those of intermittent connectivity.

Figure 3-8 shows an instance of a discontiguous network.

If there are discontiguous networks in the organization, it is important that summarization is turned off, or not configured. Summarization may not provide enough information to the routing table on the other side of the intervening NIC number to be able to appropriately route to the destination subnets. This is especially true of EIGRP, which automatically summarizes at the NIC boundary, which would in this situation be disastrous.

In OSPF and in EIGRP, manual configuration is required for any sophistication in the network design. It is not always possible to achieve summarization, because it depends entirely on the addressing scheme that has been deployed.

The key to whether summarization is configurable is determined by whether there are common high-order bits in the addresses.

In the case study used earlier, the design immediately allows for summarization, as shown in the now familiar layout in Figure 3-9. In this design, every campus within the same region will share the same high-order bits (those to the left). In California, every campus, building, floor, and host will share the bits 001. In this manner, every building in the San Jose campus will share the high-order bits of 00110. It is therefore very simple to configure summarization.

Figure 3-8 *Discontiguous Networks*

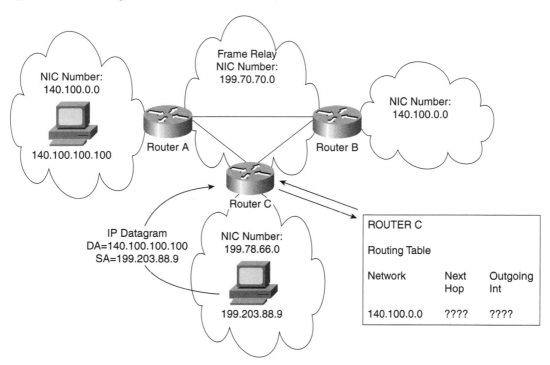

Figure 3-9 *Summarization of VLSM Addresses*

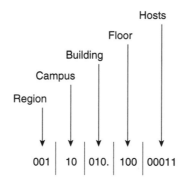

This is not necessarily the case if the addressing structure is already in place. Some analysis of the addressing scheme is required to decide whether summarization can be configured. If summarization is deemed impossible, you have the following two options:

- Not to summarize and understand the scaling limitations that have now been set on the network.

- To readdress the network. This task is not to be underestimated, although the advantages may well make it worthwhile.

VLSM also enables you to allocate the required bits for addressing a particular network.

Optimizing the IP Address Space

Particularly in the use of WANs, where there is a predominance of point-to-point connections, allocating an entire subnet is very wasteful. VLSM allows the refinement of the address space to exactly that which is needed and no more.

As demonstrated, dealing with the use of VLSM to support the hierarchical design requires the consideration of the entire network topology. When using VLSM to optimize the IP address space, the network addressing can become extremely confused if not clearly managed and documented.

In the preceding example, no consideration was given to the connections between the regions, campuses, and buildings—all of which could be point-to-point lines.

Now it is important to consider the last part of the network addressing, which will illustrate the use of VLSM for IP address optimization.

One common approach is to allocate a subnet that has not been assigned to hosts and to variably subnet it for use with connectivity between, as opposed to within, areas.

In this case study, it is sensible to take a subnet from the bits allocated to the buildings. Because there are enough bits allocated to address eight buildings, you have twice as many subnets as required. Even with the possibility of growth, one subnet would not be missed. Because the building bits come after the bits assigned to the campus, a choice must be made as to which campus will be selected for the honor of contributing a subnet of WAN addressing. This is an arbitrary decision that needs to be documented. If necessary, a building subnet can be commandeered from each campus.

In this example, if you use the bit pattern 000 as the network address for the building section, and in addition for the campus and the region, the third octet would result in a 0. The network address for all interconnectivity would be 140.100.0 . . . . The last octet would be available for further subnetting with VLSM.

Remember that the rule for not using all zeros or all ones is based on the entire subnet and not on the octet boundary. Figure 3-10 shows assigning IP VLSM subnets for WAN connections.

Figure 3-10 *Assigning IP VLSM Subnets for WAN Connections*

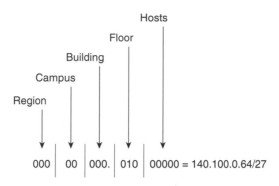

The following is an example of how the addressing might be broken down:

Between the buildings in California:

140.100.0.64/27

A 27-bit mask allows for 30 end-system addresses. This is in the expectation that the buildings are connected via FDDI or Fast Ethernet.

Between the buildings and the campuses in California:

140.100.0.32/30

140.100.0.20/30

140.100.0.24/30

140.100.0.28/30

This allows for point-to-point addresses using Frame Relay.

Between the campuses and the regions:

140.100.0.48/30

140.100.0.4/30

140.100.0.12/30

This allows for point-to-point addresses, which may also be using Frame Relay.

Between the regions:

140.100.0.96/30

140.100.0.16/30

140.100.0.8/30

This allows for point-to-point addresses, which may also be using Frame Relay or dedicated serial leased lines.

WARNING In the instance of a subnet being used to address WAN connections, it may not be possible to summarize these networks.

The rules and conditions for creating a valid and appropriate IP addressing scheme for the network are complicated. Among other things, the addressing scheme must allow for growth, to scale over time. What works today may not be flexible for next year's business requirements. You cannot build a network that will accommodate every change and addition to its environment. With careful design, however, it may be possible to anticipate some of these changes and to ensure a network with enough flexibility to survive the changes.

Designing IP Networks

The ACRC objectives mastered in this section are as follows:

ACRC Exam Objective Number	Corresponding FRS Exam Objective Number	Description
24	105	Given a network plan that includes IP addressing, explain if a route summarization is or is not possible.
25	106	Define private addressing and determine when it can be used.

Much of the design principles for an IP network have been dealt with in a practical manner in the preceding section. This section, therefore, examines the design criteria from a high-level perspective.

Certain questions should be asked before applying IP addresses to end devices. These questions include the following:

- How many networks exist currently on your network?

- How many hosts exist on each network?

- If the number of hosts varies on each subnet, how many hosts are there on the largest subnet, the smallest subnet? If there is an average number, this is also of interest.

- Where are these subnets in relation to the topology map of the network?

- In the next 3–12 months, how many more hosts will exist on each network?

- In the next 3–12 months, how many more networks will exist?

- Do you have a client/server environment?

- If so, where are the local servers located? On the same segment as the clients? On another segment and subnet?

- How much traffic is sent to the local servers?

- What is the nature of the traffic: high volume, large packet size, sensitive to delay, bursty?

- Is access required from other subnets?

- Are there any global resources that need to be accessed by everyone?

- If there are global resources on this subnet, is access required from other subnets?

- Do any security issues need to be considered?

- Are the clients mobile? Do they move around the campuses and require access from any location?

- Does the company require Internet access?

- If Internet access is required, for whom?

  Email

  Web browsing

  Remote access

  A Web page for customers

- Does your company have a NIC address from the Internet? If not, are they proposing to apply for one, or will they be connecting via an ISP?

- Is TCP/IP the only protocol on the network? If not, what are the other protocols, and is there any intention to tunnel these protocols through the WAN or core of the network using TCP/IP?

Not all of these questions may be pertinent to any particular organization. If this checklist is answered, however, the administrator or network design engineer will have a great deal of information with which to design the network. Although the questionnaire spans slightly more than the limited requirements for assigning IP addresses, the answers to these questions are crucial for the design of an IP network and to determine the traffic flow within the organization.

These questions should be considered against the topology map of the network. Without the support of the physical hierarchical design, it will not be possible to summarize the network traffic.

After the capacity of the network is understood, it is possible to design the addressing scheme. This will follow the same principles shown in the section titled "Allocating VLSM Addresses" earlier in this chapter.

Certain guidelines, or key points, should be used in the VLSM design of the network. The following section identifies these guidelines.

Keys Points to Remember When Designing an IP Network

The following list of items should be addressed when preparing the IP addressing plan for your network:

- To identify how many hosts and subnets will be required in the future requires communication with other departments in terms of the growth of personnel as well as the budget for network growth. Without the standard-issue crystal ball, a wider view must be taken at a high level to answer these questions, with the answers coming from a range of sources including the senior management and executive team of the organization.

- The design of the IP network must take into consideration the network equipment and whether consideration needs to be given to different vendor equipment. Interoperability may well be an issue, particularly with some of the features offered by each product.

- For route aggregation (summarization) to occur, the address assignments must have topological significance.

- When using VLSM, the routing protocol must send the extended prefix (subnet mask) with the routing update.

- When using VLSM, the routing protocol must do a routing table lookup, based on the longest match.

- Make certain that enough bits have been allowed for at each level of the hierarchical design to address all devices at that layer. Also be sure that growth of the network at each level has been anticipated.

TIP   Cisco offers many enhancements in their IOS. Most of these enhancements are interoperable. If they are not, they provide solutions for connecting to industry standards (which are of course fully supported by Cisco). Check with the Cisco Web page (www.cisco.com) to review the latest features and any connectivity issues.

In many cases, not enough consideration is given to IP address design with regard to the routing process making a decision based on the longest address match. This is essential to the design of a VLSM network.

Consider a network—as shown in Figure 3-10—using the Class B NIC address 140.100.0.0.

The routing table has among its entries the following:

140.100.0.0/16

140.100.1.0/20

140.100.1.192/26

A packet comes into the router destined for the end host 140.100.1.209. The router will forward it to the network 140.100.1.192 because the bit pattern matches the longest bit mask provided. The other routes are also valid, however, so the router has made a policy decision that it will always take the longest match.

The reason for this decision is the design assumption that has been made by the router. The assumption is that the longest match is either directly connected to the router or that the network is out of the identified interface. If the end host 140.100.1.209 actually resides on network 140.100.1.208/29, this network must be accessible through the interface, which has learned of the subnet 140.100.1.192. Summarization will have been configured because 140.100.1.192 is an aggregate of various networks, including the network 140.100.1.208.

If the network 140.100.1.208 resides out of the interface that has learned about 140.100.1.0, however, no traffic will ever reach this subnet 140.100.1.208 because it will always forward based on the longest match in the routing table. The only solution is to turn off summarization and list every subnet with the corresponding mask. If summarization is turned off, the subnet 140.100.1.208 will not be summarized into the network 140.100.1.0. It will consequently be the longest match in the routing table and traffic will be sent to the destination network 140.100.1.208. Figure 3-11 shows an example of route summarization.

Up to this point, this discussion has dealt with organizations that are designing an IP network for the first time. In reality, this is rarely the case unless a decision has been made to readdress the entire network.

Often the network has been up and running for some years. If this is the case, the usual task is to use some of the newer technologies now available to reduce and manage network traffic so that the network can grow without pain.

The simplest solution is to implement a more sophisticated routing protocol. Ideally, a routing protocol that supports VLSM will be chosen and summarization enabled. However, it may not be possible to use the summarization feature. As explained earlier, this capability is determined in part by how well the addressing scheme mirrors, and is supported by, the physical topology.

Figure 3-11 *Route Summarization and VLSM*

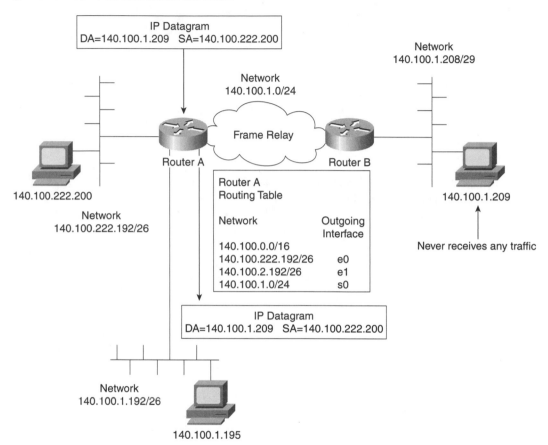

The following guidelines can be used to determine whether summarization may be configured within a particular network:

- Does the network addressing reflect the physical topology of the network?

- Is the physical and logical topology of the network hierarchical?

- Given the network addressing scheme, do the addresses to be summarized share the same high-order bits?

- If the subnet addresses are clearly set on a single binary border, this suggests a prefix mask of /21 or 255.255.248.0. Because the subnets are multiples of 8, they may be summarized by a higher subnet value that is divisible by 8, such as 140.100.64.0. The following subnets provide an example:

140.100.72.0

140.100.80.0

140.100.88.0

140.100.96.0

140.100.104.0

140.100.112.0

- The nature of the traffic flow within the network, which should reflect the hierarchical logical and physical design.

- The routing protocol used must support VLSM.

Any design of a network requires very careful analysis of the current network and a clear understanding of the organization's plans. Unfortunately, it is not always possible to determine the nature or flow of data through a network. Intranets and internal Web pages have made the nature of the traffic within an organization far more unpredictable.

The increased tendency for organizations to need flexibility or mobility in addressing can make the IP design very challenging. The design would need to include Dynamic Host Configuration Protocol (DHCP) and Domain Name System (DNS) servers to maximize the flexibility of the network.

It is also important to fully understand the nature of the traffic in the network, particularly if it is a client/server environment (where the design must allow for servers to communicate with each other and with their clients).

It may be that it is not possible to use the existing addressing of the organization. If this is the case, the decision must be made to readdress the network. The decision may be made either because the network cannot scale because of the limitations of the NIC number that has been acquired from the Internet, or because the original design did not allow for the current environment or growth.

If the addressing scheme is inadequate in size, you have several options. The first is to apply to the Internet for another address or to use private addressing.

Private Addresses on the Internet

The Internet community, realizing that there was a limitation to the number of IP addresses available on the Internet, came up with several solutions, including the following:

- VLSM

- IP version 6 with an address field of 128 bits

- CIDR addressing and prefix routing

- Private addressing

Private addressing was defined by RFC 1597 and revised in RFC 1918. It was designed as an addressing method for an organization with no intention of ever connecting to the Internet. If Internet connectivity were not required, there would be no requirement for a globally unique address from the Internet. The individual organization could address its network without any reference to the Internet, using one of the address ranges provided.

The advantage to the Internet was that none of the routers within the Internet would recognize any of the addresses designated as private addresses. Therefore, if (in error) an organization that had deployed private addressing as outlined in RFC 1918 connected to the Internet, all its traffic would be dropped. The routers of ISPs are configured to filter all network routing updates from networks using private addressing. Previously, organizations had been "inventing" addresses, which were, in fact, valid addresses that had already been allocated to another organization. There are many amusing and horrifying stories of organizations connecting to the Internet and creating duplicate addresses within the Internet. A small company inadvertently masquerading as a large state university can cause much consternation.

Table 3-5 outlines the IP address ranges reserved for private addressing, as specified in RFC 1918.

Table 3-5   *Private Address Ranges*

Address Range	Prefix Mask	Number of Classful Addresses Provided
10.0.0.0–10.255.255.2555	/8	1 Class A
172.16.0.0–172.31.255.255	/12	16 Class Bs
192.168.0.0–192.168.255.255	/16	256 Class Cs

The use of private addressing has now become widespread among companies connecting to the Internet. It has become the means by which an organization docs not have to apply to the Internet for an address, and as such has dramatically slowed, if not prevented, the exhaustion of IP addresses.

Because these addresses have no global significance, an organization cannot just connect to the Internet, but must first go through a gateway that can form a translation to a valid, globally significant address. This is called a Network Address Translation (NAT) gateway.

Configuring private addressing is no more complicated than using a globally significant address that has been obtained from the Internet and is "owned" by the organization. In many ways, it is easier because there are no longer any restrictions on the subnet allocation, particularly if you choose the Class A address 10.0.0.0.

The reasons for addressing your organization's network using private addressing include the following:

- Shortage of addressing within the organization.

- Security—the network, by virtue of having to go through a translation gateway, will not be visible to the outside world.

- Internet service provider change—If connecting to the Internet through an Internet service provider, the addresses allocated by them are just on loan or leased to your organization. If for any reason the organization decides to change its ISP, the entire network will have to be readdressed. If the addresses provided just define the external connectivity and not the internal subnets, however, the readdressing is limited and highly simplified.

The use of private addressing has been implemented by many organizations and might be said to have had a dramatic impact on the design of IP networks and the shortage of globally significant IP addresses. As ever, you should bear some things in mind when designing an IP network address plan using private addressing, including the following:

- If connections to the Internet are to be made, those hosts wanting to communicate externally will need to have some form of address translation performed.

- Because private addresses have no global meaning, routing information about private networks will not be propagated on inter-enterprise links, and packets with private source or destination addresses should not be forwarded across such links. Routers in networks not using private address space, especially those of Internet service providers, are expected to be configured to reject (filter out) routing information about private networks.

- Remember that in the future you may be connecting, merging, or in some way incorporating with another company that has also used the same private addressing range.

- Security and IP encryption do not always allow NAT.

If private addressing is deployed in your network and you are connecting to the Internet, you will be using some form of NAT translation.

The following section explains this technology.

Connecting to the Outside World

The ACRC objective mastered in this section is as follows:

ACRC Exam Objective Number	Corresponding FRS Exam Objective Number	Description
26	107	Define network address translation and determine when it can be used.

When connecting to the outside world, some filtering and address translation may be necessary. Unless an address has been obtained from the Internet or from an ISP, it is necessary to perform address translation. The RFC that defines NAT is RFC 1631.

NAT is the method of translating an address on one network into a different address for another network. It is used when a packet is traversing from one network to another and the source address on the transmitting network is not legal or valid on the destination network. The NAT software process needs to be run on a Layer 3 device or router (which is logical because it is dealing with the translation of Layer 3 addresses). It is often implemented on a device that operates at higher layers of the OSI model because of their strategic placement in the organization. NAT is often used on a firewall system, for example, which is a security device that guards the entrance into the organization from the outside world. The position of the firewall makes it an excellent choice for NAT because most translations are required for traffic exiting an organization that has used private addressing as defined in RFC 1918.

NAT had a controversial childhood, particularly when it was used for translating addresses that did not use RFC 1918 guidelines for private addressing—perhaps the organization used an address that had just been imaginatively created by a network administrator. This practice occurred when there was no glimmer of a possibility that the organization would ever connect to the Internet. This certainty of never connecting is unrealistic, even for small companies, in an era when individual homes have connectivity to the Internet.

Therefore, NAT is useful in the following circumstances:

- To connect organizations that used address space issued to other organizations on the Internet.

- To connect organizations that have used private addressing space defined in RFC 1918 and want to connect to the Internet.

- To connect two organizations that have used the same private address, in line with RFC 1918.

- The organization wants to hide its addresses and is utilizing NAT as part of the firewall capabilities or is using additional security features.

NOTE   NAT is designed for use between an organization and the outside world, as shown in Figure 3-12. Although it may be used to solve addressing problems within an organization, this should be seen as a temporary fix. In such situations, NAT is seen as a transitory solution to keep the network functional while it is designed and readdressed appropriately.

Figure 3-12   *Connecting to the Outside World Using NAT*

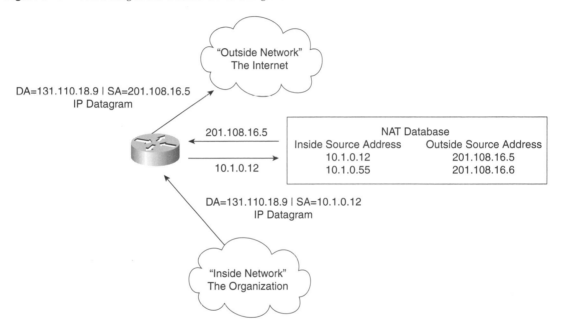

Cisco supports the use of NAT on the majority of their platforms, as well as on their firewall product, the PIX box. Various levels of support are offered, depending on the platform and IOS that has been purchased. NAT support is beginning to be bundled into the standard product offering. It started to be widely offered from IOS version 11.2. NAT is currently at version 3.0. The following section lists the main features that Cisco offers.

TIP   If you are considering implementing NAT, as opposed to studying it for academic/exam purposes, contact Cisco via their Web page. It is advisable to always contact the vendor of a product prior to purchase to fully appreciate the latest offerings and pricing.

The Main Features of NAT

The main features of NAT, as supported by Cisco, include the following:

- **Static addressing**—This one-to-one translation is manually configured.

- **Dynamic source address translation**—Here a pool of addresses is defined. These addresses are used as the product of the translation. They must be a contiguous block of addresses.

- **Port address translation (PAT)**—Different local addresses (within the organization) are translated into one address that is globally significant for use on the Internet. The additional identifier of a TCP or UDP port unravels the multiple addresses that have been mapped to single addresses. The uniqueness of the different local addresses is ensured by the use of the port number mapped to the single address.

- **Destination address rotary translation**—This is used for traffic entering the organization from the outside. The destination address is matched against an access list and replaced by an address from the rotary pool. This is only used for TCP traffic, unless other translations are in effect.

TIP   Many other features are supported by Cisco. Therefore, if you intend to implement this technology, take a look at Cisco's Web page to discover the full range of options and features of the latest IOS version; these are constantly upgrading and improving the feature set.

The basic operation of NAT is very straightforward, although the phraseology is rather confusing. The list of address definitions in Table 3-6 and the accompanying Figure 3-13 clarify the different terms.

To translate one network address into another, the process needs to differentiate between the functionality of the addresses being translated. Table 3-6 lists the categories of functions.

Table 3-6   *Categories of Functions*

Address	Definition
Inside global	The addresses that connect your organization indirectly to the Internet. Typically, these are the addresses provided by the ISP. These addresses are propagated outside the organization. They are globally unique and are the addresses used by the outside world to connect to the organization. Simply explained, they are the addresses that define how the *inside* addresses are seen *globally* by the outside.
Inside local	The addresses that allow every end device in the organization to communicate. Although these addresses are unique within the organization, they are probably not globally unique. They may well be private addresses that conform to RFC 1918. They are the *inside* addresses as seen *locally* within the organization.

Table 3-6   *Categories of Functions (Continued)*

Address	Definition
Outside global	These are the Internet addresses (all the addresses outside the domain of the organization). They are the *outside* addresses as they appear to the *global* Internet.
Outside local	These addresses are external to the organization. It is the destination address used by a host inside the organization connecting to the outside world. This will be the destination address of the packet propagated by the internal host. This is how the *outside* world is seen *locally* from inside the organization.

Figure 3-13 illustrates the terms of Table 3-6.

Figure 3-13   *The Use of the NAT Terms*

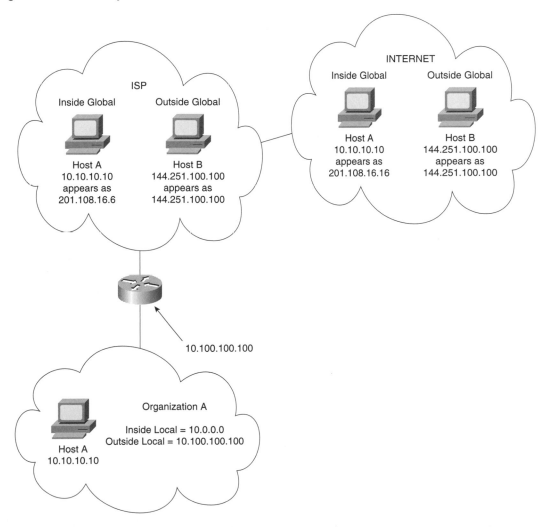

Conclusion

This chapter described various ways to conserve IP address space, as well as how to conserve memory and CPU in the network devices and bandwidth within the network itself. Despite the dramatic increase in low-cost bandwidth and computing power, these considerations are crucial to the health and well-being of your network.

Various technologies such as VLSM, summarization, private addressing, and NAT have been introduced and explained. Although these tools are useful, they are potentially deadly to your network if not administered with care and reference to a well-conceived and thought-out network design.

Q&A

The following questions test your understanding of the topics covered in this chapter. The answers appear in Appendix A, "Answers to Quizzes and Q&As," on page 459. If you get an answer wrong, review the answer and ensure that you understand the reason for your mistake. If you are confused by the answer, refer back to the text in the chapter to review the concepts.

1 Identify one criterion to help determine a subnet mask for classful addressing when designing a network-addressing scheme.

_____

_____

_____

2 What is an inside local address?

_____

_____

_____

3 With a classless address of 204.1.64.0/20, what is the range of classful addresses that are included in the address? Write your answer in both dotted decimal and the third octet in binary notation.

_____

_____

_____

4 What is a discontiguous network?

_____

_____

_____

5 For VLSM to be available as a design option in the network, what characteristic must the routing protocol possess?

_____

_____

_____

6 If summarization is to be implemented in the network, name one design criterion for the addressing scheme that must be in place.

_____

_____

_____

7 What are the networks provided in RFC 1918 and what is the prefix mask that accompanies each network?

_____

_____

_____

8 If the host portion of a subnet has been used to identify end devices, can that subnet be used again for VLSM?

_____

_____

_____

9 Give one reason for using private addressing in a network.

_____

_____

_____

10 When using NAT, configured to translate many inside addresses into one outside address, what mechanism is used to multiplex the different addresses into one address?

_____

_____

_____

11 Give one example of when route summarization would not be a good solution.

_____

_____

_____

12 Give one reason for implementing router summarization.

_____

_____

_____

13 Given an address of 133.44.0.0 and a prefix mask of /25, how many networks can be
    addressed and how many hosts on each network? Write the first and last possible subnets
    in binary and decimal notation.

_____

_____

_____

14 What class of address is 131.188.0.0, and how many hosts can be addressed if no
    subnetting is used?

_____

_____

_____

Scenarios

The following case studies and questions are designed to draw together the content of the chapter and exercise your understanding of the concepts. There is not necessarily a right answer. The thought process and practice in manipulating the concepts is the goal of this section.

The answers to the scenario questions are found at the end of this chapter.

Scenario 3-1

This scenario is concentrating on correcting an addressing scheme that was devised by a network administrator before there was any intention of connecting the company to the Internet and before the company had regional offices. Addresses were subsequently allocated without any policy or administrative control. This has led to problems in the current organization, which now needs to summarize its addresses. Using the addressing scheme in Figure 3-14, answer the following questions:

1 There are serious problems with the addressing scheme in Figure 3-14. If the network had this addressing scheme, would summarization be possible?

2 Design an alternative addressing scheme using VLSM that would summarize to the regional level.

3 Write out the addressing scheme in both binary and dotted decimal notation.

4 Could these addressing requirements be achieved with a Class C address?

5 If the answer to the preceding question is yes, write out the dotted decimal and binary notation to support it. If the answer is no, how many Class C addresses would be required (again write out the dotted decimal and binary notation to support your argument)?

Scenario 3-2

A network has a remarkably even distribution of campuses, buildings, and hosts. They have four campuses, each campus has four buildings, each building has five floors, and each floor has approximately 100 hosts. Each building also has a basement where the building servers are held.

There are eight locations distributed globally. Each location replicates this physical design. The locations are connected via dedicated leased T1 lines. Each T1 constitutes a subnet.

1 Draw the topology map for one of the locations.

2 Using the private network 10.0.0.0, design an addressing scheme that can be summarized. Apply the binary notation for the bit allocation to your diagram.

Figure 3-14   *An Addressing Scheme for Scenario 3-1*

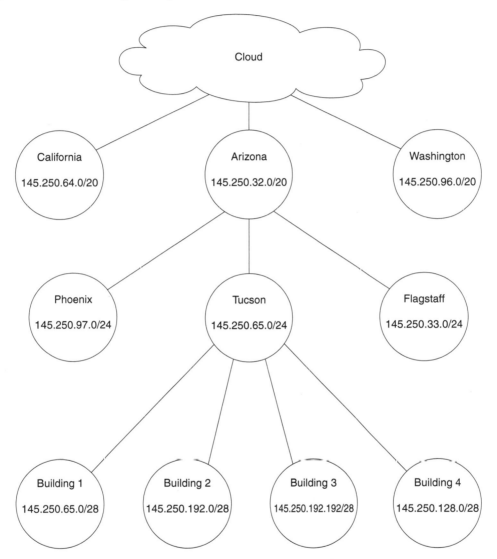

3   List the range of hosts on one of the subnets allocated to a floor in a building.

4   Indicate how summarization would work within the location.

5   Allocate a subnet to be used for VLSM to address the WAN links between the locations.

6   Is it possible to summarize the WAN subnets?

Scenario 3-3

Study Figure 3-15 and answer the questions that follow.

Figure 3-15 *Topology Map for Scenario 3-3*

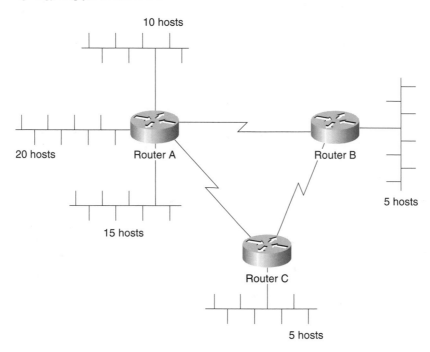

1 To address this network, what class of address would you apply to the Internet?

2 Could you use VLSM? Give reasons for your answer.

3 If you could use VLSM, write out the masks you would deploy in binary notation.

4 Could summarization be implemented?

Scenario Answers

The answers provided in this section are not necessarily the only possible answers to the questions. The questions are designed to test your knowledge and to give practical exercise in certain key areas. This section is intended to test and exercise skills and concepts detailed in the body of this chapter.

If your answer is different, ask yourself whether it follows the tenets explained in the answers provided. Your answer is correct not if it matches the solution provided in the book, but rather if it has included the principles of design laid out in the chapter.

In this way, the testing provided in these scenarios is deeper: It examines not only your knowledge, but also your understanding and ability to apply that knowledge to problems.

If you do not get the correct answer, refer back to the text and review the subject tested. Be certain to also review your notes on the question to ensure that you understand the principles of the subject.

Scenario 3-1 Answers

1 Summarization is not possible, because

- The buildings do not share the same high-order bits as the campus.

- The campuses do not share the same high-order bits as the region.

- Depending on the physical design, California campus and Building 1 could be seen as duplicate addresses.

2 See Table 3-7.

3 See Table 3-7.

Table 3-7 shows an alternative solution using the same address as before and the same bit allocation. If you have changed the bit allocation, ensure that there are enough bits for each level of the network. The requirements have not been stated, so you will have to state them for yourself or use the limited information that is provided. The question identifies three states and you can assume three campuses in each state. Each campus has four buildings.

Table 3-7   *Alternative Addressing Scheme*

Entire Address in Decimal	Third and Fourth Octets in Binary	Prefix	Subnets	Hosts
145.250.16.0	00010000.00000000	/20	14	4094
145.250.32.0	00100000.00000000	/20	14	4094

Continues

Table 3-7   *Alternative Addressing Scheme (Continued)*

Entire Address in Decimal	Third and Fourth Octets in Binary	Prefix	Subnets	Hosts
145.250.48.0	00110000.00000000	/20	14	4094
145.250.17.0	00010001.00000000	/24	254	254
145.250.18.0	00010010.00000000	/24	254	254
145.250.19.0	00010011.00000000	/24	254	254
145.250.19.16	00010011.00010000	/28	4094	14
145.250.19.32	00010011.00100000	/28	4094	14
145.250.19.48	00010011.00110000	/28	4094	14
145.250.19.64	00010011.01000000	/28	4094	14

4 It would not be possible to address this network, using a hierarchical design, with one Class C address. Given the minimum requirements shown in the question of three states, three campuses, and four buildings at each campus, seven bits would be required. A Class C address only allows eight bits in total, leaving one bit for host allocation. The rule of not using all zeros or all ones applies to the host portion of the address, and, therefore, one bit would not enable you to address any hosts.

5 It is interesting that although the first guess is that two is better than one, two Class C addresses do not really improve the situation. The need to address 12 buildings requires four bits, which would only allow 14 hosts in each building. The network could be addressed with two Class C addresses if 14 hosts in each building are all that is required. There is very little growth allowance in this scheme (therefore making it unadvisable).

The most efficient addressing scheme with Class C addresses would be to use 40 Class C addresses. Consider, for example, the addressing scheme using Class C addresses.

A Class C address would be allocated to each building. This would allow 255 hosts in each building and subnetting to the floor if necessary. The other three Class C addresses would be used with VLSM to identify the regions and campuses. Table 3-8 shows the addressing scheme for the one Class C address to address one region, three campuses, and four buildings.

Each region or state will now advertise five networks—the four Class C addresses for the buildings and the shared network for the state. One Class C network can be used for the state if the connections are point-to-point. Because there are 15 connections—four buildings per region, and three regions—this means 12 connections to the buildings plus three connections to the state. A Class C address would easily accommodate this, even with redundant connections built in to the design.

The reason that 40 Class C networks are needed is that the analysis of the state needs to be extrapolated to the entire organization. The organization covers three states, each with three regions, and each region has four buildings. Although the addressing described previously is correct, it would need to be extended to the other regions. This is calculated as follows.

The number of buildings requiring Class C networks in three states, each with three regions, and each region in turn with four buildings is 3×3×4 = 36. Add to the three states requiring Class C networks the additional network required for the core cloud that connects the states, and you have 36 + 3 + 1 = 40. In total, therefore, 40 Class C networks will be required.

Other than for academic interest in torturous addressing, this scenario would be an excellent candidate for a private Class B address.

Table 3-8   *The Bit Allocation for Class C Network to Address the Organizational Network Described in Step 5*

Entire Address in Decimal	Fourth Octet in Binary	Prefix Mask
Region: Arizona		
210.10.32.0		
Campuses		
210.10.32.32	001 00000	/27
210.10.32.64	010 00000	/27
210.10.32.96	011 00000	/27
Buildings		
Tucson		
210.10.32.36	001001 00	/30
210.10.32.40	001010 00	/30
210.10.32.44	001011 00	/30
210.10.32.48	001100 00	/30
Flagstaff		
210.10.32.68	010001 00	/30
210.10.32.72	010010 00	/30
210.10.32.76	010011 00	/30

Continues

Table 3-8 *The Bit Allocation for Class C Network to Address the Organizational Network Described in Step 5 (Continued)*

Entire Address in Decimal	Fourth Octet in Binary	Prefix Mask
210.10.32.80	010100 00	/30
Phoenix		
210.10.32.100	011001 00	/30
210.10.32.104	011010 00	/30
210.10.32.108	011011 00	/30
210.10.32.112	011100 00	/30

Table 3-9 shows how to address the departments or floors within each building. For this discussion, use 210.10.64.0 as the example Class C address. Four bits taken in the fourth octet allows 14 networks, either distributed between the floors or between departments, with 14 hosts on each subnet.

Table 3-9 *How to Address a Building Using a Class C Network Address*

Entire Address in Decimal	4th Octet in Binary	Prefix Mask
210.10.64.16	0001 0000	/28
210.10.64.32	0010 0000	/28
210.10.64.48	0011 0000	/28
210.10.64.64	0100 0000	/28
210.10.64.80	0101 0000	/28
210.10.64.96	0110 0000	/28
210.10.64.112	0111 0000	/28
210.10.64.128	1000 0000	/28
210.10.64.144	1001 0000	/28
210.10.64.160	1010 0000	/28
210.10.64.176	1011 0000	/28
210.10.64.192	1100 0000	/28
210.10.64.208	1101 0000	/28
210.10.64.224	1110 0000	/28

Scenario 3-2 Answers

Using the private network 10.0.0.0, designing a summarized addressing scheme is straightforward.

When the last three octets are written in binary notation, it is easy to determine the bit allocation needed to fulfill the requirements.

Location	|Campus	|Building	|Floor	|Hosts
0000	|0000	|.0000	|0000	|.00000000

This design provides 16 locations, 16 campuses, and 16 buildings. To conform to the rule that excludes the use of all zeros and all ones in a subnet range, you would allocate 14 subnets per building. This would allow 254 hosts per floor or building subnet. There is, therefore, a lot of flexibility in this design for future growth.

1   See Figure 3-16.

2   See Figure 3-16.

Figure 3-16   *Topology Map of One of the Locations*

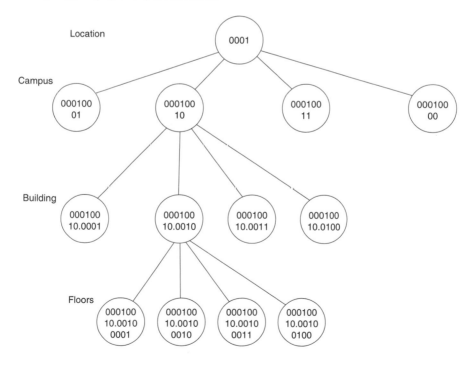

3 If one of the floors is given the subnet:

Location	|Campus	|Building	|Floor	|Hosts
0000	|0000	|.0000	|0000.	|.00000000

Subnet in binary notation:

00001010.00010010.00100010.00000000

Subnet in decimal notation:

10.18.34.0

Range of hosts on that subnet:

10.18.34.1–254

4 Summarization would work within a location because every device and subnet would share the same four high-order bits. The following example clearly demonstrates this:

Location	|Campus	|Building	|Floor	|Hosts
0000	|0000	|.0000	|0000.	|.00000000

Subnet in binary notation:

00001010.00010010.00100010.00000000

Subnet in decimal notation:

10.18.34.0

The summarized address advertised out of the location router would be

10.16.0.0/12

5 Many spare subnets are available in the addressing scheme designed. To address the WAN links, it would be sensible to select one of the subnets allocated to the floors and to reassign it to be further subnetted. For example:

Location	|Campus	|Building	|Floor	|Hosts
0000	|0000	|.0000	|0000.	|.00000000

Subnet in binary notation:

1000	0000	.1000	1000	.00000000

Subnet in decimal notation:

10.128.128.0/30

This allows 60 subnets; each subnet allowing two hosts (ideal for point-to-point lines). The use of 128.128 in the second and third octets eases network management, by readily identifying the serial connections.

6 It would not be easy to summarize these WAN subnets because they have a longer bit pattern than the other subnets beneath them. If summarization is possible, they could be summarized down to 10.128.128.0. It is equally sensible to use any easily recognizable address for WAN links (for example, 10.100.100.0).

Scenario 3-3 Answers

This is a simple network for a small company. Remember, however, that potential growth of the company should not be overlooked in the design. For your reference, the topology map has been included.

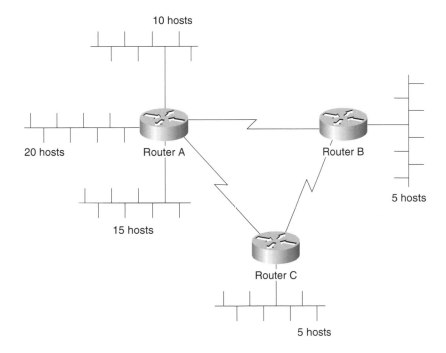

1 The network could be addressed using a Class C address.

2 VLSM can be used as long as a routing protocol is used to support the propagation of the subnet mask. It would be useful to have VLSM for the WAN links, but not essential.

3 The bit allocation could be as follows:

Remote Subnet Locations |Hosts

000 |00000

This would allow for six remote subnet locations, with thirty hosts on each subnet. The assumption that was made was that the company was more likely to expand each existing location than to increase the number of remote sites. If the reverse were true, the mask would no longer be appropriate and a single Class C may no longer be sufficient.

Because there are only three remote sites, with five networks to address and three WAN point-to-point links, and there are six available subnets, one of the subnets could be further subnetted. This subnet would be used to address the WAN links. Another alternative is to use **ip unnumbered** on the serial links.

Remote subnet locations | Hosts:

000|00000

110|00000—Taken for WAN links

New mask:

110000|00

This would allow 14 WAN links to be identified.

4 In this size of a network, summarization is not a concern and would not be possible; also, there is no hierarchy in the physical design.

It should be noted that this design does not allow for much network growth, and the organization may want to consider using a private Class B network.

The objectives for the ACRC exam for CCNP or CCDP certification are taken from the Cisco Web site at http://www.cisco.com/training under the heading "Cisco Career Certifications and Training." The following table shows the ACRC exam objectives covered in this chapter and also provides the Foundation Routing and Switching exam objective number.

ACRC Exam Objective Number	Corresponding FRS Exam Objective Number	Description
21	102	List the key information routers needed to route data.
22	103	Compare distance vector and link-state protocol operation.
27	108	Explain why OSPF is better than RIP in a large internetwork.
28	109	Explain how OSPF discovers, chooses, and maintains routes.
31	112	Describe the issues with interconnecting multiple areas and how OSPF addresses.
32	113	Explain the differences between the possible types of areas, routers, and LSAs.

CHAPTER 4

IP Routing Protocols

How to Best Use This Chapter

By taking the following steps, you can make better use of your study time:

- Keep your notes and answers for all your work with this book in one place for easy reference.

- Take the quiz, writing down your answers. Studies show that retention significantly increases by writing facts and concepts down, even if you never look at the information again!

- Use the diagram in Figure 4-1 to guide you to the next step.

"Do I Know This Already?" Quiz

These questions are designed to test not just your knowledge, but your understanding of the subject matter. It is therefore important to realize that getting the answer the same as stated in Appendix A, "Answers to Quizzes and Q&As," is less important than your answer having embodied the spirit of the question. In this manner, the questions and answers are not as open and shut as will be found on the exam. Their intention is to prepare you with the appropriate knowledge and understanding to give you mastery of the subject as opposed to limited rote knowledge.

1   Name the interior IP routing protocols that send the mask with the routing update.

_____

_____

_____

2   Name the interior IP routing protocols that send incremental updates.

_____

_____

_____

Figure 4-1   *How to Use This Chapter*

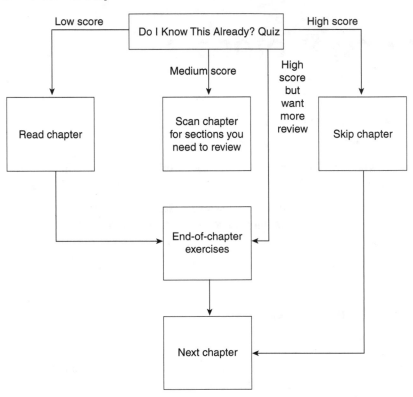

3 How often is the Hello protocol in OSPF sent out on a Cisco router?

_____

_____

_____

4 State the different LSA types.

_____

_____

_____

5 What is used in an OSPF network to discover the designated router by default?

_____

_____

_____

6 A virtual link in OSPF is used to solve what problem?

_____

_____

_____

7 Where does the backbone router reside and what is its function?

_____

_____

_____

8 What must two neighbors do to form an adjacency in OSPF?

_____

_____

_____

9 If a router has the OSPF priority set to 0, what does this indicate?

_____

_____

_____

10 An area border router must be resident in which area?

_____

_____

_____

The answers to this quiz are found in Appendix A, "Answers to Quizzes and Q&As" (see page 462). Review the answers, grade your quiz, and choose an appropriate next step in this chapter based on the suggestions diagrammed in Figure 4-1. Your choices for the next step are as follows:

- Read this chapter.
- Scan this chapter for sections you need to review.
- Skip to the exercises at the end of this chapter.
- Skip this chapter.

Foundation Topics

Introduction: What Is a Routing Protocol?

The ACRC objective mastered in this section is as follows:

ACRC Exam Objective Number	Corresponding FRS Exam Objective Number	Description
21	102	List the key information routers needed to route data.

A routing protocol is the mechanism used to update the Layer 3 routing devices in the organization. With this information, the device makes a decision about forwarding data packets to the end destination identified in the destination address of the datagram/packet. This information must be both accurate and current to ensure the data is sent by the most efficient path to the end device.

Each router makes the decision independent of the other devices. A unit is dependent on the information from the other devices, but independent in that it makes a local decision with regard to only the next hop in the journey of the datagram.

It is important to distinguish between the datagram and the routing protocol used to determine the path of the datagram. The distinction is between the *routed* and *routing* protocol.

The routed protocol is the Layer 3 protocol used to transfer data from one end device to another across the network. The routed protocol is the Layer 3 datagram that carries the application data as well as the upper-layer information.

The routing protocol is the protocol used to send updates between the routers about the networks that exist in the organization, thereby allowing the routing process to determine the path of the datagram across the network.

Table 4-1 provides a list of routed protocols and their corresponding interior routing protocols.

Table 4-1   *Routing and Routed Protocols*

Routed Protocol	Corresponding Interior Routing Protocol
AppleTalk	RTMP, AURP, Enhanced IGRP[1]
IPX	RIP, NLSP, Enhanced IGRP[1]
Vines	RTP
DECnet IV	DECnet
IP	RIP-1, OSPF, IS-IS, IGRP[1], Enhanced IGRP[1]

1. IGRP and Enhanced IGRP are Cisco Systems proprietary routing protocols.

The routing protocol is the mechanism for updating each router so that it can route the data across the best path.

Participating routers advertise the routes they know about to their neighbors in routing protocol updates. Routes learned from routing protocol updates are held in the routing table. Table 4-2 shows the fields that are present in a typical routing table.

Table 4-2 *The Routing Table*

Network	Outgoing Interface	Metric	Next Logical Hop
140.100.100.0 /24	E0	6	131.108.13.15
140.100.110.0 /24	E0	7	131.108.13.15
140.100.120.0 /24	E0	8	131.108.13.15
140.100.130.0 /24	E0	8	131.108.13.15
166.99.0.0 /16	E1	10	131.108.14.11
166.90.0.0 /16	E1	11	131.108.14.11
145.0.88.0 /24	S0	3	131.108.10.9

It is useful to look at each field in the routing table to determine the functionality of the table to the routing process. The next sections cover the following fields of the routing table:

- The Network field
- The Outgoing Interface field
- The Metric field
- The Next Logical Hop field

The Network Field

The Network field contains the networks that the router knows exist in the organization. These entries have either been entered manually as *static routes* or *default routes*, or learned via a routing protocol as *dynamic routes*.

Typically, only the network portion of the address is stored in the table. Using the hierarchical strength of the addressing keeps the routing table small and the lookup short. The routing process makes a decision based on the longest match. This ensures that if VLSM has been deployed, the most specific network is chosen. Cisco IOS code mandates that the longest match can be a /32 or 255.255.255.255 mask. This is a match based on the full host address and is used on specific situations such as an OSPF environment. It is not encouraged as a common configuration because the size of the routing table grows rapidly.

Later in this chapter in the section titled "How the Routing Table Is Kept Current and Correct," you will see how the networks are placed in the table and how path selection to a remote network is chosen.

The Outgoing Interface Field

The Outgoing Interface field tells the routing process the following:

- Which interface to send the datagram to
- Which interface the routing update came through

The Metric Field

The metric is used to determine which path to use if there are multiple paths to the remote network. The metric used is dependent on the routing protocol. Essentially, the routing process assigns a value to each path that leads to the remote network and the routing protocol uses this value to choose between different paths to the same destination. If the values are the same, the router either selects the path it heard first or it uses both paths, sending the datagrams across each route. It is the responsibility of the end device to reassemble the datagrams before sending them to the application.

Table 4-3 shows the metrics used by the different routing protocols.

Table 4-3   *Routing Protocol Metrics*

Routing Protocol	Metric
RIP-1	Hop count
IGRP	Bandwidth, delay, load, reliability, MTU
Enhanced IGRP	Bandwidth, delay, load, reliability, MTU
OSPF	Cost (The cost of an interface is inversely proportional to the bandwidth of that interface. A higher bandwidth indicates a lower cost.)
IS-IS	Cost

By default, on a Cisco router if multiple equal cost paths exist, up to six paths are used in a round-robin manner to load balance the traffic across the network.

The Next Logical Hop Field

The Next Logical Hop field is used to identify the next device that receives the datagram on its journey to the end device. Remember that once the path has been decided, the router takes a very local view of the network. This is good because it keeps the computation and memory utilization low. The reason that the logical address is stored, as opposed to the MAC address of the next hop, is to ensure that the information is accurate. The MAC address may change because of changes in the hardware; however, such changes do not affect the logical address. Also, the router is operating at Layer 3 and just examines the source address of the routing update to determine the next hop. The simplicity of this action reduces the need for extra computation and memory.

TIP   Remember that the Next Hop Logical address is the address of the device directly connected to the router that is determining the path to the end device. Therefore, the address of the next logical hop is a Layer 3 address that shares the same subnet as the determining router.

How the Routing Table Is Kept Current and Correct

The capability to send traffic from one end of the network to the other is dependent on the accuracy and currency of the routing table in every router in the network. Although all routing protocols have this written into their mission statements, the more recent routing protocols are more efficient, and therefore their networks scale more easily.

The accuracy of the table is going to be affected by how quickly it responds to changes in the network. These changes include the following:

- Learning new networks

- Learning a better path to an existing network

- Learning that a network is no longer available

- Learning an alternative route to a network

How each of these changes is achieved depends on the routing protocol.

The techniques used can be broadly divided into two groups. Routing protocols use two main technologies: *link-state* and *distance vector*.

Distance Vector and Link-State Routing Protocols

The ACRC objective mastered in this section is as follows:

ACRC Exam Objective Number	Corresponding FRS Exam Objective Number	Description
22	103	Compare distance vector and link-state protocol operation.

Distance vector protocols are the earliest protocols and include RIP-1 and IGRP. They were designed for small networks, which is why as the networks started to expand, link-state protocols were introduced.

Distance vector protocols send periodic updates. The update is periodic because it waits for the timer to expire before it sends an update. The update is the entire routing table, excluding those networks that were learned through the interface that the update is being sent from. This is in accordance to the *split horizon rule*. This reduces network overhead and also prevents information from traveling in circles through the network, which can create *routing loops*.

To prevent routing loops, distance vector routing protocols employ the following techniques:

- Split horizon
- Count to infinity
- Poison reverse
- Holddown
- Triggered updates
- Aging of routes from the routing table

The metric used by distance vector protocols is often stated as being distance measured in the number of *hand-off points* or *hops* (routers) encountered on the way to the end device. Cisco defines IGRP as a distance vector routing protocol. This muddies the original definition because IGRP uses a composite and complex metric.

The path selection is made using the Bellman Ford algorithm based on the metric or value of each available path. RFC 1058 discusses this in depth in reference to RIP-1.

TIP	If asked a question on distance vector metrics, it may be wise to use the original definition of hop count because IGRP is a proprietary protocol. Cisco also uses the original definition in their documentation.

Link-state routing protocols are used in larger networks because the method they use to update the routing tables requires fewer network resources.

A link-state routing protocol develops a relationship with an adjacent router, one that is on the same physical network. It does this by sending a simple message across the medium. When another router replies, it is identified as a *neighbor* for the routing process. This neighbor relationship is maintained as long as the simple message (Hello protocol) is received. Because the neighbor relationship is continuous, information can be exchanged between the routing processes quickly and efficiently. Therefore, changes in the network are realized very quickly.

A router knows very quickly whether the neighbor, who may also be the next logical hop, is dead, because the router no longer receives Hello protocol messages.

The routing process sends out a message immediately when it identifies a problem, without waiting for the update timer to expire. This is known as an *incremental update*. The update contains only the relevant information. The router also remains silent if there is no change in the network.

The *incremental update* improves convergence time and also reduces the amount of information that needs to be sent across the network. The network overhead on the physical media is eased, and the potential throughput of the network is improved.

A link-state protocol holds a partial map of the network and can easily update the map and routing table database, via the incremental updates. In OSPF, these are called link-state advertisements (LSAs). After an update is received and forwarded the router will compute a new topology map and from this a new path. It uses the Dijkstra algorithm to achieve this new understanding of the network.

The metric that is used is stated as cost, although many vendors supply a default that may be overridden manually. This is true of Cisco's implementation of OSPF, which uses bandwidth as its default.

Examples of link-state routing protocols for IP are OSPF and IS-IS.

A distinction also needs to be made between routing protocols that update routers within an organization and routing protocols that update routers that connect different organizations to each other or to the Internet. Routing protocols that operate within an organization are referred to as *interior routing protocols* (for example, RIP-1, IGRP, Enhanced IGRP, OSPF, and IS-IS).

The boundaries of the organization are defined as the *autonomous system*. The unique number assigned to the autonomous system then identifies the organization. The autonomous system number may be viewed as another layer of hierarchy in the IP addressing scheme because the number can represent a collection of NIC numbers.

Routing protocols that exchange routing information between organizations are known as *exterior routing protocols*. Exterior routing protocols are highly complex. The complexity arises from the need to determine policies between different organizations. Border Gateway Protocol Version 4 (BGP4) is an example of an exterior gateway protocol.

RIP Version 1

The ACRC objective mastered in this section is as follows:

ACRC Exam Objective Number	Corresponding FRS Exam Objective Number	Description
27	108	Explain why OSPF is better than RIP in a large internetwork.

Routing Information Protocol Version 1 (RIP-1) is a simple routing protocol that works well in a small environment. As a distance vector routing protocol, it sends updates every 30 seconds. These updates comprise the entire routing table.

RIP-1 will support the following:

Count to infinity—A router advertising networks heard from a neighboring router, back to the same neighboring router, could create a loop. In repeating networks to the router that informed the routing table, when a network goes down, each router may believe that there is an existing path through its neighbor. This problem is limited because each router increments the hop count before it sends out the update. When the hop count reaches 16, the network is rejected as unreachable because the diameter of a RIP-1 network cannot be greater than 15. This is called *counting to infinity*, where infinity = 16. Although the liability is controlled, it will still slow down convergence of the network.

Split horizon—This is a mechanism to prevent loops and, thereby, the necessity of count to infinity. The routing process will not send networks learned through an interface in an update out of that interface. It will not repeat information to the router that told of the networks.

Split horizon with poison reverse—Split horizon on its own may not prevent loops. Poison reverse includes all the networks that have been learned from the neighbor, but sets the metric to infinity (16). By changing the metric value to 16, the networks are reported to be unreachable. It acknowledges the network, but denies a valid path. Although this increases network overhead by increasing the update size, it can prevent loops.

Holddown—After deciding that a network in the routing table is no longer valid, the routing process waits for three routing updates (by default) before it believes a routing update with a less-favorable metric. This again is to prevent routing loops from generating false information throughout the network.

Triggered updates—As soon as the routing process changes a metric for a network in its routing table, it sends an update. This informs the other routers immediately. If there is a problem in the network, all the affected routers go into Holddown immediately, instead of waiting for the periodic timer. This increases convergence and helps prevent loops.

Load balancing—If the routing process sees multiple paths of equal cost to a remote network, it will distribute the routed (datagram) traffic evenly among the paths. It will allocate datagrams to the different paths on a round-robin basis.

WARNING   Because the metric used is hop count, one path may become saturated. A 56 kbps line and a 100 Fast Ethernet line may both offer paths of equal hop count; to divide the user traffic between them, however, may not optimize the bandwidth of the network.

Cisco has implemented all the preceding options, which are defined in RFC 1058.

RIP-1 is useful in small networks and is distributed with BSD, which makes it widely available. It may not be suitable for large environments, because the protocol was never designed with the expectation of being used in huge organizations.

As the network grows, problems will be seen with applications timing out and congestion on the network as the routers fail to adapt quickly to changes. It is necessary to either contain the growth of the network or to use a routing protocol that scales to a larger size. OSPF is designed to scale and has the added advantage of being defined by the Internet Engineering Task Force (IETF), making it an industry standard in the public domain.

OSPF

The ACRC objectives mastered in this section are as follows:

ACRC Exam Objective Number	Corresponding FRS Exam Objective Number	Description
27	108	Explain why OSPF is better than RIP in a large internetwork.
32	113	Explain the differences between the possible types of areas, routers, and LSAs.

OSPF is an improvement on RIP-1 for large networks because of the following reasons:

- It utilizes bandwidth more efficiently, sending incremental updates.

- It propagates changes in the network more quickly, with incremental updates and neighbor relationships.

- It is not limited in size by a maximum hop count of 15.

- It allows for variation in network size throughout the organization, using VLSM.

- It has security options defined in the MD5 specification.

- The metric may be defined manually, allowing for greater sophistication in the path determination.

- It is more responsive to network changes, is flexible in network addressing and design, and scales to a larger size.

The following sections discuss these key points in detail.

Key Attributes of OSPF

OSPF is designed to offer the greatest flexibility for every situation. As an open standard, it is required to offer interoperability in conjunction with this flexibility, while allowing the network to grow. These requirements make OSPF a highly complex routing protocol.

To understand this complexity, it is useful to identify the main characteristics of OSPF. These key attributes of OSPF include the following:

- Maintaining a connection-oriented relationship with other routers on the same physical segment. These are known as *adjacent neighbors*.

- Sending the minimum amount of information in an *incremental update* when there has been a change in the network.

- Adding another level of hierarchy to the IP address by designing networks into *areas*.

- Using VLSM and summarization.

- Assigning specific functionality to different routers to streamline the process of communication change in the network.

- Operating within an organization as an interior routing protocol.

To understand these key concepts, it is important to examine each of the characteristics of OSPF in detail.

OSPF has many features and each one is dealt with here in turn, starting with the simplest design of a single area. After the main concepts have been identified, the discussion turns to determining the design criteria for a multiple area network. Chapter 5, "OSPF Configuration," covers the detailed configuration of the OSPF protocol.

Hierarchy in OSPF—Areas and Routers

One of the main strengths of OSPF is its capability to scale and to support large networks. It achieves this by creating areas from groups of subtends. The area is seen internally almost as if it is a small organization or entity on its own. It communicates with the other areas, exchanging routing information; this exchange is kept to a minimum, however, allowing only that which is required for connectivity. All computation is kept within the area.

In this way, a router is not overwhelmed by the entirety of the organization's network. This is crucial because the nature of a link-state routing protocol is that it is more CPU- and memory-intensive.

Given the hierarchical nature of the OSPF network, you will see routers operating within an area, routers connecting areas, and routers connecting the organization or autonomous system to the outside world. Each of these routers will have a different set of responsibilities, depending on their position and functionality within the OSPF hierarchical design.

The following list identifies the different OSPF routers:

Internal router—Within an area, the functionality of the router is straightforward. It is responsible for maintaining a current and accurate database of every subnet within the area and to forward data to other networks by the shortest path. Flooding of routing updates will be confined to the area.

Backbone router—The design rules for OSPF require that all the areas be connected through a single area known as the *backbone area* or *area 0*. A router within this area is referred to as a *backbone router*. It may also be an internal router or an area border router.

Area border router (ABR)—This router is responsible for connecting two or more areas. It will hold a full topological database for each area it is connected to and will send LSA updates between the areas. These LSA updates will be summary updates of the subnets within an area. It is at the area border that summarization should be configured for OSPF, because this is where the LSAs make use of the reduced routing updates to minimize the routing overhead on both the network and the routers.

Autonomous system boundary router (ASBR)—To connect to the outside world, or to any other routing protocol, you need to leave the OSPF domain. OSPF is an *interior routing protocol* or *interior gateway protocol* (IGP); *gateway* is an older term for a router. The router configured for this duty is the autonomous system boundary router. Although you can place this router anywhere in the OSPF hierarchical design, it should reside in the backbone area. Because it is likely that any traffic leaving the OSPF domain will also leave the router's area, it makes sense to place the ASBR in a central location that all traffic leaving its area must traverse.

Figure 4-2 shows how the different router types are interrelated.

Figure 4-2   *Router Definitions for OSPF*

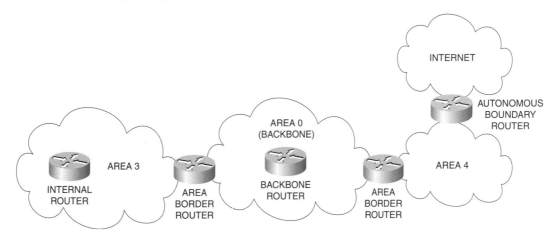

OSPF Neighbors

A router configured for OSPF sends out a small packet periodically (10 seconds is the default). This packet is known as the *Hello protocol*. It has a source address of the router and a multicast destination address set to AllSPFRouters. This is true of broadcast media. Other media require additional configuration. Any other router on the same network listens to the Hello protocol.

How an OSPF protocol communicates to a network depends on the physical medium being used. OSPF identifies the different technologies as follows:

Broadcast multiaccess—This is any LAN network such as Ethernet, Token Ring, or FDDI. In this environment, OSPF sends out multicast traffic. A designated router and backup designated router will be elected.

Point to point—Used where there is one other system, which is directly connected to the transmitting or receiving router. A typical example of this is a serial line. OSPF has no need of a designated or backup designated router in this scenario and will use unicast traffic.

Nonbroadcast multiaccess—This physically resembles a point-to-point line, but in fact, many destinations are possible. WAN clouds, including X25 and Frame Relay, are examples of this technology. This technology requires manual configuration. The configuration options have increased with the different versions of Cisco IOS.

After neighbors have been established by means of the Hello protocol, they exchange routing information. When their topology databases are the same, or synchronized, the neighbors have formed an *adjacency*. The Hello protocol continues to transmit, by default every 10 seconds. The transmitting router and its networks reside in the topology database for as long as the other routers receive the Hello protocol.

There are obvious advantages to creating neighbor relationships. These advantages include the following:

- There is another mechanism for determining that a router has gone down (obvious because its neighbor no longer receives Hello packets).

- Streamlined communication results because after the topological databases are synchronized, incremental updates will be sent to the neighbors as soon as a change is perceived.

- Adjacencies created between neighbors control the distribution of the routing protocol packets.

The use of adjacencies and a neighbor relationship result in a much faster convergence of the network than can be achieved by RIP-1, which has to wait for incremental updates and holddown timers to expire on each router before the update is sent out. Convergence on a RIP-1 network can take many minutes, and the real problem is the confusion created by the different routing tables held. This problem can result in routing loops and black holes in the network.

If there are many routers on the same segment, however, the intermesh of neighbor relationships becomes complex. On a FDDI ring, which forms the campus or building backbone, each router has to form an adjacency with every other router on the segment. Although the Hello protocol is not networking-intensive, maintaining the relationships requires additional CPU cycles. Therefore, if routers are connected to a broadcast segment, one router on the segment is assigned the duty of maintaining adjacencies with all the routers on the segment. This router is known as the *designated router* and is elected by the use of the Hello protocol. All other routers need only peer with the designated router, which informs them of any changes on the segment.

In case the designated router dies or becomes unreachable for any reason, the Hello protocol elects a backup designated router at the same time that the designated router is elected. The backup designated router maintains an adjacency with the designated router, which allows it to rapidly detect the failure of the designated router. When the designated router fails, the backup designated router assumes the role of designated router and a new backup designated router is elected.

Very little time is required to switch over from the backup designated router because the backup designated router has been listening to all the traffic sent to the designated router and is primed to take over the duties and responsibilities of the designated router. The backup designated router maintains the new status of designated router irrespective of whether the preceding incumbent designated router returns to the network.

The network administrator can manually elect the designated and backup designated routers, or they can be dynamically selected using the Hello protocol. When selected dynamically, the designated router is elected arbitrarily. The selection is made on the basis of the highest router ID, or IP address. It is wise to be aware that the highest IP address is the numerically highest number, not the class ranking of the addresses. Therefore, a remote, small router with a Class C address may end up as a designated router. This may not be the optimal choice.

If you are manually determining which routers are to be the designated and backup designated routers, it is easier to design your network to the optimum.

After the designated and backup designated routers have been elected, all routers on the broadcast medium will communicate directly with the designated routers. They will use the multicast address to all designated routers. The backup router will listen, but will not respond; remember, it is the understudy waiting in the wings. The designated router will send out multicast messages if it receives any information pertinent to the connected routers for which it is responsible.

In Figure 4-3, the 2500 router for Building A, which is connected to the San Francisco campus via a hub, would be a poor choice as the designated router. The larger, 7200 Cisco router, which connects the building routers to the campus backbone, acts as the centralized router; therefore, the 7200 Cisco router makes more sense as the router in charge of the connectivity for the segment.

Figure 4-3   *The Designated Router*

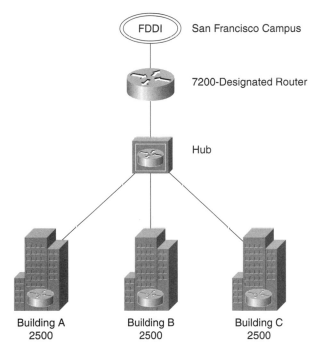

How OSPF Builds Its Routing Table

The ACRC objectives mastered in this section are as follows:

ACRC Exam Objective Number	Corresponding FRS Exam Objective Number	Description
28	109	Explain how OSPF discovers, chooses, and maintains routes.
32	113	Explain the differences between the possible types of areas, routers, and LSAs.

After a neighbor is discovered in OSPF, adjacency is formed. It is important to understand how the neighbor adjacency is formed, and in this context, to understand the other messages that the routers receive.

Routing tables are built in two different ways. The first way is for a new router to be added to the network, and for it to build a routing table by listening to the routers with complete routing tables. Remember that every router within an area will have the same topology database and will know of every network within the area. The decisions made on the best path to those networks depend on the individual router's position within the area relative to the remote destination network.

The other event that necessitates an addition to the routing table is when there is a change in the network. A particular router that notices a change floods the area with the update so that all routers can alter their routing tables to reflect the most current and accurate information, or so that they can converge.

Different techniques are used for these different routing table requirements. Essentially, the difference between the two techniques is simple:

- If a new router connects to a network, it will find a neighbor using the Hello protocol and *exchange* routing information.

- If a change occurs in an existing network, the router that sees the change will *flood* the area with the new routing information.

These two requirements for updating the routing table use different technologies and OSPF protocols. These technologies and protocols are often confused. It is worth a moment to distinguish them, however, because understanding the distinction makes the OSPF operation much clearer.

Five packets are used to build the routing table for the first time. They are as follows:

- **The Hello protocol**—Used to find neighbors and to determine the designated and backup designated router. The continued propagation of the Hello protocol maintains the transmitting router in the topology database of those that hear the message.

- **The database descriptor**—Used to send summary information to neighbors to synchronize topology databases.

- **The link-state request**—A request for more detailed information, which is sent when the router receives a database descriptor that contains new information.

- **The link-state update**—This is the link-state advertisement (LSA) packet issued in response to the request for database information in the link-state request packet. The five types of LSA are described in the following section, "The Link-State Advertisements."

- **The link-state acknowledgement**—Acknowledges the link-state update.

Consider the case of when a router joins the OSPF network for the first time. Take a look at Figure 4-4. The 2500 router in Building A at the San Francisco campus has just been connected.

Figure 4-4   *Joining an OSPF Network*

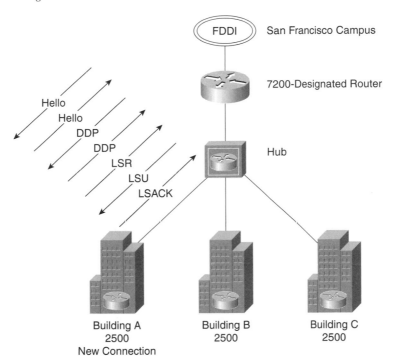

In accordance with the description of the Hello protocol, the designated router has been elected. It is the 7200 router, which connects the campus to the campus backbone. The 2500 router transmits its own Hello packets to introduce itself to the segment and to find any other OSPF-configured routers. On hearing the Hello protocol from the 2500, the designated router adds the router ID of the 2500 and replies as a unicast with its own ID and a list of any other neighbors.

The 2500 and the designated router have now established a neighbor relationship and need to ensure that the 2500 has all the relevant information about the network. The 7200 must update and synchronize the topology database of the 2500. This is achieved by using the exchange protocol, or the database description packets.

As demonstrated in Figure 4-4, both routers will send out database description packets. One of the routers will take seniority, becoming the master router. The master router will be the router with the highest router ID (probably the designated router). This designation is not significant, however, because it just determines who starts the communication. Both routers exchange their knowledge of the network. In this example, the 2500 has no knowledge and can only inform the 7200 of the networks or links to which it is directly connected.

For this example, assume that the 7200 has become the master router. As such, it will send out a series of database description packets containing the networks held in the topology database. These networks are referred to as *links*. Each link has been received from another router (the next logical hop) referred to by its router ID. The topology database will have an interface ID for the outgoing interface, a link ID, and a metric to state the value of the path, relative to others on the same remote network. This database is indeed a routing table, but a routing table for which no path decisions have been made; it is at present a topology database.

The database description packet will not contain all the necessary information, just a summary (enough for the receiving router to determine whether more information is required or whether it already contains that entry in its database).

If the receiving router, the 2500, requires more information, it will request that particular link in more detail, using the link-state request packet (LSR). The LSR will prompt the master router to send the link-state update packet (LSU). Figure 4-4 illustrates this as well. This is the same as a link-state advertisement used to flood the network with routing information when a change is perceived in the network.

The LSAs are therefore a subset of the OSPF protocol just described.

The Link-State Advertisements

There are five different types of link-state advertisements (LSAs). Although all five are listed here, this discussion focuses only on those advertisements sent between routers in the same area and on the same segment.

The five link-state advertisements are as follows:

The router link—This LSA states all the links to the router sending out the LSA. The list is of all the neighbors attached to the router. The LSA is flooded to the area.

The network link—This LSA is sent out by the designated router and lists all the routers on the segment for whom it is the designated router and has a neighbor relationship. The LSA is flooded to the whole area.

The summary link—This LSA is sent between areas and summarizes the IP networks from one area to another. It is generated by an area border router.

The summary link (autonomous system boundary router [ASBR])—This LSA is sent to a router that connects to the outside world. It is sent from the area border router to the autonomous system boundary router. The LSA contains the metric cost from the area border router to the autonomous system boundary router.

The external link—Originated by AS boundary routers and flooded throughout the AS. Each external advertisement describes a route to a destination in another autonomous system. Default routes for the AS can also be described by AS external advertisements.

Figure 4-5 clearly shows the relationship between the different LSAs. This section discusses the router and network LSAs. The LSAs concerned with communication outside an area are considered later.

Figure 4-5   *The Propagation of LSAs*

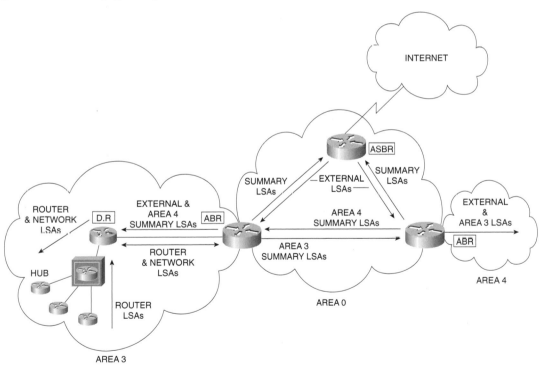

The Topology Database

The topology database is the router's view of the network within the area. It includes every OSPF router within the area and all the connected networks.

The topology database is updated by the LSAs. Each router within the area has exactly the same topology database. All routers must have the same vision of the network; otherwise, confusion, routing loops, and loss of connectivity will result.

The synchronization of the topology maps is ensured by the intricate use of time stamps and sequence numbers in the LSA headers.

From the topology map, a routing database is constructed. This database will be unique to each router, which creates a routing database by running the *shortest path first* (SPF) algorithm called the *Dijkstra algorithm*. Each router uses this algorithm to determine the best path to each network and creates an SPF tree on which it places itself at the top or root. If there are equal metrics for a remote network, OSPF includes all the paths and load balances the routed data traffic among them.

NOTE   Although RFC 2328 does not state the number of multiple, equal-cost paths that can be used at the same time, Cisco has defined a maximum of six paths that can be used simultaneously for load balancing.

Maintaining the Topological Database and the Routing Table

Now turn back to the 2500 in San Francisco—which is now happily a member of the OSPF network—and follow the process of hearing an update to the network in the form of an LSA.

As soon as a router realizes that there has been a change in the network topology, the router is responsible for informing the rest of the routers in the area. Typically, it will identify a change in the state of one of its links for one of the following reasons:

- The router loses the physical or data link layer connectivity on a connected network.

- The router fails to hear either an OSPF Hello protocol or a data link Hello protocol.

- It receives an LSA update from an adjacent neighbor, informing it of the change in the network topology.

In any of these instances, the router will generate an LSA and flood it to all its neighbors.

This discussion now turns to the process initiated when a router receives such an update. For this purpose, return to the 2500 connected to its designated router, the 7200.

When the 2500 receives a network LSA update from the designated router, it goes through the following logical steps:

1   Takes the first entry from the update—the first network with information about the state of its link.

2   Calculates the checksum for the link-state and ensures that it is a valid entry.

3   Verifies that it is a known type of LSA and one that can be accepted by this router.

4   Ensures that the update is still valid and has not aged out.

5   Having ascertained that it is a valid LSA it can receive, the router issues a lookup to its topological database.

6   If the LSA entry is *not* in the topological database, it will be flooded immediately out of all the OSPF interfaces, except for the receiving interface.

7   If the LSA entry is in the topological database, further questions are required.

Does the new LSA have a more recent time stamp?

If so, has it arrived outside the wait period, before another computation is allowed (minsLSarrival)?

If the new LSA entry passes these tests, it is flooded out of all the OSPF interfaces, except for the receiving interface.

8   The current copy replaces the old LSA entry. If there was no entry, the current copy is just placed in the database.

9   The time stamp for the new LSA entry is changed to reflect the receive time of the LSA.

10   The received LSA is acknowledged.

11   If the LSA entry was in the database, but the LSA that has just been received has an older time stamp, the process will ask whether the information in the database is the same.

12   If the information is the same and the new LSA has an older time stamp, the process just discards the packet. It may be old news, but there is no inconsistency in the database.

13   If the information is different and the newly received LSA has an older time stamp, however, the receiving router will discard the LSA update and issue its own LSA out of the receiving interface to the source address of the out-of-date LSA. The logic is that the sending router has either bad or old information and needs to be updated because its topological database is obviously not synchronized with the rest of the area.

This ensures that any packets that get out of sequence will be verified before action is taken. It also attempts to rectify a problem that it sees—that of multiple routers offering different paths because their topological databases are completely confused.

14 After the initial flood, things calm down and updates are sent only when there are changes in the area or when the 30-minute timer goes off. This timer ensures that the databases stay synchronized.

This shows some of the internal complexity of OSPF. As you can see, the internals are extremely detailed. Therefore, the design of any OSPF network should be very carefully thought out. The configuration of the routing protocol, on the other hand, is incredibly straightforward.

Figure 4-6 shows a logical flowchart of how the OSPF topological database is updated.

As you have seen, different types of LSA are propagated through the network. Figure 4-7 illustrates graphically the flooding of an LSA through the network.

Choosing the Shortest Path First and Building the Routing Table

As with any routing protocol, OSPF examines all the available paths to every network it knows about. It selects the shortest, most direct path to that destination.

As with all routing protocols, this decision will be based on the metric used by the routing protocol. RIP uses hop count. Hop count shows how many routers must be passed through to get to the destination. When CPU and memory were very expensive, the latency of traveling through the router had much higher implications on network performance. OSPF has few of those constraints and so chooses the metric of *cost*. Cost is not defined, however; it depends on the implementation of the protocol. The metric may be programmed to be either complex or simple. Cisco's implementation of a dynamic and default cost uses a predefined value based on the bandwidth of the router interface. The network administrator can manually override this default.

The cost is applied to the outgoing interface. The routing process will select the lowest accumulated cost of the interfaces to the remote network.

NOTE   If the network is manually configured, all routers connected to a particular network should agree on cost.

Also, if manually configured, the cost should be thought through very carefully; otherwise, you might seriously damage your network.

The routing process, having determined the shortest path or multiple equal-cost paths, will need to supply additional information. To forward the data down the chosen path, the next logical hop, link, and outgoing interface must be ascertained. The routing table, or *forwarding database* as it is sometimes called, requires this information.

Figure 4-6   *Updating the Topological Database*

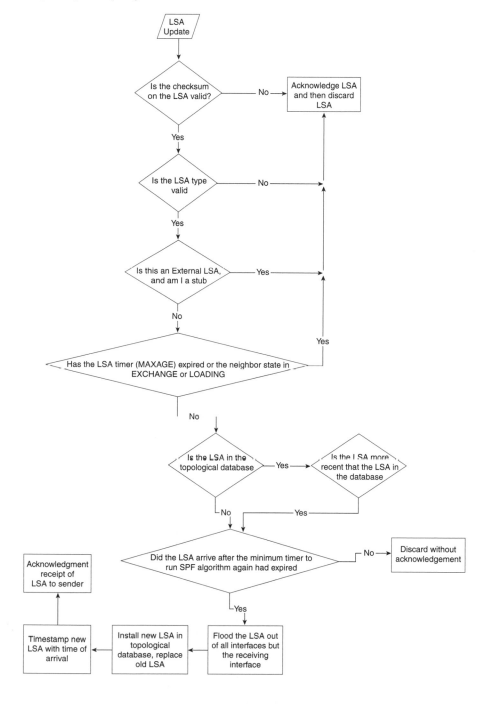

Figure 4-7 *Flooding LSAs Throughout the Area*

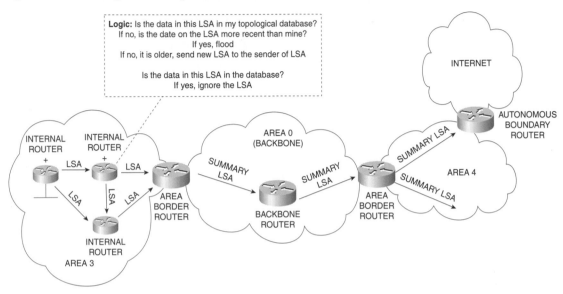

Now that you understand the mechanism of the OSPF routing protocol and how the link-state routing protocol is more efficient in large environments, it will be useful to understand how to configure the protocol on a Cisco router.

WARNING If OSPF is used in an environment across different vendor equipment, it should be researched and tested to ensure interoperability.

The following section examines the implications of a larger network.

OSPF in a Multiple Area Network

The ACRC objective mastered in this section is as follows:

ACRC Exam Objective Number	Corresponding FRS Exam Objective Number	Description
31	112	Describe the issues with interconnecting multiple areas and how OSPF addresses.

In explaining the fundamentals of OSPF, the foundation for this section has been created and reference will be made to the earlier topics in this chapter.

The first consideration must be why multiple areas are needed. There is a lot of noise about multiple areas in OSPF, and indeed it is one of the main distinguishing features among other distance vector protocols and the link-state OSPF.

Why Multiple Areas?

The creation of multiple areas solves the problem of a large network outgrowing its capacity to communicate the details of the network to the routing devices charged with maintaining control and connectivity throughout the network.

The division of the AS into areas allows routers in each area to exchange routes and maintain their own topological databases. This limits the size of the topological databases, and summary and external links ensure connectivity between areas and networks outside the AS.

Although there is an obvious need for the multiple areas, the practical question of how this is implemented arises. There are two approaches. The first approach is to grow a single area until it becomes unmanageable. The second approach is to design the network with multiple areas, which are very small, in the expectation that the networks will grow to fit comfortably into their areas.

Both approaches are valid. The first approach requires less initial work and configuration. Great care should be put into the design of the network, however, because this may cause problems in the future, particularly in addressing.

In practice, many companies convert their networks into OSPF from a distance vector routing protocol when they realize they have outgrown the existing routing protocol.

Now consider the implications of implementing the first approach to OSPF—that of configuring one area and adding others as needed. Unfortunately, life with OSPF is not that easy; and by looking at the issues, you can learn many things, beyond just how to create multiple areas.

To understand how OSPF works and the true benefit of multiple areas, consider why someone might decide to create multiple areas from one area.

The following symptoms that you will observe on the network provide a clue that a single area is becoming overpowered:

- The frequency of the SPF algorithm being run will increase. The larger the network, the greater the probability of a network change and thus a recalculation of the entire area. Each recalculation will also take longer.

- The routing table will become extremely large. The routing table is *not* sent out wholesale as in a distance vector routing protocol; however, the greater the size of the table, the longer each lookup becomes and the memory requirements on the router increase.

- The topological database will increase in size and will eventually become unmanageable for the same reasons.

- As the various databases increase in size and the calculations become increasingly frequent, the CPU utilization will increase as the available memory decreases. This will make the network response time very sluggish (not because of congestion on the line, but because of congestion within the router itself).

TIP   To check the CPU utilization on the router, use the **show cpu process** command. To check the memory utilization, issue the **show mem** command.

Now that you understand why the size of the areas should be controlled, it is important to consider the design issues for the different areas, including the technology that underpins them and their communication (both within and between the areas).

The Different Types of Areas

In addition to the backbone area, which connects the other areas together, OSPF networks use several other types of areas. The following are the different types of areas:

An ordinary or standard area—This area, described earlier, connects to the backbone. The area is seen as an entity unto itself. Every router knows about every network in the area, and each router has the same topological database. However, the routing tables will be unique to the perspective of the router and its position within the area.

A stub area—This is an area that will not accept external summary routes. The LSAs blocked are types 3 and 4 (summary link LSAs that are generated by the ABRs). The consequence is that the only way a router within the area can see outside the autonomous system is via the configuration of a default route. Every router within the area can see every network within the area and the networks (summarized or not) within other areas.

A totally stubby area—This area does not accept summary LSAs from the other areas or the external summary LSAs from outside the autonomous system. The LSAs blocked are types 3, 4, and 5. The only way out of the area is via a configured default route. This type of area is particularly useful for remote sites that have few networks and limited connectivity with the rest of the network. This is a proprietary solution offered only by Cisco. Cisco recommends this solution if you have a totally Cisco shop because it keeps the topological databases and routing tables as small as possible.

A not so stubby area (NSSA)—This area is used primarily to connect to ISPs. It accepts all LSA types except LSA type 5. This is the same as the stub area. The result is that there is full communication within the autonomous system, but no information about the outside world is communicated into the area. All external routes to the OSPF autonomous system are blocked.

Another LSA, type 7, is created for the NSSA, however. This LSA may be originated and communicated throughout the area, but will *not* be propagated into other areas, including area 0. Translating it into an LSA type 5 at the NSSA area border router allows the propagation of the information.

The purpose is to allow the area to have autonomous system boundary routers and to receive information from outside the OSPF domain while keeping the routing tables, topological databases, and, therefore, router resources to a minimum. A typical example would be of an area that has a connection to an ISP, but is not area 0. Another use would be another routing protocol sharing its information about the network with the OSPF protocol. These routes are seen as external to the autonomous system. It is not always possible to design the network and determine where redistribution is to occur. RFC 1587 deals with this subject.

The backbone area—This area is often referred to as area 0 and connects all the other areas together. It can propagate all the LSAs except for LSA type 7, which would have been translated into LSA type 5 by the ABR.

Figure 4-8 shows the connectivity and functionality of the different areas.

Figure 4-8   *The Different Types of OSPF Areas and LSA Propagation*

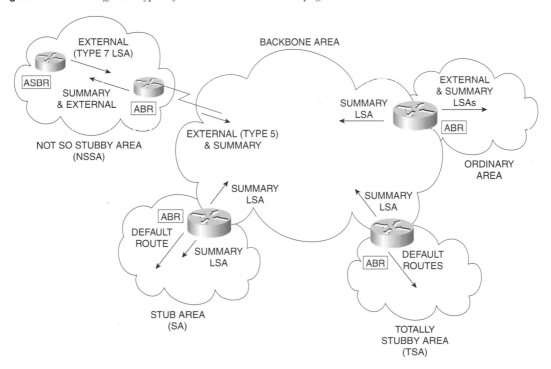

The routing table that exists on a router depends on the following factors:

- The position the router has in the area and the status of the network

- The type of area in which the router is located

- Whether there are multiple areas in the domain

- Whether there are communications outside the autonomous system

Remember the sequence of events. The router receives LSAs. It builds the topological database and then runs the Dijkstra algorithm, from which the shortest path first is chosen and entered into the routing table. The routing table is therefore the conclusion of the decision-making process. It holds information on how that decision was made by including the metric for each link. This enables the network administrator to view the operation of the network.

Different LSAs hold different weighting in the decision-making process. It is preferable to take an internal route (within the area) to a remote network rather than to traverse multiple areas just to arrive at the same place. Not only does multiple area traveling create unnecessary traffic, it also can create a loop within the network.

The routing table will reflect the network topology information and will indicate where the remote network sits in relation to the local router.

At the side of the routing table is a column indicating the source of the routing information. Typically, this is the routing protocol. In the instance of OSPF, however, it includes the LSA type that provided the path.

Table 4-4 shows the codes used in the routing table.

Table 4-4 *OSPF Routing Table Codes and Associated LSAs*

LSA Type	Routing Table Entry	Description
1 Router Link	O	Generated by the router, listing all the links it is connected to, their status, and cost. It is propagated within the area.
2 Network Link	O	Generated by the designated router on a multiaccess LAN, to the area.
3 or 4 Summary Link (between areas)	IA	LSA type 3 includes the networks or subnets within an area, which may have been summarized and are sent into the backbone and between ABRs. LSA type 4 is information set to the ASBR from the ABR. These routes are not sent into totally stubby areas.
5 Summary Link/ External Link (between autonomous systems)	E1 or E2	The routes in this LSA are external to the autonomous system. They can be configured to have one of two values. E1 will include the internal cost to the ASBR and the external cost reported by the ASBR. E2 does not compute the internal cost, just reporting the external cost to the remote destination.

Now that you understand many components of OSPF, it is important to focus on some of the design implications of creating multiple areas. This focus will reinforce the concepts detailed in the chapter.

Design Considerations in Multiple Area OSPF

The major design consideration in OSPF is how to divide the areas. This is of interest because it impacts the addressing scheme for IP within the network.

An OSPF network works best with a hierarchical design, where the movement of data from one area to another comprises only a subset of the traffic within the area itself.

It is important to remember that with all the inter-area traffic disseminated by the backbone, any reduction of overhead through a solid hierarchical design and summarization is beneficial. The lower the number of summary LSAs that need to be forwarded into the backbone area, the greater the benefit to the entire network. It will allow the network to grow more easily because the network overhead is at a minimum.

With this in mind, summarization is the natural consequence. As shown in Chapter 3, "IP Addressing," summarization is not something that can be imposed on a network. It must be part of the initial network design. The addressing scheme must be devised to support the use of summarization.

OSPF is stringent in its demand for a solid hierarchical design; so much so, it has devised some commands to deal with situations that break its rules of structure.

The main dictate in OSPF is that the multiple areas all connect directly to the backbone area. The connection to the backbone area is via an ABR, which is resident in both areas and holds a full topological database for each area.

OSPF has provided for the unhappy occasion that this rule cannot be followed. The solution is called a *virtual link*. If the new area cannot connect directly to the backbone area, a router is configured to connect to an area that does have direct connectivity.

The configuration commands create a tunnel to the ABR in the intermediary area. From the viewpoint of OSPF, it has a direct connection.

The reason such a situation may occur is because the organization has recently merged with another, or perhaps because the distant area was connected to the backbone, but has lost its physical connection.

Although this is an extremely powerful command, it is not recommended as part of the design strategy for your network; instead, it is a temporary solution to a connectivity problem. Figure 4-9 illustrates the use of a virtual link to provide a router in area 10 connectivity to the backbone in area 0.

Figure 4-9   *Virtual Links in a Multiple Area OSPF Network*

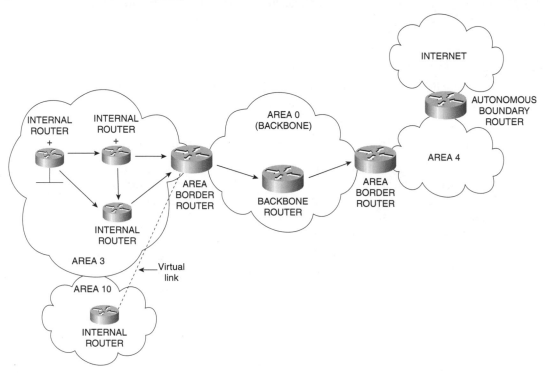

After the design of the network is in place, it is time to configure the routers. The configuration of a basic OSPF network is demonstrated in the beginning of Chapter 5, "OSPF Configuration." Chapter 5 also deals with the additional commands required to configure the router to operate in a multiple area network.

Foundation Summary

Table 4-5 summarizes the major differences between distance vector routing protocols and link-state routing protocols.

Table 4-5   *Distance Vector Routing Protocols Versus Link-State Routing Protocols*

Distance Vector	Link-State
Sends its entire routing table at periodic intervals out of all interfaces (typically this is based in seconds). It will also send triggered updates to reflect changes in the network.	Sends incremental updates when a change is detected. Will send summary information every 30 minutes if incremental updates have not been sent in that time.
Uses a metric based on how distant the remote network is to the router. (IGRP does not conform to this as a proprietary solution.)	Capable of using a complex metric.
Knowledge of the network is based on information learned from its neighbors.	Knowledge of the network is based on information learned from every router in the area.
The routing table is a database viewed from the perspective of each router.	The topological database is the same for every router in the area. The routing table that is built from this database is unique to each router.
Uses Bellman Ford algorithm for calculating the best path.	Uses the Dijkstra algorithm.
Does not consume many router resources, but is heavy in the use of network resources.	Uses many router resources, but is relatively low in its demand for network resources.
Maintains one domain in which all the routes are known.	Has a hierarchical design of areas that allow for summarization and growth.
Is not restricted by addressing scheme.	For effective use, the addressing scheme should reflect the hierarchical design of the network.
Convergence is slower in a distance vector routing protocol because information of changes must come from the entire network (but indirectly). Each routing table on every intervening router must be updated before the changes reach the remote end of the network.	Convergence is quicker because the update is flooded immediately throughout the network.

Table 4-6 summarizes the differences between RIP-1 and OSPF. Because RIP-1 is a distance vector routing protocol and OSPF is a link-state routing protocol, you will find it helpful to keep in mind the information in Table 4-5.

Table 4-6 *RIP-1 Versus OSPF*

RIP–1	OSPF
A simple protocol to design, configure, and maintain.	A complex protocol to design and, in some instances, to configure and maintain.
Does not require a hierarchical addressing scheme.	If full benefits of the protocol are to be harnessed, the IP addressing scheme should be hierarchical.
Does not pass the subnet mask in the routing update and therefore is not capable of classless routing or VLSM.	Carries the mask in the update and therefore can implement VLSM, summarization, and classless routing.
Is limited to 15-hop diameter network.	Is unlimited in the diameter of the network, although it is suggested that an area not exceed more than 50 networks.
The routing updates are not acknowledged, just repeated periodically (every 30 seconds).	The updates are acknowledged.
The routing table is sent out of every interface every 30 seconds (by default).	The updates are sent as required (when changes are seen) and every 30 minutes after no change has been seen.
RIP can transmit information about the network in two messages: the routing update and the triggered update.	OSPF has protocols for discovering neighbors and forming adjacencies as well as protocols for sending updates through the network. These protocols alone add up to nine message types.
The metric used by RIP–1 is hop count—the number of routers to process the data.	The metric used is cost. Cost is not stated in the RFCs, but it has the capacity to be a complex calculation, as seen in Cisco's implementation.

Q&A

The following questions test your understanding of the topics covered in this chapter. The answers appear in Appendix A, "Answers to Quizzes and Q&As," on page 464. If you get an answer wrong, review the answer and ensure that you understand the reason for your mistake. If you are confused by the answer, refer back to the text in the chapter to review the concepts.

1 The topological database is a map of what?

_____

_____

_____

2 Which protocol is used to elect the designated router? Which command is used to manually determine which router is elected?

_____

_____

_____

3 To achieve full adjacency, the communication between the routers will have transferred what packets?

_____

_____

_____

4 If the network is stable and sees no changes, how often will OSPF send out LSAs? Why are these updates still sent out periodically?

_____

_____

_____

5 What does ABR stand for, and what LSAs will it forward?

_____

_____

_____

6 What characteristic of an interface is used to calculate the default OSPF cost?

_____

_____

_____

7 Give three reasons why RIP-1 has problems with working in a large network.

_____

_____

_____

8 What is the Dijkstra algorithm used for?

_____

_____

_____

9 How does a stub area differ from the backbone area?

_____

_____

_____

10 How does a totally stubby area differ from a stub area?

_____

_____

_____

11 What information does a routing table give?

_____

_____

_____

Scenarios

The following case studies and questions are designed to draw together the content of the chapter and to exercise your understanding of the concepts. There is not necessarily a right answer. The thought process and practice in manipulating the concepts is the goal of this section.

The answers to the scenario questions are found at the end of this chapter.

Scenario 4-1

1 Explain the purpose of the virtual link in Figure 4-10.

Figure 4-10   *Network Diagram #1 for Scenario 4-1*

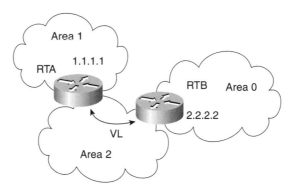

2 Is the configuration of the OSPF network shown in Figure 4-11 a valid configuration?

Figure 4-11   *Network Diagram #2 for Scenario 4-1*

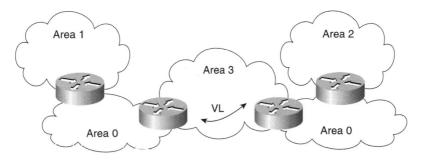

3 If the configuration shown in Figure 4-11 is a valid configuration, why would a company implement this design?

Scenario 4-2

In Figure 4-12, all routers share a common multiaccess segment. Due to the exchange of Hello packets, one router is elected DR and another is elected BDR. Use Figure 4-12 to answer the following questions.

Figure 4-12 *Network Diagram for Scenario 4-2*

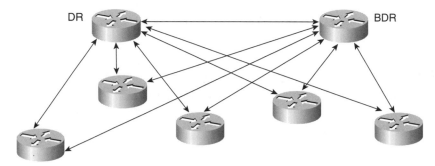

1 Which parameter determines the router that will be selected as the DR in an OSPF network?

2 Could a router with a priority value of zero assume the role of a DR or BDR in the OSPF network shown in Figure 4-12?

3 How is the OSPF router ID determined on a Cisco router?

4 What is the role of the DR and BDR in the OSPF network shown in Figure 4-12?

Scenario 4-3

Scenario 4-3 provides you with the data produced with the Cisco router IOS command **show ip route**. A legend defining the fields of the sample output is also provided to assist in answering the questions for Scenario 4-3.

Following is sample output from the **show ip route** command:

```
Codes: I - IGRP derived, R - RIP derived, H - Hello derived, O - OSPF derived
       C - connected, S - static, E - EGP derived, B - BGP derived
       * - candidate default route, IA - OSPF inter area route
       E1 - OSPF external type 1 route, E2 - OSPF external type 2 route


Gateway of last resort is 131.119.254.240 to network 129.140.0.0


O E2 150.150.0.0  [160/5]    via 131.119.254.6,    0:01:00, Ethernet2
E         192.67.131.0 [200/128] via 131.119.254.244, 0:02:22, Ethernet2
O E2 192.68.132.0 [160/5]    via 131.119.254.6,    0:00:59, Ethernet2
O E2 130.130.0.0  [160/5]    via 131.119.254.6,    0:00:59, Ethernet2
E         128.128.0.0  [200/128] via 131.119.254.244, 0:02:22, Ethernet2
E         129.129.0.0  [200/129] via 131.119.254.240, 0:02:22, Ethernet2
E         192.65.129.0 [200/128] via 131.119.254.244, 0:02:22, Ethernet2
E         131.131.0.0  [200/128] via 131.119.254.244, 0:02:22, Ethernet2
E         192.75.139.0 [200/129] via 131.119.254.240, 0:02:23, Ethernet2
```

The following information defines the fields reported in the **show ip route** command:

- The first column lists the protocol that derived the route.

- The second column may list certain protocol-specific information as defined in the display header.

- The third column lists the address of the remote network. The first number in the brackets is the administrative distance of the information source; the second number is the metric for the route.

- The fourth column specifies the address of the router that can build a route to the specified remote network.

- The fifth column specifies the last time the route was updated in hours:minutes:seconds.

- The final column specifies the interface through which the specified network can be reached.

Answer the following questions by using the output from the preceding **show ip route** command:

1 What routing protocol derived the route 130.130.0.0?

2 What router interface IP address is used to reach IP network 192.67.131.0?

3 When was the last time the route 192.65.129.0 was updated?

4 Through which router interface can the IP network 128.128.0.0 be reached?

Scenario Answers

The answers provided in this section are not necessarily the only possible answers to the questions. The questions are designed to test your knowledge and to give practical exercise in certain key areas. This section is intended to test and exercise skills and concepts detailed in the body of this chapter.

If your answer is different, ask yourself whether it follows the tenets explained in the answers provided. Your answer is correct not if it matches the solution provided in the book, but rather if it has included the principles of design laid out in the chapter.

In this way, the testing provided in these scenarios is deeper because it examines not only your knowledge, but also your understanding and ability to apply that knowledge to problems.

If you do not get the correct answer, refer back to the text and review the subject tested. Be certain to also review your notes on the question to ensure that you understand the principles of the subject.

Scenario 4-1 Answers

1   In this example, area 1 does not have a direct physical connection into area 0. A virtual link has to be configured between RTA and RTB. Area 2 is to be used as a transit area, and RTB is the entry point into area 0. This way RTA and area 1 will have a logical connection to the backbone.

2   Yes, the configuration is a valid one.

3   OSPF allows for linking discontinuous parts of the backbone using a virtual link. In some cases, different area 0s need to be linked together. This can occur if, for example, a company is trying to merge two separate OSPF networks into one network with a common area 0. In other instances, virtual links are added for redundancy in case some router failure causes the backbone to be split in two. Whatever the reason may be, a virtual link can be configured between separate ABRs that touch area 0 from each side and that have a common area.

Scenario 4-2 Answers

1   The router with the highest OSPF priority on a segment will become the DR for that segment. The default for the interface OSPF priority is one. If multiple routers have the same priority, the router with the highest RID will be selected as the DR.

2   No. A priority value of zero indicates an interface is not to be elected as a DR or BDR. The state of the interface with priority zero will be DROTHER.

3 The OSPF router ID is the highest IP address on the box, or the highest loopback address if one exists.

4 Instead of each router exchanging updates with every other router on the segment, every router will exchange the information with the DR and BDR. The DR and BDR will relay the information to everybody else. In mathematical terms, this cuts the information exchange from $O(n*n)$ to $O(n)$ where n is the number of routers on a multiaccess segment.

Scenario 4-3 Answers

1 OSPF.

2 131.119.254.244. The fourth column of the sample output specifies the address of the router that can build a route to the specified remote network.

3 0:02:22. The fifth column of the sample output specifies the last time the route was updated in hours:minutes:seconds.

4 Ethernet2. The last column in the sample output specifies the interface through which the specified network can be reached.

The objectives for the ACRC exam for CCNP or CCDP certification are taken from the Cisco Web site at http://www.cisco.com/training under the heading "Cisco Career Certifications and Training." The following table shows the ACRC exam objectives covered in this chapter and also provides the Foundation Routing and Switching exam objective number.

ACRC Exam Objective Number	Corresponding FRS Exam Objective Number	Description
18	99	Configure priority.
29	110	Configure OSPF for proper operation.
30	111	Verify OSPF operation.
33	114	Configure a multiarea OSPF network.
34	115	Verify OSPF operation (on a multiarea network).

CHAPTER 5

OSPF Configuration

How to Best Use This Chapter

By taking the following steps, you can make better use of your study time:

- Keep your notes and answers for all your work with this book in one place for easy reference.

- Take the quiz, writing down your answers. Studies show that retention significantly increases by writing facts and concepts down, even if you never look at the information again!

- Use the diagram in Figure 5-1 to guide you to the next step.

"Do I Know This Already?" Quiz

These questions are designed to test not just your knowledge, but your understanding of the subject matter. It is therefore important to realize that getting the answer the same as stated in Appendix A, "Answers to Quizzes and Q&As," is less important than your answer having embodied the spirit of the question. In this manner the questions and answers are not as open and shut as will be found on the exam: Their intention is to prepare you with the appropriate knowledge and understanding to give you mastery of the subject as opposed to limited rote knowledge.

1 Is it possible to have more than one OSPF process running on a Cisco router? How might one configure more than one process on the router?

_____

_____

_____

2 The address 192.100.56.10 has been allocated to an interface on the router. This interface alone is to be included in the OSPF process. State the command that would start the process for the interface.

_____

_____

_____

Figure 5-1   *How to Use This Chapter*

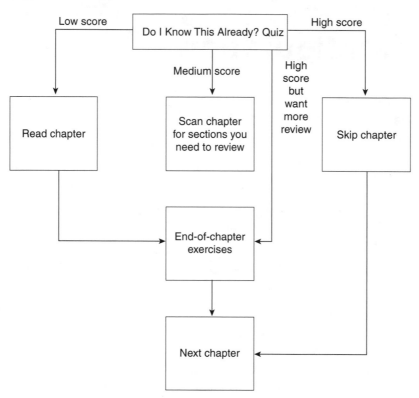

3 Why would one configure the loopback interface when configuring OSPF?

_____

_____

_____

4 What is the default method of selecting a router ID?

_____

_____

_____

5 The metric used by OSPF is cost. If the cost of an interface has not been manually configured, what default metric will be used?

_____

_____

_____

6 The designated router may be automatically selected using defaults. How would one manually determine the designated router for a LAN?

_____

_____

_____

7 Which command would identify the designated router for your LAN?

_____

_____

_____

8 What is a neighbor in OSPF?

_____

_____

_____

9 What is an adjacency in OSPF?

_____

_____

_____

10 Where would you see whether a learned network was within the same area as the router you were looking at?

_____

_____

_____

The answers to this quiz are found in Appendix A, "Answers to Quizzes and Q&As" (see page 467). Review the answers, grade your quiz, and choose an appropriate next step in this chapter based on the suggestions diagrammed in Figure 5-1. Your choices for the next step are as follows:

- Read this chapter.
- Scan this chapter for sections you need to review.
- Skip to the exercises at the end of this chapter.
- Skip this chapter.

Foundation Topics

Configuring OSPF on a Single Cisco Router

The ACRC objectives mastered in this section are as follows:

ACRC Exam Objective Number	Corresponding FRS Exam Objective Number	Description
18	99	Configure priority.
29	110	Configure OSPF for proper operation.

When configuring any device, it is important to establish why you are configuring the system and what you are trying to achieve.

This section examines the configuration of a Cisco router for OSPF within a single area. The commands are few and extremely simple; the implications are somewhat more difficult.

This section covers the following:

Configuration of OSPF

What is to be done.	Required configuration
	Optional configuration

Commands

What each configuration command achieves.	What the commands do
Reference how the configuration command achieves its goal.	How the commands do it

An example of a working configuration that uses the commands discussed in this section illustrates the use of those commands in context. A corresponding diagram graphically illustrates the configuration.

Required Commands for Configuring OSPF on an Internal Router

The router to be configured is the 2500, an internal router within a single area. The router needs to understand how to participate in the OSPF network. It therefore requires the following:

- **The OSPF process**—The routing protocol needs to be started on the router.

- **Participating router interfaces**—The router may not want to have all its interfaces send or receive OSPF routing updates. A classic example is a dial-up line to a remote office. If there were only one subnet at the remote office, it would be more efficient to use default and static route commands because any updates would dial the line.

- **Identification of the area**—The router will define which area it is in on a per interface basis.
- **A router ID**—This allows the router to be identified by the other routers in the network. The ID of the router advertising a link is used to determine the next logical hop, for example, if that link is used in the path selection to a remote network.

The following two commands are required for configuring OSPF on a single internal router:

- OSPF **process** command
- OSPF **network** command

Enabling the OSPF Routing Protocol

By default, (unless the SETUP script is used) there is no IP routing protocol running on the Cisco router. This is not true of other protocols, however; for example, if an IPX network address is configured on an interface, the IPX RIP process will be automatically started.

To configure OSPF as the routing protocol, use the following command:

```
router(config)# router ospf process number
```

process number is a number local to the router. It is possible to have more than one process running on a router, although this is an unusual and expensive configuration in terms of router resources. The process number does not have to be the same on every router in the area or the autonomous system. In the interest of sanity, many administrators make it the same number.

OSPF **network** Command

Although OSPF has been turned on, it has no information on how to operate. The networks that are to participate in the OSPF updates, and the area that they reside in, must be defined. If the following information is not specified, the process will have nothing to do and will die:

```
router(config-router)# network network number wildcard mask area area number
```

This command deserves a moment's explanation because it is the cause of many errors in configuration.

The **network** command in OSPF plays a similar role to that of the **network** command in RIP or IGRP. The difference is the level of granularity afforded to the administrator. In RIP and IGRP, the **network** command is defined at the class level. In OSPF, it is possible to identify the specific address of an interface.

After the network command has been entered, OSPF will identify which interfaces are participating in OSPF by comparing the interface IP address with the address given in the **network** command, filtered through the wildcard mask. The wildcard mask states how much of the address to pay attention to. It could just look at the class of address, such as everything in network 10.0.0.0, for example. At the other extreme, it can be more specific and identify an interface address. All interfaces that match the given network number will reside in the area specified in the **network** command.

WARNING   Take great care in the wildcard mask. Remember that it follows the same format as the wildcard mask in an access list. It is extremely easy to make errors in the configuration and those errors may be difficult to find.

Having identified the interfaces on the router that are participating in the OSPF domain, the following will happen:

- Updates will be received on the interface.

- Updates will be sent out of the interfaces.

- The interface will be placed in the defined area.

- If appropriate, the Hello protocol will be propagated.

This **network** command has many of the same characteristics as an access list. The wildcard mask has the same format and enables you to group interfaces into an area. It follows the same top-down logic of a link list that you saw before in configuring access lists in Chapter 2, "Managing Scalable Network Growth."

The following examples show how one command can cover all router interfaces and also how each individual interface can be specified.

Given a router with six interfaces, three with addresses in the 10.0.0.0 class, and three with addresses in the 172.16.0.0 class, the following would configure all interfaces to participate in OSPF area 0:

```
network 0.0.0.0 255.255.255.255 area 0
```

The following would have only the interfaces addressed from 10.0.0.0 participating in OSPF area 0:

```
network 10.0.0.0 0.255.255.255 area 0
```

Finally, this example shows only two specific interfaces participating in OSPF area 0:

```
network 10.12.0.1 0.0.0.0 area 0
network 172.16.15.1 0.0.0.0 area 0
```

As with an access list, the top-down logic should be thought through carefully. The most specific criteria must be defined before the general.

It is reasonable to ask why OSPF is so much more complex than either IGRP or RIP, in this instance. The answer is that the level of precision available in the OSPF **network** command provides the ability to place different interfaces into different areas on the same router. The need for this complexity is not obvious in this example because an internal router is being configured within a single area.

In the section titled "Configuration Commands for a Multiarea OSPF Network" later in this chapter, the flexibility in defining which interfaces reside in which area is considered.

Options for Configuring OSPF on an Internal Router

The following are not necessary to make OSPF function properly within an area. They may, however, be useful in your network design:

- The loopback interface
- The **cost** command
- The **priority** command

The Loopback Interface and the Router ID

The router needs an ID to participate in the OSPF domain. This ID takes the form of an IP address. This address can either be defined by the administrator or left to the whim of the router. Most people define the ID so that it is easier to track events in the network, for internal documentation, and for other system-administration purposes.

If no ID is stated, the router will take the highest IP address configured on the router. Although it is unlikely that this address will change, it is possible; from an administrative viewpoint, such a change would introduce an unnecessary level of chaos into the network.

There is no command to define the OSPF router ID, but the Cisco rule states that the router ID will be taken from the address of the *loopback interface*. If no loopback interface is defined, it will use the highest IP address configured on the router.

The loopback interface is a virtual interface that does not exist. This makes it very powerful: If it does not exist, it can never go down. Therefore, the OSPF network is not vulnerable to hardware interface problems.

It is important to remember that each interface requires a separate subnet. The use of a private address from RFC 1918 may be wise, both in terms of addressing issues and administrative documentation.

The following shows how to configure a loopback interface:

```
Router(config)# interface loopback interface number
Router(config-if)# ip address ip address subnet-mask
```

NOTE	When designing a network, consider whether to include the loopback interface address in the **network** commands. There are both advantages and disadvantages to this and they should be researched in any network design.

Changing the Default Metric Using the **cost** Command

Another command that may be useful is the **cost** command. This command manually overrides the default cost that the router assigns to the interface. The default cost is calculated based on the speed of the outgoing interface.

The **cost** command syntax is as follows:

```
Router(config-if)# ip ospf cost cost
```

A lower cost increases the likelihood that the interface will be selected as the best or shortest path. Considerations in using this command include the following:

- Never change defaults unless you can explain why the change is necessary. Reasons for using the **cost** option in OSPF include the following:

  Maintaining interoperability among different vendors running OSPF

  There is a design reason to choose a different path than the one selected by the Cisco default metric

- If the default is to be overridden by the manual configuration, it is important that it is done with due consideration to the physical and logical topology map of the network because any change to the metric will necessarily change the traffic patterns in the network.

Determining the Designated Router Using the **priority** Command

The last command to consider is the **priority** command. This command is used to determine the designated and backup designated routers on a multi-access link. Remember that the Hello protocol is the mechanism by which the designated routers are elected. To be "up for election," the priority must be a positive integer between 1 and 255. If the priority is 0, the router cannot participate in the election. The higher the priority, the greater the likelihood of being elected. If no priority is set, all Cisco routers have a default priority of one and the router ID is used as a tiebreaker. In effect, this means that the router ID is the determining factor.

Reasons for changing the router priority include the following:

- The router has greater CPU and memory than the others on the LAN.

- All the other routers on the LAN connect to stub networks. They all form the access layer of the network.

- There are point-to-multipoint connections in an NBMA cloud, and the hub router needs to be configured as the centralized resource requiring it to be the designated router.

- The router is an ABR and you don't want it to consume more resources as a designated router.

Seeing how these commands work in context makes their use and functionality much more apparent.

A Working Configuration of OSPF on a Single Router

Example 5-1 is a working configuration tested for verification. It should be used in conjunction with Figure 5-2.

Example 5-1 *Configuring OSPF*

```
SanJose(config)#router ospf 100
SanJose(config-router)#network 140.100.0.0 0.0.255.255 area 3
SanJose(config-router)#interface FastEthernet1/0
SanJose(config-if)#ip address 140.100.17.129 255.255.255.240
SanJose(config-if)#ip ospf priority 100
SanJose(config-if)#full-duplex
SanJose(config-if)#no shutdown
SanJose(config-if)#interface FastEthernet3/0
SanJose(config-if)#ip address 140.100.17.193 255.255.255.240
SanJose(config-if)#ip ospf cost 10
SanJose(config-if)#full-duplex
SanJose(config-if)#no shutdown
SanJose(config-if)#interface Fddi2/0
SanJose(config-if)#ip address 140.100.32.10 255.255.255.240
SanJose(config-if)#no ip directed-broadcast
SanJose(config-if)#no keepalive
SanJose(config-if)#no shutdown
```

It is imperative to check any configuration on a network device because any errors could potentially bring down the entire network. To verify the configuration, there is a wealth of Cisco commands.

Figure 5-2   *A Diagram of the Example 5-1 Network*

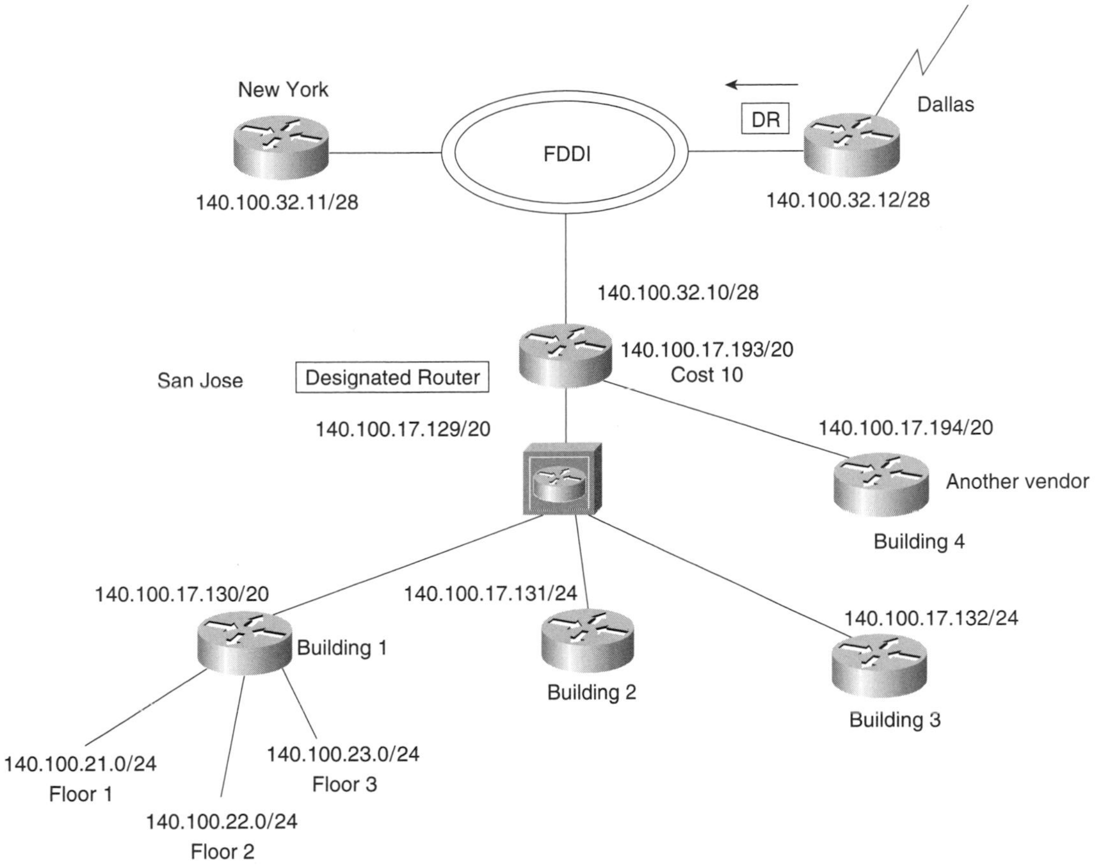

Checking the Configuration of OSPF on a Single Router

The ACRC objective mastered in this section is as follows:

ACRC Exam Objective Number	Corresponding FRS Exam Objective Number	Description
30	111	Verify OSPF operation.

The following set of commands is invaluable in both the configuration and maintenance of a live network. They are particularly useful in troubleshooting the network. As such, these commands are a necessary set of tools for use on a daily basis, for the ACRC exam, as well as the CCIE lab exam:

- **show ip protocol**—To view the IP configuration on the router. It is useful because it not only shows the interfaces, but also shows the configuration of the IP routing protocols.

- **show ip route**—Gives detailed information on the networks that the router is aware of and the preferred paths to those networks, as well as the next logical hop as the next step in the path.

- **show ip ospf interface**—Gives information on how OSPF has been configured on each interface. Typing errors are easily seen with this command.

- **show ip ospf**—Shows the OSPF process and its details—for example, how many times the router has recalculated its routing table.

- **show ip ospf neighbor** *detail*—Displays all the information about the relationship that the router has with its neighbors—for example, the status of communication, whether it is initializing or transferring DDP packets.

- **show ospf database**—Will show the contents of the topological database.

For the ACRC exam, understanding the output of these commands is important not just because the output may constitute questions on the exam, but because the ability to analyze what is happening on the network demands a thorough understanding of the concepts explained in this chapter. An understanding of the concepts in this chapter is required in interpreting the output of a **show** command.

The OSPF **show** commands are highly detailed and give a comprehensive understanding of the state of the network.

The show ip ospf **Command**

```
Router# show ip ospf process-ID
```

Example 5-2 shows the output of this command.

Example 5-2 *show ip ospf Output*

```
SanJose#sh ip ospf
 Routing Process "ospf 100" with ID 140.100.32.10
 Supports only single TOS(TOS0) routes
 SPF schedule delay 5 secs, Hold time between two SPFs 10 secs
 Minimum LSA interval 5 secs. Minimum LSA arrival 1 secs
 Number of external LSA 0. Checksum Sum 0x0
 Number of DCbitless external LSA 0
 Number of DoNotAge external LSA 0
 Number of areas in this router is 1. 1 normal 0 stub 0 nssa
    Area 3
    Number of interfaces in this area is 3
    Area has no authentication

    SPF algorithm executed 10 times
```

Example 5-2 *show ip ospf Output (Continued)*

```
Area ranges are
Link State Update Interval is 00:30:00 and due in 00:18:54
Link State Age Interval is 00:20:00 and due in 00:08:53
Number of DCbitless LSA 2
Number of indication LSA 0
Number of DoNotAge LSA 0
```

Table 5-1 explains the meanings of the important fields.

Table 5-1   *Explanation of the show ip ospf Command Output*

Field	Explanation
SPF schedule delay	How long to wait to start the SPF calculation after receiving an LSA update.
Hold time between two SPFs	Minimum amount of time between SPF calculations.
Number of DCbitless external LSA	Used with OSPF demand circuits.
Number of DoNotAge external LSA	Used with OSPF demand circuits.
Routing Process "ospf 100" with ID 140.100.32.10	This shows the local process ID for OSPF and the router ID that it will advertise.
Supports only single TOS(TOS0) routes	OSPF is capable of carrying information about the type of service (ToS) that the IP datagram has requested. This is supported by Cisco in accordance to the RFCs, but is not implemented. ToS therefore has the value of 0.
It is an Internal router	The types of router that OSPF defines include internal, area border, and autonomous system boundary router.
Summary Link update interval is 0:00:00 and the update due in 0:00:00	An area border router would transmit this link-state advertisement (LSA) into another area. Summarization occurs at the area border. As an internal router, this router is not capable of issuing this update.
External Link update interval is 0:00:00 and the update due in 0:00:00	An autonomous system boundary router would transmit this LSA into another routing protocol using redistribution. The update is external to the domain or AS. As an internal router, this router is not capable of issuing this update.
Area 3 Number of interfaces in this area is 3 Area has no authentication SPF algorithm executed 10 times Area ranges are	The number of areas of which this router is a member. As an internal router, it is configured for a single area and is a member of one area. At a glance it is possible to see how many of the router's interfaces are in an area and whether it is using MD5 security. It is very useful to see the number of times the SPF algorithm has been executed, because this is an indication of the network stability. The area ranges show any summarization that has been configured.

Continues

Table 5-1 *Explanation of the show ip ospf Command Output (Continued)*

Field	Explanation
Link State Update Interval is 00:30:00 and due in 00:18:54	The default update timer for the LSA update timer is 30 minutes. This is used to ensure the integrity of the topological databases. This field shows when the next update is and that the default has not been changed. These update timers should be the same throughout the area.
Link State Age Interval is 00:20:00 and due in 00:08:53	This specifies the MAX-AGED update deletion interval and shows when the database will next be purged of out-of-date routes.

The show ip ospf database **Command**

```
Router# show ip ospf database
```

This command displays the contents of the router's topological database and the different LSAs that have populated the database. In this example, because the router used is an internal router, the LSAs displayed will be the router and network updates. This command has many parameters that enable the user to examine very specific information. This section considers the general command.

Example 5-3 shows the output of this command.

Example 5-3 *show ip ospf database Output*

```
SanJose#sh ip ospf database

        OSPF Router with ID (140.100.32.10) (Process ID 100)


        Router Link States (Area 3)

Link ID          ADV Router       Age         Seq#        Checksum Link count
140.100.17.131   140.100.17.131   471         0x80000008 0xA469    1
140.100.17.132   140.100.17.132   215         0x80000007 0xA467    1
140.100.17.194   140.100.17.194   1489        0x8000000B 0xFF16    1
140.100.23.1     140.100.23.1     505         0x80000006 0x56B3    1
140.100.32.10    140.100.32.10    512         0x8000000C 0x46BA    3
140.100.32.11    140.100.32.11    150         0x80000006 0x6A73    1
140.100.32.12    140.100.32.12    1135        0x80000002 0x8E30    1

        Net Link States (Area 3)

Link ID          ADV Router       Age         Seq#        Checksum
140.100.17.130   140.100.23.1     220         0x80000007 0x3B42
140.100.17.194   140.100.17.194   1490        0x80000002 0x15C9
140.100.32.11    140.100.32.11    150         0x80000004 0x379E
```

Table 5-2 explains the meaning of the important fields.

Table 5-2   *Explanation of the **show ip ospf database** Command*

Field	Explanation
OSPF Router with ID (140.100.32.10) (Process ID 100)	The router ID and the process ID of the router being viewed.
Router Link States (Area 3)	The router LSAs, showing the links connecting the router to neighbors discovered via the Hello protocol.
Link ID	The link ID is the same as the OSPF router ID.
ADV Router	The OSPF router ID of the advertising router. Note that the ID is the same as the link ID when describing the router LSAs. This is because the router is advertising these links in its router LSA to the area.
Age	The age is the length of time since the last update. It is shown in seconds.
Seq#	The sequence number is used to ensure that the LSA is truly an update that is more recent than anything currently in the topological database.
Checksum	The checksum is on the entire LSA update and ensures the integrity of the update.
Link count	The number of links that the router has configured for OSPF. Note that this field is only shown for the router LSA update.
Net Link States (Area 3)	This is the information taken from the network LSAs that have been received by the router.
Summary Net Link States (Area 3)	This is information taken from the summary LSAs, which are passed between the area border routers. As an internal router in a single area, this section of the display would not appear.

The show ip ospf interface **Command**

```
Router# show ip ospf interface [type-number]
```

This command is used to show how OSPF has been configured on an interface level, as well as how it is working at the interface. This level of detail is excellent for troubleshooting configuration errors.

Example 5-4 shows the output of this command.

Example 5-4   *show ip ospf interface [type-number] Output*

```
SanJose#sh ip ospf in fastethernet1/0
FastEthernet1/0 is up, line protocol is up
  Internet Address 140.100.17.129/28, Area 3
  Process ID 100, Router ID 140.100.32.10, Network Type BROADCAST, Cost: 1
  Transmit Delay is 1 sec, State DR, Priority 100
  Designated Router (ID) 140.100.32.10, Interface address 140.100.17.129
  Backup Designated router (ID) 140.100.23.1, Interface address 140.100.17.130
  Timer intervals configured, Hello 10, Dead 40, Wait 40, Retransmit 5
    Hello due in 00:00:06
  Neighbor Count is 3, Adjacent neighbor count is 2
    Adjacent with neighbor 140.100.17.132
    Adjacent with neighbor 140.100.17.131
    Adjacent with neighbor 140.100.23.1  (Backup Designated Router)
  Suppress hello for 0 neighbor(s)
```

Table 5-3 explains the meaning of the important fields.

Table 5-3   *Explanation of the show ip ospf interface Command*

Field	Explanation
FastEthernet1/0 is up, line protocol is up	This should be seen as two statements. The first half of the sentence indicates the physical line is operational. This meaning differs with the type of interface; for Ethernet it indicates the presence of the transceiver. The second portion of the sentence indicates the data link layer is working.
Internet Address 140.100.17.129/28	The IP address and mask configured on the interface.
Area 3	The OSPF area for which the interface is configured.
Process ID 100	The autonomous system number, which is in fact the OSPF process ID.
Router ID 140.100.32.10	The router ID that will be advertised in the LSA updates.
Network Type BROADCAST	The type of network that the interface is connected to, which indicates how neighbors are found and adjacencies formed.
Cost: 1	This is the metric cost of the link, which although not stated was probably dynamically chosen using the Cisco defaults.
Transmit Delay is 1 sec	This shows the anticipated time taken to send an update to the neighbor. The default is one second.

Table 5-3   *Explanation of the **show ip ospf interface** Command (Continued)*

Field	Explanation
State DR	This shows the state of the link in reference to establishing adjacencies.
	This field is extremely useful in troubleshooting. Here are the states in order:
	DOWN—Heard from no one.
	ATTEMPT—Sent a Hello on an NBMA, but haven't heard back.
	INIT—Heard a Hello, but have not achieved neighbor status.
	TWO-WAY—Full neighbor relationship; seen self in neighbor's Hello table.
	EXSTART—Starting up the link for exchanging DDPs.
	EXCHANGE—Sending DDPs to other router.
	LOADING—Building the database and LSAs from the DDPs.
	FULL—Adjacency.
	DR—The designated router for this LAN.
Priority 100	The priority is sent in the Hello protocol and is used to determine the election of the designated router and the backup designated router. The value of 1 means that the router is prepared to be elected. If every other router has the priority of 1, the highest router ID will select the routers.
Designated Router (ID) 140.100.32.10, Interface address 140.100.17.129	This is the address of the elected designated router. Note that the ID and the interface ID differ. This is a useful field for troubleshooting misconfiguration.
Backup Designated router (ID) 140.100.23.1, Interface address 140.100.17.130	The address of the backup designated router. Note both the ID and the interface are given and they differ.
Timer intervals configured, Hello 10, Dead 40, Wait 40, Retransmit 5	It is possible to change these timers and sometimes necessary if connecting to another vendor's equipment that has different defaults. These timers should be consistent throughout the area. The defaults are as follows:
	Hello: 10
	Dead: 40
	Wait: 40
	Retransmit: 5

Continues

Table 5-3   *Explanation of the **show ip ospf interface** Command (Continued)*

Field	Explanation
Hello due in 00:00:06	When the next Hello packet is due to be sent out of the interface.
Neighbor Count is 3, Adjacent neighbor count is 2	The number of routers that have neighbor relationships.
	Note that the number of routers with which adjacency is established is less than the neighbors; this is because there is a designated router and a backup designated router, whose responsibility it is to maintain the adjacencies with all routers on the LAN.
Adjacent with neighbor 140.100.23.1 (Backup Designated Router)	The router ID of the adjacent router, which is the backup designated router in this case.

The show ip ospf neighbor **Command**

Router# **show ip ospf neighbor** [*type number*] [*neighbor-id*] [**detail**]

This command is used to show OSPF neighbors. All the neighbors known to the router may be viewed, or the command can be made more granular and the neighbors shown on a per interface basis, or indeed, one neighbor may be picked out for scrutiny. This level of detail is excellent for troubleshooting configuration errors.

Example 5-5 shows the output of this command.

Example 5-5   *show ip ospf neighbor Output*

```
SanJose#sh ip ospf neighbor

Neighbor ID     Pri   State           Dead Time   Address         Interface
140.100.17.132   1    FULL/DROTHER    00:00:36    140.100.17.132  FastEthernet1/0
140.100.17.131   1    FULL/DROTHER    00:00:37    140.100.17.131  FastEthernet1/0
140.100.23.1     1    FULL/BDR        00:00:38    140.100.17.130  FastEthernet1/0
140.100.32.12    1    FULL/DROTHER    00:00:35    140.100.32.12   Fddi2/0
140.100.32.11    1    FULL/DR         00:00:32    140.100.32.11   Fddi2/0
140.100.17.194   1    FULL/DR         00:00:31    140.100.17.194  FastEthernet3/0
```

To be more specific, in what is viewed, it is possible to look at the neighbors that have been discovered on a particular interface, as seen in Example 5-6.

Example 5-6   *The Neighbors That Have Been Discovered on a Particular Interface*

```
SanJose#sh ip ospf nei fddi 2/0

Neighbor ID     Pri   State           Dead Time   Address         Interface
140.100.32.12    1    FULL/DROTHER    00:00:36    140.100.32.12   Fddi2/0
140.100.32.11    1    FULL/DR         00:00:32    140.100.32.11   Fddi2/0
```

To see all the neighbors in as much detail as possible, however, use the command displayed in Example 5-7.

Example 5-7   *Using the **show ip ospf neighbor detail** Command*

```
SanJose#sh ip ospf neighbor detail
 Neighbor 140.100.17.132, interface address 140.100.17.132
    In the area 3 via interface FastEthernet1/0
    Neighbor priority is 1, State is FULL, 6 state changes
    DR is 140.100.17.129 BDR is 140.100.17.130
    Options 2
    Dead timer due in 00:00:35
 Neighbor 140.100.17.131, interface address 140.100.17.131
    In the area 3 via interface FastEthernet1/0
    Neighbor priority is 1, State is FULL, 6 state changes
    DR is 140.100.17.129 BDR is 140.100.17.130
    Options 2
    Dead timer due in 00:00:34
 Neighbor 140.100.23.1, interface address 140.100.17.130
    In the area 3 via interface FastEthernet1/0
    Neighbor priority is 1, State is FULL, 6 state changes
    DR is 140.100.17.129 BDR is 140.100.17.130
    Options 2
    Dead timer due in 00:00:36
 Neighbor 140.100.32.12, interface address 140.100.32.12
    In the area 3 via interface Fddi2/0
    Neighbor priority is 1, State is FULL, 6 state changes
    DR is 140.100.32.11 BDR is 140.100.32.10
    Options 2
    Dead timer due in 00:00:32
 Neighbor 140.100.32.11, interface address 140.100.32.11
    In the area 3 via interface Fddi2/0
    Neighbor priority is 1, State is FULL, 6 state changes
    DR is 140.100.32.11 BDR is 140.100.32.10
    Options 2
    Dead timer due in 00:00:38
 Neighbor 140.100.17.194, interface address 140.100.17.194
    In the area 3 via interface FastEthernet3/0
    Neighbor priority is 1, State is FULL, 9 state changes
    DR is 140.100.17.194 BDR is 140.100.17.193
    Options 2
    Dead timer due in 00:00:38
```

Table 5-4 explains the meanings of the important fields from Examples 5-5 through 5-7.

Table 5-4   *Explanation of the **show ip ospf neighbor** Command*

Field	Explanation
ID	This is the router ID.
Pri	This is the priority sent out with the Hello protocol to elect the designated router and the backup designated router.

Continues

Table 5-4 *Explanation of the **show ip ospf neighbor** Command (Continued)*

Field	Explanation
State	This shows the state, not of the link but whether the interface was elected.
	DR—Designated router.
	BDR—Backup designated router.
	DROTHER—It was not chosen as the DR or the BDR. If the priority on the interface had been set to zero, the state would always be DROTHER because it could not be elected as a DR or BDR.
Dead Time	The dead time is how long the router will wait without hearing the periodic Hello from its neighbor before it is declared dead. This timer should be consistent on the network; otherwise, there will be problems.
Address	This is the interface address of the neighbor. Note that the router ID is not the same as the interface address. If the loopback address or the highest IP address on the router has been used, the probability is that the address will differ.
Interface	This is the outgoing interface of the router, upon which the neighbor routers were heard.
Options	The option available is one of design. It identifies whether the area the neighbors inhabit is a stub area. The next section discusses this in detail.

The show ip protocol **Command**

```
Router# show ip protocol
```

This command is used to show the configuration IP routing protocols on the router. It details how the protocols were configured and how they interact with one another. This command is excellent for troubleshooting configuration errors and understanding how the network is communicating about its routes.

Example 5-8 shows the output of this command.

Example 5-8 *The **show ip protocol** Command Output*

```
SanJose#sh ip prot
Routing Protocol is "ospf 100"
  Sending updates every 0 seconds
  Invalid after 0 seconds, hold down 0, flushed after 0
  Outgoing update filter list for all interfaces is not set
  Incoming update filter list for all interfaces is not set
  Redistributing: ospf 100
```

Example 5-8 *The **show ip protocol** Command Output (Continued)*

```
Routing for Networks:
  140.100.0.0
Routing Information Sources:
  Gateway         Distance      Last Update
  140.100.17.131        110      00:50:23
  140.100.17.132        110      00:50:23
  140.100.17.194        110      00:07:39
  140.100.23.1          110      00:50:23
  140.100.32.11         110      00:07:39
  140.100.32.12         110      00:07:39
Distance: (default is 110)
```

Table 5-5 explains the meaning of the important fields.

Table 5-5   *Explanation of the **show ip protocols** Command*

Field	Explanation
Routing Protocol is "ospf 100"	This routing protocol is configured on the router. If there is more than one routing protocol configured, the details of each are listed in turn.
Sending updates every 0 seconds	The frequency of the routing update is shown. It is not relevant for a link-state routing protocol that sends updates of changes as required (incremental updates).
Invalid after 0 seconds	This field is relevant for distant vector protocols. It indicates the period of time a route is considered valid from the time of the last update. If an update on the status of the route has not been received in this defined value, the route is marked unreachable.
hold down 0	Hold-down timers are only used in distance vector protocols. If a distance vector protocol suspects a route in its table is bad, it will mark it down but not accept another path with a less-favorable metric until the hold-down timer has expired. This is to avoid loops in the network. If a link-state protocol hears an update, it acts on the information.
flushed after 0	The 0 value indicates that this is a field used by distance vector routing protocols. After marking a route as invalid, it will flush it from the routing table after this timer has expired.
Outgoing update filter list for all interfaces is not set	Access lists may be set on an interface to filter networks from the routing update. This should be used carefully because it affects connectivity.
Incoming update filter list for all interfaces is not set	The access list can filter either outgoing or incoming updates.

Continues

Table 5-5   *Explanation of the **show ip protocols** Command (Continued)*

Field	Explanation
Redistributing: ospf 100	If the routing protocol is sharing information with another routing protocol configured on the router, the information is listed here. This is a very important field because redistribution is complex and therefore easily misconfigured. If no redistribution is configured, the protocol is seen to be sharing information with itself.
Routing for Networks: 140.100.0.0	This reflects the use of the network commands when the protocol was configured. OSPF allows granularity in the use of the command. The entries here could be as specific as the interface addresses.
Routing Information Sources	This is a major heading for the gateway fields, which are the addresses of the routers sending updates to this router. They will become the next logical hop in the routing table.
Gateway	This field is a subset of the Routing Information Sources just discussed. It is the address of the router providing updates.
Distance	The administrative distance is the value given to the source of the update. Whereas the metric indicates which path to choose if there is more than one available, the administrative distance indicates which source (routing protocol) to choose if there is more than one providing a path to a remote network. The administrative distance takes precedence over the routing metric.
Last Update	The time since the last update was received from that source.
Distance: (default is 110)	The administrative distance may be changed for the entire routing protocol (the example here is OSPF), which would be listed here, or it can be changed per source, as seen earlier in the listing of each individual source (gateway).

The show ip route **Command**

```
Router# show ip route
```

This command is used to show the IP routing table on the router. It details how the network is known to the router and its sources for the information. This command is excellent for troubleshooting configuration errors and understanding how the network is communicating about its routes.

Example 5-9 shows the output of this command.

Example 5-9 *show ip route Output*

```
SanJose#show ip route
Codes: C - connected, S - static, I - IGRP, R - RIP, M - mobile, B - BGP
       D - EIGRP, EX - EIGRP external, O - OSPF, IA - OSPF inter area
       N1 - OSPF NSSA external type 1, N2 - OSPF NSSA external type 2
       E1 - OSPF external type 1, E2 - OSPF external type 2, E - EGP
       i - IS-IS, L1 - IS-IS level-1, L2 - IS-IS level-2, * - candidate default
       U - per-user static route, o - ODR
       T - traffic engineered route

Gateway of last resort is not set

     140.100.0.0/28 is subnetted, 3 subnets
C       140.100.17.192 is directly connected, FastEthernet3/0
C       140.100.17.128 is directly connected, FastEthernet1/0
C       140.100.32.0 is directly connected, Fddi2/0


Bldg_1#show ip route
Codes: C - connected, S - static, I - IGRP, R - RIP, M - mobile, B - BGP
       D - EIGRP, EX - EIGRP external, O - OSPF, IA - OSPF inter area
       N1 - OSPF NSSA external type 1, N2 - OSPF NSSA external type 2
       E1 - OSPF external type 1, E2 - OSPF external type 2, E - EGP
       i - IS-IS, L1 - IS-IS level-1, L2 - IS-IS level-2, * - candidate default
       U - per-user static route, o - ODR

Gateway of last resort is not set

     140.100.0.0/28 is subnetted, 3 subnets
O       140.100.17.192 [110/20] via 140.100.17.129, 00:07:44, Ethernet0
C       140.100.17.128 is directly connected, Ethernet0
O       140.100.32.0 [110/11] via 140.100.17.129, 00:07:44, Ethernet0
```

Table 5-6 explains the meaning of the important fields.

These commands are useful to verify that the configuration has worked and that the OSPF network is functioning correctly. In a single area environment, the full complexity of OSPF is not engaged. The full strength and complexity of OSPF come to the fore in the design and configuration of a multiarea network.

Table 5-6 *Explanation of the **show ip route** Command That Was Performed on Router Building 1*

Field	Explanation
O	Indicates protocol that derived the route. Possible values include the following: I—IGRP derived R—RIP derived O—OSPF derived C—Connected S—Static E—EGP derived B—BGP derived i—IS-IS derived
140.100.17.192	Indicates the address of the remote network.
[110/20]	The first number in the brackets is the administrative distance of the information source; the second number is the metric for the route.
via 140.100.17.129	Specifies the address of the next router to the remote network.
00:07:44	Specifies the last time the route was updated in hours:minutes:seconds.
Ethernet0	Specifies the interface through which the specified network can be reached.

Configuring OSPF on a Multiarea Network

The ACRC objective mastered in this section is as follows:

ACRC Exam Objective Number	Corresponding FRS Exam Objective Number	Description
33	114	Configure a multiarea OSPF network.

Some of these commands have been dealt with before. Therefore, they will be reviewed briefly, and the additional parameters for configuration in a multiarea environment will be explained.

Configuration Commands for a Multiarea OSPF Network

The following commands are necessary to configure a multiarea OSPF network:

- The OSPF **network** command

- The OSPF **summarization** command for an ABR

- The OSPF command for a stub area

- The OSPF command for a totally stubby area

- The OSPF command for the cost of a default route propagated into the area

The first command to consider is indeed one that was dealt with earlier in this chapter. The **network** command was explained in terms of identifying the interfaces that participated in the OSPF routing process. The command will now be used to identify not only the interfaces that are sending and receiving OSPF updates but also the area in which they reside. This configuration is used on an area border router.

The following is the syntax for the OSPF **network** command:

```
Router(config)#
network network number wildcard mask area area number
```

NOTE   The area required in the preceding syntax is the area in which the interface or interfaces configured with the network address reside.

Care must be taken now in the use of the wildcard mask. In a single area configuration, all the interfaces are in the same area; therefore, the **network** commands just identify the network numbers in use and may be configured to the Internet number, as done in IGRP and RIP. The only reason to be more specific would be to exclude some interfaces from the OSPF domain.

The need now to identify areas on an interface basis brings into use the other part of the command. Although the command itself is very simple, it adds a complexity to the use of the mask. Remember that the **network** command follows the rule of a linked list. The order of the statements is important. The most specific should be stated first because the OSPF process will act on the first match that is found.

The **summarization** command is configured on an area border router because it dictates the networks that will be advertised to the area.

There is also a command used on the autonomous system boundary router to summarize the networks to be advertised to the outside world.

The syntax for the OSPF **summarization** command for an ABR is as follows:

```
Router(config-router)# summary-address address mask
```

Use the **area router configuration** command with the **range** keyword to consolidate and summarize routes at an area boundary. Use the **no** form of this command to disable this function for the specified area:

```
area area-id range address mask
no area area-id range address mask
```

In the preceding syntax, *area-id* is the identifier (ID) of the area about which routes are to be summarized. It can be specified as either a decimal value or as an IP address. *address* is the IP address. *mask* is the IP mask.

NOTE   The area ID requested is the area from which the subnets originated. It is not the destination area. The summarization update will populate the topological databases of the routers in the destination area. These routers will need to know the source area for the summarized subnet in order to know where to send the data traffic.

The syntax for the OSPF **summarization** command for an ASBR is as follows:

```
Router(config-router)# summary-address address mask
```

In the preceding syntax, *address* is the summary address designated for a range of addresses and *mask* is the IP subnet mask used for the summary route.

The design and implementation of the addressing scheme is crucial to the success of the OSPF network and cannot be stressed too strongly. Refer to Chapter 3, "IP Addressing," for details on IP addressing and summarization.

Having designed the addressing scheme for the network, it should be clear which areas, if any, are suitable candidates for configuration as stub, totally stubby, or not so stubby areas.

NOTE   In this age of jargon and complex language, it is refreshing that the industry sense of humor allows such descriptive yet slightly ludicrous terms to have official status.

The syntax for the OSPF command for a stub area is as follows:

```
Router(config-router)# area area-id stub
```

NOTE   All OSPF routers inside a stub area have to be configured as stub routers. This is because whenever an area is configured as stub, all interfaces that belong to that area will start exchanging Hello packets with a flag that indicates that the interface is stub. Actually, this is just a bit in the Hello packet (E bit) that gets set to 0. All routers that have a common segment have to agree on that flag. If they don't, they will not become neighbors and routing will not take effect.

The syntax for the OSPF command for a totally stubby area is as follows:

```
Router(config-router)# area area-id stub no-summary
```

This addition of the **no-summary** parameter informs the ABR not to send summary updates from other areas into the area. This command need only be configured on the ABR because it is the only router with this responsibility. It is only configurable on a Cisco router because it is a proprietary command. All the other routers are configured as stub area internal routers.

As a totally stubby area, there will be no summary or external routes propagated by the ABR into the area. To reach networks and hosts outside their area, a workstation will need to send to a default route, which the ABR advertises into the area.

To define the cost to the default route, the following command is used. If the cost is not specified, the path will be calculated as the internal area cost plus one.

The syntax for the OSPF command for the cost of a default route propagated into the area is as follows:

```
Router(config-router)# area area-id default-cost cost
```

NOTE   This command need only be configured on the ABR because it is the only router with this responsibility.

Seeing how these commands work in context makes their use and functionality much more apparent.

A Working Configuration of OSPF on a Multiarea Network

Example 5-10 is a working configuration tested for verification. It includes many of the commands explained earlier in this chapter. This is so that you see an entire working configuration, as opposed to the relevant segment for configuring a particular networking nuance.

The configuration should be used in conjunction with Figure 5-3.

Figure 5-3   *Diagram of the Example 5-10 Network*

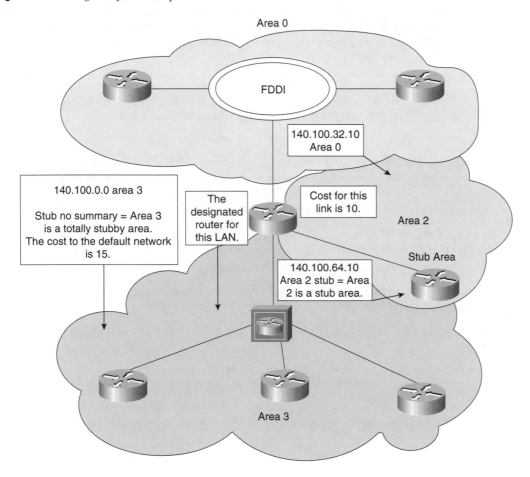

Example 5-10 *Configuring OSPF in a Multiarea Network*

```
Router(config)#router ospf 100
Router(config-router)#network 140.100.17.128 0.0.0.15 area 3
Router(config-router)#network 140.100.17.192 0.0.0.15 area 2
Router(config-router)#network 140.100.32.0 0.0.0.255 area 0
Router(config-router)#area 2 stub
Router(config-router)#area 3 stub no-summary
Router(config-router)#area 3 default-cost 15
!
Router(config-router)#interface FastEthernet0
Router(config-if)#ip address 140.100.17.129 255.255.255.240
Router(config-if)#no ip directed-broadcast
```

Example 5-10 *Configuring OSPF in a Multiarea Network (Continued)*

```
Router(config-if)#ip ospf priority 100
!
Router(config-if)#interface FastEthernet1
Router(config-if)#ip address 140.100.17.193 255.255.255.240
Router(config-if)#no ip directed-broadcast
Router(config-if)#ip ospf cost 10
!
Router(config-if)#interface Fddi0
Router(config-if)#ip address 140.100.32.10 255.255.255.240
Router(config-if)#no ip directed-broadcast
Router(config-if)#no keepalive

Router(config-if)#exit
```

It is imperative to check any configuration on a network device because any errors could potentially bring down the entire network. To verify the configuration, there is a wealth of Cisco commands.

Checking the Configuration of OSPF on a Multiarea Network

The ACRC objective mastered in this section is as follows:

ACRC Exam Objective Number	Corresponding FRS Exam Objective Number	Description
34	115	Verify OSPF operation (on a multiarea network).

The **show** commands shown here are in addition to the commands described in the section titled "Checking the Configuration of OSPF on a Single Router" earlier in this chapter. These earlier commands are also extremely useful in a multiarea configuration. They are all invaluable in both the configuration and maintenance of a live network. They are particularly useful in troubleshooting the network. The following are the additional commands you can use in conjunction with them when verifying OSPF operation on a multiarea network:

- The **show ip ospf border-routers** command
- The **show ip ospf virtual-links** command

The ability to analyze the output of a **show** command demonstrates more than rote learning; it also demonstrates an understanding of the concepts that make up the foundations of OSPF design and configuration.

The commands explained in this book constitute a small subset of the commands available in OSPF. Because the OSPF command set is very comprehensive, the ability to monitor the network and thereby maintain and troubleshoot it requires advanced OSPF knowledge.

The show ip ospf border-routers **Command**

```
Router# show ip ospf border-routers
```

This command shows the OSPF area border routers and autonomous system boundary routers that the internal router has entries for in its routing table. This command is excellent for troubleshooting configuration errors and understanding how the network is communicating about its routes.

Example 5-11 shows the output of this command.

Example 5-11 *show ip ospf border-routers Output*

```
Router# show ip ospf border-routers
OSPF Process 100 internal Routing Table
Destination      Next Hop        Cost      Type      Rte Type    Area       SPF No
160.89.97.53     144.144.1.53    10        ABR       INTRA       0.0.0.3         3
160.89.103.51    160.89.96.51    10        ABR       INTRA       0.0.0.3         3
160.89.103.52    160.89.96.51    20        ASBR      INTER       0.0.0.3         3
160.89.103.52    144.144.1.53    22        ASBR      INTER       0.0.0.3         3
```

Table 5-7 explains the meaning of the important fields.

Table 5-7   *Explanation of the **show ip ospf border-routers** Command*

Field	Explanation
OSPF Process 100 internal Routing Table	The OSPF routing process ID for the router.
Destination	This is the router ID of the destination router, be it an ABR or an ASBR.
Next Hop	If the ABR or ASBR is not directly connected, this is the address of the next logical hop in the chosen path to the ABR or ASBR.
Cost	The metric or cost of taking this path to the destination.
Type	This states whether the destination router is an ABR or ASBR or both.
Rte Type	The type of this route; it is either an intra-area or interarea route.

Table 5-7   *Explanation of the **show ip ospf border-routers** Command (Continued)*

Field	Explanation
Area	The area ID of the area that this route is learned from.
SPF No	This is the SPF calculation number that installed this route into the routing table.

The **show ip ospf border-routers** command is useful to verify that the configuration has worked and that the OSPF network is functioning correctly. In a multiarea network, **show ip ospf border-routers** command can immediately indicate why users cannot connect outside their area.

It is helpful to extract this information from what could be a long routing table, within which this information is scattered.

The show ip ospf virtual-links **Command**

```
Router# show ip ospf virtual-links
```

When it is not possible to connect an area to area 0 directly, a solution is to create an IP tunnel called a virtual link. This is remarkably easy to configure. The ease of configuration, as with many things in OSPF, belies the complexity of the technology it is using. Many things can go wrong. This command is essential to verify the configuration. The most common problem is in the address of the other end of the virtual link. Another command to use in conjunction with this is **show ip ospf neighbors**.

NOTE   The next command is potentially in the ACRC exam and for that reason is worth mentioning. In practice, virtual links are a design nightmare and are best avoided. They are useful when mending a network on a temporary basis, while awaiting a moment's peace to rectify the design of the network.

Example 5-12 shows the output of this command.

Example 5-12 *show ip ospf virtual-links Output*

```
Router# show ip ospf virtual-links
Virtual Link to router 140.100.32.10 is up
Transit area 0.0.0.1, via interface Ethernet0, Cost of using 10
Transmit Delay is 1 sec, State DROTHER
Timer intervals configured, Hello 10, Dead 40, Wait 40, Retransmit 5
Hello due in 0:00:08
Adjacency State FULL
```

Table 5-8 explains the meaning of the important fields.

Table 5-8 *Explanation of the **show ip ospf virtual-links** Command*

Field	Explanation
Virtual Link to router 140.100.32.10 is up	Shows the router ID of the other end of the virtual link, which is seen as a neighbor.
Transit area 0.0.0.1	This is the area through which the virtual link is tunneled.
via interface Ethernet0	This is the outgoing interface on the router that connects the virtual link to area 0.
Cost of using 10	The cost of reaching the OSPF neighbor through the virtual link.
Transmit Delay is 1 sec	The delay of the link. How long it will take to transit an LSA. This value must be less than the retransmit timer setting.
State DROTHER	The state of the OSPF neighbor.
Hello 10	The timed update interval for the Hello protocol in seconds. This is the default.
Dead 40	How long the router will wait without hearing a Hello from the neighbor before it declares the neighbor dead. The default is 40 seconds.
Retransmit 5	The retransmit interval is the time in seconds that the router will wait without hearing an acknowledgement for the LSA it has sent to its neighbor. The default is 5 seconds.
Hello due in 0:00:08	When the next Hello is expected from the neighbor.
Adjacency State FULL	The state of the neighbor adjacency. The two routers have fully synchronized their topological databases.

Conclusion

You may conclude that OSPF is definitely more complex than RIP. To harness the power that this complexity offers, it is important to spend time in the analysis and design of the network. In many cases, the addressing scheme must be redesigned to support the hierarchical structure that OSPF requires.

OSPF is not a routing protocol to be taken lightly. The configuration commands are simple and work well, but the work is in the old-fashioned analysis and maintenance of the system.

Foundation Summary

Table 5-9 explains how to read the information in the routing table as explained in the **show ip route** command.

Table 5-9   *Explanation of the **show ip route** Command*

Code	Protocol That Derived the Route
I	IGRP
D	EIGRP
EX	External EIGRP
R	RIP
C	Connected
S	Static
E	EGP
B	BGP
i	IS-IS
L1	IS-IS level 1
L2	IS-IS level 2
M	Mobile
U	Per user static route
O	ODR
T	Traffic-engineered route
O	OSPF networks from within the same area as the router. These are networks learned from router and network LSAs.
IA	OSPF inter-area. This is sent out by the ABRs. It is created from the summary link LSA (type 3 and type 4). These routes will not be seen on a router within a totally stubby area, because it will not receive LSAs external to the area.
N1	OSPF NSSA external type 1.
N2	OSPF NSSA external type 2.
E1	OSPF external type 1. These routes are generated by the ASBR and show routes that are external to the autonomous system. These routes will not be seen in a stub or totally stubby area.
E2	OSPF external type 2.

The metric or link cost is advertised in the LSA updates and is used to determine the shortest path. Although the standard does not state a default metric, the Cisco router has implemented a default. This is based on the bandwidth of the link, the slower lines proving more expensive. The calculation for the metric is 10^8 divided by the bandwidth. Bandwidth is an interface that can be configured.

Table 5-10 shows Cisco's default metric in OSPF for different speed links.

Table 5-10   *Cisco's Default Metric in OSPF for Different Speed Links*

Link Speed	Default Metric
56 kbps	1785
64	1562
T1 (1.544 Mbps serial link)	65
E1 (2.048 Mbps serial link)	48
4 Mbps Token Ring	25
10 Mbps Ethernet	10
16 Mbps Token Ring	6
FDDI	1

Q&A

The following questions test your understanding of the topics covered in this chapter. The answers appear in Appendix A, "Answers to Quizzes and Q&As," on page 468. If you get an answer wrong, review the answer and ensure that you understand the reason for your mistake. If you are confused by the answer, refer back to the text in the chapter to review the concepts.

1   State one command that would be used to show distribution filters have been configured in OSPF.

   _____

   _____

   _____

2   What command would show which router on the LAN is the backup designated router?

   _____

   _____

   _____

3   What command would be used to create a totally stubby area?

   _____

   _____

   _____

4   What is a virtual link and what command would be used to create it?

   _____

   _____

   _____

5   Explain briefly what the command **show ip ospf database** will show you.

   _____

   _____

   _____

6 Where would one issue the command to summarize IP subnets? State the command that would be used.

_____

_____

_____

7 How would one summarize external routes before injecting them into the OSPF domain?

_____

_____

_____

8 What command is used to show the state of adjacencies?

_____

_____

_____

9 In a totally stubby area, which routes are not propagated into the area?

_____

_____

_____

10 In the command **show ip ospf database**, a field shows the SPF delay. What does this field indicate?

_____

_____

_____

Scenarios

The following case studies and questions are designed to draw together the content of the chapter and exercise your understanding of the concepts. There is not necessarily a right answer. The thought process and practice in manipulating the concepts is the goal of this section.

The answers to the scenario questions are found at the end of this chapter.

Scenario 5-1

Refer to Figure 5-4 and write the configuration for the central router.

Figure 5-4   *The Diagram for Configuration Scenario 5-1*

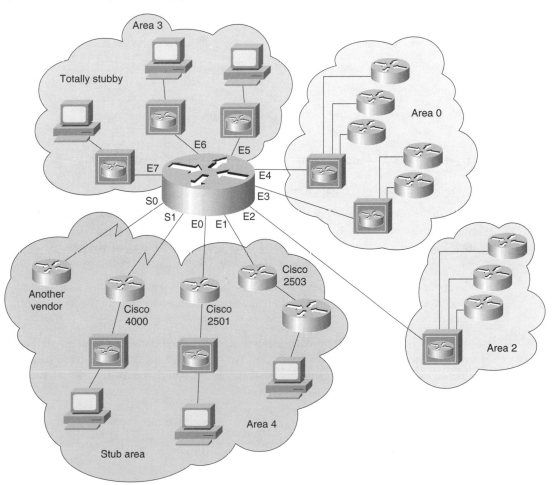

Ensure that you include the following:

- Address the network using the private network 10.0.0.0.

  Area 0 is using a prefix of 28 bits, within the area.

  Area 2 is using a prefix of 22 bits, within the area.

  Area 3 is using a prefix of 24 bits, within the area.

  Area 4 is using a prefix of 30 bits for the serial connections. It is using a 28-bit prefix for the connections to the Ethernet routers. Do not include the subnets attached to the LANs in area 4.

  Design the addressing scheme so that it allows for the summarization of addresses between areas. Show the summarization that you allocate and explain your reasons for your choices.

- The router ID.

- The network commands to place the appropriate interfaces into the correct areas.

- The configuration of the stub and totally stubby areas.

- Summarization between areas.

- The election of the central router as designated router where appropriate.

Scenario 5-2

Using Figure 5-5, answer the questions that follow.

The users in the network are complaining about the slowness of the network, particularly when trying to access the Internet. Examine the configuration in Example 5-13 in conjunction with Figure 5-5 and give reasons for any slowness or lack of connectivity that you can see on the network. Provide current configuration commands to correct any errors that you find.

1 There are problems with Router B. There is inconsistency in the routing table, and the system is extremely slow. What commands would be used to identify the problem? In examining the diagram and configuration, what problems can you see?

2 Router A is having problems connecting to Area 0, which is causing problems in other areas because this router is used to connect to Area 0. What commands would be used to identify the problem? In examining the diagram and configuration, what problems can you see?

Figure 5-5   *The Diagram for Configuration Scenario 5-2*

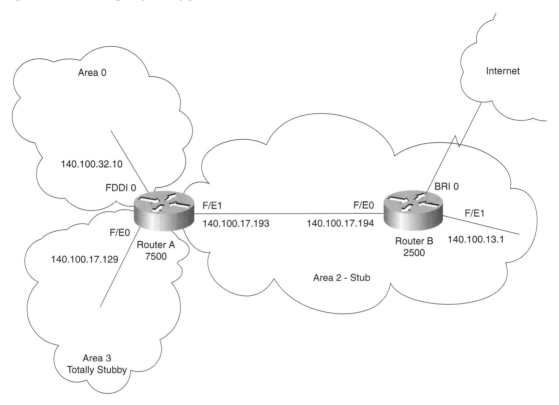

Example 5-13 *Configuring OSPF Example for Scenario 5-2*

```
ROUTER Λ
Router(config)#router ospf 100
Router(config-router)#network 140.100.17.128 0.0.0.15 area 3
Router(config-router)#network 140.100.17.192 0.0.0.15 area 2
Router(config-router)#network 140.100.32.0 0.0.0.0 area 0
Router(config-router)#area 2 stub
Router(config-router)#area 3 stub no-summary
Router(config-router)#area 3 default-cost 15
!
Router(config-router)#interface FastEthernet0
Router(config-if)#ip address 140.100.17.129 255.255.255.240
Router(config-if)#no ip directed-broadcast
!
Router(config-if)#interface FastEthernet1
Router(config-if)#ip address 140.100.17.193 255.255.255.240
Router(config-if)#no ip directed-broadcast
!
Router(config-if)#interface Fddi0
```

Continues

Example 5-13 *Configuring OSPF Example for Scenario 5-2 (Continued)*

```
Router(config-if)#ip address 140.100.32.10 255.255.255.240
Router(config-if)#no ip directed-broadcast
Router(config-if)#no keepalive

Router(config-if)#exit
ROUTER B
Router(config)#router ospf 100
Router(config-router)#network 140.100.0.0 0.0.0.15 area 2

!
Router(config-router)#interface FastEthernet0
Router(config-if)#ip address 140.100.17.194 255.255.255.240
Router(config-if)#no ip directed-broadcast
Router(config-if)#ip ospf priority 100
!
Router(config-if)#interface FastEthernet1
Router(config-if)#ip address 140.100.13.1 255.255.255.240
Router(config-if)#no ip directed-broadcast
!
Router(config-if)#exit
```

3 Issue the commands that would be used to correct the configuration problems that you see in the example configuration for Routers A and B.

4 When you issue the **show ip ospf** interface command, you notice that there is a discrepancy in the timers on the link between Routers A and B. The transmit timer on Router A is set to 5 and the retransmit timer is set to 1. What problems would this cause? What command would be used to change the timers, and what are the default settings?

5 There is an ISDN link into the Internet from Router B. The network manager has suggested that this link is the cause of some performance problems on the router. You have noticed that the interface is included in the OSPF network command. What might be the cause of the problem and how could it be fixed?

Scenario 5-3

Using the configuration in Example 5-14, draw the network that it would support (in as much detail as possible) and answer the questions that follow.

Example 5-14 *Configuration for Scenario 5-3*

```
Router(config)# router ospf 55
Router(config-router)#network 140.100.160.10  0.0.0.0 area 0
Router(config-router)#network 140.100.192.10  0.0.63.255 area 2
Router(config-router)#network 140.100.0.0  0.0.255.255 area 3
Router(config-router)#area 0 range 140.100.160.0 255.255.224.0
Router(config-router)#area 2 range 140.100.192.0 255.255.224.0
Router(config-router)#area 3 range 140.100.16.0 255.255.248.0
Router(config-router)#area 2 stub
Router(config-router)#area 3 stub no summary
Router(config-router)#area 3 default-cost 5
Router(config)#interface loopback 0
Router(config-if)#ip address 140.100.200.200 255.255.255.255
Router(config)#interface ethernet 0
Router(config-if)#ip address 140.100.9.129 255.255.255.0
Router(config-if)#ip ospf priority 64
Router(config-if)#no shut
Router(config)#interface ethernet 1
Router(config-if)#ip address 140.100.12.193 255.255.255.0
Router(config-if)#ip ospf cost 5
Router(config)#interface fddi 0
Router(config-if)#ip address 140.100.160.10 255.255.255.0
Router(config-if)#no shut
Router(config)#interface ethernet 2
Router(config-if)#ip address 140.100.216.193 255.255.255.0
Router(config-if)#no shut
Router(config)#interface ethernet 3
Router(config-if)#ip address 140.100.208.10 255.255.255.0
Router(config-if)#no shut
```

1 Explain the summarization used in this configuration.

2 It is not clear from this configuration why cost has been manually configured. Give possible reasons for the use of cost in this configuration.

3 This router is the designated router for one of the LANs; identify which one. Give reasons why it may have been configured to ensure that it was the designated router. Why are the other LANs not chosen as the designated router?

4 What is the router ID for this system, and has it been configured correctly?

5 Identify the different LSAs that will be transmitted out of each interface. Give reasons for your answers.

6 If you issued the command **show ip route**, to how many networks would the router directly be connected?

Scenario Answers

The answers provided in this section are not necessarily the only possible answers to the questions. The questions are designed to test your knowledge and to give practical exercise in certain key areas. This section is intended to test and exercise skills and concepts detailed in the body of this chapter.

If your answer is different, ask yourself whether it follows the tenets explained in the answers provided. Your answer is correct not if it matches the solution provided in the book, but rather if it has included the principles of design laid out in the chapter.

In this way, the testing provided in these scenarios is deeper: It examines not only your knowledge, but also your understanding and ability to apply that knowledge to problems.

If you do not get the correct answer, refer back to the text and review the subject tested. Be certain to also review your notes on the question to ensure that you understand the principles of the subject.

Scenario 5-1 Answers

Table 5-11 is a possible addressing scheme using the criteria stated in Scenario 5-1.

Taking the private address 10.0.0.0, there is a great deal of flexibility in the addressing scheme that can be devised. Remember, however, that careful filtering is required if the organization is to connect to the Internet.

The addressing scheme proposed here is broken out by area. It is not exhaustive in terms of designing an addressing policy down to the LAN level, as was shown in Chapter 3, but rather deals with the principles of addressing and summarization.

Table 5-11   *Allocation of Addresses for Scenario 5-1*

Area	Subnet/ Prefix	Range	Reasons
0	10.0.0.0/28	10.0.0.16– 10.0.255.224	The use of the zeros in the second octet is an easy reminder that you are in area 0. Because area 0 is a transit area, it will be small. The addressing within the area would be allocated the prefix of 28 bits, allowing the range of subnets shown.
2	10.2.0.0/22	10.2.0.0– 10.2.252.0	Again, the private addressing of 10.0.0.0 as a Class A address is so large that full use may be made of the documentation advantages of the addressing scheme. The second octet allows area 2 to be identified. The prefix of 22 bits is used within the area. This allows 1022 hosts on each network, which is good for further VLSM and VLANs in switched environments.

Table 5-11   *Allocation of Addresses for Scenario 5-1 (Continued)*

Area	Subnet/ Prefix	Range	Reasons
3	10.3.0.0/24	10.3.0.0– 10.3.255.0	The second octet identifies the area. Within the area, a 24-bit prefix is used to address the LANs.
4	10.4.0.0/28	Ethernet: 10.4.0.16– 10.4.255.176 Serial: 10.4.0.0– 10.4.0.12	The second octet identifies the area. Within the area, a 30-bit mask is used to identify the serial links where only two addresses are needed. A 28-bit mask was chosen for the Ethernet connections to allow the creation of many subnets.

Example 5-15 demonstrates a sample configuration for questions 2–6 of Scenario 5-1. The configuration file is for the central router.

Example 5-15 *Sample Configuration of Scenario 5-1*

```
Router(config)# router ospf 100
Router(config-router)# network 10.0.0.0 0.0.255.255 area 0
Router(config-router)# network 10.2.0.0 0.0.255.255 area 2
Router(config-router)# network 10.3.0.0 0.0.255.255 area 3
Router(config-router)# network 10.4.0.0 0.0.255.255 area 4
Router(config-router)# area 3 stub no-summary
Router(config-router)# area 4 stub
Router(config-router)# area 0 range 10.0.0.0 255.255.255.0
Router(config-router)# area 2 range 10.2.0.0 255.255.0.0
Router(config-router)# area 3 range 10.3.0.0 255.255.0.0
Router(config-router)# area 4 range 10.4.0.0 255.255.0.0
Router(config)# interface e0
Router(config-if)# ip address 10.4.0.33 255.255.255.240
Router(config)# interface e1
Router(config-if)# ip address 10.4.0.17 255.255.255.240
Router(config)# interface e2
Router(config-if)# ip address 10.2.4.1 255.255.252.0
Router(config-if)# ip ospf priority 64
Router(config)# interface e3
Router(config-if)# ip address 10.0.0.193 255.255.255.240
Router(config-if)# ip ospf priority 0
Router(config)# interface e4
Router(config-if)# ip address 10.0.0.129 255.255.255.240
Router(config-if)# ip ospf priority 0
Router(config)# interface e5
Router(config-if)# ip address 10.3.3.1 255.255.255.0
Router(config)# interface e6
Router(config-if)# ip address 10.3.2.1 255.255.255.0
Router(config)# interface e7
Router(config-if)# ip address 10.3.1.1 255.255.255.0
Router(config)# interface s0
Router(config-if)# ip address 10.4.0.9 255.255.255.252
Router(config)# interface s1
```

Continues

Example 5-15 *Sample Configuration of Scenario 5-1 (Continued)*

```
Router(config-if)# ip address 10.4.0.5 255.255.255.252
Router(config)# interface loopback 0
Router(config-if)# ip address 10.100.100.101 255.255.255.255
```

Scenario 5-2 Answers

The following are the answers to Scenario 5-2:

1 Router B has been configured to be the designated router for the LAN, which means it is dealing with all the traffic on the LAN associated with the management of OSPF. Given that the system is a 2500, it is a poor choice for a designated router. A better choice would be Router A, which is a larger system that connects directly to Area 0, making it a better choice from the standpoint of the network design. If Router B were a larger system than a 2500, there could be an argument for making it the designated router in order to elevate Router A, which would otherwise be functioning as the ABR as well as the designated router.

The router has not been configured as a stub, and, therefore, the communication between Router A and Router B will be confused, preventing any communication between the two routers.

2 Router A is configured incorrectly. The command that would show the problem would be either **show ip route**, **show ip protocols**, or **show ip ospf database**. The lack of LSA traffic would indicate a configuration problem. When examining the configuration, you would see that the mask on the configuration of the network command for Area 0 is wrong. Therefore, there will be no communication of OSPF LSAs between the areas.

3 The commands that would solve these problems are as follows:

On Router A:

```
router ospf 100
network 140.100.32.0 0.0.0.15 area 0
interface FastEthernet1
no ip ospf cost 10
ip ospf priority 100
```

On Router B:

```
router ospf 200
network 140.100.13.0 0.0.0.15 area 2
area 2 stub
interface FastEthernet0
no ip ospf priority 100
```

4 The default setting for the transmit timer is set to 1 second, and the retransmit timer is set to 5 seconds. The transmit timer determines the estimated number of seconds it takes to send an LSA to a neighbor. The retransmit timer states the number of seconds to wait for an acknowledgement before retransmitting an LSA.

If the transmit timer is not smaller than the retransmit timer, the interface retransmits in the belief that the other side did not receive the LSA. This leads to excess traffic, confusion in the topology database, and the possibility of flapping links. To correct the settings, issue the following subinterface commands:

```
ip ospf retransmit-interval seconds
ip ospf transmit-delay seconds
```

5 If the ISDN interface is configured for dial-on-demand routing (DDR) and is also included in OSPF network commands, you may find that the link the DDR process establishes will cause the routing updates to be propagated throughout the network, causing additional CPU utilization on the routers and flooding of packets throughout the network. The solution is to ensure that the interface is not included in the network command to the OSPF process. A more important problem is that Router B is in a stub area and will not track external routes. Router B cannot connect to the Internet as an ASBR because it will not propagate the type 5 LSAs. The BRI interface cannot partake in the OSPF network. Therefore, the network will not be slow; it will be down.

Scenario 5-3 Answers

Figure 5-6 shows the network that would be supported given the criteria in Scenario 5-3.

The following are the answers for Scenario 5-3:

1 The summarization used in Scenario 5-3 will be broken out by area and is demonstrated in Table 5-12.

2 The command **cost** manually dictates the metric for the link. It is commonly used for interoperability between vendors, or it is used to force the path taken. This suggests that there are duplicate paths.

3 The router is the designated router for the e0 link. Because it is an ABR router, it is probably serving many routers within each area. If any of those routers share a link with the ABR, it makes sense that the ABR should be the designated router.

This may not be the case in Area 0, where this router may be updating a router within Area 0 that is connected to an ASBR. The key is to position the router relative to the others on the multi-access link, in terms of the network hierarchy.

4 The router ID for this router is 140.100.200.200. This is taken from the loopback interface that was configured. It is configured correctly because OSPF supports host routing and the 255.255.255.255 mask is in fact used in a loopback configuration to save address space.

Figure 5-6 *Diagram of the Scenario 5-3 Network*

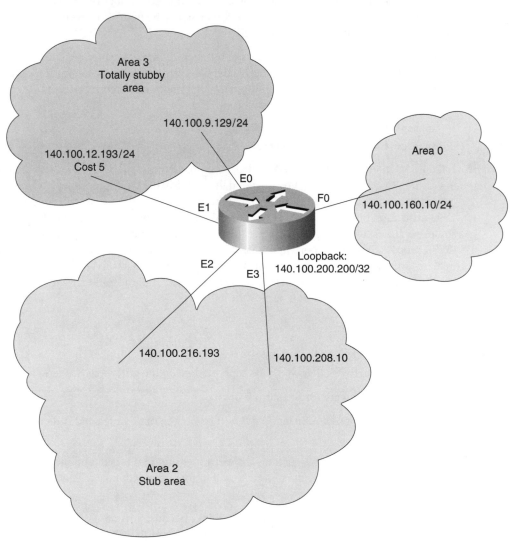

5 Table 5-13 lists the LSAs that will be propagated out of each interface.

6 It is directly connected to five interfaces, and therefore five networks and one host—the host being the loopback interface with a 32-bit mask. If the loopback interface had been configured as a host member with a mask identifying a subnet, that subnet would appear and there would be six networks directly connected.

Table 5-12   *Allocation of Addresses*

Area	Subnet/Prefix	Range	Reasons
0	140.100.160.0 /19	The actual subnet mask used is 255.255.255.0 or a prefix mask of /24. With the summarization of 101, or 160 in decimal, the range of addresses in Area 0 is 140.100.160.0–140.100.191.250.	With the use in the third octet of the bit pattern 101, there is a great deal of possible expansion, even though this is unlikely to be used in the transit Area 0.
2	140.100.192.0 /19	The actual subnet mask used is 255.255.255.0 or a prefix mask of /24. With the summarization of 110, or 192 in decimal, the range of addresses in Area 2 is 140.100.192.0–140.100.223.0.	This is a stub area, which suggests that there are non-Cisco routers within the area; otherwise, the area would probably be a totally stubby area. By using the bit pattern of 110, further use of VLSM is allowed.
3	140.100.8.0 /20	The actual subnet mask used is 255.255.255.0 or a prefix mask of /24. With the summarization of 00001, or 8 in decimal, the range of addresses in Area 3 is 140.100.16.0–140.100.31.250.	The bit pattern used is 0001. This is a smaller environment that will have less ability to grow, but can still use VLSM effectively within the LAN environment.

Table 5-13   *LSAs Propagated Out of Interfaces in Scenario 5-3*

Interface	LSA Type Propagated
E0	Type 2, network LSA
E1	Type 1 and 2, router and network LSAs
E2	Type 1 and 3, router and summary
E3	Type 1 and 3, router and summary
F0	Type 1 and 3, router and summary

The objectives for the ACRC exam for CCNP or CCDP certification are taken from the Cisco Web site at http://www.cisco.com/training under the heading "Cisco Career Certifications and Training." The following table shows the ACRC exam objectives covered in this chapter and also provides the Foundation Routing and Switching exam objective number.

ACRC Exam Objective Number	Corresponding FRS Exam Objective Number	Description
35	116	Describe Enhanced IGRP features and operation.
36	117	Configure Enhanced IGRP.
37	118	Verify Enhanced IGRP operation.
38	119	Select and configure the different ways to control route update traffic.
39	120	Configure route redistribution in a network that does not have redundant paths between dissimilar routing processes.
40	121	Configure route redistribution in a network that has redundant paths between dissimilar routing processes.
41	122	Resolve path selection problems that result in a redistributed network.
42	123	Verify route redistribution.
43	124	Describe when to use BGP to connect to an ISP.
44	125	Describe methods to connect to an ISP using static and default routes, and BGP.

CHAPTER 6

EIGRP, BGP, and Redistribution

How to Best Use This Chapter

By taking the following steps, you can make better use of your study time:

- Keep your notes and answers for all your work with this book in one place for easy reference.

- Take the quiz, writing down your answers. Studies show that retention significantly increases by writing facts and concepts down, even if you never look at the information again!

- Use the diagram in Figure 6-1 to guide you to the next step.

"Do I Know This Already?" Quiz

These questions are designed to test not just your knowledge, but your understanding of the subject matter. It is therefore important to realize that getting the answer the same as stated in Appendix A, "Answers to Quizzes and Q&As," is less important than your answer having embodied the spirit of the question. In this manner the questions and answers are not as open and shut as will be found on the exam: Their intention is to prepare you with the appropriate knowledge and understanding to give you mastery of the subject as opposed to limited rote knowledge.

1 Enhanced IGRP may be used to send information about which Layer 3 protocols?

_____

_____

_____

2 What is the advertised distance in Enhanced IGRP and how is it distinguished from the feasible distance?

_____

_____

_____

Figure 6-1 *How to Use This Chapter*

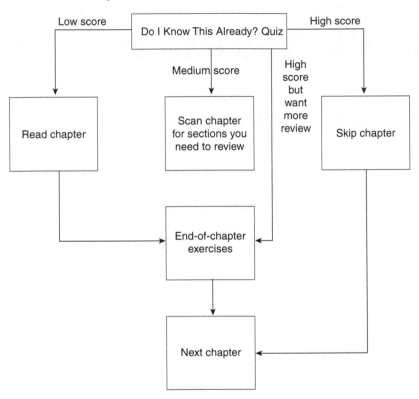

3 If a router does not have a feasible successor, what action will it take?

_____

_____

_____

4 What is an EIGRP topology table, and what does it contain?

_____

_____

_____

5 What EIGRP algorithm is run to create entries for the routing table?

_____

_____

_____

6 When does Enhanced IGRP need to be manually redistributed into another Enhanced IGRP process?

_____

_____

_____

7 When is redistribution required?

_____

_____

_____

8 What type of routing protocol is BGP classified as, and what does this mean?

_____

_____

_____

9 What is a passive interface and why is it used?

_____

_____

_____

10 What is a static route?

_____

_____

_____

11 What is the administrative distance for RIP?

_____

_____

_____

12 What is the transport protocol for BGP?

_____

_____

_____

13 What is a default route?

_____

_____

_____

The answers to this quiz are found in Appendix A, "Answers to Quizzes and Q&As" (see page 469). Review the answers, grade your quiz, and choose an appropriate next step in this chapter based on the suggestions diagrammed in Figure 6-1. Your choices for the next step are as follows:

- Read this chapter.

- Scan this chapter for sections you need to review.

- Skip to the exercises at the end of this chapter.

- Skip this chapter.

Foundation Topics

Introduction: The Alternatives to the Complexity of OSPF in Large Enterprise Networks

The ACRC objective mastered in this section is as follows:

ACRC Exam Objective Number	Corresponding FRS Exam Objective Number	Description
38	119	Select and configure the different ways to control route update traffic.

Chapters 4 and 5 deal with routing protocols in general and OSPF specifically. This chapter concentrates on the alternative routing protocols to OSPF. The focus is on the use of these sophisticated routing protocols in managing connectivity within a large enterprise network.

The major concern in scaling an organizational network is controlling the network overhead that is sent, in particular over slow WAN links. The less information about the network, its services, and networks that need to be sent, the greater the capacity available for the data between clients and servers. Although sending less routing information relieves the network, it gives the routers less information with which to make decisions. Every designer of routing protocols and every network administrator must deal continually with this trade-off. As seen with summarization, static and default routes can lead to poor routing decisions and loss of connectivity.

OSPF was the first protocol to attempt to address these problems. Unfortunately, its complexity and age have discouraged many potential users. These perceived drawbacks are not, however, the reality. It is true that OSPF has been in networks for many years, but it is constantly revised—as seen with the implementation of MOSPF, NSSAs, and other protocols. This is one of the advantages of an open standard that has the world reviewing it. Also, with regard to the concept of areas, OSPF can truly scale to large environments.

Alternatives to OSPF that offer the capability to scale to the size of modern networks are few. Static routing is one possibility, but it demands so much from the network administrator that it would never scale. IGRP offers another alternative; and as a proprietary distance vector protocol, IGRP has solved many of the problems. It does, however, face some issues with regard to scaling because of the inherent nature of distance vector. Enhanced IGRP, although still distance vector and proprietary, does address many of the problems related to scaling the network that IGRP never anticipated. BGP, as an exterior routing protocol, is extremely taciturn and communicates only the minimum information across the links. BGP is too limited for use as an interior protocol, however, where full knowledge of every network is required.

This chapter discusses Enhanced IGRP and BGP. It also deals with the practical concerns of using a proprietary routing protocol as well as managing multiple routing protocols within your IP network. To have full connectivity, every router must know about every network within the organization, irrespective of the routing protocol that first learned of it. If the organization uses more than one routing protocol, this information must be shared or redistributed between all the routing protocols. This sounds simple. In reality, however, it is complex and a potential "can of worms."

The chapter begins by covering Enhanced IGRP. As a proprietary routing protocol, Enhanced IGRP can solve many problems seen in standards-based protocols that have to please all the devices all the time. The Enhanced IGRP sections of this chapter cover the following:

- The concepts and operation of Enhanced IGRP

- The configuration of Enhanced IGRP

- The system administration of a network running Enhanced IGRP

Enhanced IGRP

The ACRC objective mastered in this section is as follows:

ACRC Exam Objective Number	Corresponding FRS Exam Objective Number	Description
35	116	Describe Enhanced IGRP features and operation.

Enhanced IGRP is a revised and improved version of IGRP. Its goal is to solve the scaling limitations that IGRP faces, using the distance vector technology from which it grew. Enhanced IGRP increases the potential growth of a network by reducing the convergence time. This is achieved by the following:

- The Diffusing Update Algorithm (DUAL)

- Loop-free networks

- Incremental updates

- Holding information about neighbors as opposed to the entire network

These features depend on proprietary technology, which centers on local computation. The DUAL algorithm diffuses this computation over multiple routers, with each router responsible for its own small calculation and making requests of neighboring routers when necessary. A full understanding of the concepts and operation of Enhanced IGRP will aid you in the design, implementation, and maintenance of Enhanced IGRP networks, and will definitely help you pass an exam on the subject.

The main concepts of Enhanced IGRP are as follows:

- Neighbor discovery
- The Diffusing Update Algorithm
- Successors, feasible and otherwise
- Passive and active routes
- Protocol independence at Layer 3
- Routing updates sent reliably
- VLSM

How Enhanced IGRP Works

Even if the computation of the network is local, the router must know about the entire network. The explanation of the routing protocol will be given through the viewpoint of one router. In seeing how it learns about the network, and its interaction with other routers, the operation of Enhanced IGRP will become clear; the concepts and terms will be placed in context. This will facilitate the memorization of the subject; rote learning is no longer necessary.

The router will send out a small Hello packet to dynamically learn of other routing devices that are in the same broadcast domain.

NOTE   A broadcast domain refers to a switched environment. It identifies devices that are within the same Layer 2 domain. Although they may not be directly connected to the same physical cable, from a logical Layer 2 or Layer 3 perspective they are on the same link.

The Hello protocol uses a multicast address of 224.0.0.10, and all routers that hear the Hello will also periodically send their own Hellos. On hearing Hellos, the router will create a table of its neighbors. The continued receipt of these packets maintains the *neighbor table*. If a Hello from a known neighbor is not heard within a predetermined amount of time, as stated in the *holdtime*, the router will decide that the neighbor is no longer operational and will take the appropriate action. The holdtime is set at the default of three times the Hello timer. Therefore, if the router misses three Hellos, the neighbor is declared dead. The Hello timer on a LAN is set to 5 seconds; the holdtime is therefore 15 seconds. On a WAN link, the Hello timer is 60 seconds and the holdtime correspondingly is 180 seconds.

The Neighbor Table

Each Layer 3 protocol has its own neighbor table—which makes sense because a neighbor may be running Enhanced IGRP for IP and IPX, while another is running Enhanced IGRP for IP only. In this case, the neighbor, topology, and routing tables would differ greatly. Although all the information could be held in one table, the different Enhanced IGRP processes would all have to access the same table, which would complicate and slow down the lookup. Separate tables for each protocol may require slightly more memory, but is a more efficient use of resources.

The neighbor table includes the following information:

- The address of the neighbor.

- The interface through which the neighbor's Hello was heard.

- The holdtime.

- The *uptime*, how long since the router first heard from the neighbor.

- The sequence number. The neighbor table tracks all the packets sent between the neighbors. It tracks both the last sequence number sent to the neighbor and the last sequence number received from the neighbor. Although the Hello protocol is a connectionless protocol, other protocols used by Enhanced IGRP are connection oriented. The sequence number is in reference to these protocols.

- *Smooth Round Trip Time (SRTT)* is used to calculate the *retransmission timeout (RTO)*. The smooth round trip is the time in milliseconds that it takes for a packet to be sent to a neighbor and a reply to be received.

- RTO, the retransmission timeout, states how long the router will wait on a connection-oriented protocol without an acknowledgement before retransmitting the packet. If the original packet that was unacknowledged was multicast, the retransmitted packets will be unicast.

After the router knows who its neighbors are, it is in a position to create a database of feasible successors. This view of the network is held in the topology table. The *topology table* is created from *updates* received from the neighboring routers. The updates are exchanged between the neighbors. Packets called *replies* will also update the topology table. Replies are sent in response to *queries* sent by the router, inquiring about suspect routes. These queries and responses are used by EIGRP for the DUAL algorithm. Figure 6-2 demonstrates building the neighbor table.

Figure 6-2   *Building the Neighbor Table*

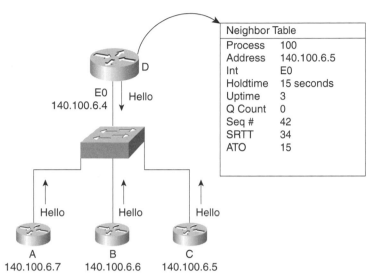

The Routing Table

The routing table is built from the topology table after DUAL has been run. The topology table is the foundation of Enhanced IGRP: This is where all the routes are stored, even after DUAL has been run. It is in the routing table that the best paths are stored and accessed by the routing process.

Now that the tables have been built, the router can make routing decisions (a process explained in the preceding chapter).

Having built the appropriate tables, the technology holds one more secret: how to maintain the tables as current and accurate.

The Topology Table

Because the routing table is the repository of valid routes, it is the topology table in Enhanced IGRP that manages the selection of routes.

The topology table has a record of all known network routes within the organization. The table is built from the update packets that are exchanged by the neighbors and by replies to queries sent by the router. When the router has an understanding of the network, it will run DUAL to determine the best path to the remote network. The result is entered into the routing table.

Maintaining the Topology Table

The topology table is updated because the router either gains or loses direct connectivity with a router or hears a change through the network communication of Enhanced IGRP.

The following four reasons may cause a topology table to be recalculated:

- **A new router (neighbor) comes online.**

  A Hello packet is received from the neighbor.

- **A new network (directly connected) comes online.**

  A Hello packet is received from the neighbor.

  Occurs if the router sees the carrier sense for a network that is configured for a Layer 3 protocol supported by Enhanced IGRP and if the routing process has been configured with the appropriate network command.

- **The router hears a change from a neighbor when a new network is available because of one of the following reasons:**

  The topology table receives an update stating that there is a new remote network.

  The topology table receives a Hello that includes the new network.

  There is local configuration of a directly connected interface.

- **The router hears a change from a neighbor when a network has become unavailable because of one of the following reasons:**

  The topology table receives an update stating that the remote network is down.

  The neighbor table does not receive a Hello within the holdtime.

  The neighbor table receives a Hello that does not include the network.

  The network is directly connected and the router senses loss of carrier.

Figure 6-3 illustrates the traffic flow seen when a router loses a direct connection.

As the neighbor table tracks the receipt of the Enhanced IGRP packets, so the topology table records the packets that have been sent by the router to the neighbors. It also identifies the status of the networks in the table. A healthy network is marked as *passive*; it will be labeled as *active* if the router is attempting to find an alternative path to the remote network that is believed to be down.

Figure 6-3   *Maintaining the Topology Table and the Traffic Flow*

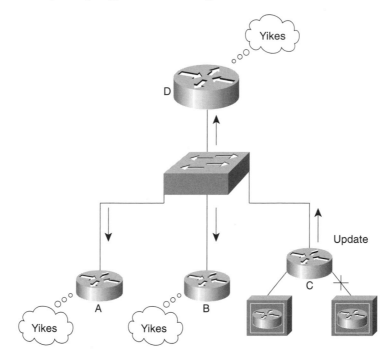

Because the routing table is built from the topology table, the topology table must have the information required by the routing table. This includes the *next logical hop*, or the address of the neighbor that sent the update with that network. It will also calculate the metric to the remote network.

Although the metric in Enhanced IGRP is very similar to IGRP, the way that the metric is used differs according to the scale used. Enhanced IGRP scales by 256.

The topology table records the metric as received from the advertising router, or next logical hop. It then adds the cost of getting to that neighbor, the one that is advertising the route.

The cost to the destination network from the advertising router plus the cost to that router equals the metric to the destination network from the router.

The metric or cost from the neighbor advertising the route is known as the *advertised distance*. The metric or cost from the router is referred to as the *feasible distance*.

Figures 6-4 and 6-5 illustrate these distances. Note that the metric shown in these figures has been simplified for the purposes of this example.

Figure 6-4 *The Use of Feasible and Advertised Distance—Passive Mode*

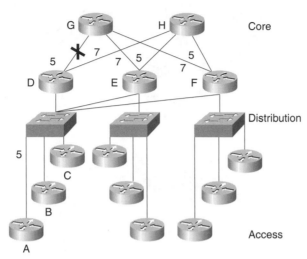

In Figure 6-4, the feasible distance (FD) from A to G is 10 (A to D to G). The advertised distance (AD) from A to G is 5 (advertised from Neighbor D). If the link between D and G were down, A would look in its topology table. The alternative routes A to D to H to E to G have an AD of 19 (7 + 5 + 7). Because 19 is greater than the original FD of 10, it does not qualify as a feasible successor. The path D to H to F to G also has an AD of 19 and cannot be a feasible successor. A to E to G has an AD of 7, however, which is less than the original 10. This is therefore a feasible successor and can be replaced as a route without Router A changing from passive to active mode. Figure 6-5 shows that the router has no acceptable route to substitute, however, and must therefore go into active mode to query its neighbors.

In Figure 6-5, the topology table of Router A has a path (successor) of A to D to G to X. The feasible distance is 20, and the advertised distance from Neighbor D is 15. When Router D dies, Router A must find an alternative path to X. The Neighbors B, C, E, and F have advertised distances of 27, 27, 20, and 21, respectively. Because all the neighbors have an AD that is the same or greater than the successor feasible distance, none of these are acceptable as feasible successors. Router A must go into active mode and send queries to the neighbors. Both Routers E and F reply with a feasible successor because both have an AD from G of 5. This is acceptable. The topology and routing tables will be updated, DUAL calculated, and the network returned to passive mode.

From this information received from Routers E and F in Figure 6-5, the router will run DUAL and determine the best paths to the remote networks. The result is placed in the routing table as valid neighboring routers to which packets may be sent as the next logical hop. Enhanced IGRP refers to these neighboring routers as *successors*.

Figure 6-5   *The Use of Feasible and Advertised Distance—Active Mode*

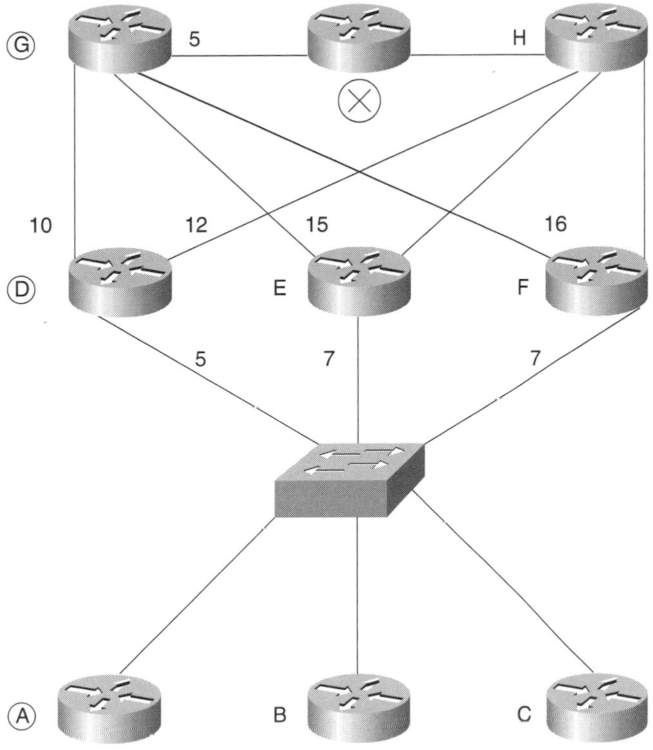

The detail on how Enhanced IGRP computes successors is complex, but the concept is fairly simple.

To determine whether a path to a remote network is feasible, Enhanced IGRP considers the *feasibility condition* (FC) of the route. Essentially, each router holds a routing table that is a list of the available networks and the best or most efficient path to each of them. The term used to describe this is the feasible distance of the successor, otherwise known as the metric for the route. The router will also hold the routing table of its neighbors, referred to as the advertised distance. If the advertised distance is within scope, this route may be identified as an alternative route, or a *feasible successor*.

A neighbor can only become a feasible successor for a route if its advertised distance (AD) is less than the feasible distance (FD). This is DUAL's fundamental key to remaining loop free; for if a route contains a loop, the advertised distance will be greater than the FD and will therefore fail the FC. By holding the routing tables of the neighbors, the amount of network overhead and computation is reduced. When a path to a remote network is lost, the router may well be able to find an alternative route, with minimal fuss, computation, or network traffic. This gives the much-advertised benefit of very fast convergence.

The new terminology can be very confusing and is best understood in context. It is easier to remember a concept or term when the function is understood. Given the overall understanding of how Enhanced IGRP works, a consideration of the topology table and its components will help explain the detail of Enhanced IGRP operation.

The topology table includes the following information:

- Whether the route is passive or active.

- That an update has been sent to the neighbors.

- That a query packet has been sent to the neighbors. If this field is positive, at least one route will be marked as active.

- If a query packet has been sent, another field will track whether any replies have been received from the neighbors.

- That a reply packet has been sent in response to a query packet received from a neighbor.

- The remote networks.

- The prefix or mask for the remote network.

- The metric for the remote network, the feasible distance.

- The metric for the remote network advertised by the next logical hop, the advertised distance.

- The next logical hop.

- The outgoing interface to be used to reach the next logical hop.

- The successors, the path to the remote network stated in hops.

Adding a Network to the Topology Table

In looking at a day in the life of a router, it is possible to put the operation of Enhanced IGRP into context. Therefore, imagine the router (Router A) that hears a new network. The administrator has plugged in another Ethernet cable to service a department that has moved into the building.

As soon as Router A becomes aware of the new network, it starts to send Hello packets out of the new interface. No one answers because this is an access router giving connectivity to the workstations and other end devices.

There are no new entries in the neighbor table because no neighbors have responded to the Hello protocol. There is a new entry in the topology table, however, because this is a new network.

EIGRP, sensing a change, is obliged to send an update to all its neighbors informing them of the new network. The sent updates are tracked in the topology table and the neighbor table because the updates are connection oriented and the acknowledgements from the neighbors must be received within a set time frame.

Router A, having added the network to the topology table, runs DUAL and adds the network to the routing table. The network will be marked as passive because it is operational.

Router A's work is done. Router D's work has just begun. Router D is the backbone router in the basement of the building acting at the distribution layer. Its neighbors are routers on each floor and the routers in the other buildings.

On hearing the update from Router A, it updates the sequence number in the neighbor table and adds the network to the topology table. It runs DUAL to calculate the feasible distance and the successor to place in the routing table. It is then in a position to send an update to all of its neighbors, except Router A.

In this manner, the new network is propagated through the network. Figure 6-6 shows this propagation. The initial bit is set in the EIGRP header to indicate that the routes in the update represent a new neighbor relationship.

Figure 6-6   *EIGRP—Updating the Topology Table with a New Router*

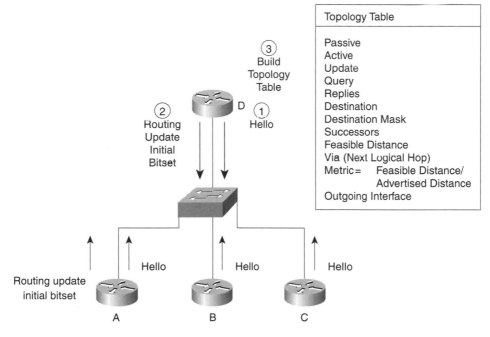

Removing a Path or Router from the Topology Table

This process is far more complex and gets to the crux of Enhanced IGRP.

If a network connected to Router A is disconnected, Router A updates its topology and routing table and sends an update to its neighbors—this discussion focuses on Router D.

When Router D receives the update, it updates the neighbor table and the topology table. As a router, it is programmed to find an alternative route to the remote network. It examines the topology table for alternatives. Because there was only one path to the remote network, no alternatives will be found.

The router then sends out a query to the neighbors requesting that they look in their tables for paths to the remote network. The route is marked active in the topology table at this time.

The query is tracked and when all the replies are in, the neighbor and topology tables are updated. DUAL, which starts to compute as soon as a network change is registered, runs to determine the best path, which is placed in the routing table. Because there is no alternative route available, however, the neighbors reply to the query stating that they have no path. Before they respond, they query their own neighbors. In this way, the search for an alternative path extends throughout the organization. When no router can supply a path to the network, all the routers remove the network from their routing and topology tables.

Figure 6-7 shows the actions taken when a router receives a query from another router asking for an alternative route to a destination. Note that if the queried router has no route to offer, it is still obliged to respond to the querying router.

Figure 6-7   *EIGRP—Maintaining the Topology Table, Router D*

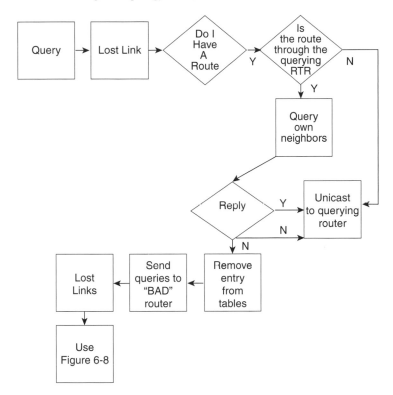

Figure 6-8 illustrates the logic flow in a router that realizes a link has been lost, which may occur because a directly connected interface has lost carrier signal or because the router has received an update or query.

Figure 6-8 *Maintaining the Topology Table—Choosing a Feasible Successor*

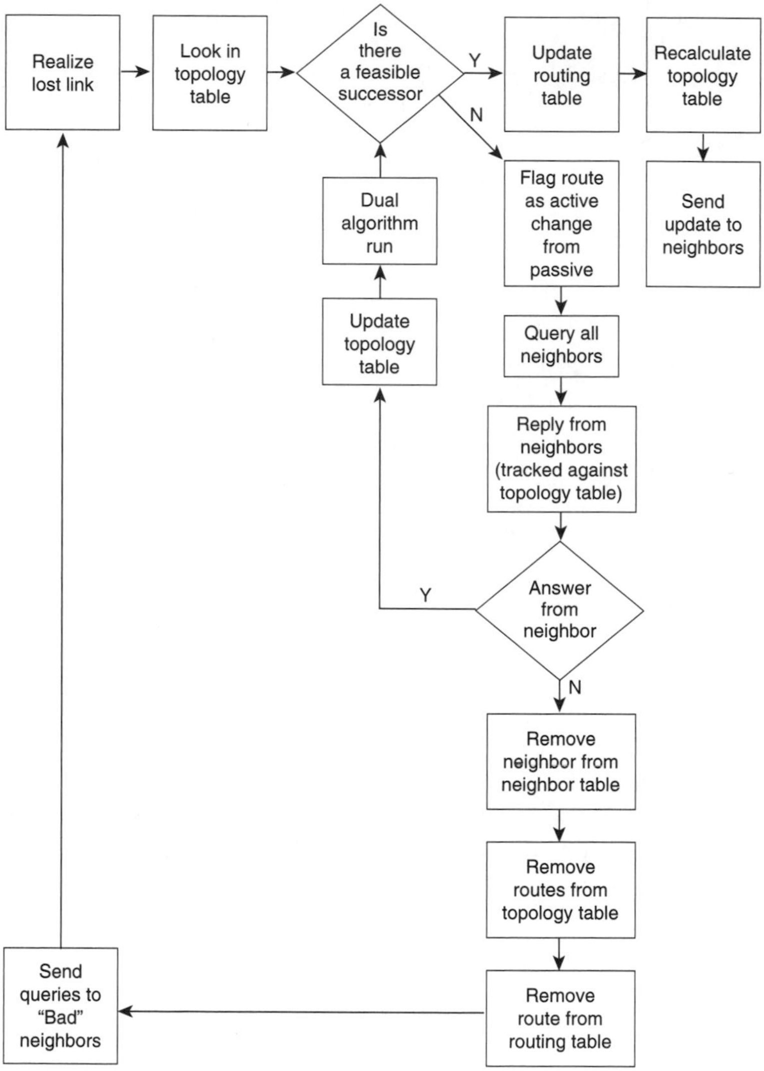

Finding an Alternative Path to a Remote Network

Using Figure 6-9 as reference for the topology of the network, you can see that when Router D
fails to hear from either Routers G or H about networks connected to Router X, which at the
core layer connects the buildings via the FDDI ring, Router B will update the neighbor table. It
then marks the routes that were reached by sending the traffic to Routers G or H as possibly

bad. It looks in the topology table, which has every network and path of the network to determine whether there is an alternative route. It is looking for a feasible successor. Note that the metric shown in Figure 6-9 has been simplified for the purposes of this example.

Figure 6-9   *Campus Topology Map Showing Alternative Path Selection*

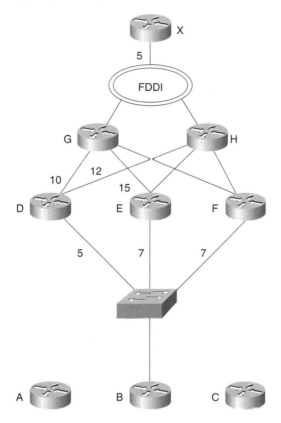

A feasible successor is determined by a clear equation. The topology table has listed for every route or successor an advertised distance and a feasible distance. This comprises the metric by which the route was selected.

Now that the chosen route to the remote network is down, a successor or new route must be found, if possible. A route that may be chosen to be the new successor is one where the advertised distance is less or equal to the feasible distance of the original route.

Updates are sent to the neighbors to inform them of a change. The neighbors recalculate the topology table to ensure that all the information is still current and accurate. The neighbors should not need to send updates to their neighbors unless the distance changes.

It is important to note that because the alternative route was found within the router's topology table, the route stayed in a passive state. Figures 6-4 and 6-5 illustrate this process.

If a feasible successor is found in the topology table, it is crowned successor and entered into the routing table. It is necessary to run DUAL on the topology table when a change in the network occurs to recalculate a new set of feasible successors to the new successor.

If the router does not have a feasible successor, it places the route into an active state, while it actively queries other routers for an alternative path. A query packet is sent to the neighbors inquiring whether they have an acceptable route. After interrogating their topology table, if a feasible route is found, the neighbor replies with the alternative path. This alternative path is then added to the topology table. Next, in the last steps of the DUAL algorithm, the routing table is updated. The network is placed back into a passive state as the router returns to sleep until the next change in the network.

If a neighbor that has been queried has no alternative path or feasible successor, it places the network into active mode and queries its neighbors. If no answer is heard, the messages are propagated until it hits a network or autonomous system boundary. Figure 6-10 illustrates the boundary for the propagation of query packets.

Figure 6-10   *The Propagation of Query Packets*

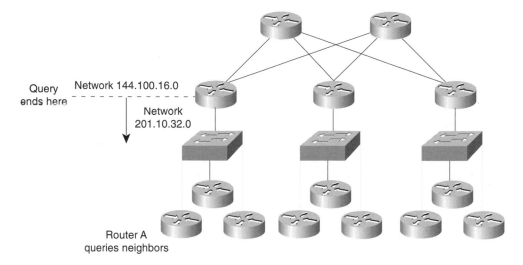

When the router sends a query packet, it is recorded in the topology table. This is to ensure a timely reply. If the router does not hear a reply within 180 seconds, the neighbor is removed from the neighbor table; all the networks held in the topology table for that neighbor are seen as suspect and the networks are queried. Occasionally, because of slow links and burdened routers in a large network, problems can occur. In particular, a router may not receive a reply from all the queries it sent out. This leads to the route being declared stuck-in-active (SIA) and the neighbor that failed to reply will be removed from the neighbor table and DUAL will assume a reply giving an infinite metric.

If you understand the principles of Enhanced IGRP functionality, configuring it is straightforward. The following section deals with the commands required to configure Enhanced IGRP. Before effective configuration can be achieved, the entire network should be analyzed from a design perspective, particularly with regard to summarization. Refer to Chapter 3, "IP Addressing," for a review of summarization.

Configuring Enhanced IGRP

The ACRC objective mastered in this section is as follows:

ACRC Exam Objective Number	Corresponding FRS Exam Objective Number	Description
36	117	Configure Enhanced IGRP.

The commands for Enhanced IGRP are consistent with the other IP routing protocols. Although IP routing is on automatically, the chosen routing protocol must be configured and the participating interfaces identified.

Enhanced IGRP allows for VLSM and therefore summarization because the mask is sent in the update packets. As with OSPF, summarization is not automatic and must be manually configured.

WARNING   Enhanced IGRP is a new protocol and has evolved over the past few years. It is essential that in a practical situation, the commands and configuration be researched for the IOS code level that is installed in your network.

This section covers the following:

- Required configuration commands of EIGRP

- Optional configuration commands of EIGRP

- What each configuration command achieves

- An example of how the configuration command achieves its goal

The Required Commands for Configuring Enhanced IGRP

The router needs to understand how to participate in the Enhanced IGRP network. It therefore requires the following:

- **The Enhanced IGRP process**—The routing protocol needs to be started on the router.

- **The Enhanced IGRP process ID**—All routers sharing routing updates and participating in the larger network must be identified as part of the same autonomous system. A router will not accept an update from a router configured with a different AS number.

- **Participating router interfaces**—The router may not want to have all its interfaces send or receive Enhanced IGRP routing updates. A classic example is a dialup line to a remote office. If there were only one subnet at the remote office, it would be more efficient to use default and static route commands because any updates would dial the line.

By default (unless the **SETUP** script is used), there is no IP routing protocol running on the Cisco router. This is not true of other protocols, however. If an IPX network address is configured on an interface, for example, the IPX RIP process will be automatically started.

To configure Enhanced IGRP as the routing protocol, the following command syntax is used:

```
Router(config)#
Router EIGRP Autonomous System Number
```

Although Enhanced IGRP has been turned on, it has no information on how to operate. The connected networks that are to be sent in the Enhanced IGRP updates and the interfaces that participate in the Enhanced IGRP updates must be defined. If the EIGRP information is not specified, the process with insufficient configuration will never start.

WARNING   Most versions of the IOS do not offer an error message, which can make troubleshooting more difficult. Refer to the section titled "Verifying the Enhanced IGRP Operation" in this chapter for more information.

The following command syntax shows the use of the **network** command:

```
Router(config-router)#network network number
```

The **network** command plays a similar role to that of the **network** command in RIP or IGRP. Unlike OSPF, where it is possible to identify the specific address of an interface, the **network** command for Enhanced IGRP is stated at the class level. Enhanced IGRP does not have the design specification of areas and is therefore without the need for granularity.

After the network has been defined to Enhanced IGRP, it will identify the interfaces directly connected to the routers that share that network address.

Having identified the interfaces on the router that are participating in the Enhanced IGRP domain, the following will happen:

- Updates will be received on the interface.
- Updates will be sent out of the interfaces.
- The network will be advertised out of all EIGRP interfaces.
- If appropriate, the Hello protocol will be propagated.

The Optional Commands for Configuring Enhanced IGRP

These commands are used to tune the way Enhanced IGRP works within your network and should be used in reference to the design of the network and its technical requirements.

This section considers the following commands:

- **ip summary address**
- **bandwidth**
- **bandwidth-percent**

Summarization with Enhanced IGRP

Summarization in Enhanced IGRP solves the same problems of scaling as seen in the section on OSPF in Chapter 5, "OSPF Configuration." For more information, refer to the section in Chapter 3 titled "Summarization."

The difference in the configuration between Enhanced IGRP and OSPF is that OSPF is only summarized at the area boundary. Enhanced IGRP does not use the concept of areas and may be configured on any router in the network. The consideration is the IP addressing scheme and how hierarchical it is. If summarization is not configured, Enhanced IGRP will automatically summarize at the class boundary.

There are two commands for summarization with Enhanced IGRP. The first command is **no auto-summary**. This command is IOS specific and research should be done on your IOS code level before configuring your live network.

The command applies to the entire router. This is very important because if there are slow serial interfaces or congested links, they will transmit all the subnets known on the router. This may significantly increase the overhead for the link. The solution is to configure the **summary** command on all interfaces, which in turn demands careful deployment of addresses.

The following shows the structure of the **no auto-summary** command:

```
Router(config-router)#no auto-summary
```

Manual summarization is configured at the interface level, as shown here:

```
Router(config)#interface S0
Router(config-if)#ip summary address eigrp autonomous-system-number address mask
```

Bandwidth Control

A perennial concern of network administrators is the amount of bandwidth used for overhead traffic. Administrators want to minimize the amount of network control traffic sent through the network to maximize the bandwidth available for user data. One of the major benefits of both Enhanced IGRP and OSPF is that they send as little network traffic as possible, which has the advantage of decreasing the convergence time of the network and ensuring that the network traffic that is sent arrives at the destination.

Enhanced IGRP will not use more than 50% of the stated bandwidth on a link. There is a **bandwidth** command used on the interfaces of a Cisco router. It allows the default settings on links to be overridden. This is often necessary on serial links because the default bandwidth is 1.544 Mbps or a T1. If Enhanced IGRP assumes a bandwidth of a T1 when in reality the link is 56 kbps, it is easy to see how Enhanced IGRP could saturate the link because it sees at 50% an upper limit that far exceeds the real bandwidth of the line. This will not only mean the dropping of data packets due to congestion, but also the dropping of Enhanced IGRP packets. This will cause confusion in the network, retransmission, and user irritation as the network slows. It is essential to configure all interfaces to reflect the true speed of the line.

NOTE   Other technologies on a Cisco router will use this value to make decisions. Therefore, you must ensure that the bandwidth stated is indeed the speed of the link. When you issue the **show interface** command, the configured bandwidth of the link will be shown. There will also be a field identifying the load on the line. The load is the amount of traffic sent out of the interface, proportional to the bandwidth of the link, where the bandwidth is the stated bandwidth and not the speed of the interface.

The bandwidth is a logical construct whose value can have wide-reaching implications on the functioning of your network. It does not affect the actual speed of the link.

When configuring the **bandwidth** command, it is important to consider the actual speed of the link. It is only practical to configure this on serial lines, where the speed of the link will vary considerably. Do not, however, confuse the speed of the interface or access line with the bandwidth of the virtual circuit (VC). If the serial interface is accessing a nonbroadcast multiaccess (NBMA) environment such as Frame Relay, the situation is complex. Your company may have five virtual circuits from your router's serial interface. Each VC is 56 kbps. The access link will need a capacity of 5 × 56 kbps, or at least 2046 kbps.

The configuration of the **bandwidth** command in an NBMA cloud depends on the design of the virtual circuits. If the serial line has many virtual circuits in a multipoint configuration, then Enhanced IGRP will evenly distribute its overhead between the virtual circuits. The **bandwidth** command should reflect the access-link speed into the Frame Relay cloud.

If possible, it is much easier to configure and manage an environment that has used subinterfaces, where each virtual circuit is logically treated as if it were a separate interface. The **bandwidth** command may be configured on each subinterface, which allows different speeds on each virtual circuit.

The following syntax shows the structure of the **bandwidth** command:

```
Router(config)#interface S0
Router(config-if)#bandwidth speed of line
```

Another command specific to Enhanced IGRP is the **bandwidth-percent** command. It is easier and simpler to use the **bandwidth** command than the **bandwidth-percent** command.

The **bandwidth-percent** command interacts with the **bandwidth** command on the interface. The reason for using this command is primarily because in your network the **bandwidth** command does not reflect the true speed of the link. The **bandwidth** command may have been altered to manipulate the routing metric and path selection of a routing protocol such as IGRP or OSPF, for example. It might be better to use other methods of controlling the routing metric and return the bandwidth to a true value. Otherwise, the **bandwidth-percent** command is available. It is possible to set a **bandwidth-percent** that is larger than the stated bandwidth. This is in the understanding that although the bandwidth may be stated to be 56 kbps, the link is in fact 256 kbps. The following shows the structure of the **bandwidth-percent** command:

```
Router(config)#interface S0

Router(config-if)#ip bandwidth-percent eigrp <autonomous-system-number>
<percent>
```

Enhanced IGRP can also be configured as a routing protocol for IPX and AppleTalk. The next section discusses this.

Configuring Enhanced IGRP for IPX

The configuration of IPX is very similar to IP. The difference is that IPX is a client/server-based protocol that was originally designed to operate in a LAN environment. Although Novell has improved their technology over the past few years to allow the networks to scale across the enterprise domain, IPX can still prove both a design and an implementation headache for the administrator. Typically, the amount of overhead generated in a client/server network is greater than that of a peer-to-peer network. This overhead becomes problematic when slower WAN links are used and bandwidth is at a premium. In this environment, Enhanced IGRP is a powerful tool.

Enhanced IGRP offers the following main features to an IPX enterprise network:

- Incremental updates for both RIP and SAP traffic

- Faster convergence of the network

- An increased diameter of the network, through the use of the metric and hop count

- A more complex and sophisticated routing metric

- Automatic redistribution of networks between IPX RIP, NLSP, and Enhanced IGRP

The operation of Enhanced IGRP for IPX is the same as IP, although the EIGRP metric uses both bandwidth and delay in calculating the best path.

Enhanced IGRP for IPX uses the same major components of

- Reliable transport mechanism for updates

- The Diffusing Update Algorithm

- Neighbor discovery/recovery

- Protocol-dependent modules

It is important to remember that IPX is still designed as a proprietary LAN client/server protocol. Enhanced IGRP is also a proprietary protocol and although there are some devices on the market that support Enhanced IGRP, it cannot be assumed that these include IPX systems.

In the design of the network using Enhanced IGRP, IPX RIP/SAP or NLSP will be running. These protocols are found on the LAN in the traditional client/server domain.

In the design of IPX in an enterprise network, Enhanced IGRP is used between Cisco routers where bandwidth is a precious commodity. Enhanced IGRP is configured in the WAN, where it is unlikely that there are any clients or servers requiring RIP/SAP updates.

When IPX is configured on a Cisco router, it is necessary to turn on IPX routing and to allocate network addresses to the appropriate interfaces. This allows the router to route IPX traffic through those interfaces and to send and receive RIP/SAP updates.

Configuring Enhanced IGRP for IPX requires some additional commands. An additional routing protocol must be identified along with the interfaces that it supports. These interfaces are then removed from the RIP/SAP update schedule. Figure 6-11 illustrates Enhanced IGRP configuration for IPX.

Figure 6-11 *Enhanced IGRP Configuration for IPX*

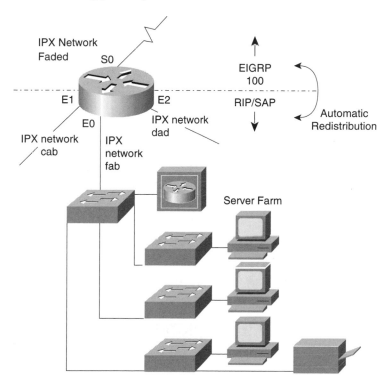

Example 6-1 is a sample configuration of the Figure 6-11 network that has both RIP/SAP and Enhanced IGRP running.

Example 6-1 *Configuring Enhanced IGRP for IPX*

```
Router(config)# ipx routing
Router(config)# ipx router eigrp 100
Router(config-router)# network FADED
Router(config)# ipx router rip
Router(config-router)#no network FADED
Router(config)#interface E0
Router(config-if)#ipx network FAB
Router(config)#interface E1
Router(config-if)#ipx network CAB
Router(config)#interface E2
Router(config-if)#ipx network DAB
Router(config)#interface s0
Router(config-if)#ipx network FADED
```

NOTE   The autonomous system number used in the configuration of Enhanced IGRP for IPX must be the same on every router that wants to share routing updates. This is the same as the configuration for IP. The IPX autonomous system number is completely independent of the IP autonomous system number.

Enhanced IGRP will automatically redistribute its routing information into RIP/SAP. It will also only send incremental updates through serial interfaces and will send periodic updates through LAN interfaces. EIGRP can be manually configured to send incremental updates out of the LAN interface, if required. Incremental updates might apply to networks that form a backbone in the network design—for example, where an FDDI ring or Fast Ethernet segments are connecting the distribution layer and forming the campus backbone.

The following is the command syntax to force a LAN interface to send incremental updates:

```
Router(config)# Interface F0
Router(config-if)#ipx sap-incremental eigrp autonomous-system-number
```

Configuring Enhanced IGRP for AppleTalk

Enhanced IGRP also supports the client/server protocol AppleTalk. Conceptually, the use of Enhanced IGRP is the same, although the configuration details differ. The main difference in configuration is that whereas in configuring IP or IPX, the autonomous system number must be the same for all routers sharing routing information, with AppleTalk every router must have a unique process ID.

The configuration details of Enhanced IGRP for AppleTalk are beyond the scope of this book. Refer to the Cisco Web site and documentation for details and design and configuration guidelines.

Moving toward IP   In reality, most organizations are porting all their client/server platforms into IP, with the support of the vendors of the client/server products. Enhanced IGRP for either IPX or AppleTalk is most powerful when transitioning your organization to IP. If you are using Enhanced IGRP, be aware of the fast development of the technology and ensure compatibility between the IOS versions by researching the Cisco Web site.

Verifying the Enhanced IGRP Operation

The ACRC objective mastered in this section is as follows:

ACRC Exam Objective Number	Corresponding FRS Exam Objective Number	Description
37	118	Verify Enhanced IGRP operation.

The following set of commands is invaluable in the configuration, maintenance, and troubleshooting of a live network. They are a necessary set of tools for use on a daily basis as well as on the CCIE lab exam.

For the preparation of the ACRC exam, understanding the output of these commands is important not just because they may constitute questions on the exam, but because the ability to analyze what is happening on the network demands a thorough understanding of the concepts explained in this chapter. This skill is required in interpreting the output of a **show** command.

This section deals with the following commands:

- **show ip eigrp neighbors**—For detailed information on the neighbors. It records the communication between the router and the neighbors as well as the interface and address by which they communicate.

- **show ip eigrp topology**—For details about the routes held in the topology table and for detailed information on the networks that the router is aware of and the preferred paths to those networks, as well as the next logical hop as the first step in the path. The router will track the EIGRP packets that have been sent to neighbors in this table.

- **show ip eigrp topology all**—For details about all the routes and alternative paths held in the topology table. The router will track the EIGRP packets that have been sent to neighbors in this table.

- **show ip eigrp traffic**—For information on the aggregate traffic sent to and from the EIGRP process.

- **show ipx route**—Shows the routing table for IPX, and the source of the information on how to reach the remote destination network.

The Enhanced IGRP **show** commands are highly detailed and give a comprehensive understanding of the state of the network. The other commands generic to IP—as described in Chapter 5—are also useful in the maintenance of Enhanced IGRP.

The show ip eigrp neighbors **Command**

This command shows the neighbor table. The syntax is as follows:

```
Router# show ip eigrp neighbors type number
```

Example 6-2 shows the output of this command. Table 6-1 explains how to read this information.

Example 6-2   *show ip eigrp neighbors Output*

```
Router# show ip eigrp neighbors
IP-EIGRP Neighbors for process 100
Address          interface    Holdtime    Uptime     Q       Seq    SRTT    RTO
                              (secs)      (h:m:s)    Count   Num    (ms)    (ms)
140.100.48.22    Ethernet1    13          0:00:41    0       11     4       20
140.100.32.22    Ethernet0    14          0:02:01    0       10     12      24
140.100.32.31    Ethernet0    12          0:02:02    0       4      5       2
```

Table 6-1 explains the meaning of the important fields.

Table 6-1   *Explanation of the show ip eigrp neighbor Command Results*

Field	Explanation
process 100	This is the autonomous system number, used to identify routers from whom to accept routing updates.
Address	IP address of the Enhanced IGRP neighbor.
interface	Interface on which the router is receiving Hello packets from the neighbor.
Holdtime	Length of time, in seconds, that the router will wait to hear from the neighbor before declaring it down. The default is 15 seconds.

Table 6-1   *Explanation of the **show ip eigrp neighbor** Command Results (Continued)*

Field	Explanation
Uptime	Time, measured in hours, minutes, and seconds, since the router first heard from this neighbor.
Q Count	Number of Enhanced IGRP packets (update, query, and reply) that the router has queued and is waiting to send.
Seq Num	The sequence number of the last packet that was received from the neighbor.
SRTT	Smooth Round Trip Time. The time is measured in milliseconds and is from the sending of the packet to the receipt of an acknowledgement from the neighbor.
RTO	Retransmission timeout, in milliseconds. This shows how long the router will wait before it retransmits the packet.

The show ip eigrp topology **Command**

This command shows the topology table and allows analysis of DUAL and whether the successor or route is in an active or passive state. The syntax is as follows:

Router# **show ip eigrp topology** [*autonomous-system-number* | [[*ip-address*] *mask*]]

Example 6-3 shows the output of this command. Table 6-2 explains how to read this information.

Example 6-3   *show ip eigrp topology Output*

```
Router# show ip eigrp topology
IP-EIGRP Topology Table for process 100
Codes:P - Passive, A - Active, U - Update, Q - Query, R - Reply, r - Reply status
P 140.100.56.0 255.255.255.0, 2 successors, FD is 0
via 140.100.32.22 (46251776/46226176), Ethernet0
via 140.100.48.22 (46251776/46226176), Ethernet1
via 140.100.32.31 (46277376/46251776), Ethernet0
P 140.100.48.0 255.255.255.0, 1 successors, FD is 307200
via Connected, Ethernet1
via 140.100.48.22 (307200/281600), Ethernet1
140.100.32.22 (307200/281600), Ethernet0
via 140.100.32.31 (332800/307200), Ethernet0
```

Table 6-2 *Explanation of the* **show ip eigrp topology** *Command Results*

Field	Explanation
P	Passive—The router has not received any EIGRP input from a neighbor and the network is assumed to be stable.
A	Active—After a route or successor is down, the router attempts to find an alternative path. After local computation, the router realizes that it must query the neighbor to see whether it can find a feasible successor or path.
U	Update—A value in this field identifies that the router has sent an update packet to a neighbor.
Q	Query—A value in this field identifies that the router has sent a query packet to a neighbor.
R	Reply—A value here shows that the router has sent a reply to the neighbor.
r	Used in conjunction with the query counter, the router has sent out a query and is awaiting a reply.
140.100.48.0	Destination IP network number.
255.255.255.0	Destination subnet mask.
successors	The number of routes or the next logical hop. The number stated here is the same as the number of routes in the routing table.
FD	Feasible distance—This is the metric or cost to the destination from the router.
Replies	Number of replies that the router is still waiting for from this neighbor. This is only relevant when the route is in an active state.
State	Enhanced IGRP state of the route. It can be the number 0, 1, 2, or 3. This is relevant when the destination is active.
via	Address of the next logical hop, or the neighbor who told the router about this route. The first N of these entries, the current successors. The remaining entries on the list are feasible successors.
(46251776/46226176)	The first number is the Enhanced IGRP metric that represents the feasible distance, or the cost to the destination. The number after the slash is the Enhanced IGRP metric that the peer advertised, or the advertised distance.
Ethernet0	Interface through which the EIGRP packets were received, and therefore the outgoing interface.

The show ip eigrp traffic **Command**

The command shows the Enhanced IGRP traffic received and generated by the router. The following is the command syntax:

```
Router# show ip eigrp traffic [autonomous-system-number]
```

Example 6-4 shows the output of this command. Table 6-3 explains how to read this information.

Example 6-4 *show ip eigrp traffic Output*

```
Router# show ip eigrp traffic
IP-EIGRP Traffic Statistics for process 100
Hellos sent/received: 218/205
Updates sent/received: 7/23
Queries sent/received: 2/0
Replies sent/received: 0/2
Acks sent/received: 21/14
```

Table 6-3 explains the meaning of the important fields.

Table 6-3   *Explanation of the **show ip eigrp traffic** Command Output*

Field	Explanation
process 100	This is the autonomous system number, used to identify routers from whom to accept routing updates.
Hellos sent/received	Number of Hello packets sent and received by the router.
Updates sent/received	Number of update packets sent and received by the router.
Queries sent/received	Number of query packets sent and received by the router.
Replies sent/received	Number of reply packets sent and received by the router.
Acks sent/received	Number of acknowledgment packets sent and received by the router.

The ability to interpret these screens in conjunction with the physical and logical topology diagrams of your organization will ensure the understanding of the operation of EIGRP.

Redistribution between Routing Protocols

The ACRC objectives mastered in this section are as follows:

ACRC Exam Objective Number	Corresponding FRS Exam Objective Number	Description
38	119	Select and configure the different ways to control route update traffic.
41	122	Resolve path selection problems that result in a redistributed network.

Unfortunately, seldom is just one routing protocol running within an organization. If the organization is running only a single routing protocol, it is necessary to find some way of passing the networks learned by one routing protocol into another so that every workstation can reach every other workstation. This process is called *redistribution*.

Although the concept of redistribution is fairly straightforward, the design and implementation is extremely tricky. It is well known that redistribution can result in "fun and games with routing loops." Although multiple routing protocols may be a necessity of life, it is critical that the implementation and maintenance be managed with a full, documented understanding of both the network and the traffic flows.

To manage the complexity of these networks and to reduce the possibility of routing loops, some level of restriction in the information sent across the various domains is often necessary.

Controlling Routing Updates

Various methods enable you to control the routing information sent between routers. These methods include the following:

- **Passive interfaces**—An interface that listens but will not send updates.

  Which interfaces participate in the routing process is controlled by the interface configuration. During configuration, the routing process is instructed via the **network** command as to which interfaces to use. Because most protocols express the networks at the major boundary, interfaces that have no reason to send this protocol's updates propagate the data across the network. This is not only a waste of bandwidth, but in many cases it can lead to confusion.

- **Default routes**—A route used if there is no entry in the routing table for the destination network. If the lookup finds no entry for the desired network and no default network is configured, the packet is dropped.

  If the routing process is denied the right to send updates, the downstream routers will have a limited understanding of the network. To resolve this, use default routes. Default routes reduce overhead, add simplicity, and can remove loops.

- **Static routes**—A route that is manually configured. It takes precedence over routes learned via a routing process.

  If there is no routing process configured, static routes may be configured to populate the routing table. This is not practical in a large network because the table cannot learn of changes in the network topology dynamically. In small environments or for stub networks, however, this is an excellent solution.

- **The null interface**—An imaginary interface that is defined as the next logical hop in a static route. All traffic destined for the remote network is carefully routed into a black hole.

  This can be used in a similar way to the passive interface, but allows for greater granularity in the denied routes.

- **Distribution lists**—Access lists applied to the routing process, determining which networks will be accepted into the routing table or sent in updates.

  When communicating to another routing process, it is important to control the information sent into the other process. This control is for security, overhead, and management reasons. Access lists afford the greatest control for determining the traffic flow in the network.

Figure 6-12 shows the use of these options in a large and complex network.

Controlling routing updates is useful for hiding certain networks from the rest of the organization, for controlling the network overhead or traffic on the wire, and for simple security reasons. However, design and control are critical in the configuration of a network that uses more than one routing protocol. This kind of network requires some level of communication between those protocols through redistribution, which can add to the complexity and confusion of the network.

Figure 6-12 *Controlling Routing Updates*

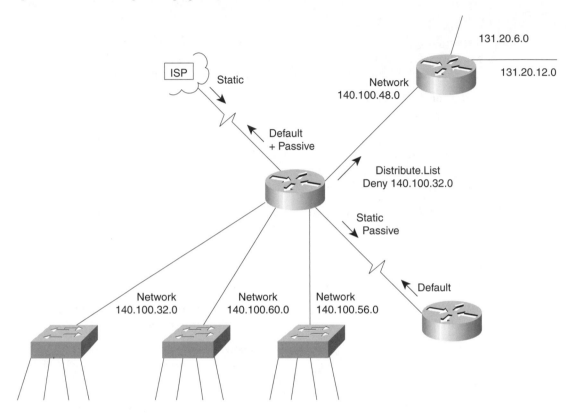

The Main Features of Redistribution

Redistribution is used when a router is receiving information about remote networks from various sources. Although all the networks are entered into the routing table and routing decisions will be made on all the networks present in the table, a routing protocol propagates only those networks that it learned through its own process. When there is no sharing of network information between the routing processes, it is referred to as *ships in the night*, or *SIN*, routing. Redistribution can only occur between processes routing the same Layer 3 protocol. There can be no network redistribution between AppleTalk and IPX, for example.

In Figure 6-13, the routing table for Router B has entries from RIP and OSPF. There are no entries for EIGRP because this is a single network directly connected to the router. You can see that the RIP updates sent out of the interfaces do not include networks from OSPF. There are no entries for EIGRP.

Figure 6-13 *Routing Updates without Using Redistribution*

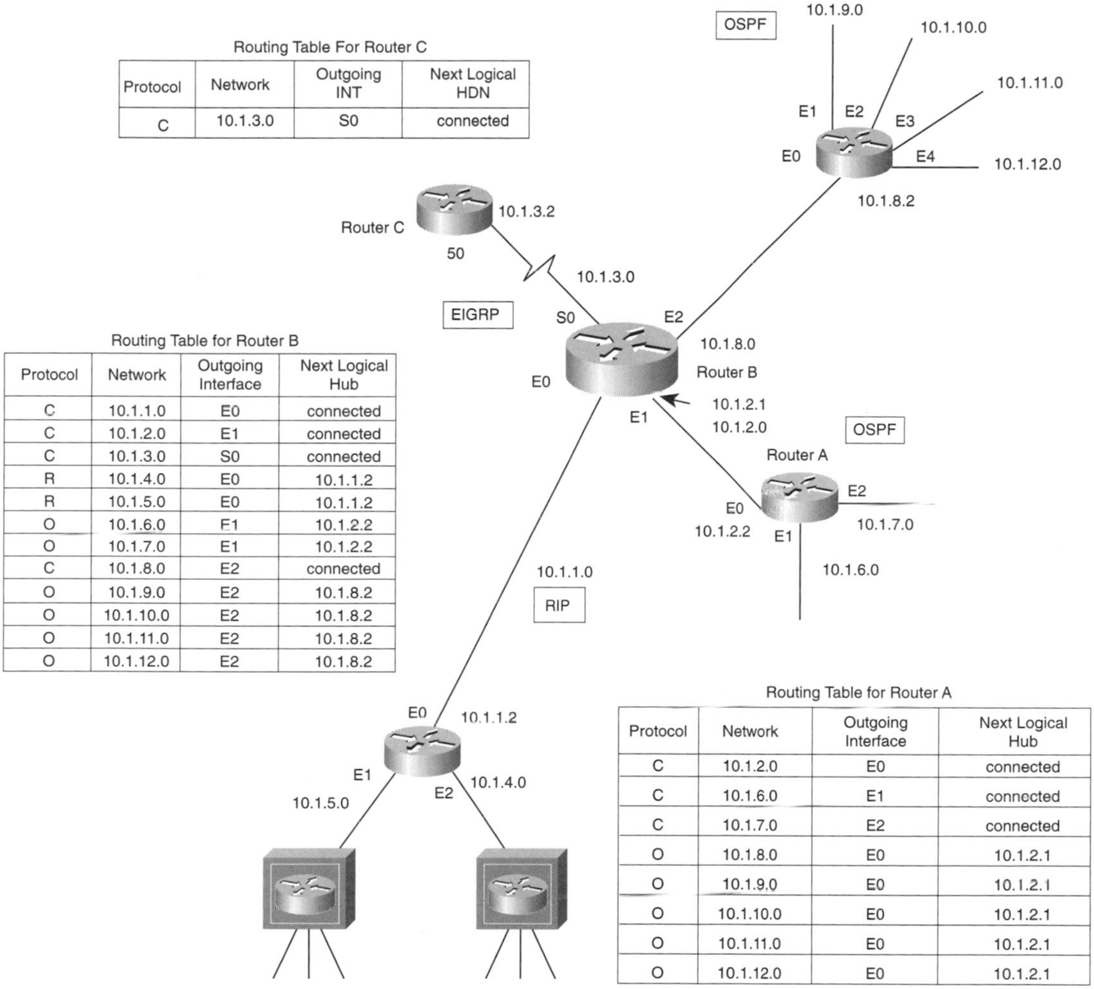

Routing Table For Router C

Protocol	Network	Outgoing INT	Next Logical HDN
C	10.1.3.0	S0	connected

Routing Table for Router B

Protocol	Network	Outgoing Interface	Next Logical Hub
C	10.1.1.0	E0	connected
C	10.1.2.0	E1	connected
C	10.1.3.0	S0	connected
R	10.1.4.0	E0	10.1.1.2
R	10.1.5.0	E0	10.1.1.2
O	10.1.6.0	F1	10.1.2.2
O	10.1.7.0	E1	10.1.2.2
C	10.1.8.0	E2	connected
O	10.1.9.0	E2	10.1.8.2
O	10.1.10.0	E2	10.1.8.2
O	10.1.11.0	E2	10.1.8.2
O	10.1.12.0	E2	10.1.8.2

Routing Table for Router A

Protocol	Network	Outgoing Interface	Next Logical Hub
C	10.1.2.0	E0	connected
C	10.1.6.0	E1	connected
C	10.1.7.0	E2	connected
O	10.1.8.0	E0	10.1.2.1
O	10.1.9.0	E0	10.1.2.1
O	10.1.10.0	E0	10.1.2.1
O	10.1.11.0	E0	10.1.2.1
O	10.1.12.0	E0	10.1.2.1

Some routing protocols will automatically exchange networks, although others require some level of configuration. Table 6-4 shows these subtleties.

Table 6-4 *Automatic Redistribution between Routing Protocols*

Routing Protocol	Redistribution Policy
Static	Requires manual redistribution into other routing protocols.
Connected	Unless included in the **network** command for the routing process, requires manual redistribution.

Continues

Table 6-4   *Automatic Redistribution between Routing Protocols (Continued)*

Routing Protocol	Redistribution Policy
RIP	Requires manual redistribution.
IGRP	Will automatically redistribute between IGRP and EIGRP if the autonomous system number is the same; otherwise, processes with different IGRP autonomous system numbers or IGRP and EIGRP processes with different autonomous system numbers require manual redistribution.
EIGRP	Will automatically redistribute between IGRP and EIGRP if the autonomous system number is the same; otherwise, it processes with different EIGRP autonomous system numbers. Or IGRP and EIGRP processes with different autonomous system numbers require manual redistribution. EIGRP for AppleTalk will automatically redistribute between EIGRP and RTMP. EIGRP for IPX will automatically redistribute between EIGRP and IPX RIP/SAP and in later versions of NLSP.
OSPF	Requires manual redistribution between different OSPF process IDs and routing protocols.

Redistribution is sometimes a necessary evil. It should be avoided if possible, however. The main reasons for multiple protocols existing within an organization are as follows:

- The organization is transitioning from one routing protocol to another because the network has grown and there is a need for a more sophisticated protocol that will scale.

- Although a vendor solution is preferred, there is a mix of different vendors within the network, so the vendor solution is used in the areas available. This is particularly true in client/server networks.

- Historically the organization was a series of small network domains that have recently been tied together to form one large enterprise network. The company may well have plans to transition to a single routing protocol in the future.

- Often after a merger or takeover, when several companies become one, it takes planning, strategy, and careful analysis to determine the best overall design for the network.

- Politically there are ideological differences between the different network administrators, which until now have not been resolved.

- In a very large environment, the various domains may have different requirements, making a single solution inefficient. A clear example is in the case of a large multinational corporation, were EIGRP is the protocol used at the access and distribution layer, but BGP is the protocol connecting the core.

If there are so many reasons why a network may have multiple routing processes for one Layer 3 protocol, why is it advisable to use one routing protocol if possible?

The reason is simple: The added complexity of having multiple routing processes can cause many problems within the network. These are typically very difficult to troubleshoot, because the symptom often appears some distance from the configuration error.

The problems experienced as a result of multiple routing processes include the following:

- The wrong or less efficient routing decision being made, referred to as the *suboptimal path*.

- A routing loop occurring, where the data traffic is sent in a circle, without ever arriving at the destination.

- The convergence time of the network increasing because of the different technologies involved. In some cases, this may result in timeouts and the temporary loss of networks.

Dealing with each of these problems in turn, the selection of the suboptimal path may occur because of the method used to make a routing decision.

Path Selection within a Routing Protocol

When a routing process does a routing table lookup for a destination network, it finds the best path in accordance with the routing decision that was made earlier. If the routing process knows of several paths to a remote network, it chooses the most efficient path based on its metric and routing algorithm and places this into the routing table. If there is more than one path with the same metric, the routing process may add up to six of these paths and distribute the traffic equally between them. This is routing protocol dependent.

Each routing protocol uses a different metric to make these decisions, as described in Chapter 3, "IP Addressing." If the different protocols now want to share information, there must be some form of translation of the metrics. This requires manual configuration in most cases—the exception being EIGRP for AppleTalk and RTMP, EIGRP for IPX, and RIP/SAP for NLSP. EIGRP and IGRP use the same metric algorithm and have no problem in automatic redistribution if the autonomous system number is the same. The configuration commands are dealt with in the section titled "Configuring Redistribution," later in this chapter.

This explains how a single routing protocol selects a single path to put into the routing table. This ensures that processing is kept to a minimum because the decisions are made before the packets arrive for routing. When the routing table is complete, the packets are just switched to the destination, based on the decisions made earlier and stored in the routing table. Figure 6-14 shows the selection of one path using the value of the metric assigned to various routes.

Figure 6-14 *The Selection of a Path Using the Metric*

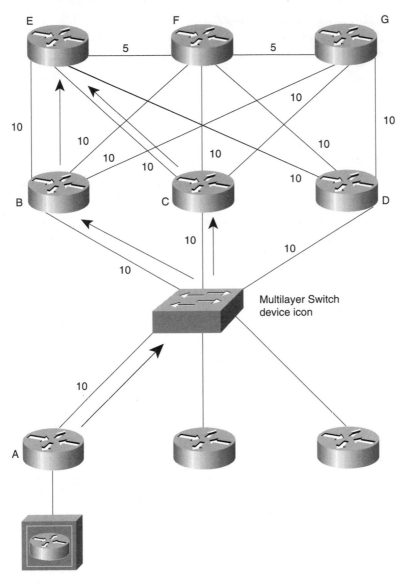

In Figure 6-14, the route from A to E will see the EIGRP path as having three equal cost routes:

A to B to E

A to C to E

A to D to E

It will load balance between these three paths. (Note that the metric shown has been simplified for the purposes of this example. EIGRP metrics will be larger numbers.)

It is slightly more complicated when there is more than one routing protocol running on the same device.

Path Selection between Routing Protocols

If there is more than one routing protocol running on the router, and they have paths to a remote destination network, the routing process must still make a decision in order to have one entry per network in the routing table. Because the metrics differ between the protocols, this method is ruled out as a solution. Instead, another method was devised to solve the problem, namely the *administrative distance*.

The administrative distance will select one path to enter into the routing table from several paths offered by multiple routing protocols.

In Figure 6-15, for example, both RIP and EIGRP have paths to the network 140.100.6.0. RIP is offering a metric of 2 hops, and EIGRP is tendering a metric of 768. Without redistribution, no conversion or choice is possible because there is no similar criteria for distinguishing the two paths. The metric is therefore ignored, and the administrative distance is used to make the selection.

In Figure 6-15, despite the speed of the Frame Relay being set at 56 kbps as opposed to the 100 Mbps of FDDI, Router D would select the Frame Relay path based on administrative distance. In this case, manually configuring the administrative distance on Router D would be advisable.

The administrative distance is a rather arbitrary set of values placed on the different sources of routing information. The defaults can be changed, but care should be taken when subverting the natural path selection and any manual configuration must be done with careful reference to the network design of the organization and its traffic flow.

The administrative distance reflects the preferred choice. The defaults are listed in the following table.

Figure 6-15   *Path Selection Using Administrative Distance*

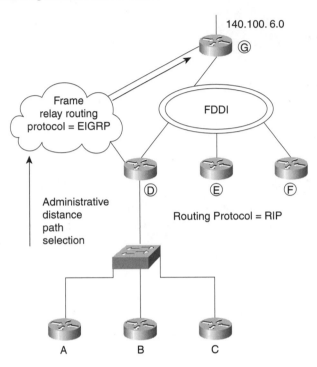

Table 6-5   *Default Administrative Distance*

Routing Source	Administrative Distance
Connected interface or static route that identifies the outgoing interface rather than the next logical hop	0
Static route	1
EIGRP summary route	5
External BGP	20
EIGRP	90
IGRP	100
OSPF	110
RIP	120
External EIGRP	170
Internal BGP	200
An unknown network	255 or infinity

The administrative distance can be manually configured. The reason for manually configuring the administrative distance for a protocol such as EIGRP is that it may have a less desirable path compared to one offered by another protocol such as RIP, which has a higher default AD.

Because the administrative distance is looked at with total disregard of the metrics, however, the Enhanced IGRP path will be selected. The other reason is that a directly connected network, which has precedence, is in fact being used as a backup link for redundancy because the directly connected network is not used on a daily basis. Backup links for redundancy are often implemented on serial connections where the network charges are based on usage. This design is called a *floating static route* and is discussed in more depth in Chapter 7, "WAN Options: ISDN, DDR, and Configuration."

Avoiding Routing Loops When Redistributing between Routing Protocols

Routing loops occur when a routing protocol is fed its own networks (for example, networks that originated within that routing process), but the routing protocol now learns from another routing protocol through redistribution. The routing protocol may now see a network that it owns as having a more favorable path even though this will send the traffic in the opposite direction, into a different routing protocol domain. This is solved by

- Changing the metric
- Changing the administrative distance
- Using default routes
- Using passive interfaces
- Using distribution lists

Redistribution and Problems with Network Convergence

To maintain consistent and coherent routing between different routing protocols, you must consider the different technologies involved. A major concern is the computation of the routing table and how long it takes the network to converge. Although Enhanced IGRP is renowned for its speed in convergence, RIP has a poorer reputation in this regard. Sharing the network information across the two technologies may cause some problems.

The first problem is just that the network takes time to converge. At some point, this will create timeouts and possibly routing loops. Adjusting the timers may solve the problems, but any routing protocol configuration must be done with a sound knowledge of the entire network and of the routers that need to be configured. Timers typically require every router in the network to be configured to the same value.

Cisco has suggested some guidelines in network design that should be considered to avoid routing loops. The principles are summarized as follows:

- Have a sound knowledge and clear documentation of the following:

  The network topology (physical and logical)

  The routing protocol domains

  The traffic flow

- Do not overlap routing protocols. It is much easier if the different protocols can be clearly delineated into separate domains, with routers acting in a similar function to area border routers in OSPF. This is often referred to as the core and edge protocols.

- If distribution is needed, ensure that it is a one-way distribution to avoid networks being fed back into the originating domain. Use default routes to facilitate the use of one-way distribution if necessary.

- If two-way distribution cannot be avoided, the mechanisms described in this section, such as the following, can help you avoid problems:

  Manually configuring the metric

  Manually configuring the administrative distance

  Using distribution access lists

The concepts of redistribution are detailed in the following examples with configuration scripts. This will reinforce the concepts and understanding of the technology.

Configuring Redistribution

The ACRC objectives mastered in this section are as follows:

ACRC Exam Objective Number	Corresponding FRS Exam Objective Number	Description
38	119	Select and configure the different ways to control route update traffic.
39	120	Configure route redistribution in a network that does not have redundant paths between dissimilar routing processes.
40	121	Configure route redistribution in a network that has redundant paths between dissimilar routing processes.

Redistribution configuration is very specific to the routing protocol itself. Before any implementation is contemplated, therefore, reference should be made to the configuration guides from Cisco.

All protocols require the following steps for redistribution:

* Configure redistribution.

* Define the default metric to be assigned to any networks that are distributed into the routing process.

The commands for redistribution are configured as subcommands to the routing process. The **redistribute** command identifies the routing protocol from which the updates are to be accepted. It identifies the source of the updates.

To configure redistribution between routing protocols, the following command syntax is used:

```
Router(config)#
redistribute protocol [process id] {level-1|level-1-2|level-2}
[metric metric-value] [metric-type type-value]
[match {internal|extrenal 1|external 2}] [tag tag-value]
[route-map map-tag] [weight weight] [subnets]
```

The command is very complex because it shows all the parameters for all the different protocols.

In accepting the new networks, the receiving process must know how to calculate the metric. It is therefore necessary to define the default metric to be assigned to the networks that are acccpted from the other routing protocol.

This metric will be assigned to all the redistributed networks from that process and will be incremented from now on as the networks are propagated throughout the new routing domain. This is sometimes referred to as a *seed metric*.

The default metric can be configured in several ways. The first is to include the metric in the **redistribute** command as shown in the preceding command syntax and as illustrated in Example 6-5.

Example 6-5   *Including the Metric in the* **redistribute** *Command*

```
Router(config)# Router EIGRP 100
Router(config-router)#redistribute rip metric 10000 100 255 1 1500
Router(config-router)#network 140.100.0.0
Router(config-router)#passive interface e1
```

This configuration shows the following:

* The use of the **redistribute** command

* The routing process from which the routes are being accepted

- The metric parameter, allowing the configuration of the EIGRP to state the new metric that the old RIP networks will use while traversing the EIGRP network.

Alternatively, it is possible to redistribute the routing protocol and then, with a separate command, to state the default metric. The advantage of this is it is a simpler configuration visually, which is helpful in troubleshooting. Also, if more than one protocol is being redistributed into the routing protocol, the default metric applies to all the protocols being redistributed.

To configure the default metric, use the following command syntax:

```
Router(config)#default-metric number
```

This is used in Example 6-6.

Example 6-6   *Configuring the Default Metric*

```
Router(config)# Router EIGRP 100
Router(config-router)#redistribute rip
Router(config-router)#redistribute ospf 10
Router(config-router)#default-metric 10000 100 255 1 1500
Router(config-router)#network 140.100.0.0
Router(config-router)#passive interface e1
```

In Example 6-6, networks from both RIP and OSPF will be assigned the same seed metric on entrance to the EIGRP process.

The default metric used is the bandwidth, delay, reliability, load, and maximum transmission unit (mtu), which reflect the compound metric used by IGRP and Enhanced IGRP. RIP and OSPF would just supply a number for hop count and cost, respectively.

To ensure that the optimal path is chosen, it is sometimes necessary to change the administrative distance, to make it less favorable. The command structure is protocol dependent in that Enhanced IGRP requires a separate command. The following command syntax is used for Enhanced IGRP:

```
Router(config)#distance eigrp internal-distance external-distance
```

To configure the administrative distance for the other IP protocols, the following command syntax is used:

```
Router(config)#distance weight [address mask] [access-list-number|name] [IP]
```

Redistribution Examples

The following examples are case studies that pull together the concepts learned in this section on redistribution. Redistribution involves complex design and configuration considerations. It is best to see the various problems and solutions illustrated in context.

This section presents three examples:

1 Route redistribution without redundant paths between different routing protocols.

2 Route redistribution with redundant paths between different routing protocols. The example also covers resolving the path selection problems that result in redistributed networks.

3 The use of a default network in a redistributed environment.

Redistribution Example 1

Refer to Figure 6-16 for this example of route redistribution without redundant paths between different routing protocols.

Figure 6-16 *Simple Redistribution between RIP and Enhanced IGRP*

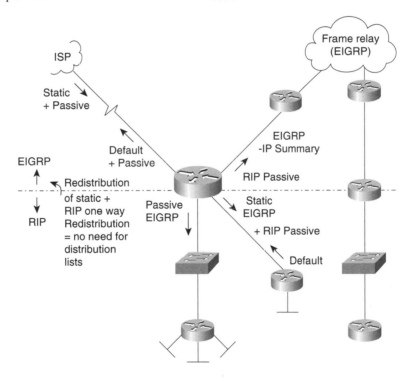

Figure 6-16 shows local offices connecting to the main office via Frame Relay. Each office has a point-to-point PVC to a router in the main office.

Enhanced IGRP is being run through the Frame Relay cloud to reduce the network overhead. The LANs are running IP for NT and there is no need for a routing protocol to be run on the LAN segments.

RIP is being run at the main office. This is to allow the corporate servers to have an understanding of the network. The servers are UNIX systems running the ROUTED daemon. ROUTED listens only to RIP updates. Redistribution allows the servers to know about the Enhanced IGRP networks.

If the Enhanced IGRP networks need to know about each other, the RIP networks would need to be redistributed into the Enhanced IGRP environment. This is unlikely because the servers are centrally held at the main office and there will be little lateral traffic flow. The configuration shown in Figure 6-16 is simple because there are no redundant links. The Frame Relay cloud uses point-to-point PVCs. In the future the company may want to add redundancy by meshing the Frame Relay cloud and consolidating the three core routers into one large router. At present the company has a simple and low-cost solution using existing equipment.

Redistribution Example 2

Refer to Figure 6-17 for this example, which covers route redistribution with redundant paths between different routing protocols and resolving path selection problems that result in redistributed networks.

Figure 6-17 *Choosing the Optimal Path, Through Administrative Distance and Distribution Lists When Redistribution Is Using Redundant Paths*

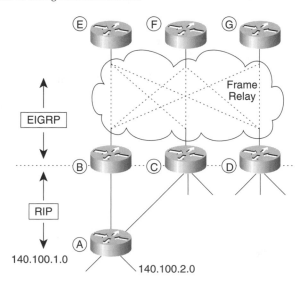

In Figure 6-17, Router A is connected to networks 140.100.1.0 and 140.100.2.0 that are advertised via RIP to Routers C and B.

The routing table of Router A will show the information presented in Table 6-6.

Table 6-6   *Router A Routing Table Information*

Routing Protocol	Network/Subnet	Next Logical Hop	Metric
Connected	140.100.1.0/24	Connected E0	0
Connected	140.100.2.0/24	Connected E1	0
Connected	140.100.3.0/24	Connected E2	0
RIP	10.10.10.8/30	140.100.3.2	1 HOP
RIP	10.10.10.12/30	140.100.3.2	1 HOP
RIP	10.10.10.16/30	140.100.3.2	1 HOP
RIP	10.10.10.20/30	140.100.3.2	1 HOP
RIP	10.10.10.24/30	140.100.3.2	1 HOP
RIP	10.10.10.28/30	140.100.3.2	1 HOP
RIP	10.10.10.32/30	140.100.3.2	1 HOP
RIP	193.144.6.0/24	140.100.3.2	1 HOP
RIP	193.144.7.0/24	140.100.3.2	1 HOP
RIP	193.144.8.0/24	140.100.3.2	1 HOP

The routing table of Router B will show the information presented in Table 6-7.

Table 6-7   *Router B Routing Table Information*

Routing Protocol	Network/Subnet	Next Logical Hop	Metric
RIP	140.100.1.0/24	140.100.3.1	0
RIP	140.100.2.0/24	140.100.3.1	0
Connected	140.100.3.0/24	Connected E0	0
Connected	10.10.10.8/30	Connected S0	1 HOP
Connected	10.10.10.12/30	Connected S0	1 HOP
Connected	10.10.10.16/30	Connected S0	1 HOP
EIGRP	10.10.10.20/30	10.10.10.9	1 HOP
EIGRP	10.10.10.24/30	10.10.10.9	1 HOP
EIGRP	10.10.10.28/30	10.10.10.13	1 HOP
EIGRP	10.10.10.32/30	10.10.10.13	1 HOP

Continues

Table 6-7 *Router B Routing Table Information (Continued)*

Routing Protocol	Network/Subnet	Next Logical Hop	Metric
EIGRP	193.144.6.0/24	10.10.10.9	1 HOP
EIGRP	193.144.7.0/24	10.10.10.13	1 HOP
EIGRP	193.144.8.0/24	10.10.10.17	1 HOP

The routing table sees all the paths as unique and, therefore, it is clear which paths are accessible through RIP or IGRP. Even after redistribution, the routing table will not change; the confusion occurs after the propagation of the IGRP updates through the network.

The IGRP updates will be sent to all the routers in the domain and Routers E, F, and G will have no confusion. Depending on the timing of the updates and convergence, however, Router C may well become confused. The Routers E, F, and G will have sent information on how to get to the networks 140.100.1.0 and 140.100.2.0. Router C will also receive information from Router A. Sending the data traffic to A is obviously the optimum path, however; because IGRP has a significantly better administrative distance, the IGRP route will be placed in the routing table as having the best path. On the assumption that the Frame Relay PCVs all have the same bandwidth, the routing table will see all three paths and distribute the traffic evenly between them.

Example 6-7 shows how to configure Routers B, C, and D to change the administrative distance to favor RIP for the LANs within its domain. The networks 140.100.1.0 and 140.100.2.0 are given an administrative distance of 200 in accordance with the access list. This ensures that the RIP path will be favored if it is available.

Example 6-7 *Changing the Administrative Distance to Favor RIP*

```
Router(config)# router rip
Router(config-router)# network 140.100.0.0
Router(config-router)#passive interface S0.1
Router(config-router)#redistribute igrp 100 metric 3
Router(config)#router igrp 100
Router(config-router)#network 140.100.0.0
Router(config-router)#passive interface E0
Router(config-router)#redistribute rip
Router(config-router)#default-metric 10000 100 255 1 1500
Router(config-router)#distance 200 0.0.0.0 255.255.255.255 3
Router(config-router)#access-list 3 permit 140.100.1.0
Router(config-router)#access-list 3 permit 140.100.2.0
```

The **distance** command sets the administrative distance for the IGRP 100 process. It changes the distance from 100 to 200, which now makes the routes RIP offers more favorable because RIP has an administrative distance of 120. The use of 0.0.0.0 with a wildcard mask of 255.255.255.255 is as a placeholder indicating that, although the command allows for a network to be specified so that the administrative distance can be applied selectively to that network, in this configuration no network has been selected. The command has been applied to all networks. You do want the administrative distance to be altered on two networks, however. This granularity cannot be stated in the **distance** command; therefore, an access list is used. In the example, the number *3* at the end of the command line points to the access list that carries that number as an identifier. The access list, by permitting networks 140.100.1.0 and 140.100.2.0, is identifying the networks to which the **distance** command is to be applied.

Redistribution Example 3

The use of the default network simplifies the configuration of a redistributed network by allowing the redistribution to be one way. This significantly reduces the possibility of feedback of networks into the originating domain. The configuration for this example is placed within Figure 6-18 because the configuration of more than one router is shown.

Figure 6-18   *The Use of a Default Network in a Redistributed Network to Resolve Problems with Path Selection*

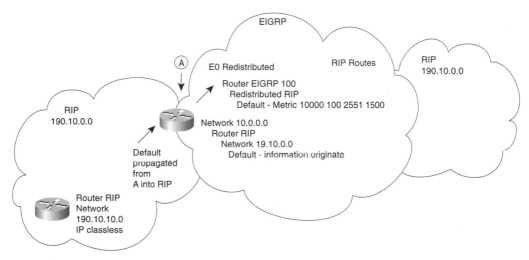

In this design, each router and workstation within the RIP domain sees its own internal networks, but all other networks are accessed via the default route.

The router that straddles both the Enhanced IGRP and RIP domain acts as an ABR in OSPF and is where the default route is configured. This is propagated throughout the RIP domain. The internal RIP-only routers must be configured to accept a default route with a destination network that they are not directly connected to; this is achieved with the **ip classless** command.

The redistribution on Router A can now be one way. Enhanced IGRP needs to know all the networks in the RIP domain; but RIP, when configured with a default route, needs no understanding of the outside world. The RIP domain works in a similar fashion to a stub network in OSPF.

Verifying, Maintaining, and Troubleshooting the Redistribution Implementation

The ACRC objective mastered in this section is as follows:

ACRC Exam Objective Number	Corresponding FRS Exam Objective Number	Description
42	123	Verify route redistribution.

The main key to maintaining and troubleshooting the redistribution within your network is to have a clear understanding of the network topology from both a physical and logical perspective. The traffic flows—the peaks and lows in the traffic volume—are also important in truly understanding the connectivity issues within the network. From this vantage point, it is possible to interpret the output presented by the various tools available.

Most of the appropriate commands in tracking redistribution problems are ones that have been examined earlier. They include the following:

- **show ip protocol**
- **show ip route**
- **show ip route** *routing protocol*
- **show ip eigrp neighbors**
- **show ip ospf database**

In addition to these commands, the use of the utilities such as **trace** and **extended ping** is also very useful.

Using trace **and** extended ping   I do not use **trace** to determine the path taken, but rather to identify where there is a problem in the network. Where the **trace** utility fails indicates a good starting point for troubleshooting a complex network.

trace is not very reliable in reflecting the routing path because path changes are not shown by **trace**. The **extended ping** command, however, is very useful because it announces every interface that it traverses. The limitation is the maximum hops it can report, which is nine.

Communicating to the Outside World—Border Gateway Protocol (BGP)

The ACRC objectives mastered in this section are as follows:

ACRC Exam Objective Number	Corresponding FRS Exam Objective Number	Description
43	124	Describe when to use BGP to connect to an ISP.
44	125	Describe methods to connect to an ISP using static and default routes, and BGP.

The ACRC course deals with connectivity to the Internet via a service provider. One of the methods used to make this connection is the exterior routing protocol BGP4.

The ACRC exam, recognizing that few administrators will be using BGP to communicate with the Internet agent, or service provider, probably only covers a conceptual overview of BGP, placing the emphasis on the common practice of connecting to the service provider via a default route.

What Is BGP?

BGP4 is an extremely complex protocol used within the Internet and multinational organizations. Its main purpose is to connect very large networks together. These networks are mainly autonomous systems. Large companies may use BGP4 as the glue between the countries; for example, a government may use it as the glue between the divisions of the administration and the military between the Army, the Navy, and the Air Force.

The routing update is the characteristic that makes it appropriate in these environments. The protocol is not interested in communicating a full knowledge of every subnet within the organization. It takes summarization to the extreme, communicating only that which is defined as necessary. The little information that it carries is extremely important and, therefore, great efforts are made to ensure the reliability of the transport carrying the updates and that the databases are synchronized. This is the pinnacle of hierarchical routing design.

The other distinctive characteristic of BGP is the concept of *policy routing*. Unlike interior routing protocols that just communicate all that they know about the networks within the routing domain, BGP can be configured to advocate one path above another in a more sophisticated and controlled manner than can the metric afforded to the interior routing protocols.

Given its complexity and role in internetworking, BGP4 is very seldom used by private organizations. Despite the rush to connect to the expanding Internet resources, service providers have emerged to set up and manage the connection. This is advantageous to everyone. For a small fee, the organization or individual has a complex connection created and maintained; the Internet's burden is also eased because it is dealing with large corporations and organizations rather than the millions of individual users.

When to Use BGP4

Although the alternatives to BGP4 are preferred in simple connections to the Internet, on some occasions it is advantageous to use the power of this complex protocol. The reasons to use BGP4 include the following:

- Your organization is connecting to multiple ISPs and actively using those links. Many organizations use this for redundancy purposes, justifying the additional cost by using all the links and reducing bottlenecks and congestion. In this case, policy routing decisions may need to be made on a link-by-link basis.

- The routing policy of the ISP and your company differ. The cost of the link depends on usage; time of day and other factors may need to be programmed into the BGP configuration to make the best use of the connection.

- The traffic in your organization needs to be distinguished from that of the ISP. They cannot logically appear as one autonomous system.

When *Not* to Use BGP4

It is a truism that a simple network is a network that is easier to manage and maintain, which is the main reason to avoid BGP4 configuration in the network. Therefore, if your network has the following characteristics, use other methods such as static and default routing to achieve connectivity to the ISP network:

- The ISP and your organization have the same routing policy.

- Although your company has multiple links to the ISP, these links are redundant and there are no future plans to activate more than one link to the Internet.

Overview of the BGP Operation

BGP is connection oriented. When a neighbor is seen, a TCP session is established and maintained. The session is maintained by BGP probes or keepalives, a 19-byte header that is sent out periodically to sustain the link.

Having established the session, the routing tables are exchanged and synchronized. The routers will now only send incremental updates when changes occur. The update refers to a single path and the networks that may be reached via that path. Having corrected the routing table, the BGP process will propagate the change to all neighbors, with a few exceptions based on an algorithm to ensure a loop-free network.

BGP4 comes in two flavors: internal and external BGP. The difference depends on the function of the routing protocol.

Internal BGP is used within an autonomous system. It conveys information to all BGP routers within the domain and ensures they have a consistent understanding of the networks available. Internal BGP is used with an ISP or large organization to coordinate the knowledge of that autonomous system. The routers are not required to be physical neighbors on the same medium, and often sit on the edges of the network. Another routing protocol, an interior routing protocol such as OSPF, is used to route the BGP packets to their remote locations. The integration of these different routing protocols can be challenging.

Exterior BGP complies with the common perception of an exterior routing protocol; it sends routing information between differing autonomous systems. Figure 6-19 shows the application of interior and exterior BGP.

Figure 6-19   *Interior and Exterior BGP*

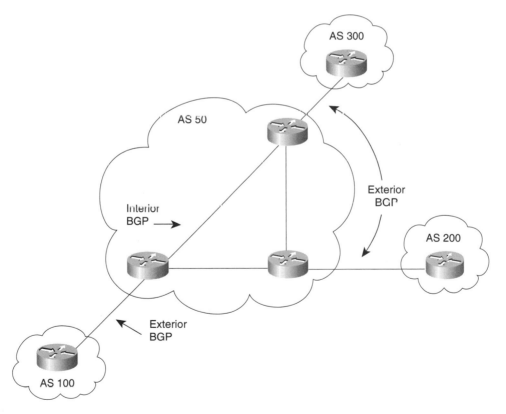

Exterior BGP4 Configuration Commands to Connect to an ISP

To connect to an ISP, it is necessary to configure the following:

- The start of the routing process

- The networks to be advertised

- The BGP neighbor that the routing process will be synchronizing routing tables with, over a TCP session

The command to configure the routing process is the same command as seen for the interior routing protocols. The syntax is as follows:

```
Router(config)# router bgp autonomous system number
```

To define the network that is to be advertised for this autonomous system, the following command is used (each network requires a separate command):

```
Router(config-router)# network network-number network-mask
```

In interior BGP, the remote autonomous system number that is defined for the BGP peer will be the same; in exterior BGP, these numbers will differ. The syntax is as follows:

```
Router(config-router)# neighbor ip-address remote-as autonomous system number
```

Because it may be necessary to redistribute BGP into the Interior Gateway Protocol (IGP), care must be taken to avoid routing loops and not to overwhelm the routing tables. The administrative distance of BGP helps prevent this problem (see Figure 6-20).

Figure 6-20 *Administrative Distance and BGP*

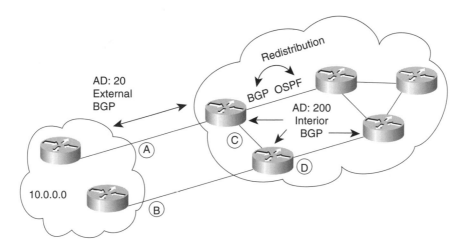

In Figure 6-20, because BGP (interior) has an administrative distance of 200, it is effectively the last choice. Router C will always choose the direct path to 10.0.0.0 through Router A because it has an administrative distance of 20. The route through D and B to find network 10.0.0.0 will have either an administrative distance of 110 or 200, depending on the configuration.

Managing and Verifying the BGP Configuration

After configuration changes in BGP, it is often necessary to reestablish the TCP session. This can be forced with the following command:

```
Router#clear ip bgp {*|address}
```

NOTE	This command is an executive command executed at the privileged level. It is not a configuration command.

The **show** commands for BGP are comprehensive and give clear information about the BGP sessions and routing options. These informative commands and their functions are as follows:

- **show ip bgp**—Displays the BGP routing table.

- **show ip bgp paths**—Displays the topology table.

- **show ip bgp summary**—Displays information about the TCP sessions.

Alternative Methods of Connecting to an ISP

If BGP is unnecessary in your network, consider the other possibilities, including the following:

- A default route into the ISP and a static route from the ISP into the organization.

- A routing protocol into the ISP, making the ISP part of your autonomous system. The ISP will be using redistribution within its domain, and it is advisable for the organization to use some form of security, either in the form of access lists or a firewall.

Typically the ISP will give you a written sheet explaining the required configuration or they will request access to your autonomous system boundary router to configure it themselves. Either way, it is useful to be cognizant of the procedure.

There are too many variations to be considered in the configuration of an interior routing protocol to detail in this chapter. The main principles are dealt with in the section on redistribution earlier in this chapter.

The use of the default and static routes is worth pondering. It is a solution that has been used for years in connecting remote satellite networks, particularly those connected via a dialup link.

The solution is simple: The smaller network defines a default route, which is propagated throughout the domain. The default route points to the exit point of the network into the ISP. The larger network, in this case the ISP, configures static routes to the organization. These routes are summarized in the master routing table to the Internet or NIC address of the IP address. The static routes must also be propagated throughout the ISP's network so that they can eventually be advertised into the Internet, connecting the smaller organization into the global internetwork. Figure 6-21 illustrates the use of default and static routes and how they would be propagated.

Figure 6-21 *Default and Static Route Configuration into the Internet*

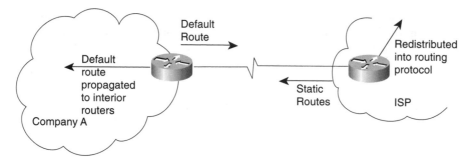

The command syntax to configure a static route is as follows:

```
Router(config)# ip route prefix mask {interface|ip-address} [distance]
```

It is possible to either specify the outgoing interface or the IP address of the next logical hop. If the outgoing interface is specified, the link is treated as if it is directly connected. The default administrative distance is 0, that of a directly connected link. If the IP address is configured, it is given the administrative distance of 1.

In either case, the administrative distance will ensure that this path will be chosen above all others. If this static route is a redundant link into the ISP and not to be used unless there is no alternative, it may be necessary to change the administrative distance.

To propagate the static routes throughout the domain, it is necessary to redistribute them in the appropriate routing protocol.

Conclusion

This chapter dealt with Enhanced IGRP, redistribution, and BGP4. It showed the complexity of the design of large networks—particularly because they seldom start as large entities; instead, they evolve. As they evolve, the needs and requirements of the different divisions change and the organizational structure often mutates or reforms. This leads to different technological requirements that have to sustain the existing structure while allowing for the development of the new environment at the same time.

The design and configuration solutions are vast. This chapter has merely introduced some of the possible solutions and pointed out the danger areas to avoid. For a true implementation on a live network, it cannot be stressed enough how important the analysis and design of the network is for an effective solution.

Foundation Summary

Tables 6-8 through 6-11 summarize the information you will need to be familiar with to master the objectives of this chapter. Table 6-8 is a summary of basic Enhanced IGRP terminology.

Table 6-8   *Enhanced IGRP Terminology[1]*

Term	Definition
Successor	A neighbor that has been selected as the next hop for a destination based on the feasibility condition.
Feasible successor (FS)	A neighbor that has satisfied the feasibility condition and has a path to the destination.
Feasibility condition (FC)	A condition that is met when the lowest of all the neighbors' costs plus the link cost to that neighbor is found, and the neighbor's advertised cost is less than the current successor's cost.
Active state	A router's state for a destination when it has no other FS available. The router is forced to compute a route to the destination.
Passive state	A router's state after losing its successor when it has an FS to the destination available in its topology table.
Hello/ACK	Periodic Hello packets are exchanged between Enhanced IGRP neighbors. ACKs are sent to acknowledge that packets were reliably received.
Update	Sent in the following circumstances: When a neighbor first comes up When a router transitions from active to passive for a destination When there is a metric change for a certain destination
Query	Sent to all neighbors when a router goes into an active state for a destination, specifically if the neighbor has an FS that the originating router can use. Unless it receives replies back from all its neighbors, the route will remain in active state for that network and not start the computation for a new successor.
Replies	Sent by every Enhanced IGRP neighbor that receives a query. If the neighbor has no information, the neighbor will query its own neighbors.
Neighbor table	This is maintained with a holdtimer ($3 \times$ the Hello timer) for each of its neighbors, based on the Hellos received from adjacent Enhanced IGRP routers (neighbors).
Topology table	Sorts routing information that neighbors exchange after the first Hello exchange. DUAL acts on the topology table to determine successors and feasible successors.
DUAL	Diffusing Update Algorithm is the convergence calculation performed on the topology table to produce a loop-free routing table.

1. This table was modified from a similar table located on the Cisco Web site (www.cisco.com).

Table 6-9 summarizes the default administrative distances configured for each IP routing protocol.

Table 6-9   *Default Values for Administrative Distance*

Routing Source	Administrative Distance
Connected interface or static route that identifies the outgoing interface rather than the next logical hop	0
Static route	1
EIGRP summary route	5
External BGP	20
EIGRP	90
IGRP	100
OSPF	110
RIP	120
External EIGRP	170
Internal BGP	200
An unknown network	255 or infinity

Table 6-10 summarizes the main concepts and terms in BGP4.

Table 6-10   *BGP4 Terminology*

Term	Definition
Autonomous system (AS)	This term defines the organizational boundary. Within the terminology of the routing protocols, it defines all the routers within an administrative domain, where each router has full knowledge of the subnets within the domain. This becomes confused with the introduction of summarization within an autonomous system. If connecting directly to the Internet using BGP, the autonomous system number must be unique and obtained from the Internet addressing committees.
External BGP	When BGP is used to connect different autonomous systems.
Internal BGP	When BGP is used to connect routers resident in the same autonomous system.
IGP	Interior Gateway Protocol. In the past, the term *gateway* was used to define a router. This is a routing protocol that runs within an autonomous system.
EGP	Exterior Gateway Protocol. This protocol runs between autonomous systems. There is a protocol with this name, which was the precursor to BGP.

Table 6-11 summarizes the commands covered in this chapter.

Table 6-11 *Summary of Commands*

Command	Function
router eigrp *autonomous system number*	Starts the Enhanced IGRP process on the router with the specified autonomous system number.
network *network number*	The networks to be advertised.
no auto-summary	Given a hierarchical addressing design, this command disables the automatic summarization to the Internet NIC network address.
ip summary address eigrp *autonomous system number address mask*	Having disabled the automatic summarization, you can manually summarize the networks.
bandwidth *speed of line*	Issued at the interface level and is a logical construct to manually determine the real bandwidth. Used mainly on serial lines. Bandwidth will influence some routing decisions and dial-on-demand implementations.
ip bandwidth-percent eigrp autonomous-system-number [percent]	Enhanced IGRP by default will only take up to 50% of bandwidth; you can change the percentage with this command.
ipx router eigrp *autonomous system number*	Configures Enhanced IGRP for IPX.
ipx sap-incremental eigrp *autonomous system number*	This states to Enhanced IGRP that incremental updates should be used. By default, the process will send periodic updates out of LAN interfaces and incremental updates through the WAN interfaces. If an FDDI ring were used as a backbone, it would be advantageous to use incremental updates if all the devices on the ring were Cisco systems.
show ip eigrp neighbors	To display information drawn from the neighbor table.
show ip eigrp topology	To display information drawn from the topology table.
show ip eigrp traffic	Shows the Enhanced IGRP traffic passing through the router.
show ipx route	Shows the IPX routing table.

Table 6-11   *Summary of Commands (Continued)*

Command	Function
redistribute *protocol* [*process-id\AS number*] {**level 1\level 1-2\level 2**} [**metric** *metric value*} [**metric-type** *type-value*] [**match**{**internal\external 1\external 2**} [**tag** *tag-value*] [**route-map** *map-tag*] [**weight** *weight*] [**subnets**]	This command has many parameters for all the different routing protocols and the subtleties of redistributing between them.
distance eigrp *internal-distance external-distance*	Manually configures the administrative distance for EIGRP configuration only.
distance *weight [address mask] [access-list-number\name]* [**IP**]	Manually configures the administrative distance and allows for the networks to be identified specifically.
router bgp *autonomous system number*	Starts the BGP routing process.
network *network-number network-mask*	Identifies the networks to be advertised by the process.
neighbor *ip-address* **remote-as** *autonomous system number*	Identifies the neighbor with whom the router is synchronizing its routing table.
clear ip bgp {**\address*}	Destroys the session between the neighbors and reestablishes it and the new configuration that has taken place.
show ip bgp	Shows the BGP connections.

Q&A

The following questions test your understanding of the topics covered in this chapter. The answers appear in Appendix A, "Answers to Quizzes and Q&As," on page 269. If you get an answer wrong, review the answer and ensure that you understand the reason for your mistake. If you are confused by the answer, refer back to the text in the chapter to review the concepts.

1 When does Enhanced IGRP recalculate the topology table?

_____

_____

_____

2 By default Enhanced IGRP summarizes at which boundary?

_____

_____

_____

3 The neighbor table is responsible for keeping track of which timers?

_____

_____

_____

4 When does Enhanced IGRP place a network in active mode?

_____

_____

_____

5 What is the difference between an update and a query?

_____

_____

_____

6 In what instances will Enhanced IGRP automatically redistribute?

_____

_____

_____

7 What problems may be experienced when redistribution is configured?

_____

_____

_____

8 What is the metric used for in a routing protocol?

_____

_____

_____

9 What is the purpose of the administrative distance?

_____

_____

_____

10 Why is it necessary to configure a default metric when redistributing between routing protocols?

_____

_____

_____

11 In BGP4, what is the purpose of the **network** command?

_____

_____

_____

12 When would you use external BGP as opposed to internal BGP?

_____

_____

_____

13 What is an alternative to using BGP as the method of connection to the ISP?

_____

_____

_____

Scenarios

The following case studies and questions are designed to draw together the content of the chapter and exercise your understanding of the concepts. There is not necessarily a right answer. The thought process and practice in manipulating the concepts is the goal of this section.

The answers to the scenario questions are found at the end of this chapter.

Scenario 6-1

The last network administrator of your company left abruptly. You were recently hired in to the position and cannot find any documentation on the network. Using a network-management tool, you now have a topology map of the network.

Refer to Figure 6-22 and answer the questions that follow.

1   Offer some reasons why the routing protocol Enhanced IGRP has recently been implemented in the network and the reasons for its deployment in that particular area of the network.

2   The ISP has decided that the company should set a default route into their domain. Write out the commands that would configure the default route.

3   Is the router connecting to the ISP the only router that needs configuration? If this is the case, explain reasons for your decision. If other routers need configuration, write out the commands required and explain why they are needed and where they would be applied.

4   The ISP router connecting into the company network will need static route(s) configured. Write out the commands to configure the router.

5   Will these routes need to be redistributed into the ISP domain? If the answer is yes, explain the reason for your decision and then write out the configuration commands. If the answer is no, explain the reasons for your decision.

6   Are filters required in this design? If so, state why and describe the type of filters required and how and where they would be applied.

7   It has been suggested that Enhanced IGRP should be configured using summarization. If this plan were to be implemented, on which routers would it be configured and why?

Figure 6-22   *Diagram of Network for Scenario 6-1*

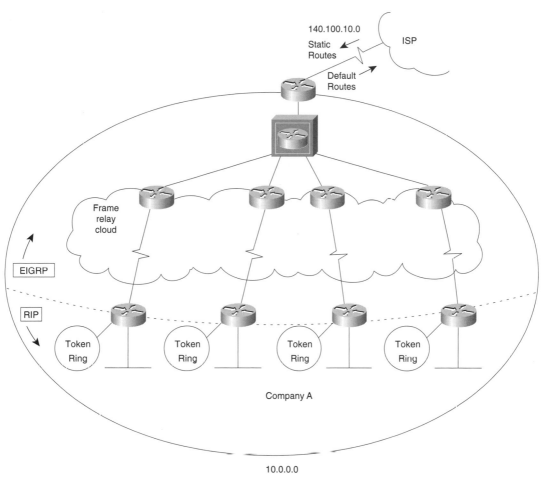

Scenario 6-2

The company has recently merged with another company that has OSPF as its routing protocol. It has been determined that this is going to be the company standard.

  1 Router A was chosen as the designated router on the LAN in the OSPF domain. Explain why this design choice was made and give the command that would ensure its selection as the designated router.

  2 Redistribution is occurring between IGRP and OSPF on Router A; state the configuration commands that would be used for both IGRP and OSPF.

3 Since the new headquarters of the merged company is in the OSPF domain, as is the connection to the Internet, it has been decided that Router A will have a default route configured to point to the OSPF domain from the IGRP domain. It will be necessary to configure the **ip classless** command for the IGRP domain. Explain why the **ip classless** command is needed and what it achieves.

4 Explain the use of the **subnet** command in OSPF and why it is required in redistribution.

5 Explain why it may be necessary to filter when redistributing and what it achieves in this network.

Scenario 6-3

Your company has decided to change its routing protocol from RIP to Enhanced IGRP. It is currently running both IPX and IP. With reference to Figure 6-23, devise a design for the new network.

Figure 6-23 *Diagram of Network for Scenario 6-3*

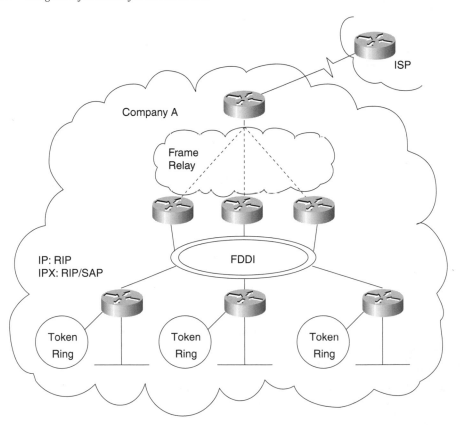

Ensure that you include the following:

1 Create a transition plan, showing how the final design will be implemented.

2 If the transition plan requires redistribution, indicate these points on the diagram and provide the configuration commands.

3 The company has also decided to connect to the Internet using Enhanced IGRP, which the ISP providing the Internet connectivity has agreed upon. Is any redistribution required? Give reasons for your answers.

4 Explain the neighbors that you see on the LAN segment and the path selection on Router B.

5 Create a diagram that shows the final network design, with **configuration** commands for Enhanced IGRP.

6 Write out the **configuration** commands for Router B.

Scenario Answers

The answers provided in this section are not necessarily the only possible answers to the questions. The questions are designed to test your knowledge and to give practical exercise in certain key areas. This section is intended to test and exercise skills and concepts detailed in the body of this chapter.

If your answer is different, ask yourself whether it follows the tenets explained in the answers provided. Your answer is correct not if it matches the solution provided in the book, but rather if it has included the principles of design laid out in the chapter.

In this way, the testing provided in these scenarios is deeper: It examines not only your knowledge, but also your understanding and ability to apply that knowledge to problems.

If you do not get the correct answer, refer back to the text and review the subject tested. Be certain to also review your notes on the question to ensure that you understand the principles of the subject.

Scenario 6-1 Answers

1   Enhanced IGRP is being run across the Frame Relay WAN in areas where there are no client or server workstations. The network routers are all Cisco devices, which understand Enhanced IGRP.

Using Enhanced IGRP is far more efficient on a WAN because incremental updates can be sent across the limited bandwidth. In particular, if either AppleTalk or IPX are running at the access level, the routing updates can be sent in Enhanced IGRP, which gives far more control and flexibility because it is a new, more sophisticated, proprietary routing protocol.

2   The configuration commands to establish a default route from the company's network to the ISP domain are as follows:

```
Router(config)# router eigrp 100
Router(config-router)# network 10.0.0.0
Router(config-router)# network 140.100.10.0
Router(config)# ip default network 140.100.0.0
```

The **network** command is also required for EIGRP to propagate the network in the updates.

3   The router connecting to the ISP is the only router that needs to be configured. The default route will be propagated to all the other EIGRP routers automatically. Although default routes redistributed into a RIP environment require that the **ip classless** command be configured, this is for routers that are downstream from the router that is dealing with the redistribution. Because the routers at the redistribution points will have routes redistributed into them by Enhanced IGRP, they will have no problem in the lookup.

4 The **configuration** commands to establish static routes from the ISP domain into the company's network are as follows:

```
Router(config)# ip route 140.100.0.0 255.255.0.0    140.100.60.3
Router(config)# ip route 200.10.20.0 255.255.255.0 140.100.60.3
Router(config)# ip route 199.56.10.0 255.255.255.0 140.100.60.3
Router(config)# ip route 222.22.10.0 255.255.255.0 140.100.60.3
```

5 The **static** commands will need to be redistributed into the ISP domain. Static routes are not redistributed automatically. Static routes configured with the outgoing interface as opposed to the next hop address are considered by the router to be directly connected.

The commands for redistribution of static routes are as follows:

```
Router(config)# Router EIGRP 100
Router(config)# redistribute static
Router(config)# default-metric 10000 100 255 1 1500
```

6 Because there are no redundant paths in the redistribution between protocols, no filters are required in the configuration of the routers because there will be no feedback between the protocols.

Because there is no routing protocol running between the company and the ISP, there is no requirement for filters here either. If any filters were required, they would be for internal security and traffic control and would be typically configured on the access routers entering the Frame Relay cloud. There could also be some distribution lists at the distribution layer to limit connectivity between the different regions.

7 Summarization would be configured at the access level to limit the number of updates that need to traverse the WAN.

Scenario 6-2 Answers

Figure 6-24 illustrates the answer for Scenario 6-2.

1 The router was selected by the administrator to be the designated router because it is an autonomous system boundary router (ASBR). This makes it the most sensible choice. All traffic must pass through it to reach another domain. It is hopefully also a more powerful router because it has to calculate redistribution and filtering and handle the role of designated router. The command to ensure that this router is chosen as the designated router is

```
router ospf 100
interface e0
ip ospf priority 100
```

Figure 6-24 *Answer Diagram for Scenario 6-2*

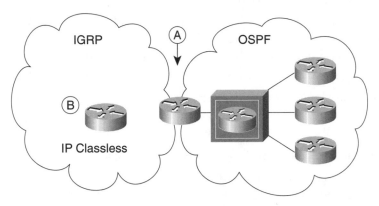

The designated router will have been selected manually by using this priority command or by configuring the router with the highest OSPF ID. This is achieved by allocating a loopback address.

2 The configuration commands for redistributing OSPF into IGRP and IGRP back into OSPF follow:

```
router igrp 100
passive int e0
network 201.100.10.0
redistribute ospf 100 metric 10000 100 255 1 1500

router ospf 100
passive interface e1
network 144.250.0.0 0.0.255.255 area 0
redistribute igrp 100 metric 30 metric-type 1 subnets
```

The use of the passive interface is unnecessary because the routing processes do not use the same Internet number. These commands will allow full connectivity between the two domains.

3 The **ip classless** command is required in a classful routing protocol that is doing a lookup in a routing table that does not contain the route, because redistribution has not propagated the route to this router. So, when a default route is redistributed into a classful routing domain, the downstream routers cannot see the network that they should forward to. This command solves that problem.

4 The **subnet** command is used to propagate subnetworks into the OSPF domain as opposed to propagating the larger classful address obtained from the InterNIC.

5 The filter prevents feedback from OSPF into IGRP and vice versa. This avoids routing loops.

Scenario 6-3 Answers

1 Figure 6-25 shows the answer to this question.

Figure 6-25   *Answer Diagram for Scenario 6-3, Question 1*

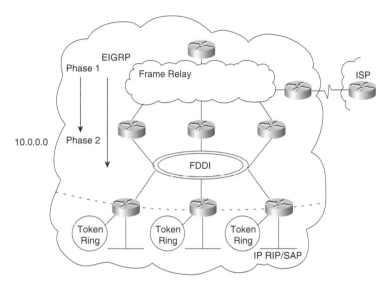

In Figure 6-25, the transition would start at the core and move down to the distribution layer routers. The first move would be to place EIGRP in the Frame Relay cloud to alleviate the network overhead. After this is operational, the second phase would be to implement EIGRP in the FDDI ring because there are no end stations on the ring that require IPX RIP/SAP.

2 The **configuration** commands that provide for the redistribution between the different routing protocols are as follows:

```
Router(config)# router rip
Router(config-router)#network  10.0.0.0
Router(config-router)#passive int E0
Router(config-router)#redistribute eigrp 100
Router(config-router)# default-metric  3
Router(config)# router eigrp 100
Router(config-router)#network  10.0.0.0
Router(config-router)#passive int  E1
Router(config-router)#passive int  Token 0
Router(config-router)#redistribute rip
Router(config-router)# default-metric 10000 100 255 1 1500
```

3 If the ISP is in the same autonomous system as the company, no redistribution is required between the company and the ISP. Within the ISP domain, however, it is likely that the router connecting to the company in question is the only router that is a part of the autonomous system of the company. This is for security reasons. Therefore, there will probably be some form of redistribution required in the ISP domain.

4 The neighbors that are seen on the LAN segment are all the routers that share the physical medium. Router B chose the path as a successor because it provided the shortest path to the networks stated.

5 Figure 6-26 shows the answer.

Figure 6-26   *Answer Diagram to Scenario 6-3, Question 5*

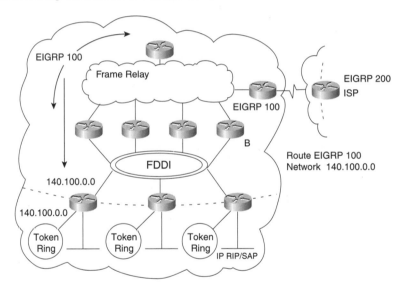

In Figure 6-26, **ip summary-address** may be configured where appropriate at the distribution layer (the routers entering the Frame Relay cloud).

6 The configuration commands for Router B are as follows:

```
Router(config)#router eigrp 100
Router(config-router)#network 140.100.0.0
Router(config-router)#no auto-summary
Router(config-router)#ip summary-address 140.100.64.0 255.255.240.0
```

The objectives for the ACRC exam for CCNP or CCDP certification are taken from the Cisco Web site at http://www.cisco.com/training under the heading of "Cisco Career Certifications and Training." The following table shows the ACRC exam objectives covered in this chapter and also provides the Foundation Routing and Switching exam objective number.

ACRC Exam Objective Number	Corresponding FRS Exam Objective Number	Description
17	98	Describe weighted fair queuing operation.
18	99	Configure priority.
19	100	Configure custom queuing.
20	101	Verify queuing operation.
45	126	Compare the differences between WAN connection types: dedicated, asynchronous dial-in, dial-on-demand, and packet switched services.
46	127	Determine when to use PPP, HDLC, LAPB, and IETF encapsulation types.
47	128	List at least four common issues to be considered when evaluating WAN services.
48	129	Describe the components that make up ISDN connectivity.
49	130	Configure ISDN BRI.
50	131	Configure Legacy dial-on-demand routing (DDR).
51	132	Configure dialer profiles.
52	133	Verify DDR operation.
53	134	Configure dial backup.
54	135	Verify dial backup operation.
55	136	Configure MultiLink PPP operation.
56	137	Verify MultiLink PPP operation.
57	138	Configure snapshot routing.
58	139	Configure IPX spoofing.

WAN Options: ISDN, DDR, and Configuration

How to Best Use This Chapter

By taking the following steps, you can make better use of your study time:

- Keep your notes and answers for all your work with this book in one place for easy reference.

- Take the quiz, writing down your answers. Studies show that retention significantly increases by writing facts and concepts down, even if you never look at the information again!

- Use the diagram in Figure 7-1 to guide you to the next step.

Figure 7-1   *How to Use This Chapter*

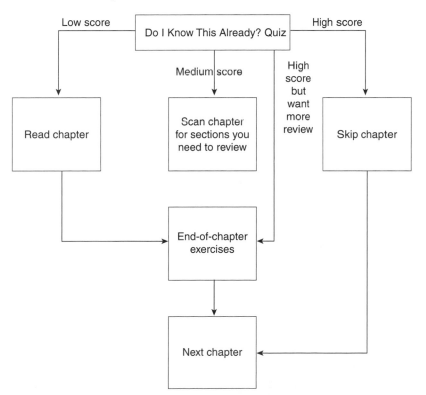

"Do I Know This Already?" Quiz

These questions are designed to test not just your knowledge, but your understanding of the subject matter. It is therefore important to realize that getting the answer the same as stated in Appendix A, "Answers to Quizzes and Q&As," is less important than your answer having embodied the spirit of the question. In this manner, the questions and answers are not as open and shut as will be found on the exam: Their intention is to prepare you with the appropriate knowledge and understanding to give you mastery of the subject as opposed to limited rote knowledge.

1 How is interesting traffic identified to the router?

_____

_____

_____

2 What is the purpose of the **dialer map** command?

_____

_____

_____

3 What is the D channel used for in ISDN?

_____

_____

_____

4 How is a static route used in DDR?

_____

_____

_____

5 What does ISDN stand for?

_____

_____

_____

6 When would you use PPP as the frame format for the link?

_____

_____

_____

7 State at least one occasion when you would choose asynchronous dial-in as the WAN option.

_____

_____

_____

8 Name two advantages of using a packet-switched service.

_____

_____

_____

9 When considering which connection to choose for the WAN, what are two important things that guide that decision?

_____

_____

_____

10 What is the difference between a BRI connection and a PRI connection?

_____

_____

_____

11 What is the purpose of the Terminal Adapter (TA) in ISDN?

_____

_____

_____

12 What command is used to determine how long the router will wait before dropping the link?

_____

_____

_____

The answers to this quiz are found in Appendix A, "Answers to Quizzes and Q&As" (see page 473). Review the answers, grade your quiz, and choose an appropriate next step in this chapter based on the suggestions diagrammed in Figure 7-1. Your choices for the next step are as follows:

- Read this chapter.
- Scan this chapter for sections you need to review.
- Skip to the exercises at the end of this chapter.
- Skip this chapter.

Foundation Topics

Introduction: The Alternatives Available in a WAN Environment

The ACRC objectives mastered in this section are as follows:

ACRC Exam Objective Number	Corresponding FRS Exam Objective Number	Description
45	126	Compare the differences between WAN connection types: dedicated, asynchronous dial-in, dial-on-demand, and packet switched services.
46	127	Determine when to use PPP, HDLC, LAPB, and IETF encapsulation types.
47	128	List at least four common issues to be considered when evaluating WAN services.

This chapter deals with wide-area networks (WANs). This chapter considers the various options available to the administrator when connecting an organization's networks across long distances. This is normally achieved by buying a carrier service; many different services are available, however. When deciding which to choose, consideration must be given to the different technologies available and the requirements of the organization.

WAN Connections: The Options Available

The options available for connecting WANs include the following:

- Dedicated lines
- Asynchronous dial-in lines
- Dial-on-demand routing (DDR)
- Packet switched

The choice of which technology to use is based on the requirements of the organization, but comes down to the amount of traffic and the constancy of the traffic (which can be continuous, bursty, or occasional).

Dedicated Lines

A dedicated line is a telephone link that you have paid to have available at any time, for a determined amount of bandwidth. It is sometimes referred to as a leased line. The speed or bandwidth usually offered is between 56 kbps and a T1/E1. A T1 is available in the United States and has an upper limit of 1.544 Mbps; an E1, on the other hand, is used in Europe and reaches 2.048 Mbps. This technology is useful when there is constant traffic on the line. There is no call setup, which means that access is fast and efficient. The line is also dedicated to your organization, unlike packet-switched services, which although they guarantee an available bandwidth, are a shared domain.

Asynchronous Dial-In

This is a useful option when the link is required only for occasional use, or as a backup to, say, a dedicated line. It is commonly used as a means of remote access for users who are travelling or need access from home.

DDR

This could be an ordinary telephone line or it could be an ISDN line. The link is established when the device connecting to the telephone sees traffic that it has been configured to recognize. This allows the link to be set up automatically and torn down when the data has been transferred.

Packet Switched

A carrier provides these services, typically a telephone company that has the infrastructure to create long-distance connections. It is a shared environment; many organizations share the resources of the packet-switched cloud. It is often an economical solution for companies with regular traffic between campuses. It also allows flexibility in changing the service as the company's needs change. Common packet-switched services include the following:

- X.25

- Frame Relay

- SMDS

- ATM

NOTE   Although the decision as to which type of WAN connection to implement is a technical one, in many respects it is also an economic or political decision. The best solution is also governed by availability in your region and by the marketing of the various technologies.

WAN Connections: The Layer 2 Encapsulations Available

Life becomes very confusing when different technologies are explained, because frequently no explanation of how the various parts fit together is given. This is often the case with the various parts of WAN technology. This section gives an overview of the options available to connect two sites using WAN technology, and then deals with the encapsulations that may be available after that choice has been made. The encapsulation refers to the Layer 2 frame type, the data unit transmitted on the link.

For some of the connectivity options available, the frame type is predetermined by the technology; for others there is a choice. Again, the decision is made based on how the link is to be used—for example, you might need to consider the level of security required.

The main available encapsulations include the following:

- High-Level Data Link Control (HDLC)
- Point-to-Point Protocol (PPP)
- Link Access Procedure, Balanced (LAPB)
- Internet Engineering Task Force (IETF)

HDLC

HDLC is an older technology that is still widely used and very efficient. It was originally designed to connect mini- or mainframe computers directly to proprietary protocol stacks that had been predefined. It was never imagined that the Layer 2 encapsulation HDLC would be used to carry a variety of Layer 3 protocols across the same link—for example, IPX, IP, AppleTalk, and DECnet. For this reason, no provision was made to identify the different possible Layer 3 protocols encapsulated inside the HDLC frame, as was done for Ethernet II with the type field or the DSAP/SSAP (destination service access point/source service access point) fields in 802.2. This is the means by which the destination source Layer 3 protocol is identified. Without this provision in the standard, each vendor solved the problem in his or her own way. The result is the irony of an industry standard that is vendor specific: Although HDLC is an industry standard, it cannot be used between different vendors.

PPP

PPP is an industry standard and is used for interoperability between different vendor's equipment. It has the type field sadly missing in HDLC. It also offers a fairly basic form of security through the use of a password handshake. In recent years, the technology has evolved to offer multilink PPP, which allows for load balancing of traffic over multiple WAN connections. It is used on dedicated or leased lines. It is available for both synchronous and asynchronous lines.

LAPB

LAPB is used by X.25 and offers a connection-oriented Layer 2 frame type. In fact, PPP and HDLC are connection oriented, but LAPB takes the task very seriously. It has strict timeouts and windowing that can be tuned to ensure an efficient use of the link. The manner in which that LAPB is configured will depend on the service purchased from the service provider.

LAPB is occasionally used in other situations, such as a point-to-point link, if it is deemed that this level of reliability is required.

IETF

IETF is a Layer 2 encapsulation method. It is an industry standard, which is why it was given the name of the standards proposal organization, the International Engineering Task Force (IETF).

This encapsulation is only used in a Frame Relay environment. It is an industry standard. As with all standards, it offers the capability to mix and match the vendor products that connect into the Frame Relay cloud. If the organization has only purchased Cisco equipment, the administrator could use the Cisco encapsulation, which requires less information in the frame header because it knows the characteristics of the destination device.

Figure 7-2 illustrates the application of the different technologies and frame encapsulation types.

Considerations When Selecting a WAN Connection Type

When considering the differences between the various options, how does one choose between them? The answer depends on several factors. Remember the hidden considerations such as the political and economic influences within the organization before you touch on the availability of the service in your region. Also note the providers' marketing and incentives on particular products.

The main considerations when selecting the most appropriate WAN connection type for your needs include the following:

- **Availability**—This is the point made earlier, as to whether the service required is available in the regions where it is required. For example, is Frame Relay available in Calcutta, India, or in the Sudan?

- **Application traffic**—What is the nature of the traffic crossing the link? Is it interactive, small packet size traffic that is tolerant of delay, or are you sending voice over this link (which is very sensitive to delay and for which there is no recovery protocol)? Perhaps the traffic is comprised of large file transfers, but only once a day, because the connection is used for evening backup of remote sites.

Figure 7-2   *The Connection Options in WAN and the Frame Encapsulations That Support Them*

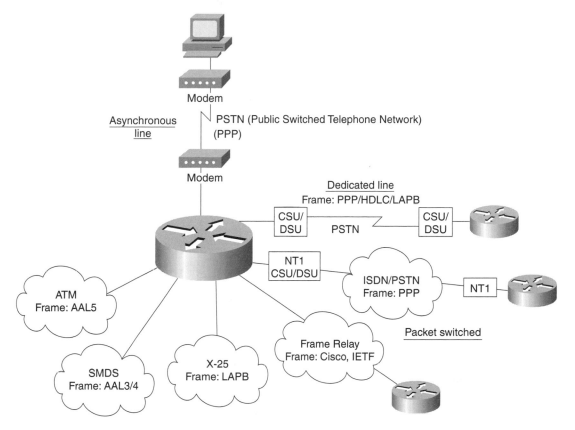

- **Bandwidth**—Having determined the character of the traffic, it should be possible to estimate the amount of bandwidth required. It may be that the traffic volume is low most of the time but peaks at certain times of the day, or during a business week. If this is the case, a technology such as Frame Relay may be useful because it enables you to buy a certain bandwidth with the provision to oversubscribe the link. Therefore, decisions will be made based on not just the quantity of traffic, but also the duration of that traffic flow.

- **Ease of management**—Some thought needs to be given to the ease of management of the WAN connection. This is a difficult area because most of the connections use the services of a third party and, therefore, WAN connection should take place at the entry point into the provider's cloud.

- **Routing protocol characteristics**—The selected routing could radically affect the monthly costs. Because many of the WAN options are based on a pay-as-you-go philosophy or are limited by bandwidth, the network overhead is of prime importance. As seen in Chapters 5 and 6, some routing protocols such as EIGRP or OSPF specialize in keeping network overhead to a minimum.

ISDN and Dial-on-Demand Routing

The ACRC objectives mastered in this section are as follows:

ACRC Exam Objective Number	Corresponding FRS Exam Objective Number	Description
48	129	Describe the components that make up ISDN connectivity.
49	130	Configure ISDN BRI.
50	131	Configure Legacy dial-on-demand routing (DDR).
51	132	Configure dialer profiles.
52	133	Verify DDR operation.

ISDN is a technology that has existed for many years, but has not been implemented in the United States because there was no perceived market. In recent years, it has gained popularity as a cheap, efficient, and fast method of connecting remote offices.

The Components of ISDN

Integrated Services Digital Network (ISDN) is just a digitized telephone system allowing both voice and data to be encoded on to the line. It is used to connect remote offices to headquarters, as well as to give workers connectivity from home. It is often used to create the home office by integrating the telephone, PC, and fax machine together on one access line.

This technology has only been widely deployed in the United States in the past few years, but it has been in use in Europe and defined as an international standard for more than a decade.

ISDN's component parts are described as follows and are reflected in Figure 7-3.

- **The channels**—ISDN has two types of channel, one to carry the data and another for signaling. The separate channels are what make ISDN so popular with the home user. It is as easy as a telephone call; because the call is set up on a line dedicated solely to the management of the call, however, it is both fast and efficient.

The *D channel* is the signaling channel, providing out-of-band signaling to set up, manage, and tear down the line. The Layer 2 signaling used is the Link Access Procedure on the D channel (LAPD). There is always one D channel. In some cases, it can also be used to carry data. This has the bandwidth of 16 kbps on a BRI and 64 kbps on a PRI.

The *B channel* is the bearer channel, which is responsible for carrying the user data. The number of B channels depends on the type of ISDN in use. The Layer 2 encapsulation on the bearer channel may either be HDLC or PPP. It is possible, although unusual, to tunnel Frame Relay or X.25 through the ISDN cloud.

- **Basic Rate Interface (BRI)**—The bandwidth for ISDN that may be purchased depends on the number of 64 kbps B channels that you require. The smallest increment that can be bought is two bearer channels at 64 kbps each. This configuration is called a BRI.

- **The Primary Rate Interface (PRI)**—A greater bandwidth is offered by PRI, which offers either 23 channels (T1) or 30 channels (E1), depending on the country of purchase. It is possible to buy a fractional T1, which allows a smaller number of channels to be allocated to your site.

- **The terminal adapter (TA)**—The terminal adapter converts signals from equipment that is not ISDN compliant into ISDN signals. This allows the telephone or fax to connect to the ISDN line.

- **Terminal endpoint 1 (TE1)**—The terminal endpoint is the end device that is ISDN compliant with an ISDN interface card. This is typically a small Cisco router, although it can be a PC, telephone, fax machine, or any device that supports ISDN.

- **Terminal endpoint 2 (TE2)**—This terminal endpoint is an end device that does not have an ISDN interface card and therefore requires a Terminal Adapter (TA) to connect up the ISDN telephone system.

- **The network termination 1 (NT1)**—This converts the signal into one understood by the ISDN switch technology. It connects the customer to the service provider. The TE1 and TA equipment connect to this device directly in small environments that require a low-bandwidth ISDN line (BRI).

- **The network termination 2 (NT2)**—This is the device that is the junction station for the lines provided by the service provider at the customer site. The NT2 supports switching of multiple TE devices, connecting them to the NT1 that interfaces with the service provider. The NT2 is required for larger businesses (for example, those using a PRI line). The NT2 supports the multiple channels of the PRI with multiplexing, allowing switching systems and the concentration of many lines from either a PBX (using voice) or LAN data traffic.

- **Local termination (LT)**—This is the first switch that the customer connects to in the service provider's cloud.

- **Exchange termination (ET)**—This is a switch that connects to other switches in the service provider's cloud.

Figure 7-3 illustrates the interaction between these devices.

Figure 7-3   *The Components of ISDN*

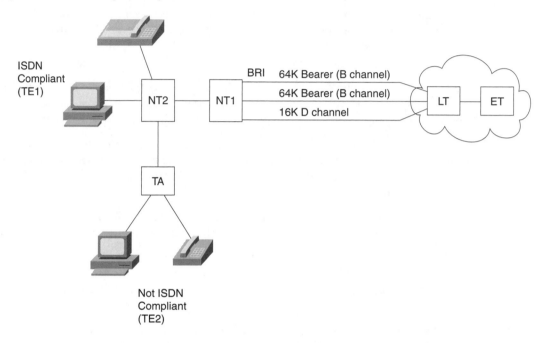

Having explained the different devices that make up the ISDN network, it is time to understand another element of the technology: the communication between the devices. The standards categorize this connection between two functions or devices as *reference types*.

The reference types of significance are as follows:

- **R interface**—This connects a non–ISDN-compliant device to a TA.

- **S interface**—Connects the customer equipment to the NT2, which allows calls between various customer devices.

- **T interface**—Identical to the S interface, it deals with the connection from the NT2 to the service provider or the NT1.

- **U interface**—Connects the NTE to the LE. It carries full-duplex communication, permitting only one device to connect. This is not a problem because it connects the aggregated traffic to the service provider.

Figure 7-4 illustrates the interaction between these devices.

Figure 7-4   *The Different Interface Types in ISDN*

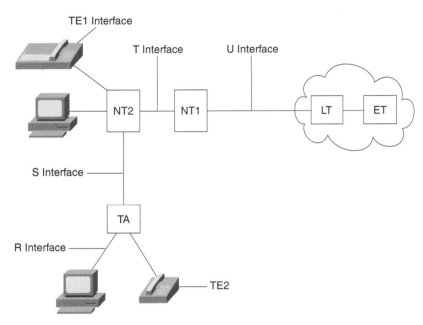

WARNING   When connecting to any service provider's cloud, ensure that you have a clear understanding of the service provider's equipment and requirements in reference to the organization connecting into their domain. This is true of all technologies. For example, in the case of ISDN, the importance of understanding equipment and requirements is clearly demonstrated in the selection of the switch type that the organization is connecting to in the cloud. The common switches that are used by the service providers are listed in the "Foundation Summary" section of this chapter. The command to identify the switch type to the Cisco equipment and thereby the signal that it should use is as follows:

```
ISDN switch-type switchtype
```

Commands for Configuring ISDN

Configuring ISDN is very straightforward. The key is in gathering all the information together and ensuring that the pieces that need to be obtained from the service provider are verified and documented. If your organization has multiple serial lines, it is easier to manage the environment if there is consistency in the configuration. Table 7-1 summarizes the commands that are used when configuring ISDN for dial-on-demand, allowing the link to be activated only when it is required to send data to the remote location. Table 7-2 summarizes the DDR EXEC command to verify ISDN configuration.

Table 7-1 *DDR Configuration Commands Using ISDN*

Command	Configuration Mode	Explanation
ip route, **ipx route**, and so on	Global	Static routes pointing out of a dial interface.
dialer-list [*list nnn*] **protocol** [*protocol-type*] **permit**|**deny**	Global	Defines types of traffic considered interesting.
dialer-group *n*	Interface	Enables dialer list on this interface.
dialer in-band	Interface	Enables dial out and dial in on this interface. This command is only used for serial lines that connect to a TA and not for native ISDN interfaces that use the out-of-band D channel.
dialer string *string*	Interface	Dial string used when dialing only one site.
dialer map *protocol next-hop* [**broadcast**] **name** *name dial-string*	Interface	Dial string to reach next hop. However, the **map** command is used when dialing more than one site. Name used for authentication. Broadcast ensures copies of broadcasts go to this next hop address.

Table 7-2 *DDR Exec Command to Verify ISDN Configuration*

Command	Function
show dialer	Lists DDR parameters. Shows whether currently dialed by indicating current status. Also shows previous attempts to dial and whether they were successful.

Configuring ISDN for DDR

There are two ways to configure DDR. The two styles of DDR configuration are called DDR legacy and DDR dialer profiles. The main difference between the two is that DDR legacy associates dial details with a physical interface, but DDR dialer profiles configuration disassociates the dial configuration from a physical interface, allowing a great deal of flexibility.

The concepts behind legacy DDR apply to DDR dialer profiles as well, but DDR legacy is a little less detailed. Therefore, in this book, DDR legacy will be used to describe the key concepts, followed by the extra details for DDR dialer profiles. When the term *DDR* is used in this book, without the legacy or dialer profile qualifier, the topic describes a fact that is true of both.

DDR can be used to cause the router to dial or to receive a dial on asynchronous and synchronous serial interfaces as well as on ISDN BRI and PRI interfaces. All examples in this chapter use ISDN.

The following list identifies the four key concepts that lay behind DDR configuration. They are detailed in this book, even in simple cases. The first two concepts are not actually related to the dial process, but to the process of choosing when to dial and when not to dial. The other two concepts relate to dialing, or signaling. The term *signaling* is used in ISDN to describe the processes of call setup and takedown, and will be used synonymously with the term *dialing* here. The four key concepts are as follows:

- Routing packets out of the dial-out interface

- Choosing which of these packets trigger the dialing process

- Dial parameters

- What happens while the link is up, and what causes it to come down

Each of these is addressed in succession, followed by a discussion of DDR legacy configuration and DDR dialer profiles configuration.

Routing Packets Out of the Dial Interface

Figure 7-5 provides the backdrop for these discussions. In these discussions, the SanFrancisco router will be dialing into the main site in LosAngeles.

Figure 7-5   *Sample DDR Network*

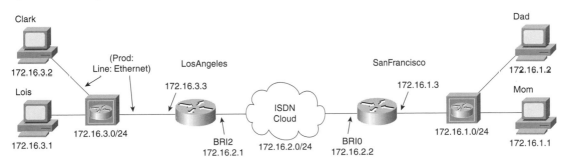

The router must choose when to dial. The first step in this process relates to the following fact:

DDR will not dial until some traffic is directed out of the dial interface.

The router needs to route packets so that they are queued to go out of the dial interface. Cisco's design for DDR defines that the router will receive some user-generated traffic, and will, through normal routing processes, decide to route the traffic out of the dial interface. The router

(SanFrancisco) can receive a packet that needs to be routed out of BRI0—routing the packet out of BRI0 triggers the IOS to cause the dial to occur.

Of course, routes are not learned over a dial link while the dial link is down. In Figure 7-5, for instance, SanFrancisco will have no routes to 172.16.3.0/24 learned via a routing protocol. Therefore, static routes are configured on SanFrancisco. This can be done for any protocol that is supported by DDR for the purpose of triggering the dial; IP will be used in the upcoming examples. Any traffic that could be routed or bridged across a leased link is supported after the link is up.

To begin the process of building a DDR configuration, IP routes are added to the configuration so that packets can be directed out of BRI0 on SanFrancisco:

```
! SanFrancisco Static routes.
ip route 172.16.3.0 255.255.255.0 172.16.2.1
```

Triggering the Dial

A packet routed out of BRI0 does not necessarily cause the dial to occur. Cisco could have designed DDR in this way; in fact, one configuration option is to state that any IP traffic routed out of BRI0 would cause the dial to occur. The logic flow works as shown in Figure 7-6.

Figure 7-6   *DDR Logic for Triggering the Dial*

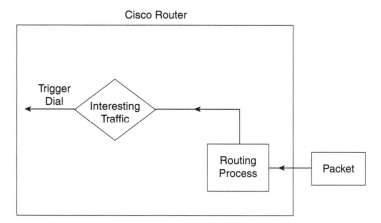

"Is this packet, which is being routed out of this dial interface, worthy of causing the dial to occur?" is the question being asked. The packets that are worthy of causing the device to dial are called *interesting packets* by Cisco. Cisco does not categorize those packets not worthy of causing the dial; in effect, they are "boring!"

Interesting can be defined as all packets of one or more Layer 3 protocols (for example, all IP packets). In that case, any user in SanFrancisco can send a packet to any host in 172.16.3.0/24 and trigger the dial connection! That may be exactly what is desired, or it may not be.

Interesting can be defined as packets permitted by an access list. If the access list permits the packet, it is considered interesting. Example 7-1 shows additional configuration on SanFrancisco, with two cases shown. One shows all IP packets being considered interesting, and the other shows all packets to the PC Lois (refer to Figure 7-5) considered interesting.

Example 7-1 *Defining Interesting Packets to Activate the Circuit from SanFrancisco to LosAngeles*

```
ip route 172.16.3.0 255.255.255.0 172.16.2.1
access-list 101 permit tcp any host 172.16.3.1 eq 80
dialer-list 1 protocol ip permit
dialer-list 2 protocol ip list 101
interface bri 0
encapsulation ppp
ip address 172.16.2.2 255.255.255.0
!Use this one if all IP is considered interesting…
dialer-group 1
! OR Use next statement to trigger for Web to Server Lois
dialer-group 2
```

The **dialer-group** interface subcommand enables the logic that determines what is interesting. It refers to a dialer list, which can either refer to an entire protocol suite or to an access list, as shown. (After the link is up, packets are not filtered using list 101—the logic is just used for determining what is interesting and what is tedious, or boring.)

Dialing and Connecting

The dialing router needs additional information before the dial can occur. First, if it is necessary to communicate the dial string to the external dialing device, signaling (dialing) must be enabled on the interface using the command **dialer in-band**. This is not necessary on a BRI interface. Table 7-3 summarizes what the command implies on different interfaces.

Table 7-3   *Effect of the **dialer in-band** Command*

Type of Interface	Type of Signaling Used as a Result of dialer in-band
Async	AT command set
Sync	V.25 bis
ISDN	ISDN D channel with Q.921/Q.931

The second piece of information needed before dialing is the ISDN phone number, and the service profile identifier (SPID) if the service provider uses SPIDs for ISDN connection establishment. With the example in Figure 7-7, the configuration is straightforward. The command is **dialer string** *string*, where *string* is the phone number. Example 7-2 completes the DDR configuration that allows the dial to occur. ISDN configuration details for the DDR configuration with asynchronous, synchronous, and ISDN interface appear later in the chapter.

Example 7-2 *SanFrancisco Configuration—Dial Can Now Occur*

```
ip route 172.16.3.0 255.255.255.0 172.16.2.1
access-list 101 permit tcp any host 172.16.3.1 eq 80
dialer-list 2 protocol ip list 101
interface bri 0
ip address 172.16.2.2 255.255.255.0
encapsulation ppp
dialer string 1404555123401
dialer-group 2
```

Several dial strings are needed when more than one site is dialed from the same interface. For example, Figure 7-7 adds a third site, GothamCity, to the network. The client's FTP connections to the server running on Commissioner will be considered interesting traffic for causing dial connections to GothamCity.

Figure 7-7 *Mapping between Next Hop and Dial String*

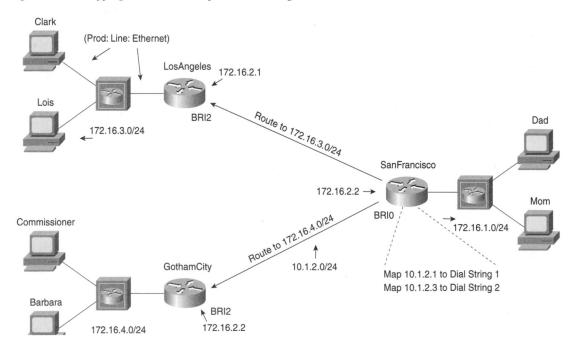

The dilemma for SanFrancisco will now be how to determine which ISDN telephone number to signal. The key is in the **ip route** commands and the new **dialer map** command. Of course, there are unique ISDN telephone numbers for both LosAngeles and GothamCity. Because the static routes will direct the router to send the packet to either 172.16.2.1 or 172.16.2.3, all that is needed is a mapping between these next hop addresses and their respective ISDN telephone numbers. The **dialer map** command does exactly that. Example 7-3 shows the mostly complete configuration.

Example 7-3 *SanFrancisco Configuration—Two Dial-to Sites, **dialer map** in Use*

```
ip route 172.16.3.0 255.255.255.0 172.16.2.1
ip route 172.16.4.0 255.255.255.0 172.16.2.3
! Added usernames for CHAP support!
username LosAngeles password Clark
username GothamCity password Bruce
access-list 101 permit tcp any host 172.16.3.1 eq 80
! Added next statement to make The Client's FTP connection interesting!
access-list 101 permit tcp any host 172.16.4.1 eq 21
dialer-list 2 protocol ip list 101
interface bri 0
ip address 172.16.2.2 255.255.255.0
encapsulation ppp
ppp authentication chap
dialer map ip 172.16.2.1 broadcast name  LosAngeles 1404555123401
dialer map ip 172.16.2.3 broadcast name GothamCity 1999999999901
dialer-group 2
router igrp 6
network 172.16.0.0
```

The map statements imply that if the interesting packet were routed to 172.16.2.1, the dial to LosAngeles would occur. Conversely, if the interesting packet were routed to 172.16.2.3, the dial to GothamCity would occur.

Two other important configuration elements are included in Example 7-2. First, CHAP authentication was configured. PAP or CHAP is required if dialing to more than one site with ISDN—and PAP and CHAP require PPP. The username expected from the other router is coded in the corresponding **dialer map** statement.

Broadcast handling is the final configuration element that needs to be addressed. Just like any other point-to-point serial link, there is no true data-link broadcast. If a broadcast needs to be sent on the interface, however, it is necessary to issue the **broadcast** command to tell the interface to forward the packet across the link.

Table 7-4 summarizes the features used to cause the dial to occur, and the features needed in conjunction with the dial features.

Table 7-4   *Dial Features and their Commands*

Feature	Command Parameters
Enable dialing on interface.	**dialer in-band [no parity|odd parity]**
Defined SPID for one site.	**isdn spid1|isdn spid2**
Defined ISDN number for multiple sites. This will configure a serial interface to map host names to next hop addresses. The speed identifies the speed to use on the line; the service provider provides this information. The **broadcast** parameter enables support for broadcasts on the dialed link.	**dialer map** *protocol next-hop-address* [**name** *hostname*] [**speed 56| 64**][**broadcast**] *dial-string*
Add CHAP configuration. The authentication protocol needs to be configured on the interface. This requires remote sites to be authenticated when connecting locally.	**ppp authentication chap**
This is a global command for CHAP to verify incoming calls.	**username** *name* **password** *password*
Defined ISDN phone number for one remote site. The **class** parameter identifies the map class to be used. The map class contains the details on how to create the call.	**dialer string** *string* **class** *class-name*

The Characteristics of the Link and What Happens to Take the Link Down

The dialed link acts just like a leased line while it is up. If a particular Layer 3 protocol is enabled on the link, it can be routed across the link. Transparent (encapsulated) bridging can be used, just like any other point-to-point link. Routing updates, IPX SAPs, AppleTalk ZIP, and other broadcasts are sent across the link if the broadcast keyword is coded. Most importantly, any access list used to define which packets are interesting does not filter the traffic on the interface. If packet filters are desired, an access list must be enabled on the interface.

Additional parallel links can be dialed if more capacity is desired. To do so, dialer profiles must be configured. Additionally, the **dialer load-threshold** *load* command is used to define the link utilization that must be exceeded for another link to be dialed.

The decision to take the link down is the most intriguing part about what happens while the link is up. Although any type of packets may be routed across the link, only interesting packets are considered worthy of keeping the link up. An idle timer counts the time since the last interesting packet went across the link. If that time expires, the link is brought down.

Two idle timers can be set. With the **dialer idle-timeout** *seconds* command, the idle time as previously described is set. If interesting traffic that needs to flow to another dial site is occurring, however, another shorter idle timer can be used. The **dialer fast-idle** *seconds* command enables you to configure a typically lower number than the idle timer so that when other sites need to be dialed, the link that is currently up, but in the process of idling out as per the **dialer idle-timeout** command, can be brought down earlier.

DDR Legacy Configuration

The network in Figure 7-7 has its DDR configuration shown in Examples 7-4 and 7-5. ISDN configuration details are not shown.

Example 7-4 *SanFrancisco Configuration—Complete*

```
ip route 172.16.3.0 255.255.255.0 172.16.2.1
ip route 172.16.4.0 255.255.255.0 172.16.2.3
! Added usernames for CHAP support!
username LosAngeles password Clark
username GothamCity password Bruce
access-list 101 permit tcp any host 172.16.3.1 eq 80
! Added next statement to make The Client's FTP connection interesting!
access-list 101 permit tcp any host 172.16.4.1 eq 21
dialer-list 2 protocol ip list 101
interface bri 0
encapsulation ppp
ppp authentication chap
dialer idle-timeout 300
dialer fast-idle 120
dialer map ip 172.16.2.1 broadcast name LosAngeles 1404555123401
dialer map ip 172.16.2.3 broadcast name GothamCity 1999999999901
dialer-group 2
router igrp 6
network 172.16.0.0
```

Example 7-5 *LosAngeles Configuration—Receive Only*

```
username SanFrancisco password Clark
interface bri 0
encapsulation ppp
ppp authentication chap
router igrp 6
network 172.16.0.0
```

The new configuration, compared to Example 7-2, is straightforward. Only the idle and fast idle parameters have been added to SanFrancisco. On LosAngeles (refer to Example 7-4), only three items of note are in the configuration. The CHAP password has been set and agrees with the configuration in SanFrancisco. And finally, PPP is the encapsulation type, as opposed to the default of HDLC. LosAngeles does not need any of the other parameters because it is not initiating a dial in this case.

DDR Dialer Profiles Configuration

Dialer profiles are used when there is a benefit to disassociating the dial configuration from the physical interface. One such example is a main-site router that dials 200 sites each night for file transfers. Five ISDN BRIs are used. Without dialer profiles, each of the five BRIs would be configured to reach 40 sites. Depending on each night's load, however, one interface might finish its 40 sites long before another BRI. There would be a benefit to letting all five BRIs be used as they become available. Dialer profiles allow all five BRIs to be used to dial any of the 200 sites.

Dialer profiles are most useful when more than one physical interface needs to be used with one set of dialing parameters.

The terminology used with dialer profiles provides a challenge. Table 7-5 summarizes the terms used with dialer profiles; Figure 7-8 helps to further illustrate these terms.

Table 7-5   *Dialer Profiles Terminology*

Term	Meaning
Dialer profiles	Term used in IOS documentation to represent three different configuration concepts, namely dialer interfaces, map classes, and dialer pools. One dialer profile is considered to correspond to each dialer interface in the configuration.
Dialer interface	Configuration entity used like a physical dial-capable interface. All **dialer** commands are subcommands on this interface.
Dialer pool	A set of physical interfaces that can be used once dial logic triggers a dial. Any B channel in the pool can be used by a dialer interface that refers to the pool.
Dialer map class	An optional definition of miscellaneous parameters, referred to by the dialer interface.

Figure 7-8   *The Use of Dialer Profiles*

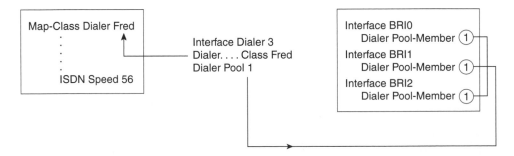

Figure 7-9 shows a sample DDR network with five sites. Figure 7-10 shows a sample DDR network with five sites and two dialer profiles. Example 7-6 is a configuration showing the use of dialer profiles to connect DDR to more than one site.

Figure 7-9 *Sample DDR Network with Five Sites*

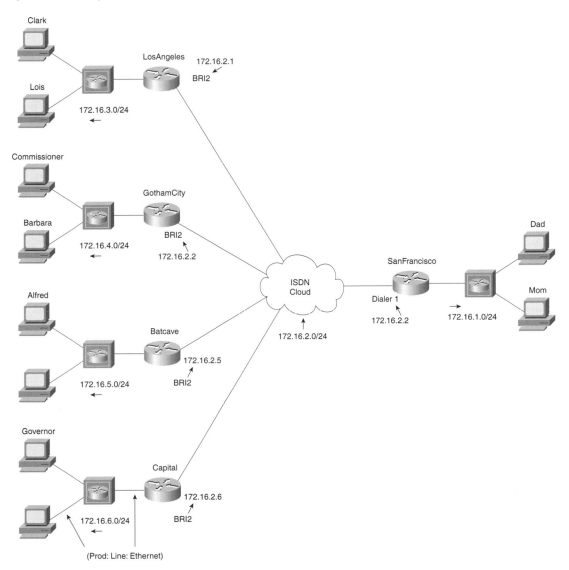

Figure 7-10 *Sample DDR Network with Five Sites and Two Dialer Profiles*

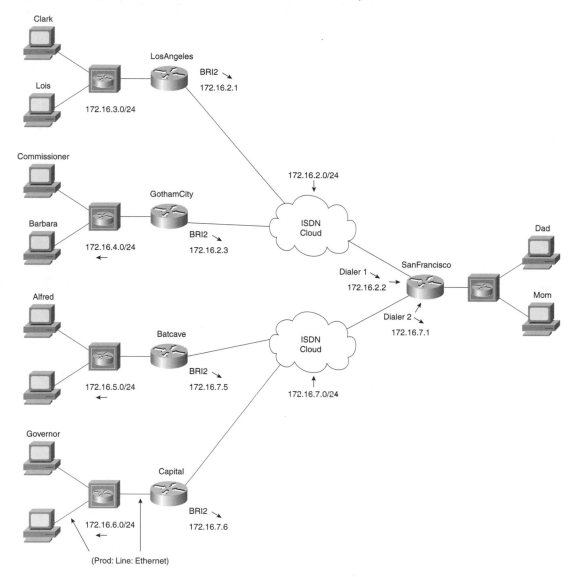

Example 7-6 *SanFrancisco Configuration—Four Sites, One Dialer Profile*

```
ip route 172.16.3.0 255.255.255.0 172.16.2.1
ip route 172.16.4.0 255.255.255.0 172.16.2.3
ip route 172.16.5.0 255.255.255.0 172.16.7.5
ip route 172.16.6.0 255.255.255.0 172.16.7.6
! Added usernames for CHAP support!
username LosAngeles password Clark
username GothamCity password Bruce
username BatCave password Alfred
username Capital password Governor
access-list 101 permit tcp any host 172.16.3.1 eq 80
! Added next statement to make The Client's FTP connection interesting!
access-list 101 permit tcp any host 172.16.4.1 eq 21
access-list 102 permit tcp any 172.16.5.0 0.0.0.255 eq 21
access-list 102 permit tcp any 172.16.6.0 0.0.0.255 eq 21
dialer-list 1 protocol ip list 101
dialer-list 2 protocol ip list 102
interface bri 1
encapsulation ppp
ppp authentication chap
dialer pool-member 1
interface bri 2
encapsulation ppp
ppp authentication chap
dialer pool-member 1
dialer pool-member 2
interface bri 3
encapsulation ppp
ppp authentication chap
dialer pool-member 1
interface dialer 1
ip address 172.16.2.2 255.255.255.0
encapsulation ppp
ppp authentication chap
dialer in-band
dialer idle-timeout 300
dialer fast-idle 120
dialer load-threshold 40 either
dialer map ip 172.16.2.1 broadcast name LosAngeles 1404555123401
dialer map ip 172.16.2.3 broadcast name GothamCity 1999999999901
dialer pool 1
dialer-group 1
interface dialer 2
ip address 172.16.7.1 255.255.255.0
encapsulation ppp
ppp authentication chap
dialer in-band
dialer idle-timeout 300
dialer fast-idle 120
dialer load-threshold 40 either
dialer map ip 172.16.7.5 broadcast name BatCave 1555555555501
dialer map ip 172.16.7.6 broadcast name Capital 1555111111101
dialer pool 2
dialer-group 2
router igrp 6
network 172.16.0.0
```

Several differences exist between the configurations in Examples 7-5 and 7-6. The first difference is that two dialer groups are used in Example 7-6 to define what is interesting and what is not. There is no need to dial on dialer interface 2 to get to LosAngeles or GothamCity—that is not the desired design. So, interesting is defined differently on each dialer interface. Another difference with Example 7-6 is that a second dialer profile, via a second dialer interface, was created; therefore, a second subnet (172.16.7.0/24) is used. The final difference is that BRI 2 is placed into both pools 1 and 2 so that it is available to be used to dial any site.

DDR for Dial Backup

The ACRC objectives mastered in this section are as follows:

ACRC Exam Objective Number	Corresponding FRS Exam Objective Number	Description
53	134	Configure dial backup.
54	135	Verify dial backup operation.

Dialing ISDN B channels to replace leased-line or Frame Relay VC connectivity is a popular feature of routers. Cisco offers two styles of configuration: dial backup and DDR. Dial backup can either just identify a secondary link that waits for the original or primary link to fail, or, with the use of DDR, it has the additional power to define the type of traffic that can dial the line.

DDR for backup is very similar to DDR, but with one additional concept. Consider Figure 7-11 and Example 7-7, which show a DDR legacy sample network and its configuration.

Figure 7-11   *DDR Legacy Sample Network*

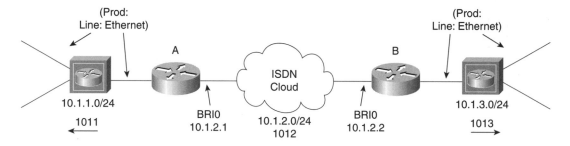

Example 7-7 *DDR Legacy Sample Network Configuration*

```
ipx routing 0200.aaaa.aaaa
username RouterB password Shhh
dialer-list 1 protocol ip permit
interface bri 0
encapsulation ppp
ip addr 10.1.2.1 255.255.255.0
ipx network 1012
ppp authentication chap
dialer map ip 10.1.2.2 broadcast name RouterB 1222555222201
dialer-group 1
interface ethernet 0
ip address 10.1.1.1 255.255.255.0
ipx network 1011
ip route 10.1.3.0 255.255.255.0 10.1.2.2
router igrp 1
network 10.0.0.0
```

In this case, all IP traffic is considered interesting. This example is perfectly valid for occasional access, except for the few additional ISDN parameters that need to be added.

If there is always a leased line between A and B in Figure 7-11, some changes need to be made to the configuration. Consider Figure 7-12, which has a leased line added.

Figure 7-12 *DDR Legacy for Backup*

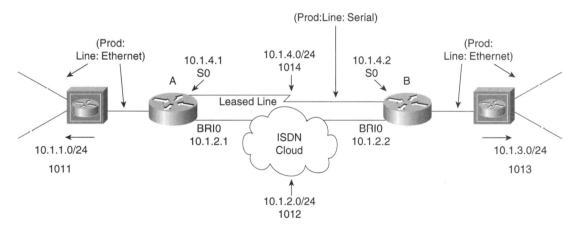

IGRP updates flow across the leased line so that a route is learned at Router A, pointing to 10.1.3.0/24, and out of serial 0. The static route in Router A pointing to 10.1.3.0 points out of BRI0 to 10.1.2.2 as the next router by default, however. Router A would place the static route to 10.1.3.0 through BRI0 in the routing table rather than the one learned by IGRP. Therefore, any IP traffic would cause the dial to occur, even if the leased line is established. No packets would be routed across the leased line.

The reason the ISDN dialup line is selected by the routing table, rather than the more sensible choice of the leased line, is due to the default *administrative distance*. When a routing table is offered multiple paths to a remote network, it uses the metric to select the best path if all the offered routes come from the same routing protocol. If different routing protocols or manual configurations have resulted in many paths to the same destination, another mechanism must be used. The IOS ranks the different sources of routing information. The defaults consider static routes to be better than any routing protocol; the logic being that if the administrator went to the trouble of typing in the command, the command should be given precedence. After static routes, routing protocols are ranked by preference. The order of preference given to the different sources of routing information is called the *administrative distance*. IGRP's default administrative distance is 100; static routes have an administrative distance of 1 by default. The lower the number, the more believable the source of the routing information. Directly connected routes are even more believable sources of routing information than static routes, having an administrative distance of 0.

To overcome the DDR for backup issue, the static route is configured with a larger administrative distance than the routing protocol. Only the static route has changed from the configuration in Example 7-7, and is as follows:

```
ip route 10.1.3.0 255.255.255.0 10.1.2.2 150
```

The static route will only be used when IGRP has not learned the route to 10.1.3.0 via updates on the serial link. When the leased link fails, IGRP will remove the route to 10.1.3.0 from the routing table, and the IOS will replace it with the static route. Likewise, when the leased line comes back up, IGRP will learn the route, which has a lower administrative distance than the static route, so the route will point out of the serial link once again. The use of static routes in this fashion is often called *floating static routes*.

Advanced Options

The ACRC objectives mastered in this section are as follows:

ACRC Exam Objective Number	Corresponding FRS Exam Objective Number	Description
17	98	Describe weighted fair queuing operation.
18	99	Configure priority.
19	100	Configure custom queuing.
20	101	Verify queuing operation.
55	136	Configure MultiLink PPP operation.
56	137	Verify MultiLink PPP operation.
57	138	Configure snapshot routing.
58	139	Configure IPX spoofing.

Configuring and Verifying Multilink PPP

Multilink PPP provides *bandwidth on demand.* As a standards-based method of multiplexing more than one B channel, multilink PPP uses the Link Control Protocol (LCP) of PPP to negotiate the link and establish that multilink PPP can be used. After the channels have been bound or *bonded,* the upper-layer protocols (Layer 3) are encapsulated into the PPP frame with a multilink PPP header that manages the sequencing of the frames. The frames are sent in a *round-robin* fashion across the links to ensure an even distribution. Round robin means that each link is given a frame in turn, rather like dealing a hand of cards. Figure 7-13 illustrates this.

The multilink PPP technology is defined in RFC 1990 and was introduced to the Cisco IOS in 11.1. In addition, IOS version 11.3, Cisco started to support Bandwidth Allocation Protocol (BACP), which allows the two sites to negotiate the link and dynamically allocate and remove extra available channels as required, thus providing dynamic bandwidth on demand.

Figure 7-13   *Multilink PPP*

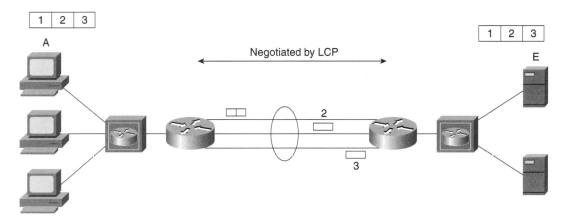

The necessary steps in establishing multilink PPP follow:

1 Bind the links together.

2 Divide the upper-level PDU's among the links; this may involve fragmentation. Create the multilink frames.

3 Negotiate the packet size to be sent across the link.

4 The remote site will be verified as a valid connection, through PPP authentication. It will also use this to determine to which bundle or group of bound links to add this link.

NOTE	The managing protocol at both ends of the link must also be capable of receiving the frames and reordering them appropriately.

Table 7-6 summarizes the commands to configure multilink PPP.

Table 7-6   *Multilink PPP Configuration Commands*

Command	Configuration Mode	Explanation
ppp multilink	Interface	Configures the dialer interface with dialer profiles. Note that the number of links cannot exceed the number of interfaces in the group interface.
dialer load-threshold *load* **[outbound|inbound|either]**	Interface	This states the load on the interface that will trigger PPP to initiate another link into the bundle. The default setting is outbound.

To verify that the configuration was successful and for basic management and troubleshooting, use the commands listed in Table 7-7.

Table 7-7   *Multilink PPP Executive Commands*

Command	Explanation
show dialer	Shows the details of the existing links in the bundle.
debug ppp multilink	Beware of the **debug** command; it is useful, however, to display PPP event information in real time.
show isdn status	This will show status and details on the ISDN links.

Having the ability to raise extra bandwidth as required is very efficient, but it should not be forgotten that the bandwidth is still limited and, in these technologies, at a premium due to the availability and cost.

The following sections offer techniques and technologies to optimize the use of the available bandwidth.

Snapshot Routing

Snapshot routing is a strange concept, but a very clever one. It allows the routers to dynamically build static routing tables.

Snapshot routing works by freezing the routing tables on either side of the link so that routes do not time out in the absence of routing updates. At either preconfigured times or whenever the dialup link is established, the routing protocol will exchange routing information. In this way, the routing tables are maintained because a snapshot of the databases are taken and the information is held as true until the next opportunity to update the tables.

Snapshot routing is a valuable utility in the ISDN DDR environment. If the routing tables at either site are large, manual configuration of the routing table is not only time-consuming, but is likely to introduce errors. Also, the table might change and this will require manual reconfiguration. This is an administrative nightmare. Snapshot routing allows the routing tables to be exchanged periodically, where periodically might mean every few days. It can also be configured to exchange routing information opportunistically, whenever the link between the two sites has been established.

This is a critical point: As seen before, the routing protocol not only consumes bandwidth, but if the updates were sent periodically, it would ensure the DDR link would be effectively transformed into a very expensive leased line. Snapshot routing gives the best of both worlds.

Snapshot routing is most effective in hub-and-spoke designs, where the central router gathers the routing table to be disseminated to the remote sites; it does not work as well in a fully-meshed environment.

WARNING   Snapshot routing has changed over various versions of the IOS. It also had some problems in earlier versions of the code. If implemented in a live network, ensure the IOS versions at the remote sites are the same and check the IOS documentation to verify configuration commands.

It is also only available for distance vector routing protocols that do not rely on a Hello protocol to maintain neighbor relationships.

To configure snapshot routing, the following are required:

- The remote router is configured to determine the update interval for exchanging routing updates.

- When the timer is reached, links to all destinations in the dialer map for snapshot routing are dialed.

- By default, if the link is made active for any other reason, the router will take the opportunity to exchange routing tables.

- A retry parameter can be configured if the link cannot be established when the active timer is reached.

To configure the remote router, the interface commands covered in Table 7-8 are required.

Table 7-8   *Configuring the Remote (Spoke) Routers for Snapshot Routing*

Command	Explanation
snapshot client *active-time* *quiet-time* [**suppress-statechange-updates**] **dialer**	*active-time* states the amount of time in minutes the line is active to allow the exchange of routing updates. There is no default for this command.
	quiet-time states the amount of time in minutes that the router is quiet and keeps the routing table in a frozen state.
	The **suppress-statechange-updates** parameter prevents the routing tables from being exchanged when the line is active for data transfer. This is because the routing tables are large and there would not be enough time to download the tables.
	The **dialer** command is an optional configuration that defines the destination to call when the active timer is reached.
dialer map snapshot *sequence-number* **name** *name* **dial-string**	This command is the same as the **map** command seen earlier. Enter this command for each remote snapshot server router that the client router calls during an active period. The only new parameter is *sequence-number*.
	The sequence number identifies the dialer map statement and will determine the order in which the remote sites are dialed in the case of multiple sites.

To configure the hub (or server) router, use the interface commands listed in Table 7-9.

Table 7-9   *Configuring the Server (Hub) Routers for Snapshot Routing*

Command	Explanation
snapshot server *active-time* [**dialer**]	This must be the same as the timer configured on the client. Note that the client controls the quiet timer.
dialer map snapshot *sequence-number* **name** *name* **dial-string**	This has the same characteristics as described in Table 7-8.

To verify the configuration, use the commands outlined in Table 7-10.

Table 7-10   *Snapshot Routing Executive Commands*

Command	Explanation
show snapshot	Shows the details of the snapshot configuration.
debug snapshot	Beware of the **debug** command; remember that it can consume all the resources of the router because it has priority 1 as a process to the CPU. However, it is useful to display snapshot event information in real time and it can be a useful tool in troubleshooting.
show ip route	This will show the routing tables and will quickly identify whether routes are missing from the tables.

To see how this configuration is implemented, see Figure 7-14.

Figure 7-14   *Configuration of Snapshot Routing*

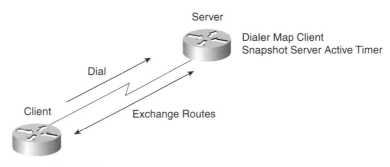

When considering a dialup line from a design perspective, you should think about any periodic traffic. Periodic traffic is a consideration because it creates overhead that takes up precious bandwidth and also triggers the line to be established. Another major source of such traffic is the client/server application traffic that is sent between the end devices.

Vendors are increasingly responsive to the overhead of their products, aware that the systems are no longer being implemented exclusively into LAN environments for which they were originally designed. There are many older networks in situ, however, as well as complicated environments that require some extra thought.

This is demonstrated clearly in the IPX world, where the server will send out a *watchdog packet* intermittently to confirm that the client is still connected. If there is a SPX connection-oriented session, SPX will also generate periodic management traffic. Where IPX has been specified as interesting traffic, the watchdog and SPX traffic would prevent the DDR call from timing out, keep the line open, and may incur high charges for the line. Cisco offers a solution to this problem; it is the age-old remedy of *spoofing*. Essentially, the way spoofing works is that the Cisco router is configured to respond on behalf of either the client or the server. Either end believes that their communication is with the other end device; whereas, in fact, it is between them and the router, removing the need to raise the line with all the cost involved. Figure 7-15 clearly shows the mechanism that is involved.

Figure 7-15 *IPX Spoofing*

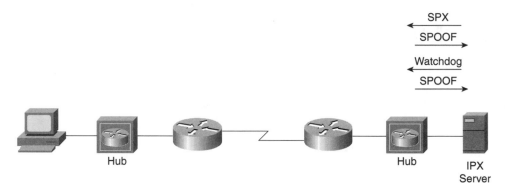

To configure IPX spoofing, use the commands in Table 7-11.

Table 7-11 *IPX Spoofing Commands for DDR. All These Commands Are Interface Commands.*

Command	Explanation
no ipx route-cache	Disables any fast or optimum caching and is required to examine the frame in sufficient detail to see that the Cisco router needs to spoof the response.
ipx spx-spoof	Enables SPX spoofing for connection-oriented sessions across the DDR line.
ipx watchdog-spoof	Enables watchdog spoofing from the server.
ipx spx-idle-time *seconds*	Sets the amount of time that transpires before the spoofing of the SPX keepalives will start. It also determines when the link will be dropped. If the link is configured to be dropped after 4 minutes of no activity, for example, and the **spx-idle-time** is set to 3 minutes, the line will disconnect after 7 minutes.

Despite all the possible configurations available to reduce the traffic on the link, it is still fairly likely that it may become saturated with traffic. As you have seen, the result of an oversubscribed line is congestion that results inevitably in the interface queues dropping packets.

Queuing

This section deals with application survival, after everything has been done to reduce the traffic load on the line. Sometimes all unnecessary traffic has been removed and still there is congestion on the line and no possibility of increasing the bandwidth capacity of the line. In this instance, it is necessary to identify which protocols will be granted access to the line first and how much of the bandwidth is available to them. This decision is made based on a solid understanding of the traffic flow in the organization and the resilience and strategic importance of the applications they support.

The solution is queuing. Three main queuing strategies are available, although it should be understood that Cisco tunes the code ceaselessly to improve the switching fabric and thus performance. A lot of these improvements occur behind the scenes.

The three queuing techniques described in this book are as follows:

- Weighted fair queuing

- Priority queuing

- Custom queuing

Weighted Fair Queuing

Weighted fair queuing is used on slow links and is on by default. It functions by sampling the traffic traversing the link and performing some basic analysis on it. Having sorted the low-volume inactive traffic from the large-volume traffic, such as terminal emulation from file transfer, it will send the terminal emulation (small packets, low-volume traffic) out of the interface first. Any remaining bandwidth is then equally divided among the higher-volume, continuous transfer traffic.

The result is hopefully that high-volume conversations cannot create *traffic trains* and monopolize the link.

Weighted fair queuing is on automatically and there is little to configure, although it is possible to set the discard threshold. The discard threshold determines the point at which the queue refuses to accept any more packets from a particular conversation until the number of queued packets drops below a certain level. The default is 64 packets in the queue. The command syntax to change this parameter is as follows:

```
Fair-queue threshold
```

Figure 7-16 illustrates the transfer of different types of data across a serial line using the intelligence of weighted fair queuing.

Figure 7-16 *Weighted Fair Queuing*

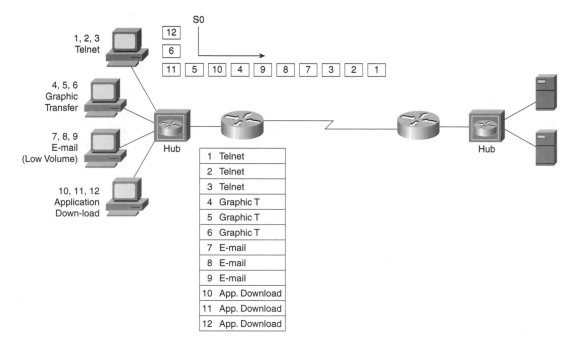

Priority queuing and custom queuing must be manually configured. They differ in function fairly subtly and, therefore, careful design consideration should be applied before implementation.

Priority Queuing

Priority queuing was the first queuing technology available on the Cisco router. It is used on slow links when all else has failed and is used to identify time-sensitive or mission-critical traffic so that it can be transmitted first. The traffic is identified via an access list, which is applied to the priority list and modifies the action of the outbound queue. Four priority queues can be configured:

- **High**—This is the first queue that is examined when the queuing process receives the attention of the CPU.

- **Medium**—This queue is examined if there is nothing in the High queue to send.

- **Normal**—This queue is examined if there is nothing in the Medium queue to send.

- **Low**—This queue is examined if there is nothing in the Normal queue to send.

When configuring priority queues, remember the following:

- When the interface queue is ready to send data, it must look in the High queue first.

- If there is anything in the High queue, it must empty the queue before it is allowed to move to the next queue.

- After it has moved to the subsequent queue, it must return to the High queue to check that there is nothing to transmit. If there is, it is required to transmit the traffic before visiting the other queues.

- The High queue should be smaller than the other queues and the Normal queue should be the largest queue. This is because the queues are processed in order and have to wait their turn. Therefore, if the High queue is large, it will hold many packets and the queue will never be emptied, starving the lower queues of attention. Applications that have data in these lower queues may well time out if this is the case. The lower queues should be larger to reflect the longer time the queue needs to wait before being processed; they will probably accumulate more packets during this time.

- Only mission-critical traffic or time-sensitive traffic should be placed in the High queue. This will minimize the amount placed in the queue and prevent the lower queues from being starved of attention.

- The result is that a preferred protocol is placed in the High queue; the other queues may never be looked at, and those protocols placed in lower queues may time out or the applications may time out.

Table 7-12 summarizes the commands to configure priority queuing.

Table 7-12   *Priority Queuing Commands*

Command	Configuration Mode	Explanation
priority-list *list-number* **protocol** *protocol-name* {**high|medium|normal|low**} *queue-keyword keyword value*	Global	This defines which protocol is to be placed into which queue. It can be very specific, identifying application or packet size in some instances.
priority-list *list-number* **interface** *interface-type interface-number* {**high|medium|normal|low**}	Global	This is included in the **priority-list** command and identifies an incoming interface. All traffic from that source interface on the router whose traffic is destined out of the interface to which this priority list is applied will be placed in the defined queue.

Continues

Table 7-12 *Priority Queuing Commands (Continued)*

Command	Configuration Mode	Explanation
priority-list *list-number* default	Global	This states what is to be done for all traffic that does not find a match in the priority list. Depending on the IOS version, this may or may not be a required statement. Therefore, it is easier to always configure it.
priority-list queue-limit **priority-list** *list-number* **queue-limit**	Global	The High, Medium, Normal, and Low queues have a default maximum number of packets that each can hold. This command enables you to change these parameters. However, the defaults make the limit in the High queue 25% the size of the Low queue. This is because the entries in the Low queue will have to wait longer to be transmitted. If the High queue has a larger number of entries, the lower queues may well be starved.
priority-group *list*	Interface	This applies the priority list to the interface. The priority queue will not take effect until the list is applied to the interface.

Figure 7-17 illustrates the commands in Table 7-12.

Priority queuing is very effective, but it has no granularity. Cisco introduced another queuing technique called *custom queuing*. This allows the bandwidth to be distributed among the different defined protocols.

Custom Queuing

Custom queuing resolves the problem seen with priority queuing in which the High queue could dominate the line if it always had traffic to transmit. In custom queuing, 16 queues are available and each queue is visited in a round-robin fashion. After a predefined threshold has been sent out of an interface, the queuing process is obliged to go to the next queue, until all the queues have been examined.

Figure 7-17   *Priority Queuing*

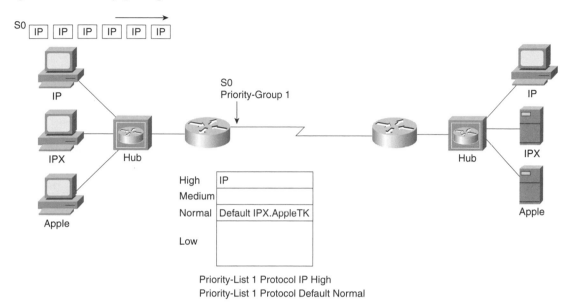

Priority-List 1 Protocol IP High
Priority-List 1 Protocol Default Normal

The threshold of how much traffic may be transmitted is manually configured; the default is set very low, at 1500 bytes. Because the amount of data sent out of the interface is determined on a queue-by-queue basis, and the protocols placed into the queues are administratively defined, it is possible to effectively allocate bandwidth on a per-protocol basis.

The defaults in custom queuing have changed since its introduction to the IOS. Originally, 10 queues were available; and if no threshold were set, the queue would be emptied. It is important to know the version of IOS you are running and to design and configure the network accordingly.

NOTE   When queuing is configured on an interface, either priority or custom queuing, it prevents the use of any router-caching techniques on the interface. This may slow the router process down because it is now making routing decisions; it may also affect system memory.

Table 7-13 lists the commands to configure custom queuing.

Table 7-13 *Custom Queuing Commands*

Command	Configuration Mode	Explanation
queue-list *list-number* **protocol** *protocol-name queue-number queue-keyword keyword value*	Global	This defines which protocol is to be placed into which queue. It can be very specific, identifying application or packet size in some instances.
queue-list *list-number* **interface** *interface-type interface-number queue-number*	Global	This is included in the **custom-list** command and identifies an incoming interface. All traffic from that source interface on the router whose traffic is destined out of the interface to which this custom list is applied will be placed in the defined queue.
queue-list *list-number* **default** *queue-number*	Global	This states what is to be done for all traffic that does not find a match in the custom list.
queue-list *list-number* **queue** *queue-number* **limit** *limit-number*	Global	The default is set to 20 packets for each queue. This command enables you to change this parameter.
queue-list *list-number* **queue** *queue-number* **byte-count**	Global	This is the command that sets the threshold on the queue, determining how traffic can be transmitted before it is required to visit the next queue.
custom-queue-list *list-number*	Interface	This applies the custom queue list to the interface. The custom queue will not take effect until the list is applied to the interface.

Figure 7-18 illustrates these commands.

Figure 7-18   *Custom Queuing*

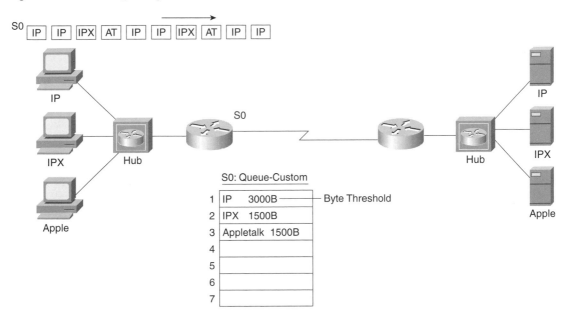

Verifying the Queuing Operation

To verify the queuing operation, issue the commands summarized in Table 7-14.

Table 7-14   *Queuing Executive Commands*

Command	Explanation
show queuing	Shows the details of the queuing configuration and status on the interfaces.
debug priority and **debug custom**	Beware of the **debug** command; it is useful, however, to display event information in real time.

Conclusion

When considering WAN connectivity, it is important to understand the nature of the traffic to be transmitted. Typically the WAN links are more expensive than LAN connections, which limits the available bandwidth. If the service provider is charging on a pay-as-you-go basis, it may be advantageous to only use the line when absolutely necessary. It will still be necessary to limit the traffic to only that which is absolutely necessary and even then to identify some traffic to be sent ahead of more robust protocols and applications. An example of time-sensitive traffic is SNA traffic that was created with the assumption that it would have a network dedicated to its own traffic. In these days of integrating SNA with the LAN data traffic, special care must be taken to ensure that the SNA sessions do not time out.

When considering DDR configuration, focus on remembering these four steps needed for DDR:

- Routing packets out of the dial-out interface
- Choosing which of these packets trigger the dialing process
- Dial parameters
- What happens while the link is up, and what causes it to come down

Foundation Summary

Table 7-15 summarizes the WAN framing options.

Table 7-15   *Summary of WAN Layer 2 Encapsulations*

Encapsulation	Connection Type	Comment
HDLC	Used on synchronous links	HDLC is bit oriented and connection oriented. It is defined by the ISO committee and may not be interoperable if used to carry multiple Layer 3 protocols.
PPP	Used on synchronous and asynchronous links	It uses LCP to negotiate and manage the link, and this allows CHAP and PAP security to be configured. It is interoperable.
Multilink PPP (a technology using a PPP encapsulation)	Used on synchronous and asynchronous links	This is PPP that allows the binding of different channels and multiplexes the traffic over the link.
LAPB	Used with X.25	This is the frame format for X.25; it is bit oriented and connection oriented.
Frame Relay IETF encapsulations (RFC 1490)	Used with Frame Relay	This is the standards body's frame type. It is similar to HDLC.

Table 7-16 summarizes some of the available WAN technologies.

Table 7-16   *Summary of WAN Technologies*

Technology	Features	Comments
Point-to-Point leased line	A telephone line dedicated to your use. It is available all the time and the bandwidth is guaranteed.	This is used for constant high-volume traffic such as between business sites.
ISDN	This is a dialup system based on a digitized telephone network.	It is used as backup and occasional connectivity such as home users and connecting remote sites.
X.25	Defined at Layer 3, this is an older technology that is available in most parts of the world. It even operates over ham radio. It is a highly reliable transport method.	This technology is still used widely for dialing up to a remote server. It is also used to connect to areas that do not have more up-to-date, bandwidth-efficient technologies available.

Continues

Table 7-16   *Summary of WAN Technologies (Continued)*

Technology	Features	Comments
Frame Relay	This is a shared resource offered by the service provider, as is X.25. Frame Relay is a more bandwidth-efficient protocol than X.25, but it is not offered as widely.	Frame Relay is offered primarily as PVCs. SVCs may be available in your region; they are a relatively new technology. Frame Relay PVCs are an excellent solution for companies that have constant traffic between remote sites.
SMDS	A cell-switching technology, based on Broadband ISDN. It is a connectionless protocol.	It is very fast but is not widely deployed, mainly due to competition with ATM.
ATM	A cell-switching technology that is connection oriented. It allows the multiplexing of different data types and offers QoS routing.	An increasingly popular solution because of its high throughput capabilities.

Table 7-17 summarizes the various queuing options available.

Table 7-17   *Summary of Queuing Options*

Weighted Fair Queuing	Priority Queuing	Custom Queuing
No queue lists	Four queues	16 queues
Low volume given priority	High queue serviced first	Round-robin service
Conversation dispatching	Packet dispatching	Threshold dispatching
Interactive traffic gets priority	Critical traffic gets priority	Allocation of available bandwidth
File transfers get balanced access	Designed for low-bandwidth links	Designed for higher-speed, low-bandwidth links
Enabled by default	Must configure	Must configure

Q&A

The following questions test your understanding of the topics covered in this chapter. The answers appear in Appendix A, "Answers to Quizzes and Q&As," on page xxx. If you get an answer wrong, review the answer and ensure that you understand the reason for your mistake. If you are confused by the answer, refer back to the text in the chapter to review the concepts.

1 Describe one key difference between what Cisco calls DDR legacy and DDR dialer profiles.

_____

_____

_____

2 Configure logic defining that traffic from FTP clients in 10.1.1.0/24 is considered interesting for DDR. Enable that logic on serial 0. Ignore other DDR parameters.

_____

_____

_____

Use Figure 7-19 to answer questions 3–10.

Figure 7-19   *Network Diagram for Use with "Q&A" Questions*

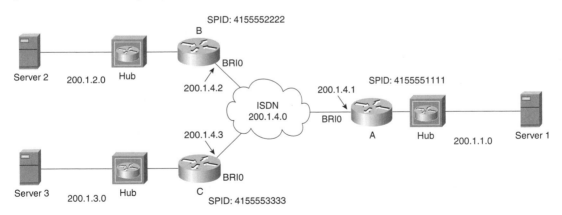

3 Configure Router A such that IP packets are directed out of BRI0 to sites B and C.

_____

_____

_____

4 Configure Router A so that packets from Web clients in 200.1.1.0, connecting to servers at sites B or C, are considered interesting. All other IP is boring.

_____

_____

_____

5 Configure DDR map statements on Router A referring to B and C. Assume CHAP is configured, and that the routers' host names are RouterA, RouterB, and RouterC.

_____

_____

_____

6 Configure commands on Router A so that the connection is taken down after 2 minutes of uninteresting traffic.

_____

_____

_____

7 Configure Router A so that IPX packets to Server2 and Server3 are directed out of BRI0 to sites B and C. The IPX addresses on the BRI interfaces are 4.0200.1111.1111 on RouterA, 4.0200.2222.2222 on RouterB, and 4.0200.3333.3333 on RouterC. The servers use internal networks 102 and 103, respectively.

_____

_____

_____

8 Configure commands on Router A so that packets from any IPX clients connecting to file services on Server 2 and Server 3 are considered interesting. Server 2 and Server 3 use internal networks 102 and 103, respectively. All other IPX is boring.

_____

_____

_____

9 Configure DDR map statements for IPX on Router A referring to B and C. Assume CHAP is configured, and that the routers' host names are RouterA, RouterB, and RouterC.

_____

_____

_____

10 Configure DDR so that the connection is taken down after 30 seconds of uninteresting traffic, but only if other interesting traffic is waiting on a B channel. Also configure to allow the second B channel to be used if the traffic load exceeds 50% in either direction on the link.

_____

_____

_____

Scenarios

The following case studies and questions are designed to draw together the content of the chapter and exercise your understanding of the concepts. There is not necessarily a right answer. The thought process and practice in manipulating the concepts is the goal of this section.

The answers to the scenario questions are found at the end of this chapter.

Scenario 7-1

In Figure 7-20, the Atlanta router will be dialing to Boston and Nashville based on DDR configuration. Examine the network diagram in Figure 7-20 and the configuration for Atlanta in Example 7-8, and answer the questions that follow.

Figure 7-20 *Network Diagram for Scenario 7-1*

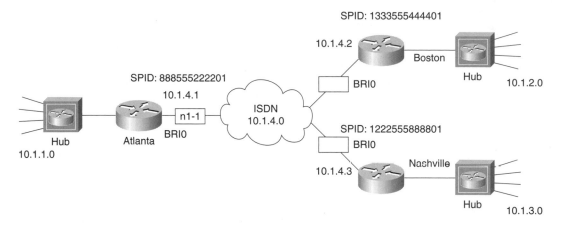

Example 7-8 *Atlanta Configuration, Scenario 7-1*

```
ip route 10.1.2.0 255.255.255.0 10.1.4.2
ip route 10.1.3.0 255.255.255.0 10.1.4.3
username Boston password Brice
username Nashville password Steph
access-list 120 permit tcp any 10.1.2.0 0.0.0.255 eq 80
access-list 120 permit tcp any 10.1.3.0 0.0.0.255 eq 21
dialer-list 5 protocol ip list 120
isdn switch-type ni-1
interface bri 0
encapsulation ppp
ip address 10.1.4.1 255.255.255.0
isdn spid1 888555222201
ppp authentication chap
```

Example 7-8 *Atlanta Configuration, Scenario 7-1 (Continued)*

```
dialer-group 4
dialer idle-timeout 600
dialer fast-idle 120
dialer load-threshold 50 either
dialer map ip 10.1.4.2 broadcast name Boston 1333555444401
dialer map ip 10.1.4.3 broadcast name Nashville 1222555888801
router igrp 6
network 10.0.0.0
```

Answer the following questions:

1 Define the type of traffic that initiates the dial to Boston and to Nashville.

2 According to Cisco IOS documentation, is this considered legacy DDR or dialer profiles DDR? Why?

3 Can both B channels be dialed to the same site at the same time with this configuration? If so, is MLPPP in use?

4 What can cause a B channel to Boston to be taken down? To Nashville?

5 What configuration command(s) would enable call screening on Atlanta to allow only calls from Boston and Nashville? Would this stop Atlanta from dialing out?

6 Create a configuration for Boston to allow:

   a Receiving calls from Atlanta

   b ISDN configuration on BRI 0; the switch is a DMS-100

   c Caller ID to allow only Atlanta to call

Scenario 7-2

The network from Scenario 7-1 has expanded to add three additional sites, as shown in Figure 7-21. Table 7-18 lists some important configuration details for the new expanded network. Create a new configuration for Atlanta using DDR dialer profiles, as detailed in the list that follows:

1 Plan your configuration. Make a list of details missing in this problem statement that you need to decide on before you create configurations.

2 Create a configuration for Atlanta based on the stated criteria. Do not add extra B channels based on load, and use only one dialer pool. Any other parameters not mentioned already can be configured with any value.

Figure 7-21 *Scenario 7-2 Network Diagram*

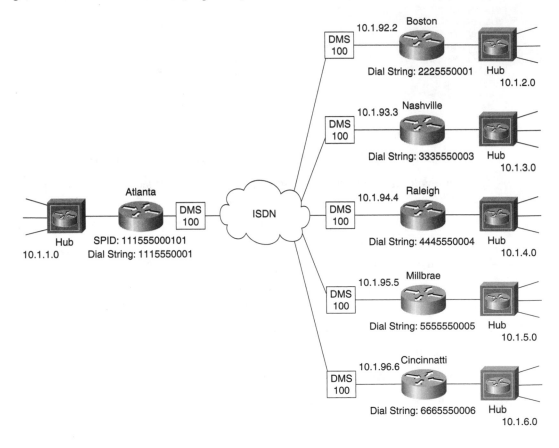

Table 7-18 *DDR Dialer Profile Configuration Details—Scenario 7-2*

Router	Configuration Item
All routers	Connected to DMS-100 switch.
All routers	Traffic from FTP clients in Atlanta reaching servers in each site is interesting. All else is boring.
Atlanta	SPID: 111555000101 Dial string: 1115550001
Boston	SPID: 222555000201 Dial string: 2225550002
Nashville	SPID: 333555000301 Dial string: 3335550003

Table 7-18   *DDR Dialer Profile Configuration Details—Scenario 7-2 (Continued)*

Router	Configuration Item
Raleigh	SPID: 444555000401 Dial string: 4445550004
Millbrae	SPID: 555555000501 Dial string: 5555550005
Cincinnati	SPID: 666555000601 Dial string: 6665550006
IP addresses	Shown in Figure 7-21.

Scenario 7-3

A dial backup strategy should be implemented for the network in Figure 7-22. When packets for NetWare servers Server1 and Server2 cannot get through the Frame Relay VC to Atlanta, each remote router should dial in to Atlanta to replace the connectivity.

Figure 7-22   *Scenario 7-3 Network Diagram*

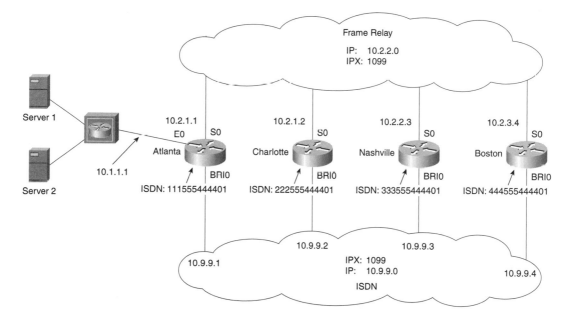

Create the additional configuration needed on Atlanta, Charlotte, Nashville, and Boston to cause them to dial Atlanta. Use DDR legacy configuration. The current configurations to be added to all four routers are in Examples 7-9, 7-10, 7-11, and 7-12. Use the following requirements as a guide to create the additional configuration:

- Only packets to file services on Server 1 and Server 2 (internal network numbers 101 and 102) are interesting.

- Dial connections should come down after 120 seconds.

- The only IP traffic allowed over the dial links is Telnet and routing updates.

- Atlanta's SPID to be used for dial is 404555111101. Nashville's is 333555333301, Charlotte's is 222555222201, and Boston's is 444555444401.

- IPX RIP is used for the IPX routing protocol.

- Use IP subnet 10.9.9.0/24 and IPX network 1099 on the BRI interfaces.

- Each router is connected to a DMS-100 switch.

- Each router has one BRI interface, BRI0.

Add to the configurations in Examples 7-9 through 7-12 to complete the scenario.

Example 7-9 *Atlanta Configuration*

```
ipx routing 0000.cafe.cafe
no ip domain-lookup
interface serial0
encapsulation frame-relay
!link to Charlotte
interface serial 0.1
interface-dlci 41
ip address 10.2.1.1 255.255.255.0
ipx network 1021
!link to Nashville
interface serial 0.2
interface-dlci 42
ip address 10.2.2.1 255.255.255.0
ipx network 1022
!link to Boston
interface serial 0.3
interface-dlci 43
ip address 10.2.3.1 255.255.255.0
ipx network 1023
!link to servers
interface ethernet 0
ip address 10.1.1.1 255.255.255.0
ipx network 1011
router igrp 1
network 10.0.0.0
```

Example 7-10 *Charlotte Configuration*

```
hostname Charlotte
ipx routing 0200.bbbb.bbbb
interface serial0
encapsulation frame-relay
!link to Atlanta
interface serial 0.1
interface-dlci 40
ip address 10.2.1.2 255.255.255.0
ipx network 1021
interface ethernet 0
ip address 10.1.2.2 255.255.255.0
ipx network 1012
router igrp 1
network 10.0.0.0
```

Example 7-11 *Nashville Configuration*

```
hostname Nashville
ipx routing 0200.cccc.ccccinterface serial0
encapsulation frame-relay
interface serial 0.1
!link to Atlanta
ip address 10.2.2.3 255.255.255.0
interface-dlci 40
ipx network 1022
interface ethernet 0
ip address 10.1.3.3 255.255.255.0
ipx network 1013
router igrp 1
network 10.0.0.0
```

Example 7-12 *Boston Configuration*

```
hostname boston
ipx routing 0200.dddd.dddd
interface serial0
encapsulation frame-relay
interface serial 0.1
!link to Atlanta
ip address 10.2.3.4 255.255.255.0
interface-dlci 40
ipx network 1023
interface ethernet 0
ip address 10.1.4.4 255.255.255.0
ipx network 1014
router igrp 1
network 10.0.0.0
```

Scenario Answers

The answers provided in this section are not necessarily the only possible answers to the questions. The questions are designed to test your knowledge and to give practical exercise in certain key areas. This section is intended to test and exercise skills and concepts detailed in the body of this chapter.

If your answer is different, ask yourself whether it follows the tenets explained in the answers provided. Your answer is correct not if it matches the solution provided in the book, but rather if it has included the principles of design laid out in the chapter.

In this way, the testing provided in these scenarios is deeper: It examines not only your knowledge, but also your understanding and ability to apply that knowledge to problems.

If you do not get the correct answer, refer back to the text and review the subject tested. Be certain to also review your notes on the question to ensure that you understand the principles of the subject.

Scenario 7-1 Answers

1 Web clients sending packets to hosts on Boston's Ethernet trigger a dial to Boston. FTP clients sending packets to Nashville's Ethernet trigger a dial to Nashville. The same access list (120) can be used for both because the access list that defines what is interesting does not tell the router the number to dial—the map statements do that.

2 Legacy DDR. Dialer profiles use the **dialer interface** command, as well as the **dialer pool-member** subcommand on the physical interface. With DDR legacy, the **dialer** commands are interface subcommands on the physical interface; with dialer profiles, the **dialer** commands are under the dialer interfaces.

3 Both B channels can be dialed to the same site because the **dialer load-threshold** command tells the router to dial if the load exceeds 50%, in either direction. MLPPP is not in use, so once the second B channel is up, multiple equal-cost routes would be in the routing tables. (The **ppp multilink** interface command is used to enable multilink.)

4 The link is taken down when no interesting traffic has exited the B channel for 10 minutes, or for 2 minutes if other interesting traffic is trying to get to Nashville. The same is true for Nashville.

5 Knowing Boston's and Nashville's ISDN telephone numbers is the tricky part of the configuration. These can be seen in the **dialer map** commands on Atlanta. Example 7-13 shows the **call screening** commands.

Example 7-13 *ISDN Caller Screening on the Atlanta Router for Scenario 7-1*

```
interface bri 0
isdn caller 333555444401
isdn caller 222555888801
```

The commands have no effect on calls out of Atlanta, which this configuration is set up to do. Therefore, call screening on Atlanta has no effect in this case.

6 The answers to all three separate questions in question 6 are shown in Example 7-14. Because only one SPID is configured on Atlanta, the assumption is that one SPID is the only SPID used as the calling number when signaling. Example 7-14 shows the comments about each answer as configuration comment lines.

Example 7-14 *Boston Configuration for Scenario 7-1*

```
! Need this to match CHAP configuration in Atlanta
username Atlanta password Brice
interface bri 0
!The interface subcommands are ordered to match the questions,
!not to match what will show up in the config file in a router…
! The next two commands are required to work with the Atlanta configuration:
encapsulation ppp
ppp authentication chap
!  Next two lines are the required ISDN parameters. A second SPID is often needed.
isdn switch-type dms-100
isdn spid1 333555444401
! The next command enables call screening.
isdn caller 888555222201
```

Scenario 7-2 Answers

1 The missing details that affect the router operation are idle timeout, fast idle timeout, CHAP passwords, how to separate the BRI's into dialer pools, and whether to dial another channel based on load. For this solution, do not add additional B channels to a site based on load, and share both BRI interfaces in a single pool of interfaces. Any other details can be configured based on your preference.

2 Example 7-15 contains the suggested solution for the configuration.

Example 7-15 *Scenario 7-2 Atlanta Configuration Using Dialer Profiles*

```
ip route 10.1.2.0 255.255.255.0 10.1.92.2
ip route 10.1.3.0 255.255.255.0 10.1.93.3
ip route 10.1.4.0 255.255.255.0 10.1.94.4
ip route 10.1.5.0 255.255.255.0 10.1.95.5
ip route 10.1.6.0 255.255.255.0 10.1.96.6
username Boston password Brice
username Nashville password Steph
username Raleigh password Lisa
username Millbrae password Greg
username Cincinnati password Lenny
```

Continues

Example 7-15 *Scenario 7-2 Atlanta Configuration Using Dialer Profiles (Continued)*

```
access-list 102 permit tcp 10.1.1.0 0.0.0.255  10.1.2.0 0.0.0.255 eq 21
access-list 103 permit tcp 10.1.1.0 0.0.0.255  10.1.3.0 0.0.0.255 eq 21
access-list 104 permit tcp 10.1.1.0 0.0.0.255  10.1.4.0 0.0.0.255 eq 21
access-list 105 permit tcp 10.1.1.0 0.0.0.255  10.1.5.0 0.0.0.255 eq 21
access-list 106 permit tcp 10.1.1.0 0.0.0.255  10.1.6.0 0.0.0.255 eq 21
dialer-list 2 protocol ip list 102
dialer-list 3 protocol ip list 103
dialer-list 4 protocol ip list 104
dialer-list 5 protocol ip list 105
dialer-list 6 protocol ip list 106
isdn switch-type dms-100
interface bri 0
no ip address
encapsulation ppp
isdn spid1111555000101
ppp authentication chap
dialer pool-member 1

!Dialer details for connection to Boston
interface dialer 1
ip address 10.1.92.1 255.255.255.0
encapsulation ppp
ppp authentication chap
dialer idle-timeout 600
dialer fast-idle 120
dialer remote-name Boston
dialer string 12225550002
dialer pool 1
dialer-group 2

!Dialer details for connection to Nashville
interface dialer 2
ip address 10.1.93.1 255.255.255.0
encapsulation ppp
ppp authentication chap
dialer idle-timeout 600
dialer fast-idle 120
dialer remote-name Nashville
dialer string 13335550003
dialer pool 1
dialer-group 3
!
!Dialer details for connection to Raleigh
interface dialer 3
ip address 10.1.94.1 255.255.255.0
encapsulation ppp
ppp authentication chap
dialer idle-timeout 600
dialer fast-idle 120
dialer remote-name Raleigh
dialer string 14445550004
dialer pool 1
dialer-group 4
```

Example 7-15 *Scenario 7-2 Atlanta Configuration Using Dialer Profiles (Continued)*

```
!
!Dialer details for connection to Millbrae
interface dialer 4
ip address 10.1.95.1 255.255.255.0
encapsulation ppp
ppp authentication chap
dialer idle-timeout 600
dialer fast-idle 120
dialer remote-name Millbrae
dialer string 15555550005
dialer pool 1
dialer-group 5
!
!Dialer details for connection to Cincinnati
interface dialer 5
ip address 10.1.96.1 255.255.255.0
encapsulation ppp
ppp authentication chap
dialer idle-timeout 600
dialer fast-idle 120
dialer remote-name Cincinnati
dialer string 16665550006
dialer pool 1
dialer-group 6

router igrp 6
network 10.0.0.0
```

Scenario 7-3 Answers

Two details in these configurations were not specifically covered earlier in the text. For IPX static routes when using dial backup DDR, there is a need for setting a higher administrative distance, but the IPX route command does not support it. The **floating-static** keyword, however, causes the static route to only be used if no routing protocol-derived route to the same network is known. The other detail is that any type of outbound access list never filters packets created by a router. Therefore, the IP access list that allows only Telnet and routing updates really only needs to permit Telnet traffic because the routing updates would flow anyway.

The full configuration for Nashville is shown in Example 7-18. The other three examples that follow just include the added configuration for DDR backup (see Examples 7-16, 7-17, and 7-19). These three examples would be combined with the configurations in the examples in the Scenario 7-3 problem statement to form the completed configuration.

Example 7-16 *Additional Atlanta Configuration for Scenario 7-3*

```
username Boston password Laurie
username Nashville password Gary
username Charlotte password Jane
isdn switch-type dms-100
interface bri 0
encapsulation ppp
ppp authentication chap
isdn spid1 111555111101
```

Example 7-17 *Additional Charlotte Configuration for Scenario 7-3*

```
username Atlanta password Jane
isdn switch-type dms-100
interface BRI 0
encapsulation ppp
ip address 10.9.9.2 255.255.255.0
ipx network 1099
isdn spid1 222555222201
ppp authentication chap
dialer-group 1
dialer idle-timeout 120
dialer map ipx 1099.0200.cafe.cafe broadcast name Charlotte 1404555111101
ip access-group 120
access-list 120 permit tcp any any eq 23
access-list 120 permit tcp any eq 23 any
access-list 900 permit any any all 101 04
access-list 900 permit any any all 102 04
ipx route 101 1099.0000.cafe.cafe floating-static
ipx route 102 1099.0000.cafe.cafe floating-static
dialer-list 1 protocol ipx list 900
```

Example 7-18 *Nashville Configuration for Scenario 7-3, DDR Dial Backup*

```
hostname Nashville
no ip domain-lookup
username Atlanta password Gary
isdn switch-type dms-100
interface BRI 0
encapsulation ppp
ip address 10.9.9.3 255.255.255.0
ipx network 1099
isdn spid1 333555333301
ppp authentication chap
dialer-group 1
dialer idle-timeout 120
dialer map ipx 1099.0200.cafe.cafe broadcast name Nashville 1404555111101
ip access-group 120
interface serial0
encapsulation frame-relay
interface serial 0.1
ip address 10.2.2.3 255.255.255.0
interface-dlci 40
```

Example 7-18 *Nashville Configuration for Scenario 7-3, DDR Dial Backup (Continued)*

```
ipx network 1022
interface ethernet 0
ip address 10.1.3.3 255.255.255.0
ipx network 1013
router igrp 1
network 10.0.0.0
access-list 120 permit tcp any any eq 23
access-list 120 permit tcp any eq 23 any
access-list 900 permit any any all 101 04
access-list 900 permit any any all 102 04
ipx route 101 1099.0000.cafe.cafe floating-static
ipx route 102 1099.0000.cafe.cafe floating-static
dialer-list 1 protocol ipx list 900
```

Example 7-19 *Additional Boston Configuration for Scenario 7-3*

```
username Atlanta password Laurie
isdn switch-type dms-100
interface BRI 0
encapsulation ppp
ip address 10.9.9.4 255.255.255.0
ipx network 1099
isdn spid1 444555444401
ppp authentication chap
dialer-group 1
dialer idle-timeout 120
dialer map ipx 1099.0200.cafe.cafe broadcast name Boston 1404555111101
ip access-group 120
access-list 120 permit tcp any any eq 23
access-list 120 permit tcp any eq 23 any
access-list 900 permit any any all 101 04
access-list 900 permit any any all 102 04
ipx route 101 1099.0000.cafe.cafe floating-static
ipx route 102 1099.0000.cafe.cafe floating-static
dialer-list 1 protocol ipx list 900
```

The objectives for the ACRC exam for CCNP or CCDP certification are taken from the Cisco Web site at http://www.cisco.com/training under the heading "Cisco Career Certifications and Training." The following table shows the ACRC exam objectives covered in this chapter and also provides the Foundation Routing and Switching exam objective number.

ACRC Exam Objective Number	Corresponding FRS Exam Objective Number	Description
59	140	Define routable and nonroutable protocols and give an example of each.
60	141	Define various bridging types and describe when to use each type.
61	142	Configure transparent bridging.
62	143	Configure integrated routing and bridging (IRB).
63	144	Describe the basic functions of source-route bridging (SRB).
64	145	Configure SRB.
65	146	Configure source-route transparent bridging (SRT).
66	147	Configure source-route translational bridging (SR/TLB).
67	148	Verify SRB operation.

CHAPTER 8

Bridging

How to Best Use This Chapter

By taking the following steps, you can make better use of your study time:

- Keep your notes and answers for all your work with this book in one place for easy reference.

- Take the quiz, writing down your answers. Studies show that retention significantly increases by writing facts and concepts down, even if you never look at the information again!

- Use the diagram in Figure 8-1 to guide you to the next step.

"Do I Know This Already?" Quiz

These questions are designed to test not just your knowledge, but your understanding of the subject matter. It is therefore important to realize that getting the answer the same as stated in Appendix A, "Answers to Quizzes and Q&As," is less important than your answer having embodied the spirit of the question. In this manner the questions and answers are not as open and shut as will be found on the exam. Their intention is to prepare you with the appropriate knowledge and understanding to give you mastery of the subject as opposed to limited rote knowledge.

1 At which layer does a bridge function?

_____

_____

_____

2 What is transparent bridging?

_____

_____

_____

Figure 8-1 *How to Use This Chapter*

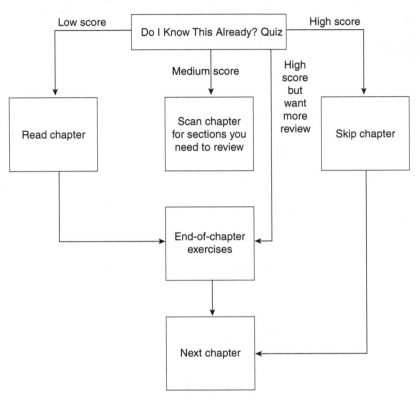

3 Which bridge technologies are used on Token Ring?

_____

_____

_____

4 In transparent bridging, what are the Spanning-Tree Protocols that may be configured?

_____

_____

_____

5 The command **source-bridge transparent** is used to configure which bridging technology?

_____

_____

_____

6 What is the RIF, and what is its purpose?

_____

_____

_____

7 What command is used to manually determine the root bridge in a transparently bridged network?

_____

_____

_____

8 State one difference between source-route bridging and transparent bridging?

_____

_____

_____

9 When would you implement source-route translational bridging?

_____

_____

_____

10 What is the purpose of a root bridge?

_____

_____

_____

11 What does RII stand for and what is its purpose?

_____

_____

_____

12 When SR/TLB is configured, it performs many conversions. State two things that it converts.

_____

_____

_____

13 What is a proxy explorer?

_____

_____

_____

The answers to this quiz are found in Appendix A, "Answers to Quizzes and Q&As" (see page 476). Review the answers, grade your quiz, and choose an appropriate next step in this chapter based on the suggestions diagrammed in Figure 8-1. Your choices for the next step are as follows:

- Read this chapter.
- Scan this chapter for sections you need to review.
- Skip to the exercises at the end of this chapter.
- Skip this chapter.

Foundation Topics

Introduction: The Difference between Routed and Nonrouted Protocols

The ACRC objectives mastered in this section are as follows:

ACRC Exam Objective Number	Corresponding FRS Exam Objective Number	Description
59	140	Define routable and nonroutable protocols and give an example of each.
60	141	Define various bridging types and describe when to use each type.

This chapter deals with those protocols that cannot be routed at Layer 3—either through the router or a Layer 3 device. These protocols must be bridged because they operate at Layer 2 and there is no information that the router can use to make a routing decision. This chapter explains how to incorporate these protocols within the organizational network that has a complex configuration of Layer 3 protocols. Typically, these protocols are older and may have their own quirks and characteristics that must be accommodated, such as sensitivity to time delay. The latest changes in technology and network design and the advent of the high-speed switch operating at Layer 2, however, have led administrators to be very creative in the designs of their networks and, therefore, the configuration of the devices that support that design.

It is important in this context to fully appreciate the differences between the functionality of Layer 2 and Layer 3 of the OSI seven-layer model. A moment's review is appropriate, particularly in view of the re-emergence of Layer 2 within the networks of today.

Layer 2 and Layer 3 Functions

The main difference between Layer 2 and Layer 3 is that Layer 3 has a hierarchical address structure of *network.host*. This allows the following to occur:

- Traffic is directed to a specific destination.
- Traffic is reduced on the network.
- Broadcast traffic is not forwarded across the router.

- The ability to increase the size of the network is easier due to the control afforded at Layer 3.

- Greater control of traffic is attained because the traffic can be identified by address.

- Traffic through the network propagates more slowly because the processing of packets requires more consideration and, therefore, more memory and CPU cycles.

At Layer 2, however, there is less information and less to do. Speed is the essential advantage of forwarding traffic at Layer 2. The following characteristics identify the Layer 2 network:

- A name or address that is not hierarchical

- Limited control or means of making decisions about the forwarding of traffic

- Traffic flooding the network to find its destination end device

- Broadcast traffic, typically network overhead, consuming the network resources

- A difficulty in increasing the size of the network because of broadcast traffic saturating the bandwidth

- High-speed networks

- Ability to work well in small environments and in networks that have implemented VLANs

When designing a network to function at Layer 2 or Layer 3, you must consider not only the requirements of the users and the application traffic, but also the characteristics from the preceding list. The devices used at Layer 2 and Layer 3 are very different—even though the Cisco router has bridging capabilities, the router is essentially coexisting with a bridge within the same chassis. The following section explains the differences.

Bridging Versus Routing

You know what a router is. A router operates at Layer 3 and forwards traffic based on the network portion of the hierarchical Layer 3 address. The traffic is only forwarded so long as no other conditions associated with that address are programmed into the logic of the router.

A bridge was the precursor to the router. A bridge operates at Layer 2 and also forwards traffic based on the address (but in this case, the Layer 2 address). Because the address is without any hierarchy, there can be no concept of directed traffic. Therefore, frames may have to traverse the entire network to find the destination end device. This may generate delays because of a greater demand on the network resources. As networks grow, delay-sensitive applications may start to timeout.

Originally, the function of a bridge was to extend the physical network. It allowed a greater number of devices to share the same logical network, while limiting the physical domain. This meant that although all the devices could see each other and communicate, they were not constrained by the physical restrictions of either Ethernet or Token Ring.

In recent years, bridging has been reintroduced (and now uses sophisticated high-speed devices called *switches*). It is now possible to either use a high-speed device at Layer 2 or a device that offers more control of the network at Layer 3; many of today's network environments actually have a mixture of both technologies. The switched environment is carefully limited and controlled. It is typically used in both the access and core layers of the Cisco design model. At the access layer, for instance, switching is often implemented within the building, enabling users to access their local servers at speed. At the core of the network, a switched environment is found after all the filtering and controls within the network have been applied and it is necessary to shift large volumes of aggregated traffic as quickly as possible.

When deciding whether to use routing or switching in your network design, you must consider many factors such as bandwidth requirements, traffic type, and protocols supported. Protocols such as IP, IPX, AppleTalk, and DECnet can take advantage of features provided by Layer 3 network services covered earlier in the chapter. Some older protocols that still exist were never defined with a Layer 3 address and are, therefore, nonroutable (having no option but to be switched or bridged). These protocols include NetBIOS, MOP, and LAT and SNA traffic.

Many different forms of bridging exist, including the following:

- **Transparent**—This technology is used mainly in an Ethernet environment, although the Institute of Electrical and Electronic Engineers (IEEE) has also defined it to work with other media, such as FDDI and Token Ring. The name *transparent bridging* is derived from the fact that the frame passes through the bridge unchanged, and the end devices are unaware of the existence of the bridge.

- **Integrated routing and bridging (IRB)**—This is a Cisco solution implemented in 11.2 of the IOS. It allows the Cisco router to be configured for both routing and bridging at the same time, providing great flexibility in the design and configuration of the network. This replaced the earlier function that allowed either routing or bridging of a protocol. With IRB, a protocol such as IP can enter an interface that is bridging IP and be switched by the router out of an interface that is routing that protocol. This is an extremely useful feature in a switched environment.

- **Source-route bridging (SRB)**—This technology was created by IBM and is used only in the Token Ring environment. The name accurately describes the functionality of the technology. The source end device provides information on the path to the destination. Hence, the name became known as source-route bridging. It works very simply. The source device provides information in the frame header, within the Routing Information

Field (RIF), as to which bridges and rings are to be traversed to find the destination host. This prevents the frame from having to visit the entire network in search of a particular address that has no group or hierarchical qualities.

- **Source-route transparent (SRT)**—The standards body determined that a bridge capable of only SRB complicated the network design and, therefore, ruled that every source-route bridge must also be capable of transparent bridging. These two functions act independently of one another, demanding separate processes within the bridge. When the frame enters the bridge, it is examined to determine whether it should be source routed or transparently bridged. This is easily decided by looking for the RIF; if there is a RIF present, the frame is sent to the source-route bridging process.

- **Source-route translational (SR/TLB)**—Although SRT allows both transparent and source-route bridge traffic to be forwarded by a bridge, source-route translational bridging converts or translates a transparent frame into a source-route frame and vice versa. This is a complex procedure and is not an industry standard. Although many vendors offer this functionality, care should be taken in interoperability.

The following sections explain how to configure these different bridging technologies.

Configuring Transparent and Integrated Routing and Bridging (IRB)

The ACRC objectives mastered in this section are as follows:

ACRC Exam Objective Number	Corresponding FRS Exam Objective Number	Description
61	142	Configure transparent bridging.
62	143	Configure integrated routing and bridging (IRB).

Although transparent bridging is easy to configure, you should take care because the implications of activating the bridging process affects the flow of traffic in the network and should be done with a full knowledge of the network topology. An understanding of the bridging operation is also useful. The following section discusses these subjects.

A transparent bridge sits between two or more physical segments. For this discussion, Ethernet segments are considered because the technology was originally designed for this medium and the majority of installations are Ethernet.

A bridge acts as a means of connectivity between the various segments. It operates at the data link layer (Layer 2). The decision whether to forward or drop frames is determined by the following criteria:

- Is the destination address in the bridge table sometimes referred to as the content-addressable memory (CAM) table?

- Is the interface associated with the destination address the same as the interface that the frame was heard on?

  If so, discard the frame because the source and destinations are on the same segment. Transparent bridging works on broadcast media. Therefore, the frame has been delivered to the destination at the same time as the bridge.

  If the destination address is on another segment, send the frame to the outgoing interface. There may be some filters that the frame needs to pass through before it can be queued to the next segment in its journey.

- If the destination address is not in the CAM table, the bridge process forwards the frame out of every interface, except for the interface through which the frame was received.

- If the destination address is a broadcast address, the bridge process forwards the frame out of all interfaces, except for the interface through which the frame was received.

How the bridge, or CAM, table is built explains the other name that a transparent bridge is known by: a learning bridge. From the moment a transparent bridge takes on life, it listens to the network. It listens to every frame that passes its way. Because transparent bridges work on broadcast media, it listens to every transmitted frame.

As the bridge listens, it updates its CAM table. It takes the source address and the interface on which the address was heard and stores these two pieces of information along with a timer in the table. In this way the bridge eventually learns the address of every active or transmitting device on the network. Figure 8-2 shows this.

The implications of the operation of the bridging process just described are those caused by saturating the network resources. There is an additional technology that helps prevent any problems from occurring, particularly when the network grows. This technology is a protocol called Spanning-Tree Protocol. Radia Perlman created it while she was working for DEC in the 1980s.

Figure 8-2   *The Operation of a Transparent Bridge*

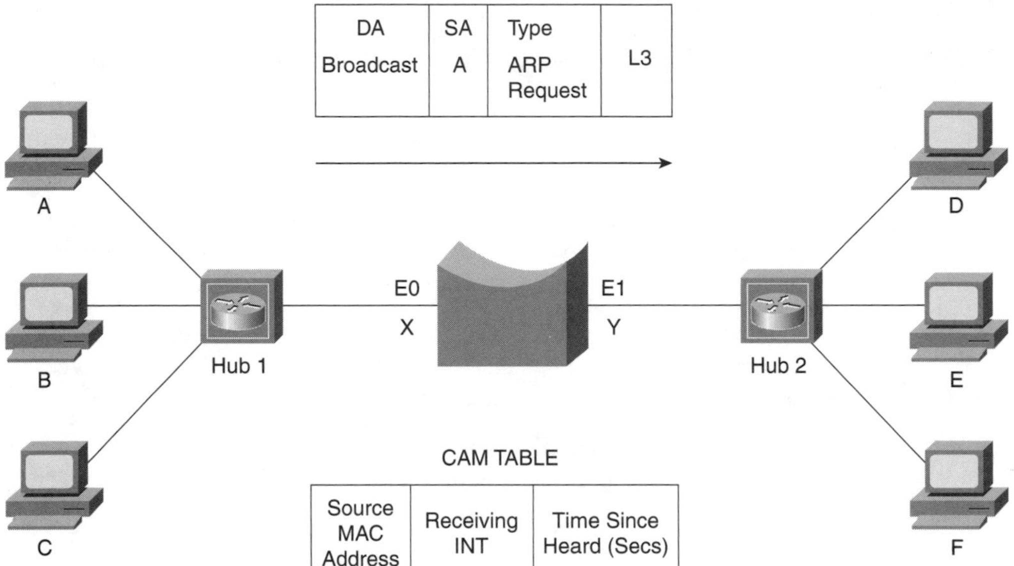

DA	SA	Type	
Broadcast	A	ARP Request	L3

CAM TABLE

Source MAC Address	Receiving INT	Time Since Heard (Secs)
A	E0	1
B	E0	13
C	E0	17
D	E1	5
E	E1	15
F	E1	8

The Spanning-Tree Protocol

The Spanning-Tree Protocol was devised to overcome problems seen in flat networks (networks that function at Layer 2). The majority of the problems derived from the use of loops in the physical topology of the network. These problems occurred when broadcasts were transmitted as every bridge forwarded them out of every interface, which resulted in a broadcast storm and eventual network death. Figure 8-3 illustrates this. Figure 8-3 demonstrates how a broadcast packet from PC A is handled after it is placed on the network. The following events occur:

1   PC A attached to shared Hub 1 sends out a broadcast packet.

2   Bridges 1 and 2 receive the broadcast frame and review the destination address.

3   Bridges 1 and 2 both forward the broadcast packet to the network attached to Hub 2.

4 Bridges 1 and 2 both receive the broadcast packets that were sent by the opposite bridge.

5 Bridges 1 and 2 review the destination address and forward the broadcast packet back to the network attached to Hub 1.

6 Events 2–5 continue to repeat.

Figure 8-3   *Bridge Loops*

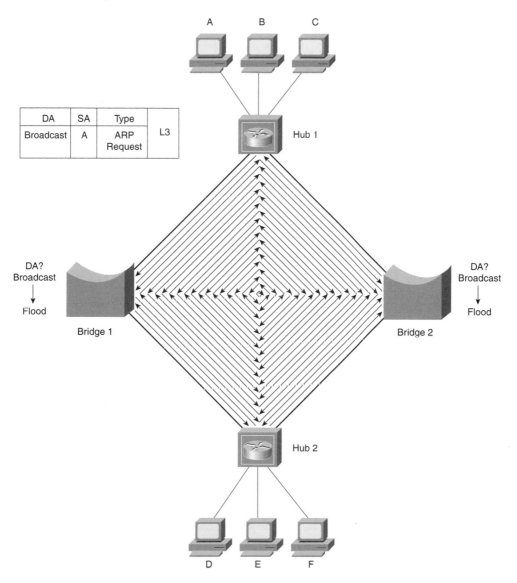

The Spanning-Tree Protocol solves bridge loop problems by communicating between bridges and shutting down redundant or alternative paths in the network. These paths are only shut down for the bridging process—for all other communication, they are still fully functional.

The decision as to which path should be removed is based on the spanning-tree algorithm. The Spanning-Tree Protocol elects a root bridge, which is a bridge that serves as a focus within the network. The Spanning-Tree Protocol then determines the best path back to the root bridge, shutting down the less-optimal path. The election of the root bridge is determined automatically by the MAC address, as is the decision of which path to utilize in the network. Both of these choices may be overridden manually on a Cisco router.

When the bridge process is configured, a Spanning-Tree Protocol must be selected. When the process is invoked, the Spanning-Tree Protocol has six separate stages before the network is stable. These stages include the following:

1 Disabled

2 Forwarding

3 Learning

4 Listening

5 Blocking

6 Bridging

When configuring a Cisco router to create a bridge process, the Spanning-Tree Protocol must be selected and then configured on a per-interface basis. It is possible to turn off the Spanning-Tree Protocol, although this is not advised because a loop in a bridged environment can spell death to your network.

Configuring a Transparent Bridge

When configuring a transparent bridge, the following steps are taken (**bold** indicates a required configuration step, the others are optional):

1 **Turn on the bridge process as a global command and select the Spanning-Tree Protocol. If in doubt, always choose the standards option.**

2 Define the priority of the bridge, which determines the likelihood of it being selected as the root bridge.

3 **Assign the bridging process to the required interfaces.**

4 Assign a cost to the interface, which determines the likelihood of that path being selected as the chosen path in a loop condition.

Table 8-1 shows a summary of the commands that can be used to enable the support for bridging:

Table 8-1   *Summary of Bridging Commands*

Command	Configuration Mode	Explanation
bridge *bridge-group-number* **protocol** {**ieee**|**dec**}	Global	Turns on the bridging process for transparent bridging and selects the Spanning-Tree Protocol to be used.
bridge *bridge-group-number* **priority** *number*	Global	Determines the priority of the bridge, and thus the likelihood of it being selected as the root bridge. The lower the number, the more likely the bridge will be chosen as root. When the IEEE Spanning-Tree Protocol is enabled on the router, values range from 0 through 65535; the default is 32768. When Digital Spanning-Tree Protocol is enabled, values range from 0 through 255; the default is 128.
bridge-group *bridge-group-number*	Interface	Identifies the interface as a member of the bridging process. All incoming frames will be examined and their source addresses added to the CAM table.
bridge-group *bridge-group* **path-cost** *cost*	Interface	This command states the cost of the outgoing interface as used by the spanning-tree algorithm. The cost is used to decide which path is chosen in the event of multiple paths to the root bridge. Referred to in the bridging world as a loop. The interface with the lowest cost will be placed in a forwarding mode and all other interfaces will be placed in a blocking mode.

Figure 8-4 illustrates the use of these configuration commands.

NOTE   With the current trend of introducing switched environments into the networks, the use of the spanning tree and the fundamentals of transparent bridging are re-emerging. Although the commands as described here are principally for use in legacy networks, the technology described is the same in the switched VLAN networks.

Figure 8-4   *Configuring a Transparent Bridge*

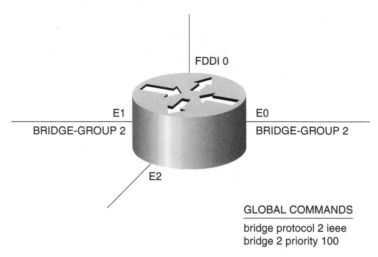

Having configured the router for transparent bridging, it is necessary to monitor the process. Table 8-2 is a summary of the most useful commands available.

Table 8-2   *Executive Commands to Verify the Transparent Bridging Process*

Command	Explanation
show bridge	The command shows:
	The size of the bridge table in blocks.
	How many entries the bridge table currently holds—This is an indication as to the available memory on the system and may be used in conjunction with the commands that display system memory utilization.
	Address—Each MAC address that is entered.
	Action—Whether a frame to that destination should be forwarded.
	Interface—The interface associated with that MAC address.
	Age—The number of minutes since a frame was seen with that address as either its source or destination.
	RX/TX count—The number of frames received or transmitted from that address.

Table 8-2   *Executive Commands to Verify the Transparent Bridging Process (Continued)*

Command	Explanation
show span	The command shows:
	The Spanning-Tree Protocol that was selected (IEEE or DEC).
	The priority of the bridge.
	The path cost of the interfaces.
	The state of the interfaces.
	The root bridge.
	The priority of the root bridge.
	How the bridge parameters are configured, for example, hello time, max age, and forward delay timers.

Transparent bridging can also be configured on a Cisco router to run integrated routing and bridging (IRB). The following section explains this.

Configuring IRB on a Cisco Router

IRB was introduced in version 11.2 of the IOS. It was designed to integrate with the switched environments that are being implemented. A switched environment is essentially a Layer 2, flat network operating in a similar fashion to a bridged network, but at a higher speed and with some additional utilities and protocols.

IRB allows a Cisco router to forward packets from a bridged interface by acting at Layer 2 and by a routed interface acting at Layer 3. To work, these must be separate interfaces. The power that this gives to the administrator is great. It is now possible to connect the switched or bridged network to the routed network.

The main reasons to implement IRB are as follows:

- To transition a bridged environment into a routed environment

- To segment the physical network

- To use VLANs and switches

The user should be aware of certain limitations when designing networks utilizing IRB, including the following:

- The same protocol cannot be used on the same interface for both bridging and routing.

- This utility cannot be used on older routers with cbuses.

- IRB cannot be configured on an X.25 or ISDN interface.

- IRB can be used only with transparent bridging.

- IRB cannot be used in conjunction with concurrent routing and bridging, which was its precursor.

If the purpose of IRB is understood, only explaining how it works and how to configure it remains.

The IRB operation requires that the interfaces configured for bridging a Layer 3 protocol and the interfaces required to route the Layer 3 protocol communicate with one another. The mechanism that connects these two disparate technologies is a virtual interface called a Bridge-Group Virtual Interface (BVI). BVI enables IRB to work. It is the collection of the bridging interfaces in one virtual interface, which is assigned a logical address so that the routing process can identify it. Figure 8-5 illustrates this.

The BVI is configured to include the bridge group number of the bridging interfaces as well as a Layer 3 address for the protocol. The BVI as an interface to the router not only needs a Layer 3 address, but also an associated MAC address; it takes this address from one of the bridging interfaces.

Configuring IRB for Traffic Entering One of the Bridging Interfaces

The technology for configuring IRB for traffic entering one of the bridging interfaces works in the following way.

The frame is sent from a remote host to its default gateway. The default gateway is the address of the BVI, a virtual interface within the router. The frame entering the router on a bridging interface sees that the MAC address is an address of one of its own interfaces. The frame is indeed addressed to the router. The normal routing process now takes effect.

After checking that the frame is valid, the type field is examined to identify the destination Layer 3 protocol. If that Layer 3 protocol is configured as a routable protocol on the router, the Layer 2 frame header and trailer are removed and the datagram is handed to the Layer 3 process.

Because the destination Layer 3 address is not that of the router, it sends the datagram to the routing process. The routing process issues a lookup in the routing table. If the remote network has an entry in the table, the appropriate outgoing interface is identified along with the next logical hop address. The datagram is forwarded to the Layer 2 or data link layer and queued to the outgoing interface. The outgoing interface is either a routed interface or another BVI for another bridge group.

If the frame received by the bridged interface is not a MAC address configured on the router, the router knows that this is a frame that must be bridged. It sends the frame to the bridging process that performs the normal bridging function. The bridging process issues a lookup in the bridging (CAM) table. If the MAC address has an entry in the table and the outgoing interface differs from the receiving interface, the frame is forwarded to the appropriate outgoing interface. If the MAC address has an entry in the table and the outgoing interface is the same as the receiving interface, the frame is dropped. If there is no entry in the bridge table, the frame is flooded out of all the interfaces in the bridge group, except for the receiving interface.

Figure 8-5 *The Bridge-Group Virtual Interface*

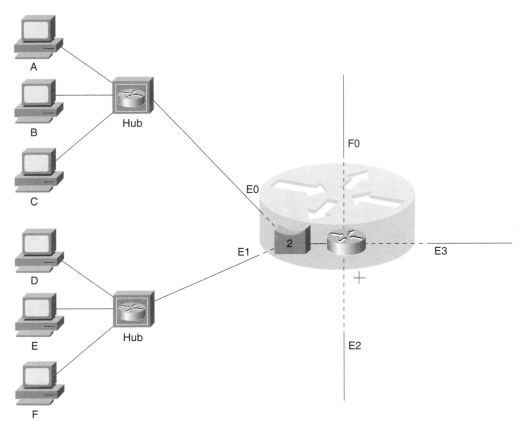

BRIDGE/CAM TABLE		
Source MAC Address	Receiving Interface	Timer (Secs)
A	E0	10
D	E1	15
B	E0	7
C	E0	9
E	E1	11
F	E1	13

ROUTING TABLE		
NET	Outgoing Int	Next Logical Hop
10.1.1.0	BVI 2	DIRECTLY CONNECTED
10.1.2.0	E2	DIRECTLY CONNECTED
10.1.3.0	E3	DIRECTLY CONNECTED
10.1.4.0	F0	DIRECTLY CONNECTED

Figure 8-6 illustrates this logic.

Figure 8-6 *Forwarding a Frame Using IRB*

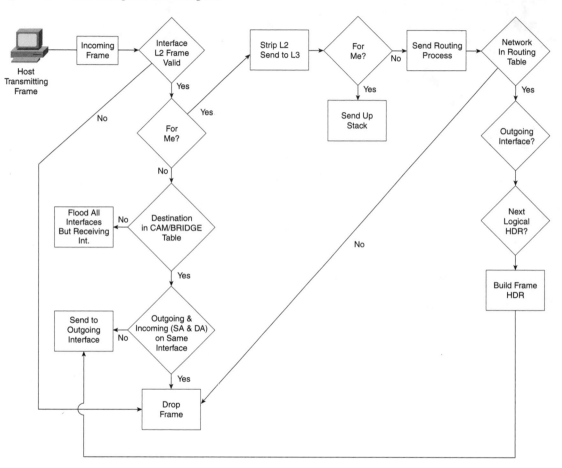

The process for forwarding a frame from a routed interface to a bridged interface is equally straightforward.

Configuring IRB for Traffic Entering One of the Routed Interfaces

The technology for configuring IRB for traffic entering one of the routed interfaces works in the following way.

The frame is sent from the transmitting host to its default gateway, which is the interface on the router.

The interface, on the router, upon receiving a frame addressed to its own MAC address, validates the frame, strips off the header and trailer, and hands the Layer 3 datagram up to the appropriate protocol. Because the destination Layer 3 address is not that of the router, it sends the datagram to the routing process. The routing process issues a lookup in the routing table. If the remote network has an entry in the table, the appropriate outgoing interface is identified along with the next logical hop address. The address of the next logical hop is now going to be that of the BVI.

Because the next logical hop at Layer 3 is an interface on the router, it knows that this destination Layer 3 address is directly connected and looks into the ARP cache for the MAC address of the destination Layer 3 address. If there is an entry, the outgoing interface is identified; the frame is built and queued to the interface. If there is no entry in the ARP cache, an ARP request is sent out of every interface in the bridge group.

Figure 8-6 also illustrates this logic.

To configure this technology on the router, the following steps must be taken:

1 Enable IRB.

2 Create the BVI using the interface number to reflect the bridge group number with which it is associated.

3 Configure the BVI to forward frames between the routed and bridged interfaces.

4 Assign a Layer 3 address to the BVI to start the Layer 3 routing process on the interface.

5 Configure any other characteristics for the protocol on the interface, such as access lists.

Table 8-3 shows a summary of the commands that can be used.

Table 8-3   *Summary of IRB Commands*

Command	Configuration Mode	Explanation
interface bvi *bridge-group-number*	Global	This command creates the virtual interface and associates it with the appropriate bridge group.
bridge irb	Global	This command turns on the capability to both route and bridge Layer 3 traffic between different interfaces.

Continues

Table 8-3 *Summary of IRB Commands (Continued)*

Command	Configuration Mode	Explanation
bridge *bridge-group-number* **route** *Layer 3 protocol*	Global	This command turns on routing for a particular Layer 3 protocol over a particular bridge group.
no bridge *bridge-group-number* **bridge** *Layer 3 protocol*	Global	This command removes the capability to route a particular Layer 3 protocol for a bridge group. It is used in association with the preceding command.

Figure 8-7 illustrates a sample network on which this chapter uses the IRB configuration commands.

Figure 8-7 *Sample Network for IRB Configuration*

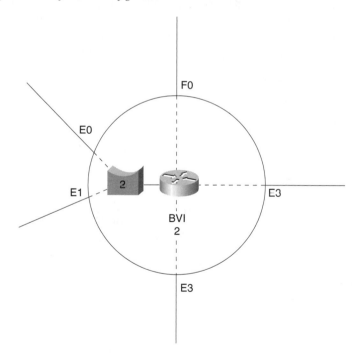

Example 8-1 demonstrates the configuration of the Figure 8-7 network.

Example 8-1 *Configuring IRB*

```
bridge irbbridge 2 protocol ieee
bridge 2 route ip
interface bvi 2
ip address 10.1.1.10
interface e2
ip address 10.1.2.10
interface e3
ip address 10.1.3.10
interface fddi 0
ip address 10.1.4.10
interface e0
bridge-group 2
interface e1
bridge-group 2
```

Having configured the router for IRB, it is necessary to monitor the process. Table 8-4 summarizes the most useful commands available.

Table 8-4 *Executive Commands to Verify the IRB Process*

Command	Explanation
show interface bvi *bridge-group-number*	The command shows:
	The MAC address of the interface
	All the statistics of the interface as if it were a physical interface
show interface *interface-type interface-number* **irb**	This command shows:
	The protocols bridged across the interface
	The protocols routed across the interface

When bridging over Token-Ring interfaces, a completely different technology is used—one that was invented by IBM. The following section describes the technology known as source-route bridging and explains how to configure it on a Cisco router.

Source-Route Bridging

The ACRC objectives mastered in this section are as follows:

ACRC Exam Objective Number	Corresponding FRS Exam Objective Number	Description
63	144	Describe the basic functions of source-route bridging (SRB).
64	145	Configure SRB.
67	148	Verify SRB operation.

Source-route bridging works completely differently from transparent bridging. In transparent bridging, the intelligence is in the bridge; the host is completely unaware that any additional operation is happening within the network. In source-route bridging, the intelligence and responsibility for finding the destination host is that of the source host. Essentially, when the host transmits data to the destination in the form of frames at Layer 2, there is additional information in the header stating the path to be taken through the network.

There must obviously be a mechanism by which the path to the destination is discovered in order for the source to be able to insert the path into the frame header. There are actually four methods, summarized as follows:

- **The local test frame**—This is an ordinary frame that is transmitted with the destination MAC address in the header. The trailer of the frame has a field that contains Acknowledgement and Copy (A/C) bits. The receiving host sets these to acknowledge that it has received and copied the frame into the buffer. When the transmitting host sees the frame return from its journey around the ring, it can immediately see whether the frame was successfully delivered. If the frame was not acknowledged, the source host can assume that the destination is not on the local ring and take the appropriate action.

- **The all-routes explorer**—The transmitting or source host, upon realizing that the destination is on another ring, must find the location and a path to the remote host. This may be done with an all-routes explorer. The host transmits a frame that has a Routing Information Field (RIF). The frame is sent across every available path once. Each bridge is responsible for forwarding the frame, ensuring that it never visits the same ring more than once, and adding its own information into the RIF.

- **The single-route explorer**—This is often known as the spanning explorer or the limited-route explorer. This is where the IBM Spanning-Tree Protocol is running on the network and the bridge treats the frame as if it were an all-routes explorer frame, but only receives and transmits on interfaces within the spanning-tree domain.

- **The routed frame**—This is a confusing term because the word *routed* suggests a Layer 3 operation. This is not the case; the bridges and hosts are working at Layer 2. This just indicates that the path has been discovered by the use of the explorer frames, also confusingly referred to as packets, and that the RIF is complete. This frame is therefore the reason for the explorer frames; this is a frame carrying data and traversing the network by means of a complete RIF.

These different frames are used when the source wants to communicate with a remote host. The actions of the two hosts are as follows:

1 The application on the source host sends data to the network application and data link layer. The host sends out a local test frame.

2 The source host hears the transmitted return and notes that the A/C have not been set.

3 The source host either sends out an all-routes explorer or a spanning explorer, depending on its configuration.

4 Each intermediary bridge adds to the RIF.

5 The destination host sees the destination MAC address as its own and takes the frame into the buffer.

6 Each explorer frame received by the destination host is sent back to the source host. The path back through the network is found by reading the RIF backward. Remember that by the time the frame has found the destination, the RIF is complete.

7 The source host receives the returning explorer frames and caches one of the frames, discarding the others. The selection of the RIF to be used is not stated in the standard's documentation, but many vendors use the method of race contention—that is, the first frame back contains the winning RIF.

8 Data can now be sent to the remote host. Each frame sent out has a RIF indicating the path to be taken.

Figure 8-8 shows the journey of an explorer frame through the network.

In Figure 8-8, because there are nine possible paths between A and B when A sends out an explorer packet, B will receive nine explorer frames, each with a unique RIF.

To simplify the operation of the bridges in the network, a bit in the header is used to indicate whether a RIF is present. If there is no RIF, this is a transparently bridged frame and the source-route bridge drops the frame. If the bit indicates that there is a RIF, the bridge looks further into the frame and invokes the source-route bridging logic. Figure 8-9 shows the 802.5 frame.

Figure 8-8   *The Explorer Frames*

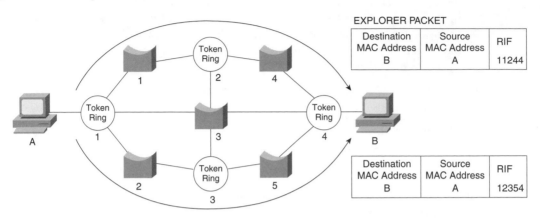

EXPLORER PACKET

Destination MAC Address B	Source MAC Address A	RIF 11244

Destination MAC Address B	Source MAC Address A	RIF 12354

Figure 8-9   *The 802.5 Frame*

OCTETS:	1	1	1	2 or 6	1 BIT	2 or 6	2	≥0	4	1	1
	Starting Delimiter (SD)	Access Control (AC)	Frame Control (FC)	Destination MAC Address (DA)	Routing Information Indicator (RII)	Source MAC Address (SA)	Routing Information Field (RIF)	Data	Frame Check Sequence (FCS)	Ending Delimiter (ED)	Frame Status (FS)

Each bridge in the path is responsible for building the RIF by inserting its own information. To ensure that the path is unique, the bridge number must be unique between the two rings or LANs that it connects. Thus, if there are parallel paths, there can be no confusion. The ring number must be unique, however, for the entire network. In Figure 8-10, the RIF shows how this information is stored.

Now that the fundamentals of source-route bridging have been covered, the explanation of how to configure the bridge will make sense.

Figure 8-10   *The RIF*

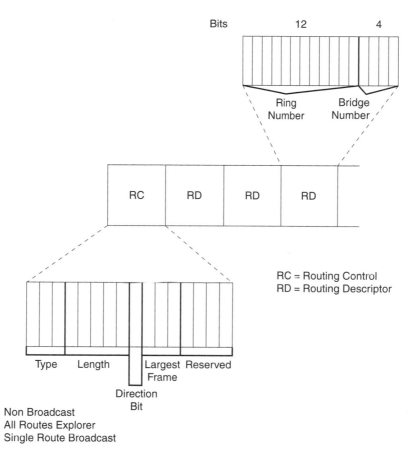

Configuring Source-Route Bridging on a Cisco Router

Table 8-5 contains a summary of the commands used by source-route bridging.

Table 8-5 *Summary Table of Source-Route Bridging Commands*

Command	Configuration Mode	Explanation
source-bridge *local-ring bridge-number target-ring*	Interface	This configures the router for source-route bridging. It states the ring the router is directly connected to on that interface (a number between 1 and 4,095). The bridge number states the number of the ring connecting the two rings (a number between 1 and 15). The target ring is a decimal ring number of the destination ring on this router. It must be unique within the bridged Token Ring network.
source-bridge spanning	Interface	This command manually instructs the interface to look for spanning-tree explorers in addition to the all-routes explorers.
bridge *bridge-group-number* **protocol ibm**	Global	This enables the automatic Spanning-Tree Protocol to run through the network and determine the path for the explorers to take. Note that this Spanning-Tree Protocol is not the same as the IEEE 802.1D Spanning-Tree Protocol defined for transparent bridging. This command is only available in the later IOS versions.
source-bridge spanning *bridge-group-number* [**path-cost** *path-cost*]	Interface	Having globally configured the Spanning-Tree Protocol to run automatically, it needs to be applied to the interface that it is to operate through. The bridge group number identifies the bridge process that was globally created.
source-bridge ring-group *ring-group-number*	Global	This configures source-route bridging on the router to deal with more than two interfaces. Originally, source-route bridging expected a bridge to be a PC with two interfaces. Therefore, when dealing with a multiport Cisco router, this command is required. The router becomes a virtual ring that connects the two physical rings. The ring group number is the number of the virtual ring that is configured. This number must be unique.

Table 8-5   *Summary Table of Source-Route Bridging Commands (Continued)*

Command	Configuration Mode	Explanation
source-bridge proxy-explorer	Interface	This command enables the interface to listen to returning explorer frames and cache them. When a host on the other side of the router sends out explorer frames with the same source and destination, the cache lookup provides the appropriate specifically routed frame with an already filled-in RIF and forwards it to the destination host. This reduces the amount of explorer frames on the network and thus network overhead.
multiring {*protocol-keyword*[**all-routes**|**spanning**] |**all**|**other**}	Interface	In a routed environment, source-route bridging cannot work because all the information sent between the bridges at Layer 2 is immediately lost when a router strips the frame and sends it to Layer 3. If there is no Layer 3 device available to make a decision and forward the frame and no information at Layer 2 to source-route bridge, the solution is to configure the **multiring** command on the router interface that connects to the source-route bridge. The **multiring** command allows the collection and use of RIF information.

The *protocol* keyword specifies the routed protocol that needs to be taken down to Layer 2 and provided an RIF.

The **all-routes** command states that all route explorers are to be used, because the router's interface now acts as a source host.

spanning states conversely that spanning-tree explorers are to be used.

all configures all frame types to be used.

other provides RIFs for Layer 3 protocols that are not stated as supported by the IOS. |

Figure 8-11 shows a sample for which Example 8-2 shows the configuration.

Figure 8-11 *Sample for Demonstrating Configuring Source-Route Bridging Using the Automatic Spanning-Tree Protocol*

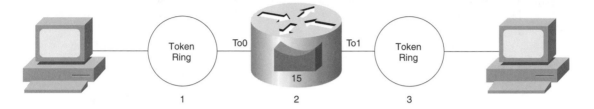

Example 8-2 demonstrates the configuration of the Figure 8-11 sample.

Example 8-2 *Configuring Source-Route Bridging Using the Automatic Spanning-Tree Protocol*

```
bridge 15 protocol ibm
interface to0
source-bridge 123
source-bridge spanning 15
interface to1
source-bridge 321
source-bridge spanning 15
```

To verify the configuration and for basic system management and troubleshooting, use the commands summarized in Table 8-6.

Table 8-6 *Source-Route Bridging EXEC Commands to Verify Configuration*

Command	Function
show source-bridge	This command will show:
	The maximum size of the RD, or the breadth of the network. IBM originally stated that this could be only seven bridges and eight rings in size; the 802.1D committee stated the limit should be 12 bridges and 13 rings. Most implementations use the smaller size for fear of finding an older bridge in the network.
	The number of received, transmitted, and dropped frames.
	Ring and bridge numbers for the router, with detail on whether they are virtual, local, or remote.
	Information on the explorer frames, and whether they are spanning-tree frames or all-routes explorers.
show rif	This command states:
	How the RIF is learned.
	How long ago the RIF was learned.
	How the RIF is written out in full.

It must by now be apparent that transparent bridging and source-route bridging are completely different technologies that have evolved separately and exist in different environments. Because small LANs were connected together to create corporate or enterprise networks, these separate bridging solutions had to learn to coexist. Two solutions are available: one is an IEEE standard; the other is not.

Source-Route Transparent and Source-Route Translational Bridging

The ACRC objectives mastered in this section are as follows:

ACRC Exam Objective Number	Corresponding FRS Exam Objective Number	Description
65	146	Configure source-route transparent bridging (SRT).
66	147	Configure source-route translational bridging (SR/TLB).

The standard's solution for connecting a source-route bridged network and a transparently bridged network is to allow the two technologies to coexist in the same bridge as separate processes that have no communication between them. This is called source-route transparent bridging (SRT).

The other solution that is available to interconnect two technologies is source-route translational bridging—where, as the name suggests, there is a translation between the technologies. Although many vendors provide this solution, it has never been ratified as a standard and, therefore, each vendor's solution is proprietary.

Source-Route Transparent Bridging

This solution allows for both technologies to be present in the same bridge as two separate processes. The incoming interface looks at the incoming frame and, if an RIF is present, forwards the frame to the source-route bridging process. If no RIF is present, it forwards the frame to the transparent bridging process. It does not translate between the two technologies; it just provides for both to coexist in the same bridge.

NOTE   The source-route transparent bridge is an addition to the original SRB bridge and is only available between Token Ring interfaces.

There are no special commands for configuring source-route transparent bridging. All that is required is that both bridging technologies are configured. Because it is in compliance with the 802.1D standard, all SRB bridges must be SRT bridges. The bridge, or in this case the router running the bridging process, works it out.

Figure 8-12 illustrates the configuration and process.

Figure 8-12   *Source-Route Transparent Bridging Example*

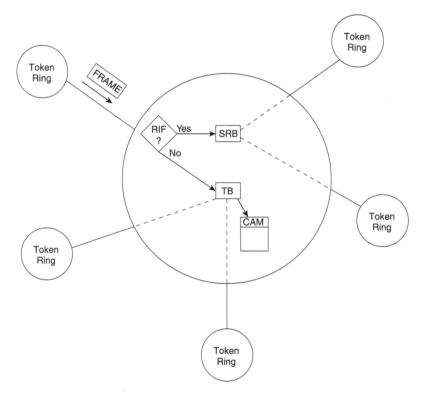

Source-Route Translational Bridging (SR/TLB)

Source-route translational bridging examines the incoming frame, determines whether it should be forwarded, and if so, determines out of which interface to propagate the frame. It then knows whether a translation is required and adds or removes the RIF as appropriate.

This technology works between Ethernet and Token Ring, but it requires more than just adding or removing a field. The considerations on translating between bridging technologies and media include the following:

*   Whether to add or remove the RIF.

*   The MTU of the frame may need to be changed because the MTU of Token Ring is much larger than that of Ethernet.

- Clocking at the physical level because the speed of Ethernet and Token Ring differ.

- The bit ordering of the MAC address: Although the entire frame header is changed to reflect the different media, the translation process must be aware that the different technologies read the addresses differently.

In addition to these translational problems that must be solved, there is the concern of how the different processes perceive the other bridging technology. In source-route bridging, this perception is also relevant to the source host.

Essentially, the configuration of the router fools the source-route bridging process into thinking that it is still sending into a source-route bridging environment. Likewise, the transparent bridging process is equally unaware of the "man behind the curtain" making the magic.

The source-route bridging process sees the transparent bridging domain as a pseudo ring, while the transparent bridging process views the source-route bridging domain as a virtual bridge group.

Figure 8-13 illustrates the logic of the translational bridging process.

To configure source-route translational bridging, use the following command syntax:

```
Router(config)# source-bridge transparent
ring-group
pseudo-ring
bridge-number
transparent-bridge-group-number [oui]
```

An explanation of the various parts of the command follows:

- The first part of the command indicates the two technologies that need to be tied together, source-route bridging and transparent bridging.

- *ring-group* is the virtual ring that was created in the multiport command to accommodate the source-route bridging process seeing more than two interfaces.

- *pseudo-ring* is the ring number given to represent the transparent bridging process to the source-route bridging process.

- *bridge-number* is the bridge number assigned to the source-route bridging process.

- *transparent-bridge-group-number* is the transparent bridge group that is being tied into the translation process.

- The *oui* parameter is used in the 802.2 oui field and determines interoperability between vendors. If Cisco equipment is being used, the value entered would be **90-compatible**; **standard** invokes the standard OUI form value, and the word **cisco** allows for future equipment.

Figure 8-13   *The Logic Flow Used in Source-Route Translational Bridging*

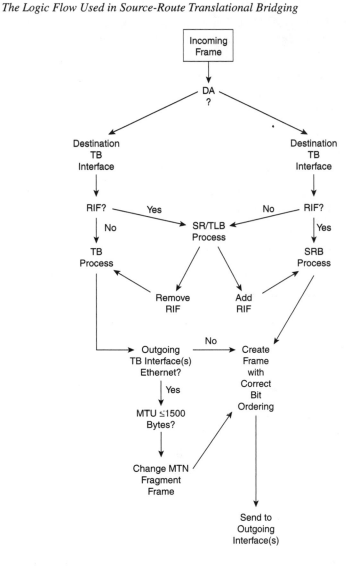

Figure 8-14 illustrates the diagram on which the sample configuration in Example 8-3 is based.

Figure 8-14   *Sample Network for Source-Route Translational Bridging*

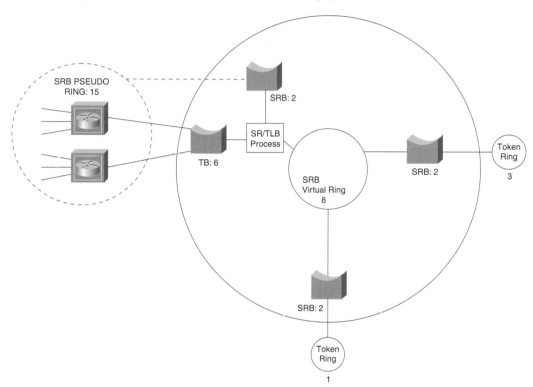

Example 8-3   *Configuring Source-Route Translational Bridging*

```
source-bridge transparent 8 15 2 6
bridge 6 protocol ieee
source-bridge ring-group 15
bridge 7 protocol ibm
interface e0
bridge-group 6
interface e1
bridge-group 6
interface to0
source-bridge 1 2 15
source-bridge spanning 7
interface to1
source-bridge 3 2 15
source-bridge spanning 7
```

Conclusion

Many thought that bridging was an old technology that was to be found in older environments and replaced with a routing solution as quickly as possible. It is true that as networks grow they are more difficult to manage and become increasing unstable when Layer 2 is the only means of control available. With the advent of the switched network design (which is a fast bridge [Layer 2] design), however, many of these problems have been overcome with a more efficient design that integrates both Layer 2 and Layer 3, as well as more efficient hardware and software.

Different bridging technologies are available, and much has been done to allow these different solutions to integrate into one network as the organizations merge and consolidate.

Foundation Summary

Table 8-7 contains a summary of routed and nonrouted protocols.

Table 8-7   *Examples of Nonrouted and Routed Protocols*

Nonrouted	Routed
LAT	TCP/IP
LAST	IPX
MOP	DECnet
SNA	XNS
NetBIOS	AppleTalk
	Vines

Table 8-8 contains a summary of the various bridging methods available on a Cisco router.

Table 8-8   *Bridging Options Available on a Cisco Router*

Technology	Description
Transparent bridging (802.1D IEEE standard)	Available on Ethernet, Token Ring, or FDDI. The intelligence is in the bridge, the end hosts being unaware of the bridging process. Also, the frame is unchanged when it is forwarded. The bridge learns the MAC addresses of the network, builds a lookup table, and forwards based on the result of the lookup.
Integrated routing and bridging (IRB) (Cisco solution)	IRB makes it possible to have a mixture of routed and bridged interfaces on a Cisco router for the same protocol. It does this by configuring a BVI, which includes all the interfaces in a bridge group, and allocating them a Layer 3 address.
Source-route bridging (SRB) (802.1D and originally 802.5 IEEE standard)	Available only for Token Ring and created by IBM. The intelligence is in the end hosts, who discover a path between them by sending explorer frames through the network. The frames build a map or RIF as they journey through the bridges. The bridges add to the RIF their bridge number and the ring number to which they are connected.

Continues

Table 8-8 *Bridging Options Available on a Cisco Router (Continued)*

Technology	Description
Source-route transparent bridging (SRT) (802.1D IEEE standard)	This is part of the 802.1D standard, which states that SRB is an optional enhancement to transparent bridges and that pure SRB bridges are no longer a part of the 802.5 standard. An SRT bridge is two bridges in one and will handle both transparently bridged traffic as well as source-route bridged traffic. It will not translate between the two technologies.
Source-route translational bridging (SR/TLB) (A vendor solution. There is no standard for this technology.)	Source-route translational bridging allows transparent bridging frames to be translated into source-route bridging frames. It will either add the RIF or remove it. Many other considerations are involved in the conversion, including MTU size, clocking, and bit ordering. It was introduced to allow SRB to communicate across WAN connections that used encapsulated bridging. (Transparent bridged frames tunneled through the WAN Layer 2 frame.) It was also necessary to introduce this technology for the FDDI backbones that were installed to connect the different buildings or campuses.

Q&A

The following questions test your understanding of the topics covered in this chapter. The answers appear in Appendix A, "Answers to Quizzes and Q&As," on page 478. If you get an answer wrong, review the answer and ensure that you understand the reason for your mistake. If you are confused by the answer, refer back to the text in the chapter to review the concepts.

1 Which of the bridging technologies are stated as standards?

\

\

\

2 Which command is used to configure source-route translational bridging on a Cisco router?

\

\

\

\

3 In an SR/TLB bridging configuration, how does the source-route bridging network appear to the transparently bridged network?

\

\

\

4 What does the Cisco command **multiring** achieve?

\

\

\

5 What is the purpose of the routing descriptor in the RIF?

\

\

\

6 How does an SRT bridge know whether to forward a frame to an SRB process or a transparent bridge process?

_____

_____

_____

7 State two restrictions that apply when using the IRB technology on a Cisco router.

_____

_____

_____

8 What does BVI stand for, and what is its function?

_____

_____

_____

9 The routing control field in the RIF performs what functions in source-route bridging?

_____

_____

_____

10 State one command that can be used to verify the configuration of transparent bridging.

_____

_____

_____

11 What is the purpose of the multiport command, and what command is used to configure this utility?

_____

_____

_____

12 What is the purpose of the Spanning-Tree Protocol in transparent bridging?

_____

_____

_____

Scenarios

The following case studies and questions are designed to draw together the content of the chapter and exercise your understanding of the concepts. There is not necessarily a right answer. The thought process and practice in manipulating the concepts is the goal of this section.

The answers to the scenario questions are found at the end of this chapter.

Scenario 8-1

The company is migrating from Token Ring System Network Architecture (SNA) to Ethernet and TCP/IP. The first stage will be to continue bridging until Ethernet is completely installed. This continuation of bridging will allow the upgrade of the mainframes and applications. Your company has recommended the use of source-route translational bridging (SR/TLB) as the Token Ring is swapped over to Ethernet. They have concluded that they should change the hosts last, but should otherwise follow the guidelines of converting the edges of the network first. This order will minimize the impact of problems that may occur.

Using Figure 8-15, answer the following questions:

1   Give the existing configuration for Router B, which is using SRB between the Token-Ring interfaces.

2   List the contents of the RD that would be created by an explorer packet that was taking a path through Routers A, B, and C.

3   Because this network is running SNA, it will be using all-routes explorer packets/frames. Given the physical topology shown in Figure 8-15, how many paths would be discovered, or how many explorer frames would reach the Mainframe 2?

Figure 8-15 *Diagram for Scenario 8-1*

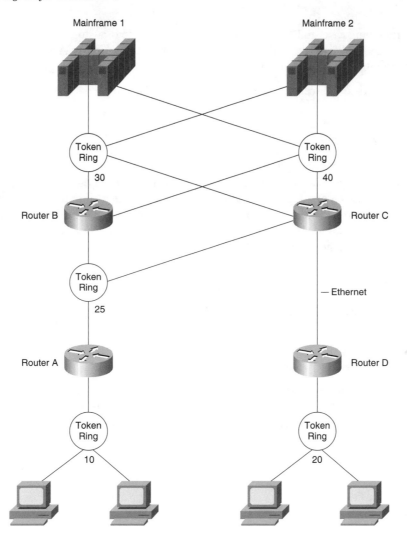

Scenario 8-2

The company in Scenario 8-1 has successfully achieved the first stage of the changeover to Ethernet and TCP/IP. While they still have some Token Ring in place, the network is running transparent bridging, except for the very edges of the network where the hosts reside.

Using Figure 8-16, answer the following questions:

1 Issue the configuration commands for Router B for IRB. Ensure that you include the following:

— IP addressing

— Transparent bridging configuration

— Bridge-Group Virtual Interface

Figure 8-16   *Diagram for Scenario 8-2*

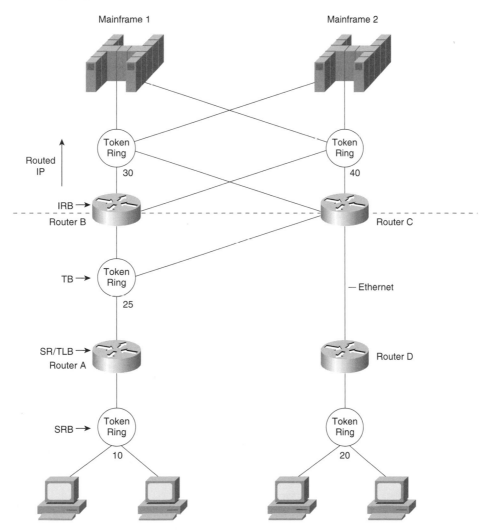

2 Configure Router A for SR/TLB. Ensure that you include the following:

— Transparent and source-route bridging configuration

— The use of the multiport utility

— SR/TLB configuration

3 Given the configurations that you have just written, explain why it was necessary to configure SRB for a multiport configuration on Router A.

4 What type of bridging technology will be configured on Router C? Give reasons for your answer.

5 If the network failed to work in a remote department and it was discovered that they had an old IBM SRB bridge that you were unaware of, what configuration commands could be used to solve the problem?

Scenario 8-3

A company is having problems on their network, which is transparently bridged. You have determined that it needs some reconfiguration. Given the information provided in Figure 8-17, answer the following questions.

1 Configure Router A to be the root bridge.

2 Provide the configuration commands and state where they should be applied to ensure that the path through Router B and Router C is chosen as the primary path.

3 Routing has been configured on Router A; is IRB necessary? Give reasons for your answer.

4 What commands would you issue to test the configuration of the network?

Figure 8-17   *Diagram for Scenario 8-3*

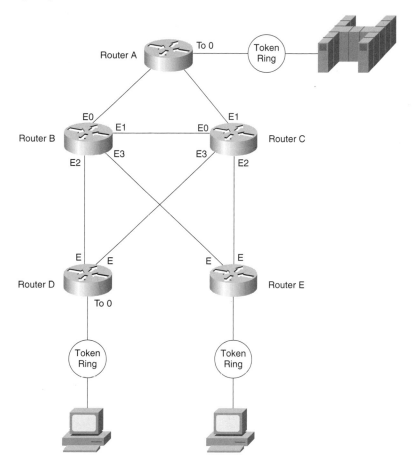

Scenario Answers

The answers provided in this section are not necessarily the only possible answers to the questions. The questions are designed to test your knowledge and to give practical exercise in certain key areas. This section is intended to test and exercise skills and concepts detailed in the body of this chapter.

If your answer is different, ask yourself whether it follows the tenets explained in the answers provided. Your answer is correct not if it matches the solution provided in the book, but rather if it has included the principles of design laid out in this chapter.

In this way, the testing provided in these scenarios is deeper: It examines not only your knowledge, but also your understanding and ability to apply that knowledge to problems.

If you do not get the correct answer, refer back to the text and review the subject tested. Be certain to also review your notes on the question to ensure that you understand the principles of the subject.

Scenario 8-1 Answers

1   Sample the existing configuration for Router B, which is using SRB between the Token Ring interfaces. Because there are more than two Token Ring interfaces, however, it will be necessary to configure a virtual ring with the **source-bridge ring-group** command.

```
source-bridge ring-group 5
interface to0
source-bridge 25  1   5interface to1
source-bridge 30   1  5
interface to2
source-bridge 40   1  5
```

2   Each route descriptor (RD) field carries a ring number-bridge number pair that specifies a portion of a route. Routes, then, are just alternating sequences of LAN and bridge numbers that start and end with LAN numbers. The RD that would be built taking a path through Routers A, B, and C would contain the following information:

```
Ring number 10
Router A bridge number
Ring number 25
Router B bridge number
Ring number 30
Router C bridge number
Ring number 40
```

3 The number of paths or explorer frames that the destination host would receive is eight. The frames are all-routes explorers and, therefore, although the bridges would examine each RIF to ensure that it did not propagate the same explorer on a ring twice, each path would have an explorer frame travel across it.

Scenario 8-2 Answers

1 Sample configuration commands for Router B using IRB:

```
bridge irb
bridge 3 protocol ieee
bridge 3 route ip
interface  t0
ip address 140.100.16.5 255.255.255.0
interface  t1
ip address 140.100.32.5 255.255.255.0
interface t2
bridge-group 3

interface bvi 3
ip address 140.100.48.5 255.255.255.0
```

2 Sample configuration for SR/TLB on Router D:

```
bridge 3 protocol ieee
source-bridge ring-group 5
source-bridge transparent 5 7 1 3
interface  e0
bridge-group 3
interface to0
source-bridge 20 1 5
```

Note that Spanning-Tree Protocol has not been configured because SNA will use the all-routes explorers.

3 It is necessary to configure the multiport utility on Router A because the SRB host was designed to understand configurations that included only two interfaces. This design has created three interfaces: the two Token Ring interfaces and the transparent bridge-group, which appears as a Token Ring interface to SRB.

4 Router C will be configured for transparent bridging. This is because the company is migrating to Ethernet only as the first step to the implementation of IP routing.

5 If the network failed to work in a remote department and it was discovered that they had an old IBM SRB bridge that you were unaware of, the configuration command that would be used is the **multiring** command:

```
interface to0
multiring ip
```

Scenario 8-3 Answers

1 Sample configuration for Router A:

```
bridge 3 protocol ieee
bridge 3 priority 100
interface e0
bridge-group 3
interface e1
bridge-group 3
```

2 The configuration commands that would ensure that the path through Routers B and C is the chosen path are as follows:

```
interface e0
bridge-group 3
bridge-group 3 path-cost 10
```

These commands would be applied to the interfaces E0 and E1 on both Routers B and C, forcing the path to go through E2 in both cases.

3 IRB is not necessary, because there is no Layer 3 protocol running on the router for SNA. That is to say, it is not being tunneled. All the Layer 3 protocols are independent of the SNA Layer 2 traffic.

4 The commands to issue to test the configuration of the network are **show span** and **show bridge**.

The objectives for the ACRC exam for CCNP or CCDP certification are taken from the Cisco Web site at http://www.cisco.com/training under the heading "Cisco Career Certifications and Training." The following table shows the ACRC exam objectives covered in this chapter and also provides the corresponding Foundation Routing and Switching exam objective number. The objective(s) that are explained within a chapter section are also listed at the beginning of that section.

ACRC Exam Objective Number	Corresponding FRS Exam Objective Number	Description
68	149	Identify potential sources of congestion in an AppleTalk network.
69	150	Configure zone filters.
70	151	Configure RTMP filters.
71	152	Configure NBP filters.
72	153	Identify channelized T1 and E1 configuration.
73	154	Identify ISDN PRI configuration commands.

CHAPTER 9

AppleTalk and ISDN Options

How to Best Use This Chapter

By taking the following steps, you can make better use of your study time:

- Keep your notes and answers for all your work with this book in one place for easy reference.

- Take the quiz, writing down your answers. Studies show that retention significantly increases by writing facts and concepts down, even if you never look at the information again!

- Use the diagram in Figure 9-1 to guide you to the next step.

Figure 9-1 *How to Use This Chapter*

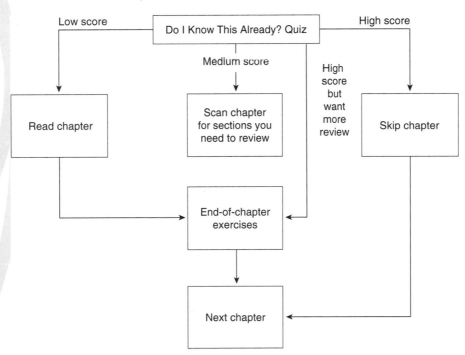

"Do I Know This Already?" Quiz

These questions are designed to test not just your knowledge, but also your understanding of the subject matter. It is therefore important to realize that getting the answer the same as stated in Appendix A, "Answers to Quizzes and Q&As," is less important than your answer having embodied the spirit of the question. In this manner, the questions and answers are not as open and shut as will be found on the exam. Their intention is to prepare you with the appropriate knowledge and understanding to give you mastery of the subject as opposed to limited rote knowledge.

1   What is the original routing protocol used for AppleTalk and how often are the updates sent out?

_____

_____

_____

2   How are services organized or grouped in AppleTalk networks and what protocol is used to maintain the service tables?

_____

_____

_____

3   State what the letters NBP stand for and briefly explain the purpose of the protocol.

_____

_____

_____

4   How do AppleTalk clients get network addresses?

_____

_____

_____

5   When and where would a GetZoneList filter be used?

_____

_____

_____

6 When and where would a ZIP reply filter be used?

_____

_____

_____

7 How many channels are provided in an E1 line?

_____

_____

_____

8 How many channels are provided in a T1 line?

_____

_____

_____

9 Some Cisco models support a MIP card. What does the acronym MIP stand for and what is its purpose?

_____

_____

_____

10 Which WAN protocols do T1 and E1 lines support?

_____

_____

_____

11 What is the bearer channel and the D channel in ISDN?

_____

_____

_____

12 What do the letters PRI represent?

_____

_____

_____

The answers to this quiz are found in Appendix A, "Answers to Quizzes and Q&As" (see page 481). Review the answers, grade your quiz, and choose an appropriate next step in this chapter based on the suggestions diagrammed in Figure 9-1. Your choices for the next step are as follow:

- Read this chapter.

- Scan this chapter for sections you need to review.

- Skip to the exercises at the end of this chapter.

- Skip this chapter.

Foundation Topics

Introduction to Managing AppleTalk Traffic and Advanced WAN Configurations

This chapter covers filtering techniques for controlling access to the AppleTalk network and for reducing unwanted traffic in an AppleTalk network, as well as how to configure T1 and E1 WAN lines. Understanding how to control your AppleTalk traffic will help ensure the best performance on your network. In larger networks it may be required to ensure the network stability. Covered Cisco IOS filtering options include zone filters, RTMP filters, and NBP filters.

Because network congestion is a particular concern over WAN links, it may be necessary to increase the bandwidth available by using T1 or E1 lines to remote sites; this is often implemented over ISDN links. This chapter describes this configuration.

AppleTalk Traffic Overview

The ACRC objective mastered in this section is as follows:

ACRC Exam Objective Number	Corresponding FRS Exam Objective Number	Description
68	149	Identify potential sources of congestion in an AppleTalk network.

AppleTalk was designed to be a "plug-and-play" network. This means that an AppleTalk user can plug a computing device into the network and use it immediately with little or no configuration. Locating network-wide services in an AppleTalk network is extremely easy. Several AppleTalk features account for this ease-of-use capability: for example, *dynamic address acquisition*, which is the capability of a client to learn an address when it boots up; and *automatic name lookup*, which locates devices on the network. This level of automation requires communication between the devices, which naturally generates network traffic. It is a truism to state that the greater the transparency of the network to the user, the greater the network traffic generated to automatically configure devices while ensuring unique addressing at Layer 3.

Apple's native routing protocol is the *Routing Table Maintenance Protocol* (RTMP). By default, RTMP broadcasts its entire routing table every 10 seconds. RTMP broadcasts can cause congestion on the network.

As AppleTalk networks grow, so does the associated traffic that occurs when hosts attempt to locate servers and printers and when routers exchange routing updates. By using Cisco IOS filters, a network manager can preserve the easy-to-use nature of AppleTalk networks and at the same time create AppleTalk networks that scale.

Before you learn how to control AppleTalk traffic, you must understand AppleTalk functions and services. The next section gives a brief overview/review of AppleTalk technology.

AppleTalk Protocol Stack

At the hardware layers, most standard media types are supported. Many Apple products contain a LocalTalk interface that operates over twisted-pair cable at 230 kbps. LocalTalk is an older protocol and is rarely seen in today's networks. For this reason, no LocalTalk interface is available on Cisco products. LocalTalk devices can be adapted to Ethernet, Token Ring, or FDDI where the physical media are referred to as EtherTalk, TokenTalk, and FDDITalk.

As compared to the OSI network layer, the *Datagram Delivery Protocol* (DDP) provides a connectionless datagram service. Running on top of DDP are several protocols. These include the following:

- The *Name Binding Protocol* (NBP) provides name-to-address association.

- The *Zone Information Protocol* (ZIP) provides a means of maintaining zone name mappings to network numbers.

- The *Routing Table Maintenance Protocol* (RTMP) provides a means of maintaining routing table information.

This chapter focuses on the protocols RTMP, NBP, and ZIP. As AppleTalk networks grow, filtering these protocols may be necessary to control excessive broadcast and multicast traffic or to prohibit unwanted access. The Cisco IOS software offers extensive AppleTalk filtering capabilities for each of these protocols.

AppleTalk Services

Hosts and servers are assembled in logical groups called *zones*, as shown in Figure 9-2.

When a Macintosh user requires a service, the Chooser provides a list of zones and types of services (including AppleShare file servers, printers, and fax services). After the zone and type of service are selected, the device names of available matching services are presented. The user selects the preferred device, and a logical link for that service is retained in the Macintosh for future reference.

Figure 9-2   *Zones Provide a Logical Grouping of Hosts and Servers*

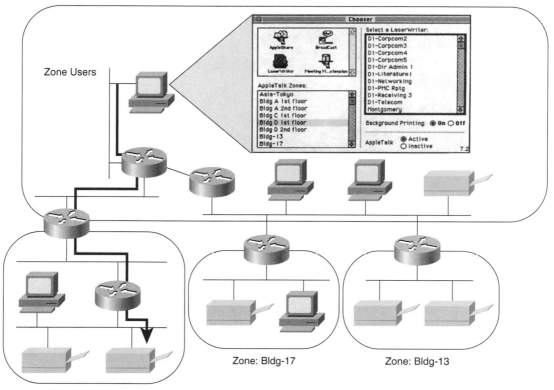

The underlying AppleTalk protocols provide user-selectable network services, as follows. When the Chooser is opened, a GetZoneList query goes to a router, which populates the zone list in the lower-left section of the Chooser. The box at the upper left is populated with all the network drivers loaded on the Macintosh. The user selects a zone and a driver, and an NBP query goes out. The responses to the NBP query populate the window on the right with the names of the networked devices that offer the selected service in the selected zone.

In the past, the Chooser created considerable amounts of traffic because it generated an NBP broadcast every 10 seconds while the window was open and a zone and device driver were selected. In 1989, Apple released version System 7.0 of the Mac OS, which includes an exponential timing backoff algorithm so that NBP broadcasts go out far less frequently.

Nonextended/Extended Networks

AppleTalk supports two network types: Nonextended (Phase 1) and Extended (Phase 2), as shown in Figure 9-3.

Figure 9-3   *Nonextended and Extended Networks*

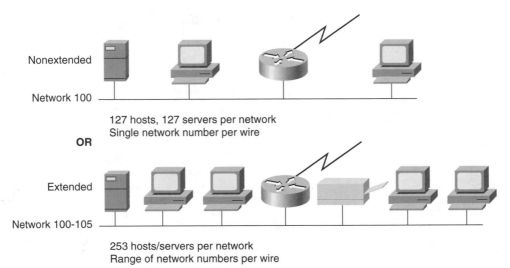

These two networks are distinguished as follows:

- Nonextended (AppleTalk Phase 1) networks allow 127 hosts and 127 servers per network. Only a single network number is allowed per wire, and only a single zone is allowed per wire. The data-link encapsulation type is Ethernet II. If this is too limiting, companies use extended networks.

- Extended (AppleTalk Phase 2) networks allow a total of 253 devices (in any combination of hosts and servers) per wire. A range of network numbers, called a *cable range*, is allowed per wire. The data-link encapsulation type is Ethernet Subnetwork Access Protocol (SNAP).

NOTE   I was upgrading Phase 1 networks to Phase 2 in the early 1990s. The use of Phase 1 networks is extremely rare nowadays.

Extended AppleTalk Internetwork

An AppleTalk Phase 2 internetwork can have multiple zones per cable range. In Figure 9-4, both Zone A and Zone B are located on cable range 101-101. Zone B is also located on cable range 110-110, illustrating the concept that zones can cross noncontiguous cable ranges.

Figure 9-4   *Extended Networks May Have Multiple Zones Per Cable Range and Multiple Cable Ranges Per Zone*

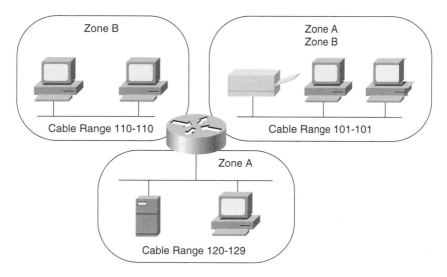

An AppleTalk Phase 2 network can also have multiple cable ranges per zone. In Figure 9-4, Zone A includes some devices on cable range 101-101 and all devices on cable range 120-129. This allows AppleTalk to decrease the possibility of a host selecting an address that has already been acquired because the number of available addresses was dramatically increased with the introduction of the extended cable range.

AppleTalk Zones

AppleTalk zones provide a way to localize broadcast traffic and to create *communities of interest*. A community of interest in the context of an AppleTalk network is a group of users that is typically collocated and shares local resources, such as servers and printers.

As the network grows, more zones and more users per zone are added, and therefore more traffic is generated to locate and track services. Therefore, filtering "unnecessary" traffic becomes an integral part of maintaining the overall health of the network. What constitutes unnecessary traffic is relative: What is considered unwanted traffic to users on one zone is essential for accessing services for users on another zone. Understanding these communities of interest is the basis of defining filtering systems for service-location traffic.

NOTE	Because the allocation of the zones determines the traffic flow of the NBP requests and replies, traffic management may be achieved by careful design. Refer to Chapter 2, "Managing Scalable Network Growth," for more detail on this subject.

AppleTalk Filtering Options

The ACRC objectives mastered in this section are as follows:

ACRC Exam Objective Number	Corresponding FRS Exam Objective Number	Description
69	150	Configure zone filters.
70	151	Configure RTMP filters.
71	152	Configure NBP filters.

Design of the zone structure in AppleTalk environments is not always sufficient to effectively manage the traffic congestion in your environment. It is therefore necessary to implement filters. There are four types of filters to isolate network, zone, and name information in an AppleTalk network, as follows:

- GetZoneList filter

  Filters ZIP information locally between a router and hosts.

- Used to hide specific zones from users on specific networks.

- ZIP reply filter

  Cisco IOS software Release 10.2 feature used to hide zone information between routers.

  Does not prevent hosts from getting zones lists.

- Distribute list

  Controls RTMP broadcasts between routers.

  Used to block the advertisement of cable ranges/network numbers or the acceptance of cable ranges/network numbers into the routing table.

  Recommended not to be used to hide zones because it can cause complex iterations.

- NBP filter

  The Cisco IOS software Release 11.0 (and later) feature used to filter NBP packets to hide services, reduce traffic, and control dial-on-demand routing (DDR).

AppleTalk filters, like other filters, have two fundamental tasks, as shown in Figure 9-5.

Figure 9-5   *Configuring AppleTalk Filters*

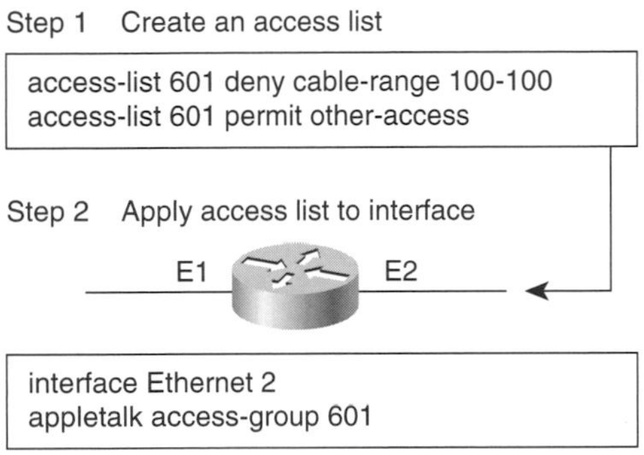

Step 1   Create an access list

```
access-list 601 deny cable-range 100-100
access-list 601 permit other-access
```

Step 2   Apply access list to interface

E1   E2

```
interface Ethernet 2
appletalk access-group 601
```

The two fundamental tasks of the AppleTalk filters are as follows:

1 Create an access list filter in global configuration mode. (All AppleTalk access lists are from 600-699.)

Define which zones, networks, or names should be filtered (or denied access) if the access list conditions are matched.

In Figure 9-5, the access list 601 is created and cable range 100-100 denied with the following command:

```
access-list 601 deny cable-range 100-100
```

Define the default action to take for all zones, networks, or names not explicitly enumerated in the access list.

In Figure 9-5, the default action to permit access for all other networks and cable ranges besides 100-100 is established with the following command:

```
access-list 601 permit other-access
```

2 Apply the access list you created to an interface in interface configuration mode.

In Figure 9-5, access list 601 is assigned to E2 with the following command:

```
appletalk access-group 601
```

The syntax of the command that assigns the access list to an interface varies from filter to filter.

GetZoneList Filtering

When the Chooser is opened, the Macintosh sends a GetZoneList (GZL) request to its router to obtain a list of all zones on the internetwork, as shown in Figure 9-6. An AppleTalk device selects a router dynamically by listening to RTMP packets. In this way, an AppleTalk device also can dynamically find redundant routers.

Figure 9-6 *The GetZoneList Request Is Sent When Chooser Is Opened*

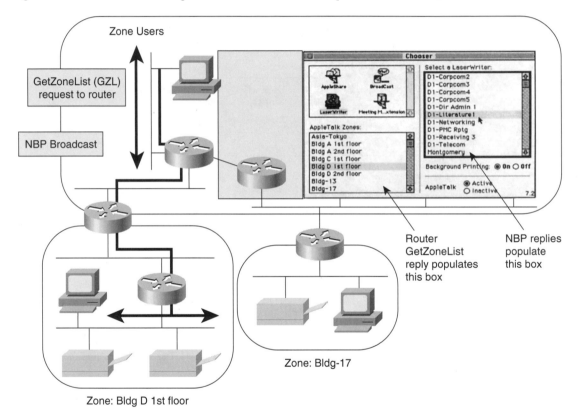

After a device has a session open with a remote device, it uses what Apple calls the *best routing algorithm*, which means that the device keeps track of the router through which it is receiving packets from the remote device. It uses that router for sending packets to the remote device for the duration of a session. If that router goes away, the local device can try a different router.

The router's GZL reply contains a list of all the (unfiltered) zones on the internetwork. This response populates the Chooser's lower-left window with zones.

When the user selects a device type (LaserWriter or AppleShare server) and zone name, the user's Macintosh sends out an NBP request looking for the names of all such devices in the specified zone. The router forwards this lookup into the requested zone. Devices implementing the service respond to the originator, and their NBP replies populate the right box of the user's Chooser with the device names. Figure 9-7 illustrates this traffic flow.

Figure 9-7   *Opening the Chooser*

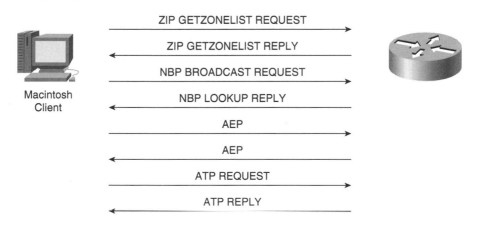

Macintosh
Client

ZIP GETZONELIST REQUEST

ZIP GETZONELIST REPLY

NBP BROADCAST REQUEST

NBP LOOKUP REPLY

AEP

AEP

ATP REQUEST

ATP REPLY

1. When a client user opens the chooser, a request is sent
   from the client requesting a server or router to supply a list
   of available zones.
2. Once a zone is selected in the chooser, a request is sent to all
   cable-ranges within the zone asking all servers to advertise their services.
3. After a service has been chosen an Apple Echo Protocol request (the
   equivalent of a TCP/IP PING) is sent in order to appropriately set the
   network timers.
4. Finally, a request to attack to the service is made.

If the requirement is to prevent users in one zone (such as the Operation zone in Figure 9-8) from accessing users in another zone (such as the Accounting zone) through the Chooser, a GZL filter can be used, as described next.

GZL Filter Hides Zones from Users

A GZL filter filters ZIP information locally between a router and hosts, as shown in Figure 9-8. It is used to hide specific zones from users.

A Macintosh's default router is chosen dynamically. If multiple routers exist on the same cable segment, the Macintosh's default router can be any one of them. Therefore, when you implement a GZL filter on a given cable segment, you must configure all routers on that segment with identical GZL filters. For this reason, a GZL filter is not a scalable solution for cable segments containing several routers.

Figure 9-8   *Using a GZL Filter, the Router Does Not Include Accounting in GZL Reply*

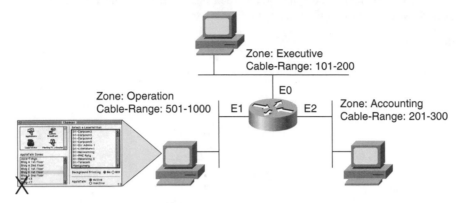

A GZL filter is not completely secure. By using a device alias, users can still access a device even if it is not listed in the Chooser.

GetZoneList Filtering Commands

Use the **access-list zone** command to create an entry in the zone filter list:

```
router(config)#access-list access-list-number {deny | permit} zone zone-name
```

access-list zone Command	Description
access-list-number	The number of the access list; a number in the range of 600 to 699.
deny | **permit**	Denies or permits access if conditions are matched.
zone-name	The name assigned to the zone being filtered.

Use the **access-list additional-zones** command to specify the default action for all other zones not specified in the access list. If not specified, the implicit deny all is in effect, so a given router will not include any zones in the GZL reply. The syntax of this command is as follows:

```
router(config)#access-list access-list-number {deny | permit} additional-zones
```

Use the **appletalk getzonelist-filter** command to assign the access list to an interface. The access list should be placed on the interface on which the request arrives, but the filter controls what zones are sent out. The syntax of this command is as follows:

```
router(config-if)#appletalk getzonelist-filter access-list-number
```

where *access-list-number* is the number of the access list; a number in the range of 600 to 699.

GetZoneList Filtering Example

Figure 9-9 illustrates a GetZoneList filtering example.

Figure 9-9   *GetZoneList Filtering Example*

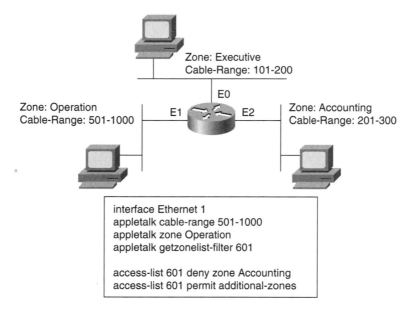

```
interface Ethernet 1
appletalk cable-range 501-1000
appletalk zone Operation
appletalk getzonelist-filter 601

access-list 601 deny zone Accounting
access-list 601 permit additional-zones
```

The requirement is to prevent users in the Operation zone from accessing the Accounting zone. To accomplish this requirement, you can create a GZL filter denying the Accounting zone.

Access list 601 is created and specifies the following:

- **access-list 601 deny zone Accounting**—The Accounting zone is not included in the router's GZL reply and is therefore invisible to the user.

- **access-list 601 permit additional-zones**—All other zones besides Accounting are accessible (in this example, the Executive zone).

Access list 601 is linked to Ethernet 1 with the **appletalk getzonelist-filter 601** command.

The result of this configuration is as follows.

- When users on cable range 501-1000 in the Operation zone open the Chooser and request a list of zones from the router, the router will not include the denied Accounting zone in its reply.

- The router will include all other zones it knows about (in this example, Executive and Operation).

- The Accounting zone will not be visible from the user's Chooser.

ZIP Reply Filtering

GZL filtering will satisfy ZIP GZL requests only from the Chooser to the router. To filter zone information exchange between routers, you should use ZIP reply filtering. When a router has a routing entry without any zone name associated with it (either because of a new route or the zone name has been aged out), the router will send a ZIP query to the next-hop router for that network to find out the zone names. (Typically this query is not a broadcast unless the router is first coming online and does not know its own network number and zones for its own cable.)

As a result, the other routers on the same cable segment will reply with a ZIP reply packet with the correct zone name. ZIP reply filtering can be done on the replying routers to hide zones. It is useful when connecting two AppleTalk administrative domains.

The ZIP reply filter allows RTMP details to propagate between RTMP peers, but blocks specific zones when the routers reach back for zone information. The filtered zones are invisible to all downstream routers and nodes.

In Figure 9-10, the zone information is gained through the following steps:

1 R1 sends RTMP update with network numbers.

2 R2 sends a ZIP request asking for the associated zones.

3 R1 sends a Zone Information Table (ZIT).

Figure 9-10 *Hiding Paris_Acct from R2*

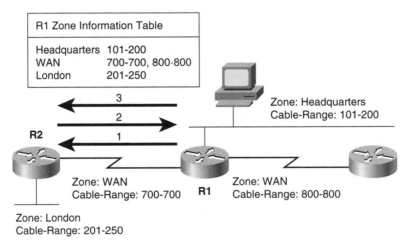

In Figure 9-11, the requirement is to hide Paris_Acct zone from R2. A ZIP reply filter preventing R1 from including Paris_Acct zone in response to R2's ZIP request will accomplish this requirement.

Figure 9-11   *Use ZIP Reply Filter on R1 So That R2 Won't Know about Paris_Acct Zone*

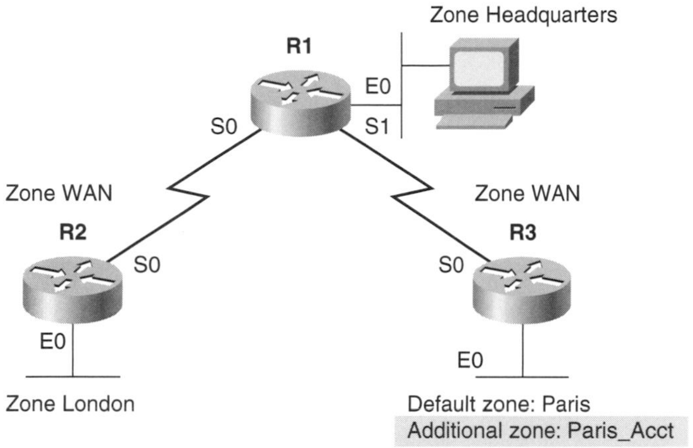

Because of the complexity involved, adhere to the following rules when implementing a ZIP reply filter:

- If multiple routers exist on the cable segment, you should implement the ZIP reply filter on all routers on that segment.

- You should not filter a network segment's zone name if the segment only has one zone defined. Otherwise, connectivity problems may appear because the cable range of the filtered zone segment will be deleted from the routing table to prevent ZIP storms.

If you deny a zone, the adjacent routers may still have the zone name in their Zone Information Table (ZIT). Therefore, you should restart the AppleTalk routing process on the adjacent routers. (Waiting for the zone name to age out may not work if there is a loop situation where a packet can be forwarded back and forth between parallel routers.)

NOTE   The default zone is the first one configured on the router.

Use the **access-list zone** command to create an entry in the zone filter list. It must use an access list number in the range 600 to 699.

```
router(config)#access-list access-list-number {deny | permit} zone zone-name
```

access-list zone Command	Description
access-list-number	The number of the access list; a number in the range of 600 to 699.
zone-name	The name assigned to the zone being filtered.

Use the **access-list additional-zones** command to specify the default action for all other zones not specified in the access list. If not specified, the implicit deny all is in effect, so a given router will not include any zones in the ZIP reply. The syntax of this command is as follows:

```
router(config)#access-list access-list-number {deny | permit} additional-zones
```

Use the **appletalk zip-reply-filter** command to assign the access list to an interface. The syntax of this command is as follows:

```
router(config-if)#appletalk zip-reply-filter access-list-number
```

where *access-list-number* is the number of the access list; a number in the range of 600 to 699.

In Figure 9-12, the requirement is to hide Paris_Acct zone from R2 and any downstream routers and users. To accomplish this requirement, you can use a ZIP reply filter.

Figure 9-12   *ZIP Reply Filtering Example*

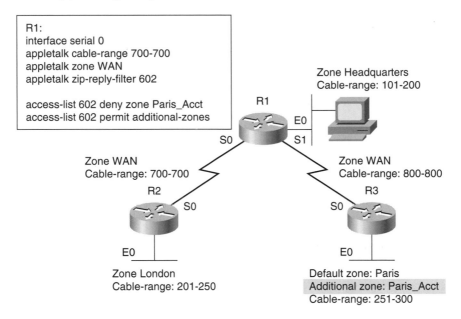

Access list 602 is created and specifies the following:

- **access-list 602 deny zone Paris_Acct**—The Paris_Acct zone is not included in R1's ZIP reply on serial 0 and is therefore invisible to R2 and users in the London zone.

- **access-list 602 permit additional-zones**—R1 includes all other zones besides Paris_Acct in its ZIP reply and they are therefore accessible (in this example, the Paris, WAN, and Headquarters zones).

Access list 602 is linked to R1's serial 0 interface with the **appletalk zip-reply-filter 602** command. Note that the filter was not placed on R3 because you want Headquarters to see Paris_Acct.

The result of this configuration is as follows. When R1 advertises cable range 251-300 to R2, R2 will respond with a ZIP query requesting all zones associated with network 251-300. R1's ZIP reply will not include the denied Paris_Acct zone, but will include the Paris zone because of the inclusion of the **permit additional-zones** command, which specifies the default action to take for zones not specified in the access list.

Use the **show appletalk zone** command to display the contents of the zone table and to verify the effect of a ZIP reply filter as shown here:

```
Tokyo#show appletalk zone
Name      Network(s)
Ozone     12810-12819
Azone     3210-3219 3230-3230 3220-3220
Fzone     11250-11259
Total of 3 zones
```

If you are performing this command on any router downstream from the router where you configured your ZIP reply filter denying one or more zones, you should not see the denied zone appearing in the ZIT.

Other useful commands are the **show appletalk access-lists** command, which checks access list statements, and the **show appletalk interface** command, which ensures that the access lists have been applied to the intended interface.

RTMP Filtering

AppleTalk's routing protocol is RTMP. RTMP, like RIP, is a distance-vector protocol. It has the following operation characteristics:

- Follows split horizon.

- The maximum hop count is 15.

- RTMP updates occur every 10 seconds.

- A routing packet contains routing tuples. A *tuple* consists of a cable range and a hop count. Zone names are not included in RTMP packets.

An RTMP filter can be used to reduce the number of AppleTalk routing table updates or prevent knowledge of routes. Alternatively, the Enhanced IGRP routing protocol can be used to reduce routing overhead. Enhanced IGRP is covered in Chapter 6, "EIGRP, BGP, and Redistribution."

RTMP Filtering Examples

In Figure 9-13, for example, R1 broadcasts its routing tables out all active interfaces every 10 seconds. If the requirement is to block the highlighted cable range 251-300 so that it does not appear in R2's routing table, you can configure an RTMP filter with the **distribute-list** command.

Figure 9-13 *Use **distribute-list** Filter So That R1 Does Not Advertise Cable Range 251-300*

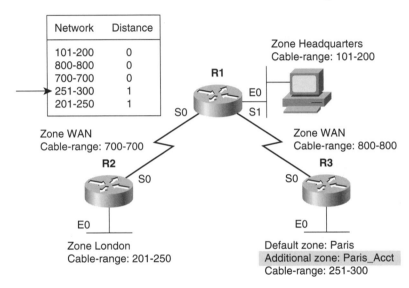

The **distribute-list** filter controls RTMP broadcasts between routers and can be used to reduce broadcasts or block cable ranges. Using the **distribute-list** command to hide zones is not recommended because this can cause complex iterations.

Use the **access-list network** command to define access for a single (nonextended) network number, as in the following:

```
router(config)#access-list access-list-number {deny | permit} network network
```

access-list network Command	Description
access-list-number	The number of the access list; a number in the range of 600 to 699.
network	AppleTalk network number.

Use the **access-list cable-range** command to define an access list for a cable range (for extended networks only), as in the following:

```
router(config)#access-list access-list-number {deny | permit} cable-range cable-
range
```

access-list cable-range Command	Description
access-list-number	The number of the access list; a number in the range of 600 to 699.
cable-range	Start-end values of the cable range (from 1-65279) separated by a hyphen. Starting values must be less than or equal to ending values.

Use the **access-list other-access** command to specify the default action for network numbers or cable ranges not specified in the access list:

```
router(config)#access-list access-list-number {deny | permit} other-access
```

where *access-list-number* is the number of the access list; a number in the range of 600 to 699.

Use the **appletalk distribute-list in** command to control which routing updates the local routing table accepts. Filters for incoming routing updates use access lists that define conditions for networks and cable ranges only. The syntax for this command is as follows:

```
router(config-if)#appletalk distribute-list access-list-number in
```

Use the **appletalk distribute-list out** command to filter which routes the local router advertises in its routing updates. Filters for outgoing routing updates use access lists that define conditions for networks and cable ranges, and for zones. The syntax for this command is as follows:

```
router(config-if)#appletalk distribute-list access-list-number out
```

It is important to note that the access list referred to in **access-list-number** is applied to the contents of the update and not to the source or destination of the routing update packets. The router decides whether to include those contents in its routing table based on those access lists.

In Figure 9-14, the requirement is to prevent cable range 251-300 from being advertised to R2.

Access list 603 is created in Figure 9-14 and specifies the following:

- **access-list 603 deny cable-range 251-300**—Cable range 251-300 is not included in the routing update R1 sends out the serial 0 interface (even though R1 has the route in its routing table).

- **access-list 603 permit other-access**—Other network numbers are included in R1's routing update (in this example, 800-800, and 101-200).

- **access-list 603 permit additional-zones**—All other zones not part of 251-300 are permitted.

Figure 9-14 *RTMP Filtering Example*

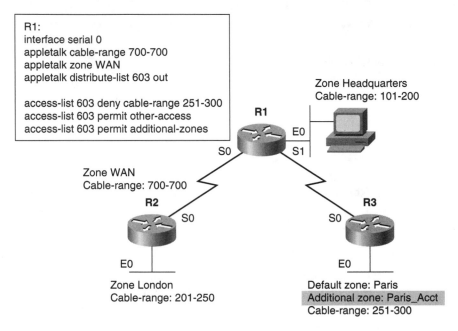

```
R1:
interface serial 0
appletalk cable-range 700-700
appletalk zone WAN
appletalk distribute-list 603 out

access-list 603 deny cable-range 251-300
access-list 603 permit other-access
access-list 603 permit additional-zones
```

Zone Headquarters
Cable-range: 101-200

R1
E0
S0   S1

Zone WAN
Cable-range: 700-700

R2   R3
S0   S0

E0   E0

Zone London   Default zone: Paris
Cable-range: 201-250   Additional zone: Paris_Acct
                                Cable-range: 251-300

Access list 603 is linked to R1's serial 0 interface with the **appletalk distribute-list 603 out** command.

The result of this configuration is as follows. When R1 sends its RTMP broadcast to R2, it sends all known network numbers except the denied 251-300. Users in the London zone will be unable to access users in either the Paris or Paris_Acct zones. In fact, users in the London zone will probably not see either of these zones in their Chooser. If R2 already has Paris and Paris_Acct in its ZIT and there are more routes in London, the zones may still be seen in London. These are called *phantom zones*. You must restart AppleTalk routing on R2 to clear the phantom zones.

Figure 9-15, for example, shows a **distribute-list** filter denying R2 from including cable range 301-301 in its routing table. If access to any network in a zone is denied, access to that zone is also denied by default. Because cable range 301-301 is denied and is located in Operation zone, cable range 201-201 would also be denied because it is also located in Operation zone. By using the **appletalk permit-partial-zones** global configuration command, cable range 201-201 is still accepted into R2's routing table and would therefore be accessible to users in the Accounting zone.

Figure 9-15 *If Access to Any Network in a Zone Is Denied, Access to That Zone Is Also Denied by Default*

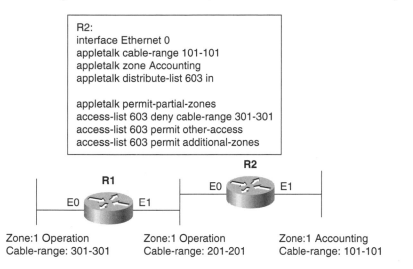

R2:
interface Ethernet 0
appletalk cable-range 101-101
appletalk zone Accounting
appletalk distribute-list 603 in

appletalk permit-partial-zones
access-list 603 deny cable-range 301-301
access-list 603 permit other-access
access-list 603 permit additional-zones

R2

R1

EO   E1   EO   E1

Zone:1 Operation   Zone:1 Operation   Zone:1 Accounting
Cable-range: 301-301   Cable-range: 201-201   Cable-range: 101-101

RTMP Filtering Considerations

You should address some considerations before configuring RTMP filters.

Use the **show appletalk route** command to display the contents of the AppleTalk routing table. This command is useful for verifying that a **distribute-list in** filter has been correctly configured and that any denied routes are not in the routing table, as follows:

```
Tokyo#show appletalk route
Codes: R—RTMP derived, E—EIGRP derived, C—connected, A—AURP, S—static P—
➡ proxy
5 routes in internet
The first zone listed for each entry is its default (primary) zone.
C Net 3210-3219 directly connected, Ethernet0, zone Azone
C Net 3220-3220 directly connected, Serial0, zone Azone
C Net 3230-3230 directly connected, Serial1, zone Azone
R Net 11250-11259 [1/G] via 3211.4, 7 sec, Ethernet0, zone Fzone
C Net 12810-12819 directly connected, Ethernet1, zone Ozone
```

Use the **show appletalk access-lists** command to check access list statements, and use the **show appletalk interface** command to ensure that the access lists have been applied to the intended interface.

NBP Filtering

Users prefer to use the names of networked devices rather than their network numbers. To communicate with the named entity, the name must be converted into an address for use by the lower-layer protocols. In AppleTalk, the NBP handles this conversion.

The NBP process has four stages in AppleTalk. When the Chooser is activated to search for a service, the software sends a broadcast request packet to the local router because only routers know which networks are in which zones. The router looks in its ZIT and forwards the request to a router for each network listed in the table as being associated with the specified zone. Each router then sends a multicast frame on its network, specifying that a node is looking for a service. The nodes that implement the service respond to the originator.

The NBP lookup process can generate considerable overhead traffic in an AppleTalk network.

NBP filters can be used to manage traffic in an AppleTalk network, as shown in Figure 9-16. They offer better network bandwidth utilization by filtering unwanted NBP traffic and improved security by hiding AppleTalk devices. The NBP filter can be applied to the AppleTalk access list to filter NBP packets. With NBP filters, access can be denied to a single device such as a Macintosh or laser printer or to all such devices within a zone.

Figure 9-16   *NBP Filters Can Deny Access to a Single Device or to All Devices within a Zone*

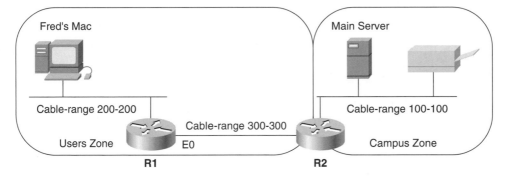

Identifying the Network-Visible Entities (NVEs)

To configure an NBP filter, you must know how to identify an AppleTalk object. Apple refers to a node service accessible over an AppleTalk network as a *network-visible entity* (NVE). The actual nodes are not considered NVEs, but the socket through which the node offers a service is an NVE.

NVEs can be referred to by an entity name. An entity name is an ASCII string with three fields: object, type, and zone. The form of the entity name is object:type@zone. The object field is the name of the device: for example, Fred's Mac. The type field is an attribute associated with the entity: for example, Workstation. The zone field is the location of the entity: for example, Users Zone. Taken together, the entity name is Fred's Mac:Workstation@Users Zone.

Special characters can be used as wildcards in place of defined character strings. An equal sign (=) in the object or type fields means "any." For example, =:AFP Server@Campus Zone means any AFPServer located in the Campus zone. An asterisk (*) in the zone field means the local zone to the user requesting the name.

Following is a list of some common entity types:

Type	Description
AFPServer	AppleShare servers or System 7 file sharing enabled
LaserWriter	Any AppleTalk PostScript laser printer
Workstation	Any Macintosh with System 7 loaded
2.0Mail Server	Microsoft Mail Server
ciscoRouter	Cisco router with AppleTalk routing enabled

NBP Filtering Commands

Use the **access-list nbp** command in global configuration mode to define access for a class of NBP entities (**type**), a particular name (**object**), or location of the entity (**zone**). The syntax for this command is as follows:

```
router(config)#access-list access-list-number {deny | permit} nbp seq
    {type | object | zone} string
```

access-list nbp Command	Description
access-list-number	The number of the access list; a number in the range of 600 to 699.
seq	A number used to tie the object, type, and zone together. Each command entry must have a sequence number. Use the same sequence number for tuples that are part of the same named entity.
string	The character string of the object, type, or zone. Each string can be up to 32 characters in length.

Use the **access-list other-nbps** command in global configuration mode to define the default action to take for NBP named entities not specified in the list. The syntax for this command is as follows:

```
route(config)#access-list access-list-number {deny | permit} other-nbps
```

Use the **appletalk access-group** command in interface configuration mode to apply the NBP filter to an interface for any type of incoming NBP packet. The syntax for this command is as follows:

```
route(config-if)#appletalk access-group access-list-number
```

In Figure 9-17, the requirement is to deny access to Color Laser from devices in Users Zone. To accomplish this requirement, you can create an NBP filter.

Figure 9-17 *NBP Filtering Example*

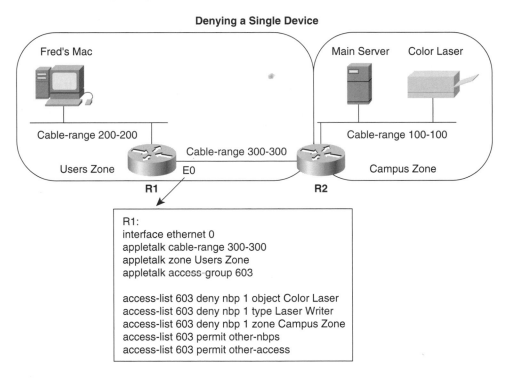

AppleTalk access list 603 is created for this purpose. Because NBP filters apply to incoming traffic, the access list is placed in R1's Ethernet 0 interface. The number 1 after the keyword "nbp" in the access list is a sequence number that ties together all three portions (object, type, and zone) of the named entity. Therefore, the entity that is inaccessible is Color Laser:LaserWriter@Campus Zone. Access list 603 also specifies the following:

- **access-list 603 permit other-nbps**—Allows users to access the Main Server

- **access-list 603 permit other-access**—Must be included or no DDP traffic (data packets) will be allowed

Access list 603 is linked to R1's Ethernet 0 interface with the **appletalk access-group 603** command specifying the number of the access list. An NBP filter is applied against the inbound traffic when the filter is used with the **appletalk access-group** command. When used with dialer lists, the NBP filter is applied against outbound traffic and controls what traffic type initiates a DDR call. Because the NBP filter works on all incoming NBP packets—broadcast request, forward request and lookup, and reply—carefully select the proper router and interface on which to place the NBP filter.

The effect of this filter is that when users on cable range 200-200 send NBP broadcasts to router R1 looking for LaserWriters, R1 forwards the request to R2, which sends an NBP lookup into the Campus Zone. The device Color Laser replies, R2 forwards the reply to R1, and the reply gets dropped at R1 Ethernet 0. As a result, users in the Users Zone do not see Color Laser in their Chooser nor are they able to access it through an alias.

Use the **show appletalk access-lists** and **show appletalk interface** commands to verify the settings on your NBP filter. Additionally, use the **show appletalk nbp** command to verify the named entities known to the router. This command shows information associated with the device, including the network number, name, type, and zone. This information is useful when creating NBP filters and, once created, for verifying that the filter you created had the intended results on downstream routers.

The remainder of this "Foundation Topics" section covers T1/E1 (including channelized T1/E1 configuration commands and examples) and ISDN PRI (including controller options, configuration examples, and configuration commands).

Configuring T1 and E1

The ACRC objective mastered in this section is as follows:

ACRC Exam Objective Number	Corresponding FRS Exam Objective Number	Description
72	153	Identify channelized T1 and E1 configuration.

Wide-area connectivity has become an integral part of large corporate networking. Dedicated serial lines can connect to digital carrier facilities to transmit data through the telephone hierarchy. Several technologies include key features of this WAN connectivity. They include the following:

- **T1**—A digital WAN service that transfers data at 1.544 Mbps through a switching network, as shown in Figure 9-18. T1 service is provided in the United States and Japan.

- **E1**—Wide-area digital transmission scheme used predominantly in Europe and Australia that carries data at a rate of 2.048 Mbps, as shown in Figure 9-18.

- **Channelized T1**—Access link operating at 1.544 Mbps that is subdivided into 24 channels of 64 kbps each. The individual channels or groups of channels connect to different destinations. Channelized T1 supports PPP, HDLC, Frame Relay, and X.25. Also referred to as fractional T1.

- **Channelized E1**—Access link operating at 2.048 Mbps that is subdivided into 30 B channels and 1 D channel. Channelized E1 supports PPP, HDLC, Frame Relay, and X.25.

- **DS-0 (digital signal level 0)**—Framing specification used in transmitting digital signals over a single channel at 64 kbps on a T1/E1 facility. DS-0 is the data rate of each T1/E1 channel.

- **DS-1 (digital signal level 1)**—Framing specification used in transmitting digital signals at 1.544 Mbps.

- **Multiplexer/demultiplexer (MUX/DMUX)**—A method of combining multiple input ports to run over a trunk line and splitting them apart again at the other end. T1 multiplexers use time-division multiplexing (TDM) to combine multiple channels into a single byte stream.

Figure 9-18   *DS-1 Framing for a Single T1 Offers 1.544 Mbps; E1 Offers 2.048 Mbps*

Many organizations have based their WAN structures on dedicated lines using individual CSU/DSUs. Each of these lines is located on a multiple-port synchronous serial interface card. The port density of the interface card and the backplane capacity are limiting factors in how many WAN connections a router can support. T1 and E1 support increases the port density and overall throughput for WAN implementations.

The framing structure and number of channels available limit the transmission rates. The European T1 (E1) supports a different framing and synchronization method, which accounts for the difference in actual data transmission rates.

The Cisco 7000 models support the MultiChannel Interface Processor (MIP) that contains two full T1/E1 ports, as shown in Figure 9-19. The Cisco 4000 models support a single-port interface for channelized T1/E1. Each port can be channelized to generate 24 DS-0 (64 kbps) lines for T1 or 30 DS-0 lines for E1. Multiple MIP cards can be configured into the Cisco 7000 chassis. Each line (subchannel) is individually configurable just as if it were a dedicated interface.

Figure 9-19   *Channelizing T1/E1 Example*

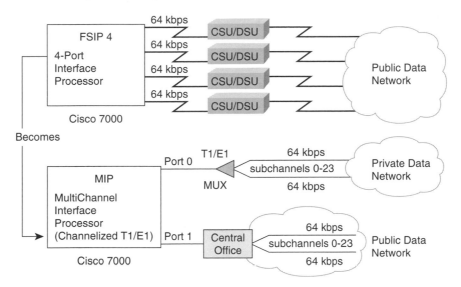

A private data network can carry the output of a port on the MIP card. Alternatively, the MIP card can be connected directly to the service provider's facility, and a private or public data network can carry the channel output.

T1 and E1 support the following WAN protocols:

X.25

LAPB

Frame Relay

HDLC

PPP

SMDS

ATM-DXI

Channelized T1/E1 Configuration Commands

Use the **controller** [**t1** | **e1**] command to configure a T1 or E1 controller and to enter the controller configuration mode, as in the following:

```
router(config)#controller [t1 | e1] [slot/port | number]
```

The components of the **controller** [**t1** | **e1**] command are as follows:

controller Command	Description
slot/port	Specifies MIP slot and port number.
number	Specifies the network interface module (NIM) number.

To configure the MIP in slot 4, port 0 of a Cisco 7000 as a T1 controller, for example, use the **controller t1 4/0** command. To configure NIM 0 of a Cisco 4000 as a T1 controller, use the **controller t1 0** command.

Use the **channel-group** command to define the time slots that belong to each T1/E1 circuit, as in the following:

```
router(config-controller)#channel-group number timeslots range speed {48 | 56 | 64}
```

The components of the **channel-group** command are as follows:

channel-group Command	Description
number	Channel-group number from 0 to 23 for T1 and 0 to 31 for E1.
timeslots *range*	Time slot or range of time slots belonging to the channel group. For a T1 controller, the time slot range is from 1 to 24. For an E1 controller, the time slot range is from 1 to 31.
speed {**48**	**56**	**64**}	Speed in kbps. The default line speed for a T1 controller is 56 kbps. For an E1 controller, the default is 64 kbps.

The channel-group number may be arbitrarily assigned and must be unique for the controller. The time slot range must match the time slots assigned to the channel group. The service provider defines the time slots that comprise a channel group. The time slots assigned depend on the level of service and bandwidth that a company orders as well as the company's current bandwidth needs.

Use the **framing** command to select the frame type for the T1 line, as in the following:

```
router(config-controller)#framing {sf | esf}
```

The components of the **framing** command are as follows:

framing Command	Description
sf	This specifies Super Frame as the T1 frame type. Super Frame is the default.
esf	This specifies Extended Super Frame as the T1 frame type. AT&T proposed the Extended Superframe Format be implemented on its T1 circuits to provide in-service diagnostic capabilities.

Use the **linecode** command to select the line-code type for the T1 line, as in the following:

```
router(config-controller)#linecode {ami | b8zs}
```

The components of the **linecode** command are as follows:

linecode Command	Description
ami	This specifies alternate mark inversion (AMI) as the line-code type. **ami** is the default.
b8zs	This specifies B8ZS as the line-code type. B8ZS (Binary Eight Zero Substitution) is an improvement to the **ami** line-code technique.

The service provider determines the framing type and the line code.

When you are connecting to a public network, the clock source originates from the T1 line rather than the router interface. On a private network, however, clocking may need to be provided by the routers. Use the **clock source** command to set the T1 line clock source for the controller. Unless you are connecting to a private network where you control the clocking, this command is required only when connecting two devices back-to-back for testing purposes. The syntax of this command is as follows:

```
router(config-controller)#clock source {line | internal}
```

The components of the **clock source** command are as follows:

clock source Command	Description
internal	Specifies that the interface will clock its transmitted data from its internal clock.
line	Specifies the T1 line as the clock source. This is the default condition.

Channelized T1 Configuration Example

The MIP card allows up to 24 (T1) subchannels to be configured independently on one physical port. Subchannels have all the same configuration options and characteristics as ordinary serial ports. Channel groups are assigned from one or several DS-0s, which are assigned by the carrier and are usually numbered contiguously. Figure 9-20 shows a channelized T1 example. The commands shown are defined as follows:

Command	Description
controller t1 4/1	This specifies the MIP card in slot 4, port 1 of a Cisco 7000.
framing esf	This specifies Extended Super Frame as the T1 frame type.
line code b8zs	This specifies B8ZS as the line-code type.
channel-group 0 timeslots 1	This specifies that circuit 0 is a single time slot.
channel-group 8 timeslots 6-11	This specifies that channel-group 8 will have six time slots (6 to 11). The line speed is the T1 default speed, 56 kbps.

The controller card in slot 4 has port 1 configured for the appropriate frame and line-code types. Channel group 0 has a single time slot running at the default (56 kbps) speed. Channel group 8 has been assigned six time slots, all operating at the default 56 kbps. Subchannel 0 has been assigned an encapsulation type of PPP. Channel group 8 assumes the default encapsulation. Both subchannels are assigned to different subnets.

The line encoding and framing must be set to match the carrier equipment.

After you define T1 channel groups, you can configure each channel group as a serial interface. In this example, the **interface serial 4/1:0** command configures channel group 0 for PPP.

Figure 9-20   *Channelized T1 Configuration Example*

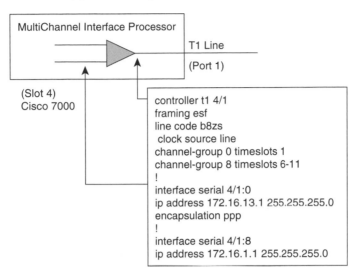

TIP   Cisco MC3810 can also support a T1/E1 trunk interface with the multiflex trunk module (MFT). The MFT provides an RJ-48 connector for the network interface and a T1.403-compliant, onboard channel service unit/data service unit (CSU/DSU). The T1/E1 trunk interface to a Frame Relay network is capable of handling time-division multiplexing (TDM) trunk services.

Channelized E1 Configuration

Use the **framing** command to select the frame type for the E1 line, as in the following:

```
router(config-controller)#framing {crc4 | no-crc4} [australia]
```

The components of the **framing** command are as follows:

framing Command	Description
crc4	Specifies crc4 as the E1 frame type, the default.
no-crc4	Specifies that CRC checking is disabled in the E1 frame type.
australia	(Optional) Specifies the frame type for E1 lines in Australia.

Use the **linecode** command to select the line-code type for the E1 line, as in the following:

```
router(config-controller)#linecode {ami | hdb3}
```

linecode Command	Description
ami	Specifies AMI as the line-code type, the default.
hdb3	Specifies high-density bipolar 3 (HDB3) as the line-code type. Use **hdb3** for E1 controllers only.

Channelized E1 Configuration Example

The MIP card allows up to 30 (E1) subchannels to be configured independently on one physical port. Subchannels have all the same configuration options and characteristics as ordinary serial ports. Channel groups are assigned from one or several 64-kbps DS-0s, which are assigned by the carrier and are usually numbered contiguously. Figure 9-21 shows a channelized E1 example. The commands shown there are defined as follows:

Command	Description
controller e1 4/1	Specifies the MIP card in slot 4, port 1 of a Cisco 7000.
framing crc4	Specifies Extended Super Frame as the E1 frame type.
line code hdb3	Specifies HDB3 as the line-code type.
channel-group 0 timeslots 1	Specifies that circuit 0 is a single time slot.
channel-group 8 timeslots 5,7,12-15, 28	Specifies that channel-group 8 will have seven time slots (5, 7, 12–15, and 28). The line speed is the E1 default speed, 64 kbps.

The controller card in slot 4 has port 1 configured for the appropriate frame and line-code types. Channel group 0 has a single time slot running at the default (64 kbps) speed. Channel group 8 has been assigned various time slot ranges, totaling seven, all operating at the default rate of 64 kbps. Subchannel 0 has been assigned an encapsulation type of PPP. Subchannel 8 assumes the default encapsulation. Both subchannels are assigned to different subnets.

The line encoding and framing must be set to match the carrier equipment. The channel-group speed you choose must match the speed specified by your service provider.

The **interface serial 4/1:8** command configures channel group 8 as a serial interface.

Figure 9-21   *Channelized E1 Configuration Example*

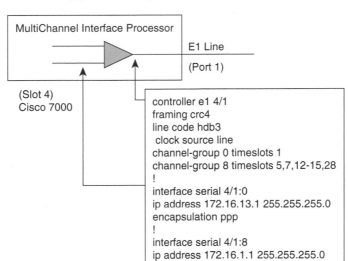

Configuring Primary Rate Interface

The ACRC objective mastered in this section is as follows:

ACRC Exam Objective Number	Corresponding FRS Exam Objective Number	Description
73	154	Identify ISDN PRI configuration commands.

The Primary Rate Interface (PRI) is an ISDN interface that multiplexes multiple channels across a single transmission medium, as shown in Figure 9-22.

PRI is sometimes described as 23B+D, or as 30B+D, and has the following configurations:

- ISDN PRI in North America and Japan offers 23 B channels and 1 D channel, yielding a combined rate of 1.544 Mbps.

- ISDN PRI in Europe provides 30 B channels and 1 D channel with a combined rate of 2.048 Mbps.

Unlike ISDN BRI, PRI does not connect to an NT1 device. The physical interface is the same as for a T1 or an E1—that is, a CSU/DSU function bundled into the router. D-channel packet data is not available for PRI.

Figure 9-22 *ISDN PRI Multiplexes Multiple Channels across a Single Transmission Medium*

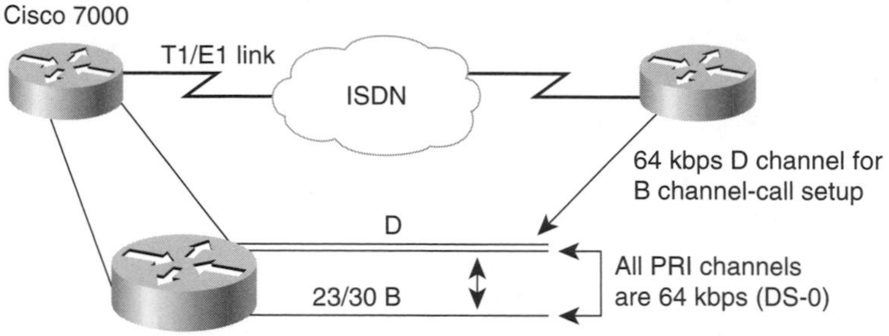

Interface	B Channels	Where used
T1 PRI	23	North America and Japan
E1 PRI	30	Europe and rest of the world

Use PRI configuration tasks in addition to the DDR-derived commands you saw earlier in BRI configurations. These PRI tasks are as follows:

1. Specify the correct PRI switch type that the router interfaces at the provider's central office.
2. Specify the T1/E1 controller, framing type, and line coding for the provider's facility.
3. Set a PRI group time slot for the T1/E1 facility and indicate the speed used.
4. Identify the interface that you will configure to act with DDR.
   - — On a Cisco 7000 series router, indicate the slot and port.
   - — On a Cisco 4000 series router, indicate the unit number.
   - — For both Cisco 7000 and Cisco 4000 routers, include a number that designates the PRI D channel.

ISDN PRI Configuration Commands

Use the **isdn switch-type** command to specify the central office PRI switch to which the router connects, as in the following:

```
router(config)#isdn switch-type primary rate switch type
```

The components of the **isdn switch-type** command are as follows:

isdn switch-type Command	Description
pri-4ess	AT&T 4ESS-Primary switches (United States).
pri-5ess	AT&T 5ESS-Primary switches (United States).
pri-dms100	NT DSM-100 PRI switches (North America).
pri-ntt	NTT ISDN PRI switches (Japan).
pri-net5	European ISDN PRI switches.
none	No switch defined.

The **controller** {**t1** | **e1**} *slot* {**0** | **1**} | *unit number* global command identifies a Cisco 7000 series controller using the MIP card. Use a *single unit number* for the Cisco 4000 series controller using the network processor module (NPM), as in the following:

```
router(config)#controller {t1 | e1} slot/ {0 | 1}
```

The components of the **controller** {**t1** | **e1**} *slot* {**0** | **1**} | *unit number* global command are as follows:

controller {t1	e1} slot	unit number Command	Description
t1	Select a controller interface for North American and Japanese facility interfaces.
e1	Controller interface for European facilities and facilities used in much of the rest of the world.

T1/E1 Controller Options for PRI

Use the **framing** controller configuration to specify the time slot frame type to use with the T1 or E1 facility, as in the following:

```
router(config-controller)#framing {esf | crc4}
```

The components of the **framing** controller configuration are as follows:

framing Command	Description
esf	Extended Super Frame. Use for T1 PRI configurations.
crc4	Cyclic redundancy check 4. Use for E1 PRI configurations.

Verify that the ISDN PRI circuits default to 64-kbps speed for each channel, which is why there are only two frame types.

Use the **linecode** controller configuration to specify the physical layer line coding to use with the provider's T1 or E1 facility, as in the following:

```
router(config-controller)#linecode {b8zs | hdb3}
```

The components of the **linecode** controller configuration are as follows:

linecode Command	Description
b8zs	Binary 8-zero substitution. Use for T1 PRI configurations.
hdb3	High-density bipolar 3. Use for E1 PRI configurations.

ISDN PRI Configuration

The **pri-group** command configures the specified interface for PRI operation, as in the following:

```
router(config-controller)#pri-group [timeslots range]
```

timeslots *range* is the number of time slots allocated. For T1, use a value in the range of 1 to 23, and for E1 use a value from 1 to 31.

CAUTION   PRI is not available in every country.

The **interface serial** *slot/port* | *unit*: {**23** | **15**} command specifies an interface for PRI operation. The interface can be a serial interface to a T1/E1 on the Cisco 7000 or Cisco 4000 series router configured, as shown previously.

```
router(config)#interface serial slot/port :{23 | 15}
```

or

```
router(config)#interface serial unit :{23 | 15}
```

The components of the **interface serial** command are as follows:

interface serial Command	Description
slot/port	A slot/port designated on the Cisco 7000 series router served by the MIP controller.
unit	A unit number designated on the Cisco 4000 series router served by the NPM.
23	A T1 interface that designates channelized DS-0s 0 to 22 are B channels and DS-0 23 is the D channel.
15	An E1 interface that designates 30 DS-0s are B channels and DS-0 15 is the D channel.

Additional commands pertain to T1 and E1 operation. For T1, enter the commands **framing esf** and **linecode b8zs**. For E1, enter the commands **framing crc4** and **linecode hdb3**.

PRI Configuration Example

Figure 9-23 shows a PRI configuration example. The commands shown there are defined as follows:

Command	Description
isdn switch-type primary-4ess	Selects a switch type of 4ESS to use on the Cisco 7000.
controller t1 2/0	Selects the T1 controller for slot 2.
pri-group timeslots 1-23	Establishes the interface port to function as PRI with 23 time slots designated to operate at a speed of 64 kbps.
framing esf	Selects Extended Super Frame, a T1 choice.
linecode b8zs	Selects line-code binary 8-zero substitution for T1.
interface serial 2/0:23	Uses serial interface slot 2, port 0. Channel 23 has the D channel (T1).

Figure 9-23   *PRI Configuration Example*

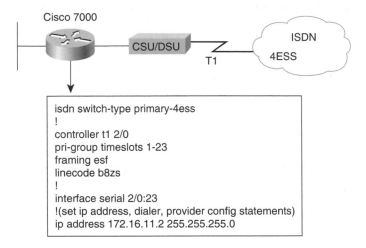

Cisco 7000

CSU/DSU

T1

ISDN
4ESS

```
isdn switch-type primary-4ess
!
controller t1 2/0
pri-group timeslots 1-23
framing esf
linecode b8zs
!
interface serial 2/0:23
!(set ip address, dialer, provider config statements)
ip address 172.16.11.2 255.255.255.0
```

TIP   Static mapping and DDR commands are also used for configuring PRI. Although they are also required for ISDN operation, they are omitted from this example.

Conclusion

In this chapter, you learned about both the management of AppleTalk traffic within the network and as well as the configuration of WAN links using specific E1 or T1 links.

In AppleTalk it became clear that the locating services and routing updates cause overhead in an AppleTalk network. Understanding groups of common interest is key to controlling service-location traffic. You also learned that filtering strategies must ensure that routing information needed for service location is accessible to routers. Cisco's IOS software provides many features for reducing the volume of service-location and routing traffic, and for controlling access.

This chapter also presented channelized T1, channelized E1, and ISDN PRI configuration commands and examples. Channelized T1 contains an access link operating at 1.544 Mbps that is subdivided into 24 channels of 64 kbps each. The individual channels or groups of channels connect to different destinations. Channelized E1 contains an access link operating at 2.048 Mbps that is subdivided into 30 B channels and 1 D channel. Channelized E1 supports PPP, HDLC, Frame Relay, and X.25. ISDN PRI multiplexes multiple channels across a single transmission medium.

Q&A

The following questions test your understanding of the topics covered in this chapter. After you have answered the questions, you will find the answers in Appendix A, "Answers to Quizzes and Q&As." If you get an answer wrong, review the answer and ensure that you understand the reason for your mistake. If you are confused by the answer, refer back to the text in the chapter to review the concepts

1 What traffic does the GetZoneList filter prevent?

2 What NBP traffic is generated when the Chooser is opened?

3 What does NVE stand for and what does it mean?

4 Between whom are the Zone Information Tables communicated?

5 Which command is used to permit all other cable ranges and networks?

6 What does the command **appletalk permit partial zones** achieve?

7 What is the use of the **timeslots** command in the configuration of an E1 or T1 line?

_____

_____

_____

8 When would the **clock source** command be used?

_____

_____

_____

9 What is the default framing used on a T1 line?

_____

_____

_____

10 In configuring a T1 line for ISDN, what are the main configuration tasks?

_____

_____

_____

11 When configuring the E1 or T1 line, is one configuring the hardware or the software?

_____

_____

_____

12 The switch that is identified in the configuration of the E1 or T1 line belongs to whom?

_____

_____

_____

Scenarios

The following case studies and questions are designed to draw together the content of the chapter and exercise your understanding of the concepts. There is not necessarily a right answer. The thought process and practice in manipulating the concepts is the goal of this section.

The answers to the scenario questions are found at the end of this chapter.

Scenario 9-1

Using Figure 9-24, answer the following questions.

Figure 9-24   *Diagram for Scenario 9-1*

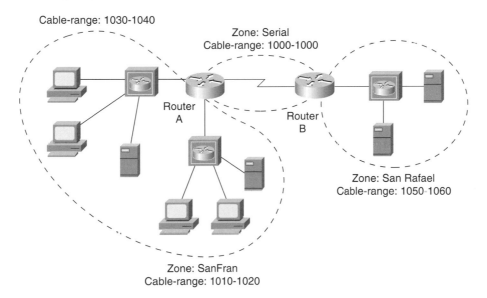

Cable-range: 1030-1040

Zone: Serial
Cable-range: 1000-1000

Router
A

Router
B

Zone: San Rafael
Cable-range: 1050-1060

Zone: SanFran
Cable-range: 1010-1020

1 Design an AppleTalk filter for Router A that restricts traffic within the San Fran zone to existing servers in the San Rafael zone and the servers within their own zone. Where would this filter be applied?

2 Write a filter that prevents the Serial zone from being seen by any hosts. Where would this filter be applied?

3 The serial link is a PRI interface. State the commands that will be required to set up the controller to use all the available channels. The framing to be used is Extended Super Frame and the line code binary 8-zero substitution.

Scenario 9-2

Using Figure 9-25, answer the following questions.

Figure 9-25 *Diagram for Scenario 9-2*

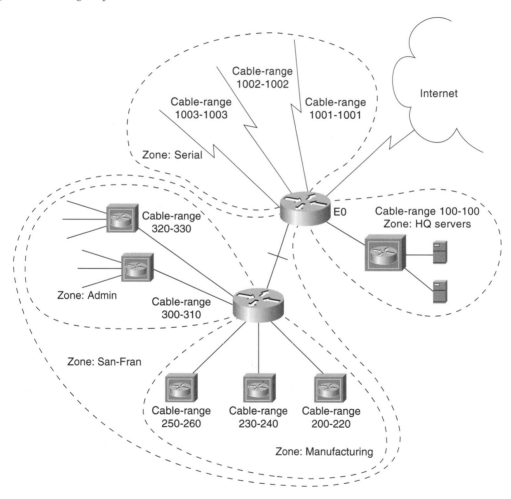

1   The link into the Internet is a T1 link. Configure the interface using PPP and the IP address of 201.100.16.5 with a 30-bit mask.

2   The company has another T1 link; using a MIP card, the link has been channelized to allow connectivity to remote sites. Using esf framing and b8zs for the line code, configure two interfaces, where one of the interfaces supports a 64-kbps line and the other a 512-kbps line.

3 Write an AppleTalk filter that prevents all zone information except for the HQServers zone across serial lines.

4 Suggest a way to prevent AppleTalk traffic from traversing the link to the Internet.

Scenario 9-3

Using Figure 9-26, answer the following questions.

Figure 9-26   *Diagram for Scenario 9-3*

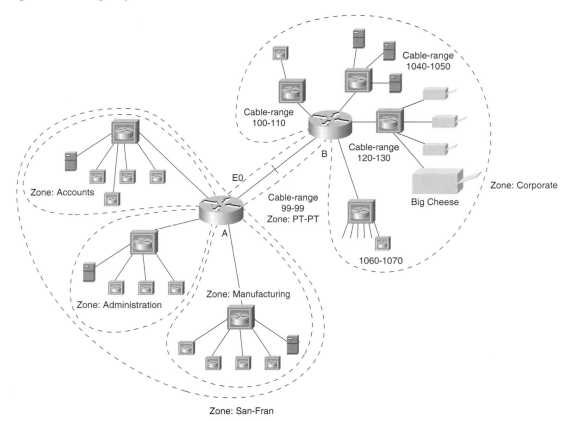

1 Write an AppleTalk filter that only allows the cable ranges for the servers and the printers to be transmitted to the other zones.

2 Write an AppleTalk filter that allows all servers and printers to be advertised in the Chooser of the client host machine, except for the president's printer (named BIGCHEESE).

3 Write a filter for AppleTalk that prevents the local servers in the Manufacturing zone from being advertised to other zones. Where would this filter be placed?

Scenario Answers

The answers provided in this section are not necessarily the only possible answers to the questions. The questions are designed to test your knowledge and to give practical exercise in certain key areas. This section is intended to test and exercise skills and concepts detailed in the body of this chapter.

If your answer is different, ask yourself whether it follows the tenets explained in the answers provided. Your answer is correct not if it matches the solution provided in the book, but rather if it has included the principles of design laid out in this chapter.

In this way, the testing provided in these scenarios is deeper: It examines not only your knowledge, but also your understanding and ability to apply that knowledge to problems.

If you do not get the correct answer, refer back to the text and review the subject tested. Be certain to also review your notes on the question to ensure that you understand the principles of the subject.

Scenario 9-1 Answers

1 The following filter would restrict the traffic to servers within the San Rafael zone and servers in their own zone. The filter would be applied to the serial interface on Router A.

```
Access-list 609 permit nbp 3 object Mail Server
Access-list 609 permit nbp 3 type 2.0MailServer
Access-list 609 permit nbp 3 zone San Rafael
Access-list 609 permit nbp 3 object Databases
Access-list 609 permit nbp 3 type AFPServer
Access-list 609 permit nbp 3 zone San Rafael
Access-list 609 permit other-access
```

Remember that the NBP filter applies to incoming traffic. Therefore, by placing the filter on the serial interface, the local traffic is unaffected but remote traffic is managed in accordance with the access list. By identifying the servers that will be allowed to advertise across the router, you are ensuring that the advertisements are restricted to current servers only.

2 The following filter prevents the Serial zone from being seen by anyone else. The filter will be a GetZoneList filter. It cannot be a ZIP reply filter because the zone connects the two routers.

```
Access-list 607 deny zone serial
Access-list 607 permit additional-zones
```

This filter would be applied to the Ethernet interfaces. The reason for denying the Serial zone is to prevent NBP broadcast from swamping the serial line when the Chooser is open and a user selects the zone.

3 The commands to set up the controller would be similar regardless of whether the link used ISDN technology:

```
Controller t1 1/0
Pri-group timeslots 1-23
Framing esf
Linecode b8zs
```

It would be necessary to configure the interface for ISDN callup in addition to configuring the hardware. Configuration at the global level for the ISN switch at the service provider's central office would also be required.

Scenario 9-2 Answers

1 Configuring thc interface that connects to the Internet requires just an IP address and the Layer 2 (data link) protocol to be identified. This is not an ISDN DDR line, and therefore additional configuration is not necessary.

```
Interface serial 1/1
IP address 201.100.16.5 255.255.255.252
Encapsulation ppp
No shutdown
```

2 The commands to configure the MIP card would be done at the controller level and are as follows:

```
Controller t1 1/1
Framing esf
Line code b8zs
Clock source line
Channel-group 0 timeslots 1
Channel-group 1 timeslots 2-9
```

This allows for two links, one with a bandwidth of 64 kbps, the other with a bandwidth of 512 kbps, which is eight channels.

3 The filter that would prevent all zone information except for the HQServers zone traversing the serial line follows:

```
Access-list 666 permit zone HQServers
Interface serial 1/1
Appletalk zip-reply-filter 666
```

This filter would be applied to the serial interfaces as a ZIP reply filter. All other zones will be denied. Additional cable ranges will be added to the HQServers zone because RTMP updates will still be sent out.

4 The easiest way to prevent AppleTalk traffic traversing the link to the Internet is to configure AppleTalk on all interfaces except the serial link to the Internet.

Scenario 9-3 Answers

1 A distribute-list filter would allow the cable ranges for the servers and the printers to be transmitted to the other zones. This filter would need to be a one-way filter or the routers in the HQServers zone would not know how to reply to requests for services. The filter follows:

```
Access-list 622 permit cable-range 100-100
```

The access list would be configured to the interface with the following command:

```
Interface serial 1/1
Appletalk distribute-list 622 out
```

The filter is applied as an outgoing list to prevent the traffic from traversing the serial line. If the cable range is not sent to the remote router, all associated zones will be eventually dropped from the ZIT. If additional cable ranges are added to the HQServers zone, the following global command is required:

```
Appletalk permit-partial-zones
```

2 The filter required to filter only the president's printer is an NBP filter, which would deny the printer BIGCHEESE and permit all other access. The following commands would achieve the desired result:

```
Access-list 644 deny nbp 3 object BIGCHEESE
Access-list 644 deny nbp 3 type LaserWriter
Access-list 644 deny nbp zone HQServers
Access-list 644 permit other-nbps
Access-list 644 permit other-access
```

Because the filter applies to incoming traffic, it would be applied to the E0 interface of the router connecting to the HQServers zone.

3 The filter that would be used to keep the local traffic within the Manufacturing zone and prevent the other zones from seeing the local servers would be a ZIP reply filter. This would still allow the cable ranges to be propagated, so communication between the client and server could be realized without advertising services held on servers that could not support a lot of access requests. The filter follows:

```
Access-list 655 deny zone MANUFACTURING
Access-list 655 permit additional-zones
```

It would be applied to interface E0 on Router A:

```
Interface E0
Appletalk zip-reply-filter 655
```

Answers to Quizzes and Q&As

This appendix contains the answers to each chapter's "Do I Know This Already?" quiz and "Q&A" section.

There may be more than one answer to some of the questions, and some of the questions may not have definite answers. Given the advanced nature of this book, the answers provided are sometimes used to point you in the right direction.

The questions are designed to test not just your knowledge, but also your understanding of the subject matter. It is therefore important to realize that getting the answer the same as stated in this book is less important than your answer having embodied the spirit of the question. In this manner the questions and answers are not as open and shut as will be found on the exam: Their intent is to prepare you with the appropriate knowledge and understanding to give you mastery of the subject as opposed to limited rote knowledge.

Chapter 2

Answers to Chapter 2 "Do I Know This Already?" Quiz

1 List four symptoms of network congestion.

The following are just some of the symptoms seen when network congestion is experienced:

— Excessive traffic seen on the network-management tools

— Packets being dropped, seen on the router interfaces

— The retransmission of packets, seen on the network-management tools

— Incomplete routing tables, seen on the router

— Incomplete service tables, seen on servers and routers

— Broadcast storms caused by spanning tree

— Applications timing out at end stations

— Clients not being able to connect to network resources

2 Which of the queuing techniques offered by the Cisco IOS are manually configured?

The queuing techniques manually configured on a Cisco system are custom and priority queuing.

3 In an IP standard access list, what is the default wildcard mask?

The default wildcard mask in an IP standard access list is 0.0.0.0.

4 At which layer of the OSI model do standard access lists work?

Standard access lists function at Layer 3 of the OSI model.

5 State three uses of access lists.

The following are all valid uses for access lists:

— Restricting networks sent out in routing updates

— Restricting connectivity to remote networks

— Restricting the services advertised in an IPX network

— Restricting large packet sizes from traversing the network

6 In the hierarchical design suggested by Cisco, at which layer are access lists not recommended?

In the hierarchical design suggested by Cisco, access lists are not recommended at the core layer because this layer should be devoted to transferring the data as efficiently as possible. All decisions should have been made at the access and distribution layers.

7 What does the established keyword do in an extended access list?

The established keyword in an extended access list will allow the user to create a TCP connection from his or her network to a system on a remote network, but it will not allow a TCP connection to be created into the network from a remote system. It checks to see whether the ACK or RST bits are set. They are normally not set in the first step of the TCP handshake, and therefore will not allow a connection to be initiated into the system.

8 What is the access list number range for SAP filter access lists?

The SAP access list number range is 1000-1099.

9 Explain the **ip helper address**. What is its function?

The **ip helper address** is a command that has the router forward User Datagram Protocol (UDP) broadcasts received on an interface to a directed or specific destination on another network.

Combined with the **ip forward-protocol** global configuration command, the **ip helper-address** command enables you to control which broadcast packets and which protocols are forwarded. One common application that requires helper addresses is Dynamic Host

Configuration Protocol (DHCP). DHCP is defined in RFC 1531. DHCP protocol information is carried inside BOOTP packets. To enable BOOTP broadcast forwarding for a set of clients, configure a helper address on the router interface closest to the client. The helper address should specify the address of the DHCP server. If you have multiple servers, you can configure one helper address for each server. Because BOOTP packets are forwarded by default, the router can now forward DHCP information. The DHCP server now receives broadcasts from the DHCP clients.

10 If a packet does not match any of the criteria in an access list, what action will be taken?

If the packet being tested against the access list does not match any of the criteria, it will hit the implicit deny all at the bottom of the access list and be discarded, generating an ICMP message to the sending station.

11 On a LAN, where does the IPX node/host address come from?

On a LAN, the node or host address of the IPX address will be taken from the Layer 2 MAC address. It is a 48-bit quantity, represented by dotted triplets of four-digit hexadecimal numbers.

The following is an example of an IPX network address:

4a.0000.0c00.23fe

12 How would you restrict Telnet connectivity to the router that you were configuring?

To restrict Telnet connections to the router that you are configuring, use access lists that are applied to the terminal lines with the **access-class** command.

Answers to Chapter 2 Q&A Questions

1 State two reasons to use an IP tunnel.

The following are reasons to use an IP tunnel:

To solve problems with discontiguous networks

To simplify network administration

To tunnel desktop protocols through an IP-only backbone

2 Will EIGRP carry SAP updates?

If IPX enhanced IGRP peers are found on an interface, you can configure the router to send SAP updates, either periodically or when a change occurs in the SAP table. When no IPX enhanced IGRP peer is present on the interface, periodic SAPs are always sent.

3 Why is it important to ensure the RIP/SAP update timers are synchronized?

It is important to ensure the RIP/SAP update timers are synchronized because a SAP service will not be advertised until the associated network is known. Entries will drop out of tables periodically to be re-entered later and drop out yet again.

4 In configuring an IP tunnel, how many IP tunnels may be created with the same source and destination address?

By default, only one tunnel is allowed with the same source and destination address.

5 Associate the appropriate IOS feature to solve the network congestion problems presented experienced on the network in the following table.

To find the answer, match the numbers.

Network Congestion Problem		Correct IOS Solution	
1	Large SAP tables on the routers	4	Routing access list
2	Clients cannot connect to the centralized servers	6	Prioritization on the interface
3	Cisco environment in a large network, with a large number of WAN connections	5	Reduce the size of the broadcast domain by adding a router
4	Large routing tables, using RIP for IP	2	IP helper address
5	Spanning tree is failing	3	EIGRP
6	SNA sessions are failing	1	SAP filters

6 Which command would prevent the router from forwarding data to a remote network without generating an ICMP message?

The command that would prevent the router from forwarding data to a remote network without generating an ICMP message is the **interface null 0** command.

7 Identify two commands that might be used to verify the configuration of an IP access list configuration.

Two commands that might be used to verify the configuration of an IP access list configuration could be taken from the following list:

— **show ip interface**

— **show access-list**

— **show running config**

— **show startup config**

8 What UDP ports will the IP helper address forward automatically?

UDP ports that the IP helper address will forward automatically are TFTP, DNS, BOOTP server, BOOTP client, Time, TACACS, NetBIOS name server, and NetBIOS datagram service.

9 If the number of workstations increases on a physical segment, the user may experience delays. Give two reasons why this might occur.

As the number of workstations increases on a physical segment, the user may experience delays because of the following reasons:

— There are collisions that require retransmission.

— There is packet loss due to buffers on devices overflowing and requiring retransmission.

— The end systems could be slowing down because of excessive broadcast traffic.

10 State three things to consider when deciding where to place extended IP access lists.

You should consider at least three of the following:

— Minimize the distance that denied traffic has to travel. Place the access list as close to the source as possible.

— Keep the denied traffic off the backbone connecting buildings or campuses.

— Ensure the router chosen can deal easily with the additional CPU requirements.

— Consider the CPU utilization because an inbound access list does not have to do a routing update on denied traffic. However, the interface may have to match the access list against more traffic.

— Consider the number of interfaces affected.

— Consider the number of nodes affected. Outbound access lists may afford greater granularity.

— Consider access list management.

— Consider the network growth and the effect on the management of the interfaces and the changing needs in connectivity.

11 What is the function of the access layer?

The function of the access layer is to act as the first point of contact for the end devices or workstations. It also acts as a filter layer to ensure that all local traffic stays local and does not unnecessarily clog the network.

12 What is the access list number range for IP extended access lists?

The extended access list number range is 100-199.

13   What is priority queuing?

Priority queuing enables network managers to define how they want traffic to be prioritized in the network. By defining a series of filters based on packet characteristics, traffic is placed into a number of queues; the queue with the highest priority is serviced first, and then the lower queues are serviced in sequence. If the highest-priority queue is always full, this queue will continually be serviced and packets from the other queues will queue up and be dropped. In this queuing algorithm, one particular kind of network traffic can dominate all others. Priority queuing assigns traffic to one of four queues: High, Medium, Normal, and Low.

Chapter 3

Answers to Chapter 3 "Do I Know This Already?" Quiz

1   If given a Class C address with the requirement to accommodate 14 subnets and 10 hosts on each subnet, what subnet mask would you use?

The mask is 255.255.255.240 or the prefix mask of /28.

2   What sort of design scheme does route summarization require?

Route summarization requires a hierarchical addressing scheme.

3   Identify two private addresses defined in RFC 1918.

The RFC 1918 addresses you can use are as follows:

— Class A: 10.x.x.x

— Class B range: 172.16.0.0 through 172.31.0.0

— Class C range: 192.168.1.x through 192.168.254.x

4   Briefly define route summarization.

Route summarization is the method of including many subnets in a few routing entries.

5   In route summarization, to where is the subnet mask moved?

In route summarization, the subnet mask is moved to the left.

6   What does VLSM stand for?

VLSM stands for variable-length subnet mask.

7   Where can the software program NAT run?

NAT is a software program that can run on a Cisco PIX box or from 11.2 of the IOS of a router.

8 When is NAT useful?

NAT is useful when your organization wants to connect to the Internet and has used a private address (or an illegal address, which they did not obtain from the Internet).

9 When is NAT required?

NAT is required if your organization is connecting to another organization that has deployed the same private address.

10 How does summarization allow for smaller routing tables?

Summarizing is the consolidation of multiple routes into one single advertisement.

11 List the range of hosts available on the 136.122.10.192/28 subnet.

The range of hosts available on the subnet 136.122.10.192/28 are 136.122.10.193–206.

12 Convert the subnet address 56.98.5.0/24 to binary notation and state the class to which it belongs.

The Class A subnet 56.98.5.0 when converted to binary notation is as follows:

00111000.01100010.00000101.00000000

Answers to Chapter 3 Q&A Questions

1 Identify one criterion to help determine a subnet mask for classful addressing when designing a network-addressing scheme.

Questions to ask include the following:

How many networks are there in the network?

How many hosts are there on the largest subnet?

2 What is an inside local address?

An inside local address is a term used in NAT. It refers to the addresses within an organization that are used to communicate between end devices. These addresses are unique to the organization, but not necessarily unique to the world.

3 With a classless address of 204.1.64.0/20, what is the range of classful addresses that are included in the address? Write your answer in both dotted decimal and the third octet in binary notation.

The address 204.1.64.0 /20 includes the Class C addresses 204.1.64.0–204.1.79.0; this is illustrated in both dotted decimal and binary notation in Table A-1.

Table A-1 *Binary to Decimal Conversion to Determine CIDR Addresses*

Binary Notation	Decimal Notation
01000000	204.1.64.0
01000001	204.1.65.0
01000010	204.1.66.0
01000011	204.1.67.0
01000100	204.1.68.0
01000101	204.1.69.0
01000110	204.1.70.0
01000111	204.1.71.0
01001000	204.1.72.0
01001001	204.1.73.0
01001010	204.1.74.0
01001011	204.1.75.0
01001100	204.1.76.0
01001101	204.1.77.0
01001110	204.1.78.0
01001111	204.1.79.0

4 What is a discontiguous network?

A discontiguous network is when a NIC address is separated by another NIC address. Therefore, the original NIC address is no longer contiguous because an intervening NIC number has interrupted it.

5 For VLSM to be available as a design option in the network, what characteristic must the routing protocol possess?

The routing protocol must send the prefix or subnet mask as part of the routing update.

6 If summarization is to be implemented in the network, what is one design criterion for the addressing scheme that must be in place?

For VLSM to work, the addressing scheme must be hierarchical, allowing the upstream devices to share the same high-order bits as the downstream devices.

7 What are the networks provided in RFC 1918 and what is the prefix mask that accompanies each network?

The private addresses provided in RFC 1918 are as follows:

10.0.0.0 /8–255.0.0.0

172.16.0.0 /12–255.240.0.0

192.168.0.0 /16–255.255.0.0

8 If the host portion of a subnet has been used to identify end devices, can that subnet be used again for VLSM?

It is not possible to use a subnet for addressing hosts as well as using it to further subnet the network using VLSM. The addresses would be seen as duplicate addresses.

9 Give one reason for using private addressing in a network.

There are many reasons for using private addressing, including the following:

— Hiding the organization network from the rest of the world.

— The organization has no intention of connecting to the Internet, or there are only a few hosts that need Internet connectivity.

— The organization is unsure of the growth pattern of its network and therefore wants to deploy a large address space that it would not be able to acquire from the Internet.

10 When using NAT, configured to translate many inside addresses into one outside address, what mechanism is used to multiplex the different addresses into one address?

The ability to multiplex many inside addresses to one outside address is achieved using the UDP or TCP port number as the distinguishing parameter.

11 Give one example of when route summarization would not be a good solution.

Route summarization is not useful in the following circumstances:

— There are discontiguous networks in the organization.

— A specific subnet needs to be seen throughout the network.

— The addressing scheme does not support summarization. There are no common high-order bits shared in the network-addressing scheme.

— Access lists require detailed information.

12 Give one reason for implementing router summarization.

Route summarization is useful for the following reasons:

— To keep the routing tables small

— To keep the network overhead low

— To hide the network details from the rest of the organization

— To prevent flapping links from affecting the rest of the network

13 Given an address of 133.44.0.0 and a prefix mask of /25, how many networks can be addressed and how many hosts on each network? Write the first and last possible subnets in binary and decimal notation.

For the network address of 133.44.0.0, the subnet mask of 255.255.255.128 would enable you to address 510 subnets with 126 hosts on each subnet. This complies with the subnetting rule of not allocating addresses with all zeros or all ones. Table A-2 illustrates the first and last subnet in their binary and decimal notation formats.

Table A-2 *Determining Subnet When Using a Prefix Mask of /25*

Binary Notation	Decimal Notation
00000000.10000000	133.44.0.128
11111111.00000000	133.44.255.0

14 What class of address is 131.188.0.0, and how many hosts can be addressed if no subnetting is used?

131.188.0.0 is a Class B address and can address more than 65,000 hosts on one network if no subnetting is utilized.

Chapter 4

Answers to Chapter 4 "Do I Know This Already?" Quiz

1 Name the interior IP routing protocols that send the mask with the routing update.

The interior IP routing protocols that send the mask with the routing update are RIPV2, OSPF, and EIGRP.

2 Name the interior IP routing protocols that send incremental updates.

The interior IP routing protocols that send incremental updates are OSPF and EIGRP.

3 How often is the Hello protocol in OSPF sent out on a Cisco router?

The Hello protocol in OSPF is sent out on a Cisco router every 10 seconds.

4 State the different LSA types.

The different LSA update types are as follows:

Router link—Sent by the router, stating the links directly connected. These are flooded through the area.

Network link—Sent by the designated router. It states the links for the LAN for which it is the designated router. These LSAs are flooded throughout the area.

Summary link—Sent by the ABR into the backbone. It states the IP subnets within the area that are to be advertised into other areas. This is where summarization would be configured.

Summary link(to an ASBR)—Sent from an ABR to a router that connects to the outside world (ABSR). It contains the metric cost from the ABR to the ASBR.

External link—Sent to the autonomous system boundary routers to which the organization is directly connected.

5 What is used in an OSPF network to discover the designated router by default?

DR election is done via the Hello protocol. Hello packets are exchanged via IP multicast packets on each segment. The router with the highest OSPF priority on a segment will become the DR for that segment. In case of a tie, the router with the highest router ID (RID) will win. The default for the interface OSPF priority is one. The OSPF router ID is usually the highest IP address on the box, or the highest loopback address if one exists. The router ID is only calculated at boot time or anytime the OSPF process is restarted.

6 A virtual link in OSPF is used to solve what problem?

In some rare cases when it is impossible to have an area physically connected to the backbone, a virtual link is used. The virtual link will provide the disconnected area a logical path to the backbone. The virtual link has to be established between two ABRs that have a common area, with one ABR connected to the backbone.

7 Where does the backbone router reside and what is its function?

OSPF has special restrictions when multiple areas are involved. If more than one area is configured, one of these areas has be to be area 0. This is called the backbone. When designing networks, it is good practice to start with area 0 and then expand into other areas later on.

The backbone has to be at the center of all other areas; that is, all areas have to be physically connected to the backbone. The reasoning behind this is that OSPF expects all areas to inject routing information into the backbone and, in turn, the backbone will disseminate that information into other areas.

8   What must two neighbors do to form an adjacency in OSPF?

An adjacency is formed in OSPF when two neighbors have synchronized their topological databases by exchanging DDPs and LSUs.

9   If a router has the OSPF priority set to 0, what does this indicate?

A router with the OSPF priority set to 0 is one that cannot participate in the election of a designated router. It can become neither a designated nor a backup designated router.

10   An area border router must be resident in which area?

An area border router must be resident in area 0, as well as the area that is connecting to the backbone area. It will have two topological databases, one for each area it is resident in, so that it knows how to forward traffic.

Answers to Chapter 4 Q&A Questions

1   The topological database is a map of what?

The topological database is a map of the routes within the area. It includes every path to the remote networks known in the area.

2   Which protocol is used to elect the designated router? Which command is used to manually determine which router is elected?

The Hello protocol is used to elect the designated router. If the designated router is elected by manual configuration, the command **priority** states the priority of the router for that link. The higher the number, the greater the likelihood of the router's election.

3   To achieve full adjacency, the communication between the routers will have transferred what packets?

To achieve full adjacency, the communication between the routers will have transferred the following packets:

Hello protocol—This establishes the neighbor relationship.

DDP—The database description packets transfer the contents of the topological database from the master router to the slave.

LSR—The link-state request is the request for more detailed information about routes learned from the DDP. This may be a network sent in a DDP that is unknown to the receiving router.

LSU—In response to the request, the neighbor will send a link-state update. The update will be one of the five LSAs defined in the chapter.

LSA—This is a link-state acknowledgement, not the link-state advertisement. It is used to acknowledge the receipt of the LSU.

4 If the network is stable and sees no changes, how often will OSPF send out LSAs? Why are these updates still sent out periodically?

If the network is stable, OSPF will still send out LSAs every 30 minutes by default. This is to ensure the integrity of the topological databases.

5 What does ABR stand for and what LSAs will it forward?

ABR stands for area border router and it will forward summary LSAs. It will forward both type 3 LSAs and type 4 LSAs. Type 3 LSAs will be forwarded to the other ABRs, and the type 4 LSAs will be forward to the ASBRs. It will also forward type 3 LSAs from other areas into its own area.

6 What characteristic of an interface is used to calculate the default OSPF cost?

The cost (also called metric) of an interface in OSPF is an indication of the overhead required to send packets across a certain interface. The cost of an interface is inversely proportional to the bandwidth of that interface. A higher bandwidth indicates a lower cost. There is more overhead (higher cost) and time delays involved in crossing a 56-kbps serial line than crossing a 10-Mbps Ethernet line. The formula used to calculate the cost is as follows:

Cost = 100,000,000/bandwidth in bps

For example, it will cost $10^8/10^7 = 10$ to cross a 10-Mbps Ethernet line and will cost $10^8/1544000 = 64$ to cross a T1 line.

Table A-3 lists the default values used.

Table A-3   *The Cisco Defaults for OSPF Cost*

Speed of Link	Default Cost
56 kbps	1785
64 kbps	1562
T1	65
E1	48
Token Ring (4 Mbps)	25
Ethernet (10Base)	10
Token Ring (16 Mbps)	6
FDDI	1

7 Give three reasons why RIP-1 has problems with working in a large network.

RIP-1 has problems working in a large network because of the following reasons:

— It has a maximum hop count of 15.

— It sends updates of its routing table out of every interface every 30 seconds, which increases the network overhead on a network and leads to link congestion.

— To avoid routing loops, it uses holddown and poison reverse, and thereby increases the time it takes to propagate the changes in the network.

8 What is the Dijkstra algorithm used for?

The Dijkstra algorithm is used to calculate the shortest path first from the topological database. It examines the topological database and creates the routing table with the best path to each remote subnet. If there is more than one equal-cost path, it will load balance among them.

9 How does a stub area differ from the backbone area?

A stub area differs from the backbone area in that it does not propagate external routes into its area. The backbone is obliged to forward these LSAs to ensure connectivity throughout the network.

10 How does a totally stubby area differ from a stub area?

A totally stubby area differs from a stub area in that it propagates neither external routes nor summary routes from other areas. This is a Cisco solution to minimize the amount of CPU and memory required of the routers within the area. Connectivity is achieved by the use of default routes, which are advertised to the internal routers.

11 What information does a routing table give?

A routing table will contain certain information. The format used to display that information differs depending on the routing protocol.

Remote network—The address of the remote network and prefix or mask.

Outgoing interface— The interface on the router to which to send the outgoing datagram/frame.

Next logical hop—The Layer 3 address of the router that shares the same link to which the frame is to be sent. The next step in the journey.

Metric to the remote network—The value or cost of taking this path to the remote network. This is used to compare new paths that are learned about, to ensure that the best path is always chosen.

Chapter 5

Answers to Chapter 5 "Do I Know This Already?" Quiz

1 Is it possible to have more than one OSPF process running on a Cisco router? How might one configure more than one process on the router?

Yes, it is possible to have more than one process, although it is rarely configured. The process ID in the command **router OSPF** *process id* not only starts the process but will also identify the process; repeating the command with another ID number will create another process. One possible scenario for this configuration is a service provider that wants to separate its OSPF domain from its customer.

2 The address of 192.100.56.10 has been allocated to an interface on the router. This interface alone is to be included in the OSPF process. State the command that would start the process for the interface.

The are several ways to configure the process to include the interface. The command **network** *network number wildcard mask* **area** *area number* would be a subcommand to the global command **router ospf** *process-id*. The **network** command is used in both possible solutions; the difference is in the wildcard mask.

Network 192.100.56.10 0.0.0.0 area 2—This will match every bit in the interface address.

Network 192.100.56.10 0.0.7.255 area 2—This will also match the interface because it will resolve to the subnet assigned to the wire connected to the interface. This bit allocation was chosen merely to demonstrate the technique. The allocation that I have assumed is the subnet mask of 255.255.248.0. Note that the wildcard mask is the inverse of the subnet mask, ensuring that the individual subnet is selected for the interface.

3 Why would one configure the loopback interface when configuring OSPF?

The loopback interface is used in the configuration of OSPF as the router ID in the OSPF domain. Every router needs to identify itself in the exchange of LSAs. The loopback interface is, by definition, always up. If OSPF is stopped and then restarted, or the router resets, the router ID could change. This will not happen if there is a loopback interface configured.

4 What is the default method of selecting a router ID?

If there is no loopback interface configured, the highest IP address on the router is used as the router ID in all updates.

5 The metric used by OSPF is cost. If the cost of an interface has not been manually configured, what default metric will be used?

The default metric that is used by Cisco is 10^8 divided by the bandwidth, resulting in the fastest links being preferred.

6 The designated router may be automatically selected using defaults. How would one manually determine the designated router for a LAN?

The way to influence the election of the designated router is to set the priority of the router with the **set priority** *priority* command. The highest number becomes the designated router.

7 Which command would identify the designated router for your LAN?

sh ip ospf neighbor will show the designated and the backup routers. Another command that will show the designated router is the **show ip ospf interface** command.

8 What is a neighbor in OSPF?

A neighbor is a system that is on the same network link.

9 What is an adjacency in OSPF?

An adjacency is the state that two neighbors can achieve after they have synchronized their databases.

10 Where would you see whether a learned network was within the same area as the router you were looking at?

The **sh ip route** command will identify how the route was learned. If it is a network from another area, it will have the code IA next to it.

Answers to Chapter 5 Q&A Questions

1 State one command that would be used to show distribution filters that have been configured in OSPF.

The command **show ip protocol** will show any distribution filters that have been configured. The **show access lists** command will show the content of the list. To display both the access list and its application in propagating routing updates, you would display the entire configuration file with **show runn** or **show startup**.

2 What command would show which router on the LAN is the backup designated router?

The command **show ip ospf interface** will show the designated and backup designated routers.

3 What command would be used to create a totally stubby area?

The command **area** *area-id* **stub no-summary** will create a totally stubby area. This is a subcommand to the **router ospf** *process-id* command. It is only necessary on the ABR.

4 What is a virtual link and what command would be used to create it?

A virtual link is a link that creates a tunnel through an area to the backbone area. This allows an area that cannot connect directly to the backbone to do so virtually. The command to create the link is **area** *area-id* **virtual-link** *router-id*.

5 Explain briefly what the command **show ip ospf database** will show you.

The command **show ip ospf database** will show the contents of the topology database and give a status on the LSAs that have been sent and received.

6 Where would one issue the command to summarize IP subnets and state the command that would be used?

Summarization is done at area boundaries. The command to start summarization is the **area range** command with the syntax **area** *area-id* **range** *address mask*.

7 How would one summarize external routes before injecting them into the OSPF domain?

The command **summary-address** *address mask* is the command that would be used.

8 What command is used to show the state of adjacencies?

The command **show ip ospf interface** will show the adjacencies that exist with neighbors.

9 In a totally stubby area, which routes arc not propagated into the area?

There will be no summary or external routes propagated by the ABR into the area.

10 In the command **show ip ospf database**, there is a field that shows the SPF delay. What does this field indicate?

The field indicates how long to wait to start the SPF calculation after receiving an LSA update.

Chapter 6

Answers to Chapter 6 "Do I Know This Already?" Quiz

1 Enhanced IGRP may be used to send information about which Layer 3 protocols?

Enhanced IGRP can be used as a routing protocol for IP, IPX, and AppleTalk.

2   What is the advertised distance in Enhanced IGRP and how is it distinguished from the feasible distance?

Advertised distance is that metric reported by the neighbor router(s). Feasible distance is the metric reported by neighbor router(s) plus the cost associated with forwarding the link from the local interface to the neighbor router(s).

3   If a router does not have a feasible successor, what action will it take?

If the router does not have a feasible successor in its topology table it sends a query packet to its neighbors asking whether they have a feasible successor.

4   What is an EIGRP topology table, and what does it contain?

The topology table contains every network and every path to every network in the domain. The metric for every path is held, as well as the metric from the next logical hop or neighbor. The table contains the outgoing interface on the router through which to reach the remote network and the IP address of the next hop address. The status of the route (passive or active) is also recorded. The topology table also keeps track of the routing packets that have been sent to the neighbors.

5   What EIGRP algorithm is run to create entries for the routing table?

The Diffusing Update Algorithm (DUAL) is run on the topology table. It is used to determine the best path and to build the routing table.

6   When does Enhanced IGRP need to be manually redistributed into Enhanced IGRP?

Enhanced IGRP needs to be manually redistributed into another Enhanced IGRP process when the autonomous system number is different.

7   When is redistribution required?

Redistribution is required when there is more than one routing protocol for IP running within the organization and every part of the network needs connectivity to all the networks.

8   What type of routing protocol is BGP classified as, and what does this mean?

BGP is classified as an exterior routing protocol. It sends only a summary of the networks known within an organization to maximize security and minimize bandwidth overhead. It is used to convey routing information between autonomous systems.

9   What is a passive interface and why is it used?

A passive interface is an interface that will listen to routing updates but will not propagate any updates for the protocol configured. It is used to prevent unnecessary traffic from being sent out of an interface. Usually a passive interface is configured when there are no routers to hear the updates on that network.

10 What is a static route?

A static route is a route that has been manually configured. It has the lowest administrative distance, which means it will always take precedence and it must be redistributed into a routing protocol for other routers to make use of it.

11 What is the administrative distance for RIP?

The administrative distance for RIP is 120; it has the highest distance of interior routing protocols, and is therefore the least likely to be selected.

12 What is the transport protocol for BGP?

The transport protocol for BGP is TCP.

13 What is a default route?

A default route is a route used when there is no entry for the remote network in the routing table. It is used to connect to the Internet and other routing domains when it is not practical to know all the available networks. It is sufficient to have an exit point from your network identified.

Answers to Chapter 6 Q&A Questions

1 When does Enhanced IGRP recalculate the topology table?

Enhanced IGRP recalculates the topology table whenever it receives a change input to the topology table. This could be a change of metric for a physically connected link, change of status of a physically connected link, or an Enhanced IGRP routing packet, either an update, query, or reply packet.

2 By default Enhanced IGRP summarizes at which boundary?

By default, Enhanced IGRP summarizes at the NIC or major network boundary.

3 The neighbor table is responsible for keeping track of which timers?

The timers the neighbor table keeps track of are the hold time, the SRTT (smooth round-trip timer), and the RTO (retransmission timer).

4 When does Enhanced IGRP place a network in active mode?

Enhanced IGRP places a network into active mode when there is no feasible successor in its topology table.

5 What is the difference between an update and a query?

An update is the routing information packet that a router will send out to inform its neighbors of a change in the network. A query is when the router has no feasible successor in its topology table for a network that is down. At this point, it queries its neighbors to ascertain whether they have a feasible successor. If they do, this route becomes the feasible successor for the original router.

6 In what instances will Enhanced IGRP automatically redistribute?

Enhanced IGRP will automatically redistribute between itself and IGRP as long as both processes are running the same autonomous system number.

Enhanced IGRP also automatically redistributes between the LAN protocol and Enhanced IGRP. Enhanced IGRP for IPX automatically redistributes int0; IPX for RIP/SAP and Enhanced IGRP for AppleTalk similarly redistribute automatically into RTMP.

7 What problems may be experienced when redistribution is configured?

A suboptimal route may be chosen, routing loops may occur, and slow convergence may occur.

8 What is the metric used for in a routing protocol?

The metric is used to select the best path when multiple paths are available to a remote network.

9 What is the purpose of the administrative distance?

When the routing table is populated with networks that are provided by multiple routing protocols, the administrative distance is used to choose the best path to the remote network.

10 Why is it necessary to configure a default metric when redistributing between routing protocols?

The metric is used within a routing protocol to select the best path to a remote network when there are multiple paths. When redistributing, it is not always possible to port the metric across because the metric is protocol specific. The default metric throws the original metric away and substitutes a new metric for the new routing protocol.

11 In BGP4, what is the purpose of the **network** command?

The **network** command defines the network to be advertised in the BGP update. It does not identify the interfaces through which to send BGP traffic. In addition, the network does not need to be directly connected to the router.

12 When would you use external BGP as opposed to internal BGP?

External BGP is used to connect different autonomous systems, and the routers are usually neighbors. Internal BGP is used within the same autonomous system to communicate information that has been learned from the external BGP processes.

External BGP is used between the organization and the ISP or the Internet, and internal BGP is used within the ISP or the Internet.

13 What is an alternative to using BGP as the method of connection to the ISP?

The alternative method, suggested by Cisco, is to use a default route into the ISP and for the ISP to configure static routes into your autonomous system.

Chapter 7

Answers to Chapter 7 "Do I Know This Already?" Quiz

1 How is interesting traffic identified to the router?

Interesting traffic is traffic that is allowed to trigger the router to set up the link to the remote site. Configuring a dialer list identifies interesting traffic. That which is permitted in the dialer list is traffic that is deemed interesting.

2 What is the purpose of the **dialer map** command?

The **dialer map** command is used to identify the remote destinations to connect to. The command maps a telephone number to a network number. This is used when there is more than one destination to connect to; it is similar in function to the **map** commands used in X.25 and Frame Relay.

3 What is the D channel used for in ISDN?

The D channel is used for out-of-band signaling, to initialize and manage the ISDN link. In some instances, it is available for data transfer.

4 How is a static route used in DDR?

The static route is used to identify the remote location to the router, without requiring the necessity of the routing protocol traversing the link. If the routing protocol were required to transmit this information, the line would be up the majority of the time, which would render ISDN an extremely expensive solution.

5 What does ISDN stand for?

ISDN stands for Integrated Services Digital Network.

6 When would you use PPP as the frame format for the link?

PPP would be used if the remote location were using a device from a different vendor. It is also necessary if the securities of CHAP or PAP are to be utilized.

7 State at least one occasion when you would choose asynchronous dial-in as the WAN option.

Asynchronous dial-in would be used to connect networks across the existing telephone infrastructure. It requires few resources and is simple to implement. It is used in small environments to connect intermittent low-volume sites. It is often used to connect home users to the network at work.

8 Name two advantages of using a packet-switched service.

A packet-switched service is useful in providing occasional connectivity to remote locations. It is a service managed by the service provider, so theoretically the maintenance should be low. As a shared resource owned by the service provider, it is easy to change the service parameters, such as the bandwidth, in accordance to the organizational needs.

9 When considering which connection to choose for the WAN, what are two important things that guide that decision?

You should consider the availability of the resource in the remote area, the bandwidth requirements of the users and network, the application traffic, the ease of managing the network, and the routing protocol that will be used across the link.

10 What is the difference between a BRI connection and a PRI connection?

A BRI connection offers two bearer channels at 64 kbps and one D channel at 16 kbps.

A PRI connection offers between 23 and 30 bearer channels and one D channel at 64 kbps.

11 What is the purpose of the Terminal Adapter (TA) in ISDN?

The TA is used to connect end devices that do not speak native ISDN.

12 What command is used to determine how long the router will wait before dropping the link?

Two commands are used to configure the length of time the router will wait before dropping the link: the **dialer idle-timeout** *seconds* command and the **dialer fast-idle** *seconds* command.

Answers to Chapter 7 Q&A Questions

1 Describe one key difference between what Cisco calls DDR legacy and DDR dialer profiles.

DDR legacy does not use dialer profiles; dialer profiles include the use of dialer interfaces and pools of physical interfaces. Dialer profiles use the dialer interfaces and dial pools.

Dialer profiles separate the dial logic from the physical interface configuration, providing a much more flexible configuration.

2 Configure logic that defines that traffic from FTP clients in 10.1.1.0/24 is considered interesting for DDR. Enable that logic on serial 0. Ignore other DDR parameters.

```
Access-list 101 permit tcp 10.1.1.0 0.0.0.255 any eq 21
Dialer-list 1 protocol ip list 101
Interface serial 0
Dialer-group 1
```

The **dialer-group** command enables the logic on the interface. Only enabling the access list with an **ip access-group 101** command would have just filtered packets after the link was brought up. No packets are actually filtered by this logic.

Refer to Figure 7-20 in Chapter 7 for questions 3–10.

3 Configure Router A such that IP packets are directed out of BRI0 to sites B and C.

```
ip route 200.1.2.0 255.255.255.0 200.1.4.2
ip route 200.1.3.0 255.255.255.0 200.1.4.3
```

These statements direct the packets out of BRI0 because it is in the same subnet as the next hop addresses in these two **ip route** commands.

4 Configure Router A so that packets from Web clients in 200.1.1.0, connecting to servers at sites B or C, are considered interesting. All other IP is boring.

```
Access-list 101 permit tcp 200.1.1.0 0.0.0.255 any  eq 80
Dialer-list 1 protocol ip list 101
```

The second command enables the logic in the access list to be used for determining whether a packet is interesting or boring.

5 Configure DDR map statements on Router A referring to B and C. Assume CHAP is configured and that the routers' host names are RouterA, RouterB, and RouterC.

```
Dialer map ip 200.1.4.2 broadcast name RouterB 4045552222
Dialer map ip 200.1.4.3 broadcast name RouterC 4045553333
```

The broadcast keyword was not requested in the question, but it is typically needed.

6 Configure commands on Router A so that the connection is taken down after 2 minutes of uninteresting traffic.

```
Interface bri0
Dialer idle-timeout 120
```

7 Configure Router A so that IPX packets to Server2 and Server3 are directed out of BRI0 to sites B and C. The IPX addresses on the BRI interfaces are 4.0200.1111.1111 on RouterA, 4.0200.2222.2222 on RouterB, and 4.0200.3333.3333 on RouterC. The servers use internal networks 102 and 103, respectively.

```
ipx route 102 4.0200.2222.2222
ipx route 103 4.0200.3333.3333
```

Routes to IPX networks 2 and 3 are not needed because that traffic will not be considered interesting. Those routes will be learned by RIP after the link is up.

8 Configure commands on RouterA so that packets from any IPX clients connecting to file services on Server 2 and Server 3 are considered interesting. Server 2 and Server 3 use internal networks 102 and 103, respectively. All other IPX is boring.

```
Access-list 902 permit any any all 101 04
Access-list 902 permit any any all 102 04
Dialer-list 3 protocol ipx list 902
```

9   Configure DDR map statements for IPX on Router A referring to B and C. Assume CHAP
    is configured and that the routers' host names are RouterA, RouterB, and RouterC.

```
Dialer map ipx 2.0200.2222.2222 broadcast name RouterB 4045552222
Dialer map ipx 2.0200.3333.3333 broadcast name RouterC 4045553333
```

10 Configure DDR so that the connection is taken down after 30 seconds of uninteresting
    traffic, but only if other interesting traffic is waiting on a B channel. Also configure to
    allow the second B channel to be used if the traffic load exceeds 50% in either direction
    on the link.

```
Dialer fast-idle 30
Dialer load-threshold 50 either
```

Chapter 8

Answers to Chapter 8 "Do I Know This Already?" Quiz

1   At which layer does a bridge function?

    A bridge functions at Layer 2.

2   What is transparent bridging?

    Transparent bridging is a learning bridge that listens and learns Layer 2 MAC addresses.
    Using this MAC address table, it forwards Layer 2 frames. It does this transparently, in
    that it does not change the frame that is forwarded, nor do the end devices have to be aware
    of the bridge.

3   Which bridge technologies are used on Token Ring?

    Transparent and source-route bridging are used on Token Ring. The router may therefore
    be configured to use source-route transparent or source-route translational.

4   In transparent bridging, what are the Spanning-Tree Protocols that may be configured?

    The IEEE spanning tree is the protocol that is offered by the standards body. The DEC
    Spanning-Tree Protocol is the original spanning tree and may need to be used in some
    environments that have older DEC equipment in place.

5   The command **source-bridge transparent** is used to configure which bridging
    technology?

    This command is used to configure source-route translational bridging on a Cisco router.

6 What is the RIF, and what is its purpose?

The RIF is the Routing Information Field that is used in source-route bridging to tell the intermediary bridges how to forward the frame to the destination host. It is a list of bridges and rings, held in the header of the frame.

7 What command is used to manually determine the root bridge in a transparently bridged network?

The command is as follows:

```
bridge bridge-number priority priority-number
```

It is stated after transparent bridging has been configured and the Spanning-Tree Protocol selected.

8 State one difference between source-route bridging and transparent bridging.

Table A-4 shows the differences between source-route bridging and transparent bridging.

Table A-4   *Transparent Versus Source-Route Bridging*

Transparent Bridging	Source-Route Bridging
Used on Ethernet, Token Ring, and FDDI LANs.	Used on Token Ring.
Ease of configuration.	Configuration required on hosts and bridges, configuration more complex.
The host is unaware of the bridge. The intelligence is in the bridge.	The host creates the frame header that the bridges use to forward traffic. The intelligence is in the host as well as the bridge.
The bridge learns the location of MAC addresses by listening to the frame source address.	The bridge does not learn by default; it just acts on information provided in the RIF of the frame.
The bridge filters frames if the destination is known to exist on another interface, forwarding it to the specified interface, but dropping it if the frame source and destination addresses were heard on the same interface. If the destination is unknown or is a broadcast, the bridge floods the frame out of all interfaces except the receiving interface.	Explorer packets flood the network initially. After the path to the remote destination is discovered, this path is recorded in the RIF.

9 When would you implement source-route translational bridging?

Source-route translational bridging would be implemented if you needed to connect LANs that supported different bridge technologies. This may be necessary in an environment that includes both Ethernet and Token Ring. A host configured for source-route bridging on a Token Ring segment that wants to connect to a server that is connected to an Ethernet segment would need to be stripped of its RIF because this would cause it to be discarded in the Ethernet domain.

10 What is the purpose of a root bridge?

A root bridge is a bridge that has been elected as the focus point of the flat network. All other bridges calculate the cost of the paths back to the root bridge. The result of the calculation allows the selection of one path to any destination that exists; if other paths exist, they are shut down for bridging. This ensures a unique path to every destination and eliminates loops within the flat network.

11 What does RII stand for and what is its purpose?

RII stands for Routing Information Indicator. It is the most significant bit of the source MAC address. It signals to the source-route bridge process that there is a RIF further in the header of the frame.

12 When SR/TLB is configured, it performs many conversions. State two things that it converts.

Source-route translational bridging converts the following:

— Change in the frame MTU

— The physical clocking

— Bit ordering in the Layer 2 frame

— Removal or insertion of the RIF

— The frame header

13 What is a proxy explorer?

A proxy explorer is a cache that can be configured on a Cisco router. It enables the source-route process on the router to listen to explorer packets returning to the source-route host. The RIF contained in the explorer packet is cached. When another host transmits explorer packets to the destination host, the router does not propagate the packets, but sends a frame to the destination with the completed RIF.

Answers to Chapter 8 Q&A Questions

1 Which of the bridging technologies are stated as standards?

Transparent bridging

Source-route transparent bridging

Source-route bridging is included in the source-route transparent standard. They are all defined in 802.1D by the IEEE.

2 Which command is used to configure source-route translational bridging on a Cisco router?

To configure source-route translational bridging, use the following command:

```
Router(config)# source-bridge transparent
ring-group
pseudo-ring
bridge-number
transparent-bridge-group-number [oui]
```

3 In an SR/TLB bridging configuration, how does the source-route bridging network appear to the transparently bridged network?

The SRB network appears as a transparent bridge group.

4 What does the Cisco command **multiring** achieve?

The **multiring** command is used when a routed network has an SRB bridge in the path. There will be no RIF information available for the SRB bridge, and it cannot forward the Layer 3 information of which it is ignorant. The **multiring** command configures the interface connecting to the SRB bridge for SRB and acts as an SRB source host. It can now provide RIF information to the Layer 3 datagrams that have to forward the Layer 2 SRB domain.

5 What is the purpose of the routing descriptor in the RIF?

The routing descriptor includes the ring numbers of the Token Rings and the bridge numbers. Each bridge will examine the RD field to decide how to forward the frame and will insert its own information if the frame is an explorer frame.

6 How does an SRT bridge know whether to forward a frame to an SRB process or a transparent bridge process?

The SRT will examine the frame header, and if it sees an RII field, it knows that there is a RIF indicating SRB; if there is no RII and therefore no RIF, the frame will be sent to the transparent bridge process.

7 State two restrictions that apply when using the IRB technology on a Cisco router.

IRB is not supported on the following:

— An AGS+ or 7000 series routers (systems using a cbus)

— X.25 bridged interfaces

— ISDN bridged interfaces

— Systems running Cisco's older concurrent bridging and routing

— Systems running source-route bridging

8 What does BVI stand for, and what is its function?

BVI stands for Bridge-Group Virtual Interface. It takes all the bridged interfaces in a bridge group on a Cisco router and allows them to appear as an interface at Layer 3, with the entire configuration options available for that routable protocol. It is this virtual interface that allows the routed interfaces to communicate to the bridging interfaces.

9 The Routing Control field in the RIF performs what functions in source-route bridging?

The RC field is used to identify the following:

— **The type of frame**—A specifically routed frame, an all-routes explorer, or a spanning-tree explorer.

— **The length of the RIF**—Five bits.

— **The direction the RIF is to be read**—Is it going to the destination or returning to the source?

— **The largest frame**—The MTU of the frame through the network.

10 State one command that can be used to verify the configuration of transparent bridging.

show bridge will show the addresses in the bridge table and related information.

or

show span will show the Spanning-Tree Protocol being used and how it operates, including the cost of the path, the designated router, and the bridge priority.

11 What is the purpose of the **multiport** command, and what command is used to configure this utility?

To configure the multiport utility, issue the following command:

```
Source-bridge ring-group ring-group-number
```

This configures source-route bridging on the router to deal with more than two interfaces. Originally, source-route bridging expected a bridge to be a PC with two interfaces. The router becomes a virtual ring that connects the two physical rings. The ring-group number is the number of the virtual ring that is configured. This number must be unique.

12 What is the purpose of the Spanning-Tree Protocol in transparent bridging?

The purpose of the Spanning-Tree Protocol in transparent bridging is to avoid loops in a Layer 2 or flat network. If there are physical loops in a large network, broadcast traffic will be propagated continually around the loop. The severe congestion that this can cause may create many problems in the network.

Chapter 9

Answers to Chapter 9 "Do I Know This Already?" Quiz

1 What is the original routing protocol used for AppleTalk and how often are the updates sent out?   .

RTMP, or Routing Table Maintenance Protocol, is the original routing protocol used for AppleTalk. The updates are sent out every 10 seconds by default.

2 How are services organized or grouped in AppleTalk networks and what protocol is used to maintain the service tables?

The AppleTalk services are organized into zones, and the Zone Information Protocol (ZIP) is used to maintain the Zone Information Tables.

3 State what the letters NBP stand for and briefly explain the purpose of the protocol.

The letters NBP stand for Name Binding Protocol. It is used to query every AppleTalk server in a zone for services that it may be offering. NBP responses from the server to the requesting client will state the services that are offered by the server.

4 How do AppleTalk clients get network addresses?

The AppleTalk client is allocated a network address through automatic address acquisition. This takes place when the client inquires across the network at boot up time, looking for the cable range of the local segment. Any router of the AppleTalk server will answer the request with the configured cable range. The client then will randomly pick a host address, which it sends out across the local segment to ensure that the address has not been used by another host and that it is indeed correct.

5 When and where would a GetZoneList filter be used?

The GetZoneList filter is used on the access layer routers. These are the routers used to service the local clients. When a user opens the Chooser on a client, the client sends out a GetZoneList request to all routers and servers, requiring them to respond with a list of zones available on the network. The GetZoneList filter is used to restrict the zones advertised on the network to a client host.

6 When and where would a ZIP reply filter be used?

The ZIP reply filter is used to restrict the communication of zones between routers.

7 How many channels are provided in an E1 line?

There are 30 channels on the line, each offering 64 kbps, giving a bandwidth of 2.048 Mbps.

8 How many channels are provided in a T1 line?

There are 24 channels on the line, each offering 64 kbps, giving a bandwidth of 1.544 Mbps.

9   Some Cisco models support a MIP card. What does the acronym MIP stand for and what is its purpose?

The acronym MIP stands for MultiChannel Interface Processor. The MIP card allows the multiplexing and demultiplexing of the channels of a T1 line within the Cisco system. This allows a T1 line to be channelized at the customer site.

10   Which WAN protocols do T1 and E1 lines support?

The protocols supported are X.25, LAPB, Frame Relay, HDLC, PPP, SMDS, and ATM-DXI.

11   What is the bearer channel and the D channel in ISDN?

The bearer channel is a channel in ISDN that carries data across the network. The D channel is used for call setup and management data. In some instances, it can also be used for data.

12   What do the letters PRI represent?

The letters PRI stand for Primary Rate Interface, and it is an ISDN offering of either 23 bearer channels or 30 bearer channels.

Answers to Chapter 9 Q&A Questions

1   What traffic does the GetZoneList filter prevent?

The GetZoneList filter prevents zone information contained in the Zone Information Table from being communicated to the requesting device. The zones sent in the reply to the request depend on what has been permitted in the filter.

2   What NBP traffic is generated when the Chooser is open?

When the Chooser is opened, a GetZoneList query goes to a router, which populates the zone list in the lower-left section of the Chooser. The box at the upper left is populated with all the network drivers loaded on the Macintosh computer. The user selects a zone and a driver, and an NBP query goes out. The responses to the NBP query populate the window on the right with the names of the networked devices that offer the selected service in the selected zone.

3   What does NVE stand for and what does it mean?

NVE stands for network-visible entity, and it refers to a node service accessible over an AppleTalk network.

4   Between whom are the Zone Information Tables communicated?

The Zone Information Tables (ZITs) are sent between the routers and servers.

5 Which command is used to permit all other cable ranges and networks?

access-list *access-list number* **permit other-access**.

6 What does the command **appletalk permit partial zones** achieve?

If a network is denied in an AppleTalk filter, the entire zone to which the network was a member would also be denied. This command allows the other networks and zone to be included in the updates.

7 What is the use of the **timeslots** command in the configuration of an E1 or T1 line?

The **timeslot** command identifies the channels that are to be associated with a channel group. In this way, it is possible to configure portions of the E1 or T1 and effectively create multiple fractional E1 or T1 links.

8 When would the **clock source** command be used?

The **clock source** command is used when the T1 or E1 line is being connected directly to another router. This is typically used to test the circuit. Otherwise, the default command clock source line is used.

9 What is the default framing used on a T1 line?

The default framing used on a T1 line is Super Frame (SF).

10 In configuring a T1 line for ISDN, what are the main configuration tasks?

These are in addition to the DDR commands seen earlier:

— Specify the PRI switch

— Specify the T1 or E1 controller, framing, and line for the service provider

— Specify a group and timeslot

— Indicate the router interface

11 When configuring the E1 or T1 line, is one configuring the hardware or the software?

The configuration identifies the controller or the hardware interface. When the interface is ready to be configured for ISDN, the serial interface is configured.

12 The switch that is identified in the configuration of the E1 or T1 line belongs to whom?

The switch is located in the central office of the service provider, and the switch type is provided to you from this office.

INDEX

A

Cisco Press

Staying Connected to Networkers

We want to hear from **you**! Help Cisco Press **stay connected** to the issues and challenges you face on a daily basis by registering your book and filling out our brief survey.

Complete and mail this form, or better yet, jump to **www.ciscopress.com** and do it online. Each complete entry will be eligible for our monthly drawing to **win a FREE book** from the Cisco Press Library.

Thank you for choosing Cisco Press to help you work the network.

Name _____

Address _____

City _____ State/Province _____

Country _____ Zip/Post code _____

E-mail address _____

May we contact you via e-mail for product updates and customer benefits?
- ❏ Yes
- ❏ No

Where did you buy this product?
- ❏ Bookstore
- ❏ Online retailer
- ❏ Mail order
- ❏ Computer store
- ❏ Office supply store
- ❏ Class/Seminar
- ❏ Electronics store
- ❏ Discount store
- ❏ Other _____

When did you buy this product? _____ **Month** _____ **Year**

What price did you pay for this product?
- ❏ Full retail price
- ❏ Discounted price
- ❏ Gift

How did you learn about this product?
- ❏ Friend
- ❏ Catalog
- ❏ Magazine ad
- ❏ School
- ❏ Store personnel
- ❏ Postcard in the mail
- ❏ Article or review
- ❏ Professional Organization
- ❏ In-store ad
- ❏ Saw it on the shelf
- ❏ Used other products
- ❏ Other _____

What will this product be used for?
- ❏ Business use
- ❏ Personal use
- ❏ School/Education
- ❏ Other _____

How many years have you been employed in a computer-related industry?
- ❏ 2 years or less
- ❏ 3-5 years
- ❏ 5+ years

CISCO SYSTEMS

CISCO PRESS

www.ciscopress.com

www.ciscopress.com

Which best describes your job function?

- ❑ Corporate Management
- ❑ Network Design
- ❑ Marketing/Sales
- ❑ Professor/Teacher
- ❑ Systems Engineering
- ❑ Network Support
- ❑ Consultant
- ❑ IS Management
- ❑ Webmaster
- ❑ Student

- ❑ Other _____

What is your formal education background?

- ❑ High school
- ❑ College degree
- ❑ Vocational/Technical degree
- ❑ Masters degree
- ❑ Some college
- ❑ Professional or Doctoral degree

Have you purchased a Cisco Press product before?

- ❑ Yes
- ❑ No

On what topics would you like to see more coverage?

_____

_____

Do you have any additional comments or suggestions?

_____

_____

ACRC Exam Certification Guide   0-7357-0075-3

Cisco Press

201 West 103rd Street
Indianapolis, IN 46290
www.ciscopress.com

Place
Stamp
Here

Cisco Press
Customer Registration
P.O. Box 189014
Battle Creek, MI 49018-9947